Happy Sugar Life 4

Tomiyaki Kagisora

Happy Sugar Life

Tomiyaki
Kagisora

Lifelog ★

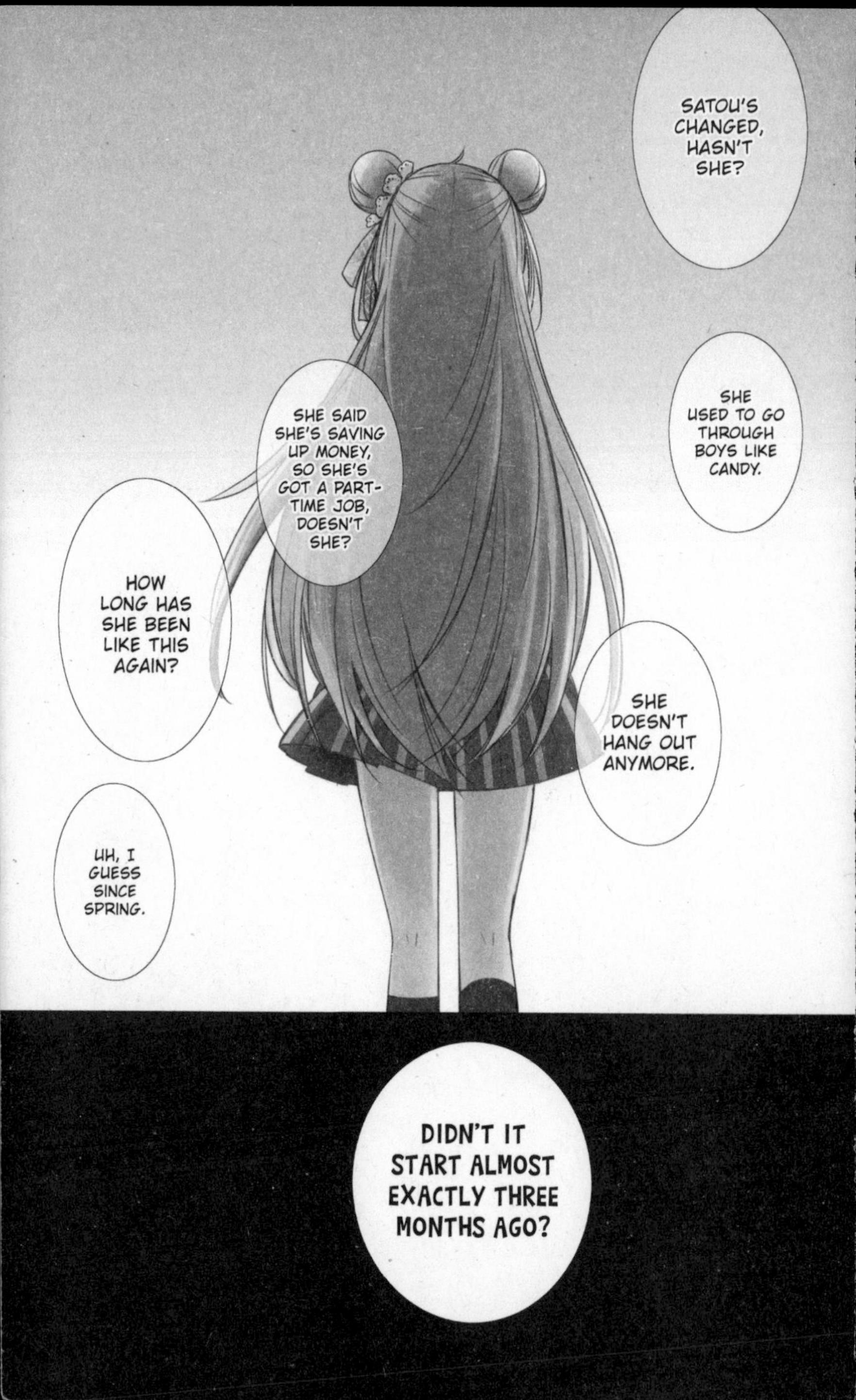
SATOU'S CHANGED, HASN'T SHE?
SHE USED TO GO THROUGH BOYS LIKE CANDY.
SHE DOESN'T HANG OUT ANYMORE.
SHE SAID SHE'S SAVING UP MONEY, SO SHE'S GOT A PART-TIME JOB, DOESN'T SHE?
HOW LONG HAS SHE BEEN LIKE THIS AGAIN?
UH, I GUESS SINCE SPRING.
DIDN'T IT START ALMOST EXACTLY THREE MONTHS AGO?

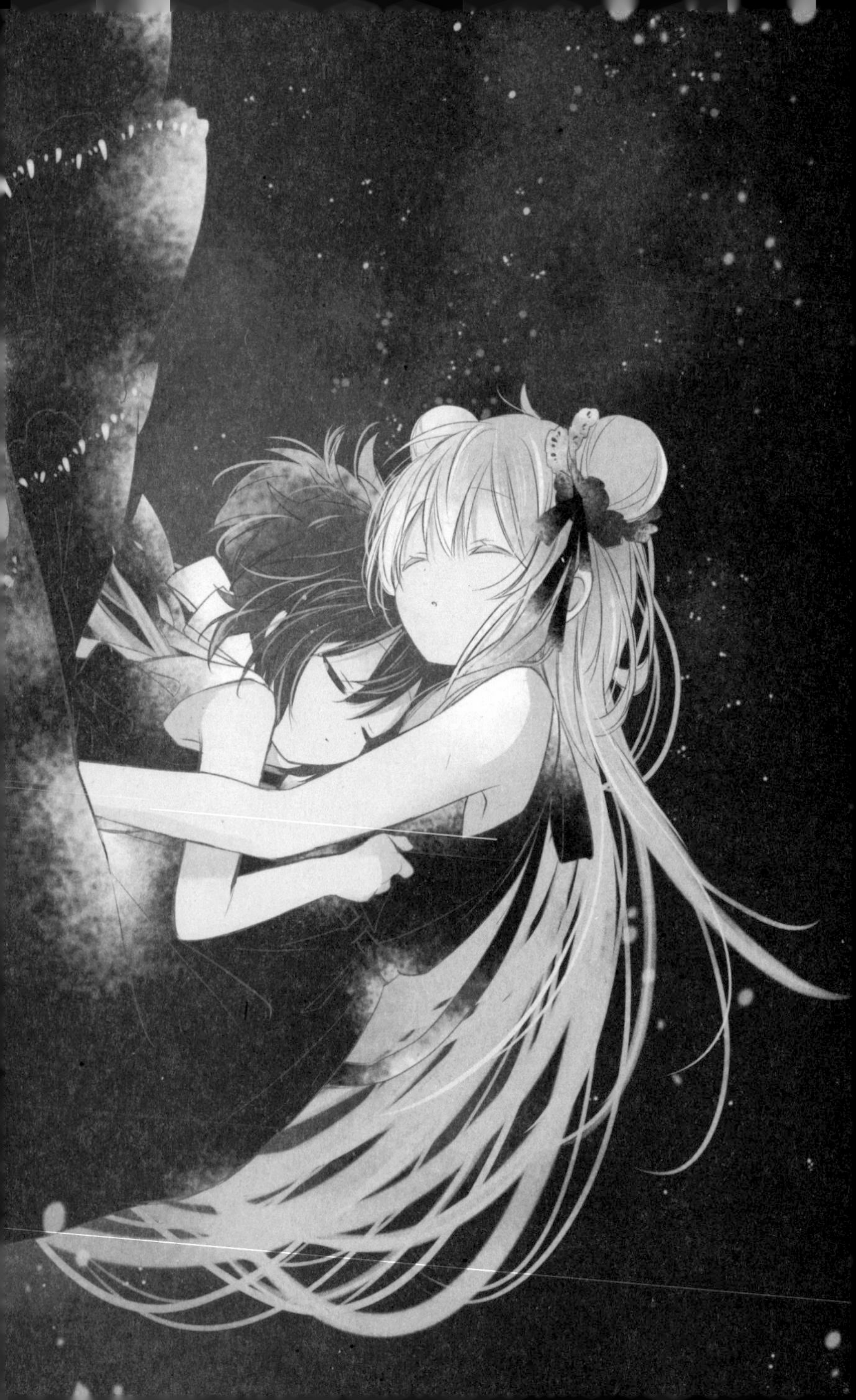

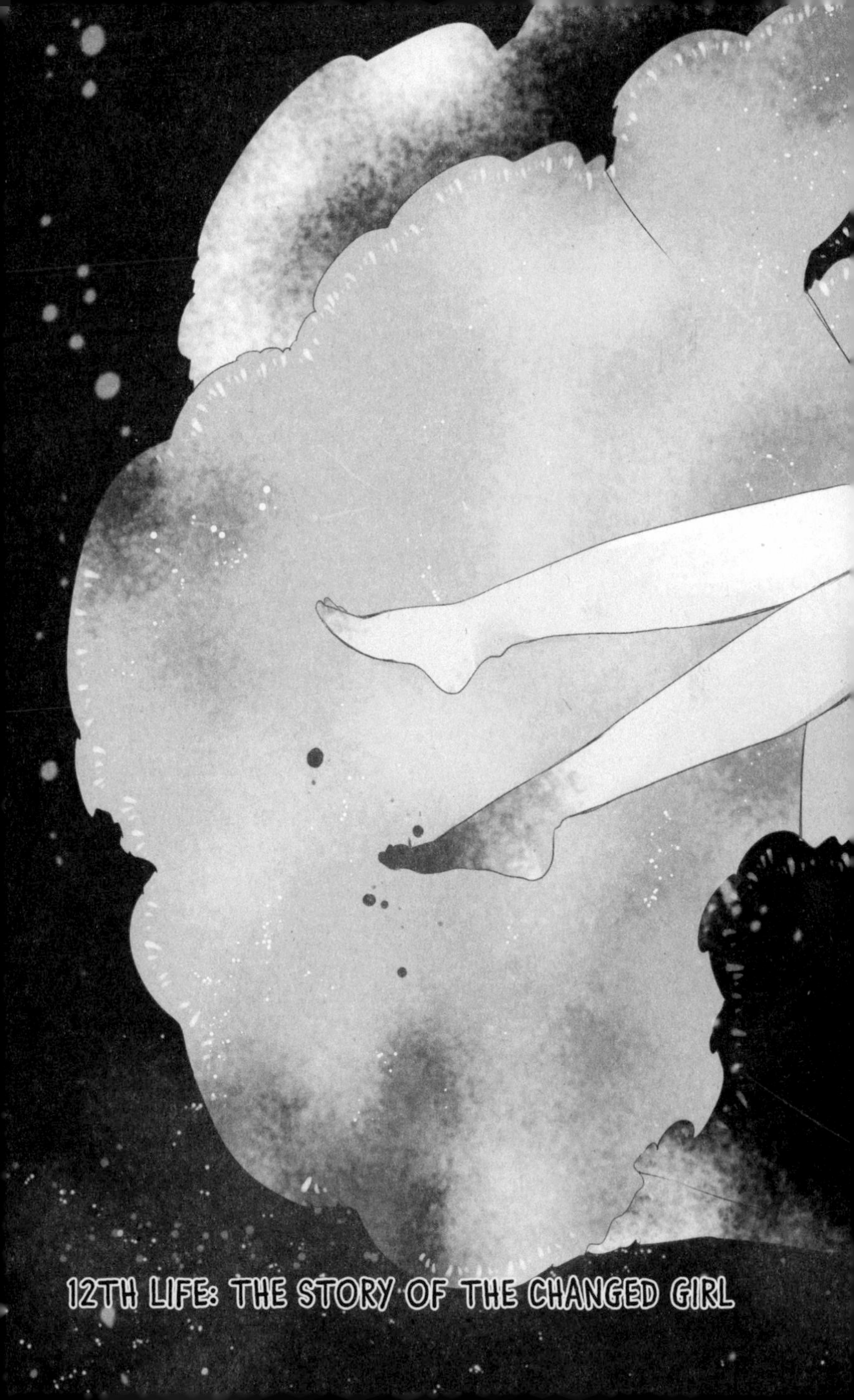

12TH LIFE: THE STORY OF THE CHANGED GIRL

Happy
Sugar
Life

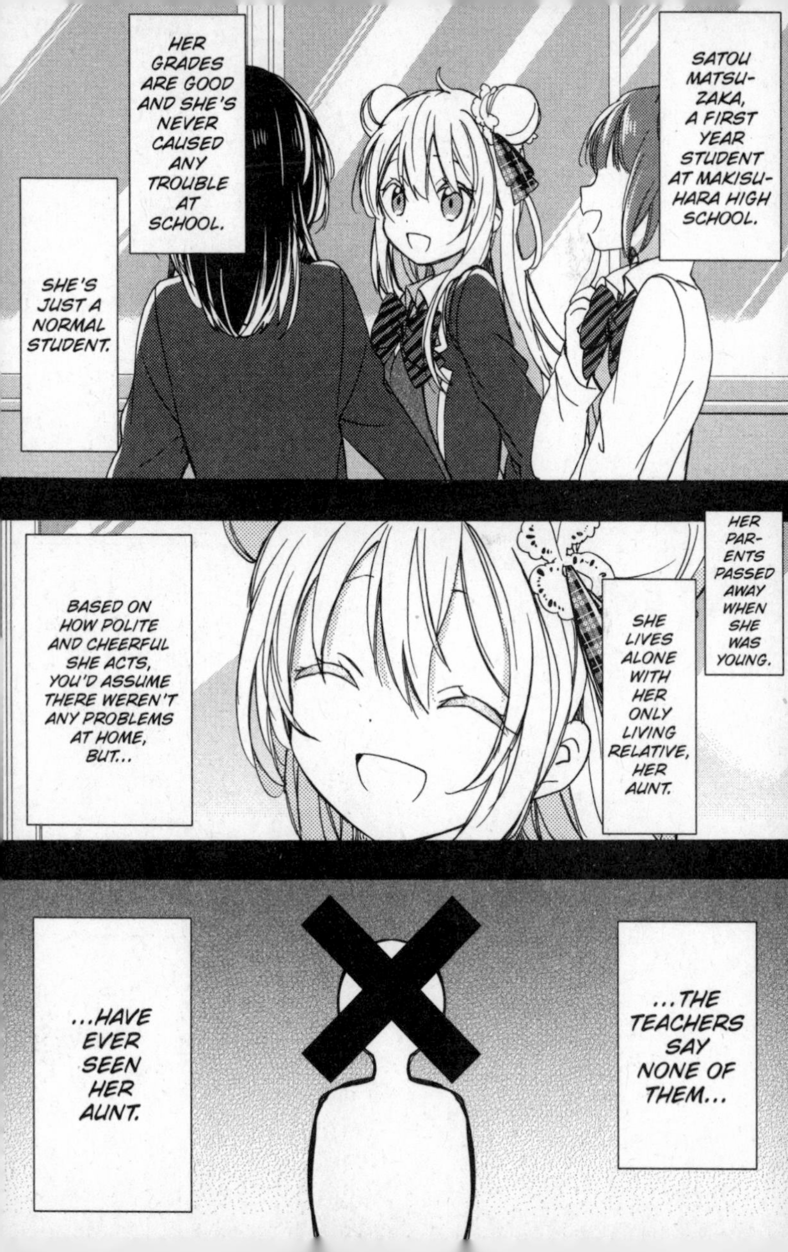
SATOU MATSUZAKA, A FIRST YEAR STUDENT AT MAKISUHARA HIGH SCHOOL.
HER GRADES ARE GOOD AND SHE'S NEVER CAUSED ANY TROUBLE AT SCHOOL.
SHE'S JUST A NORMAL STUDENT.
HER PARENTS PASSED AWAY WHEN SHE WAS YOUNG.
SHE LIVES ALONE WITH HER ONLY LIVING RELATIVE, HER AUNT.
BASED ON HOW POLITE AND CHEERFUL SHE ACTS, YOU'D ASSUME THERE WEREN'T ANY PROBLEMS AT HOME, BUT...
...THE TEACHERS SAY NONE OF THEM...
...HAVE EVER SEEN HER AUNT.

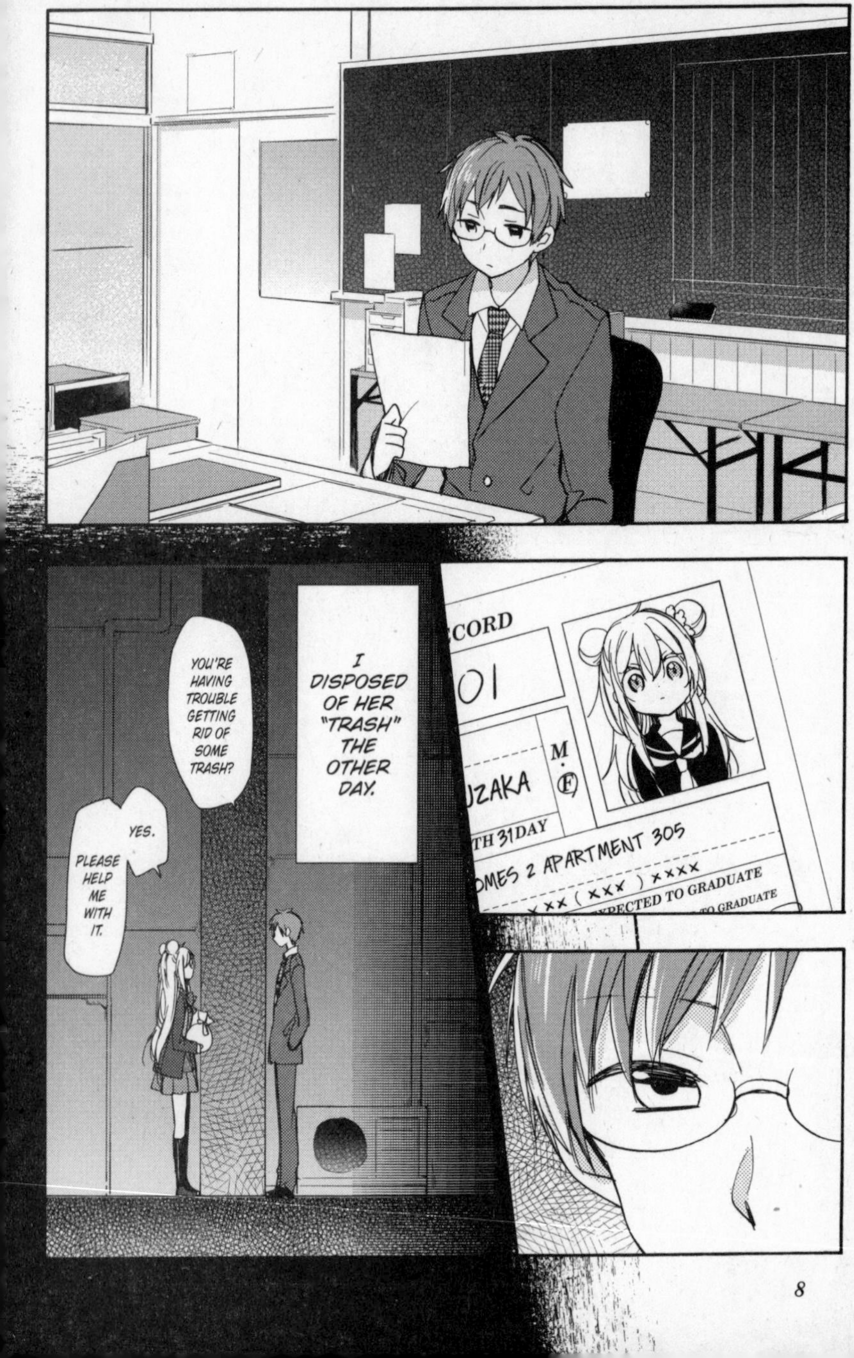
CORD
01
M
F
UZAKA
TH 31DAY
OMES 2 APARTMENT 305
EXPECTED TO GRADUATE
I DISPOSED OF HER "TRASH" THE OTHER DAY.
YOU'RE HAVING TROUBLE GETTING RID OF SOME TRASH?
YES.
PLEASE HELP ME WITH IT.

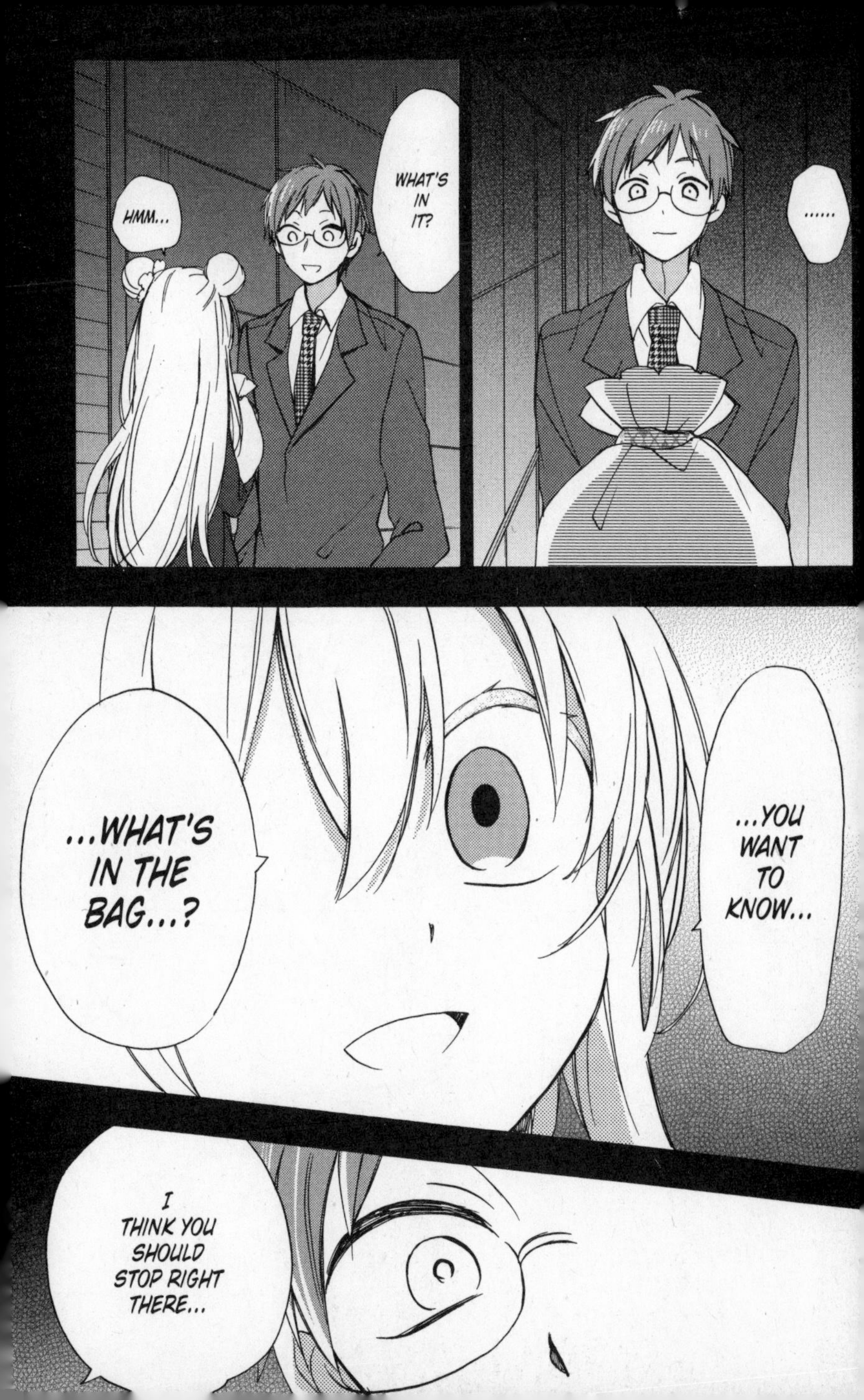
......
WHAT'S IN IT?
HMM...
...YOU WANT TO KNOW...
...WHAT'S IN THE BAG...?
I THINK YOU SHOULD STOP RIGHT THERE...

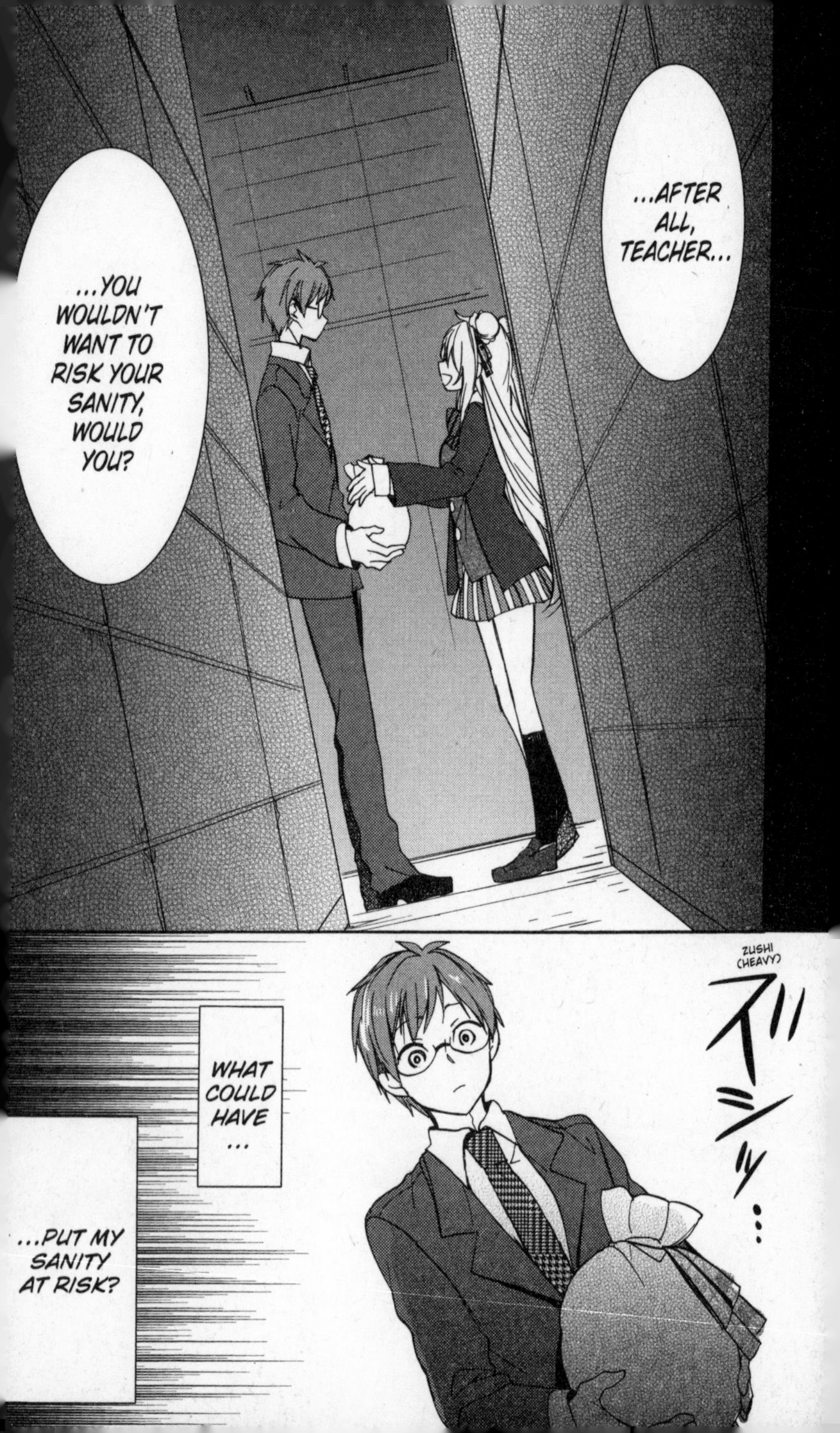
...AFTER ALL, TEACHER...
...YOU WOULDN'T WANT TO RISK YOUR SANITY, WOULD YOU?
ZUSHI (HEAVY)
WHAT COULD HAVE ...
...PUT MY SANITY AT RISK?

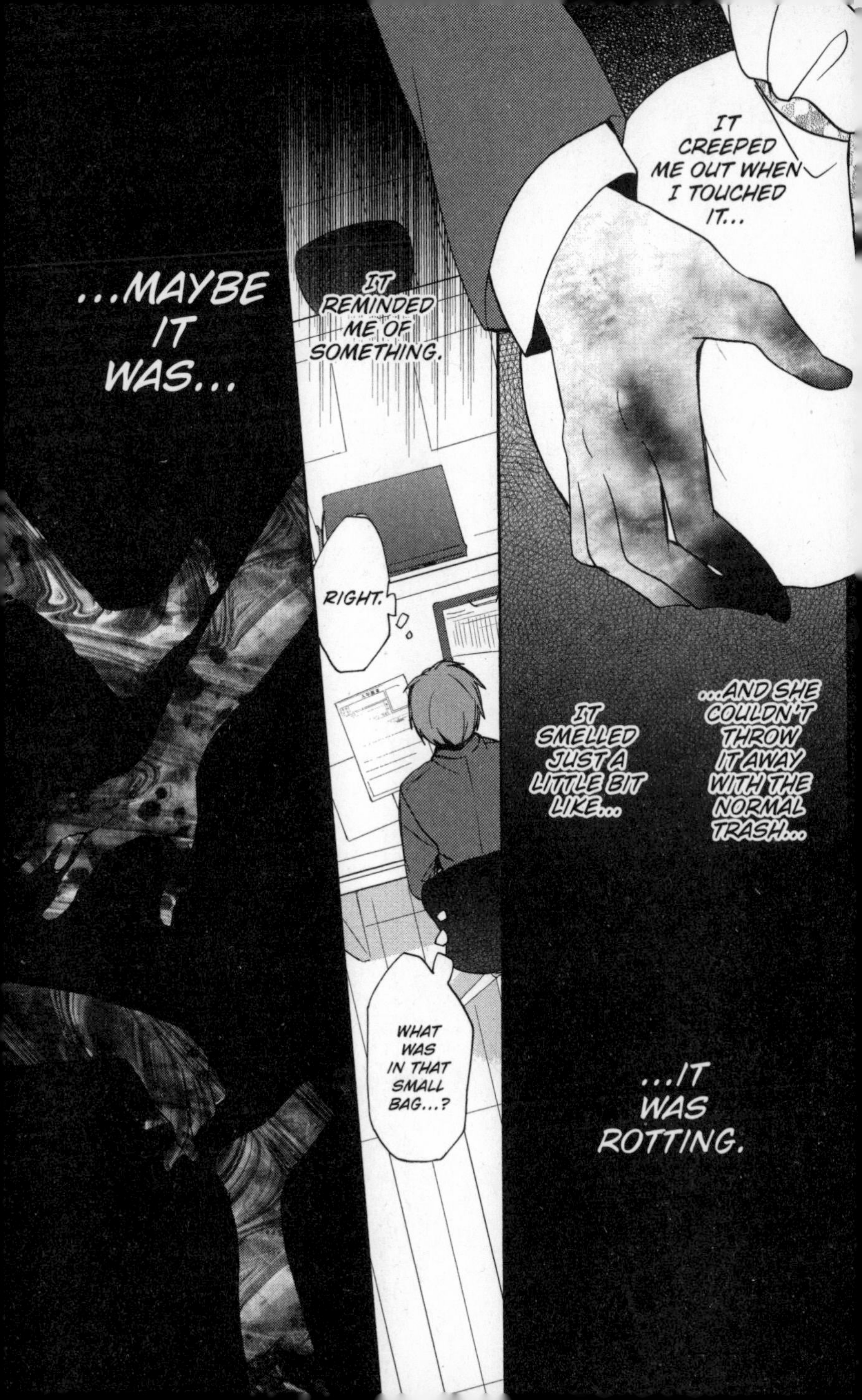
IT CREEPED ME OUT WHEN I TOUCHED IT...
...AND SHE COULDN'T THROW IT AWAY WITH THE NORMAL TRASH...
IT SMELLED JUST A LITTLE BIT LIKE...
...IT WAS ROTTING.
IT REMINDED ME OF SOMETHING.
RIGHT.
WHAT WAS IN THAT SMALL BAG...?
...MAYBE IT WAS...

HER
AUNT?

...
THEN "WHO"
WAS
IT...?

EVEN
IF IT
WAS
...

BUT
WHY?

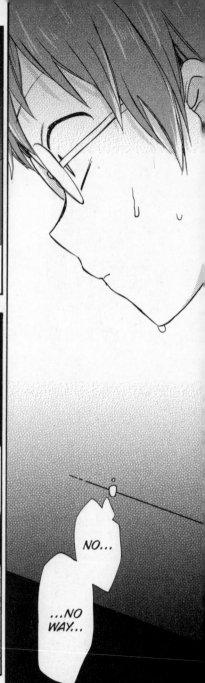

NO.

SHE'S
JUST
A
CHILD.

IS
SHE
EVEN
CAPABLE
OF
THAT?

NO...

...NO
WAY...

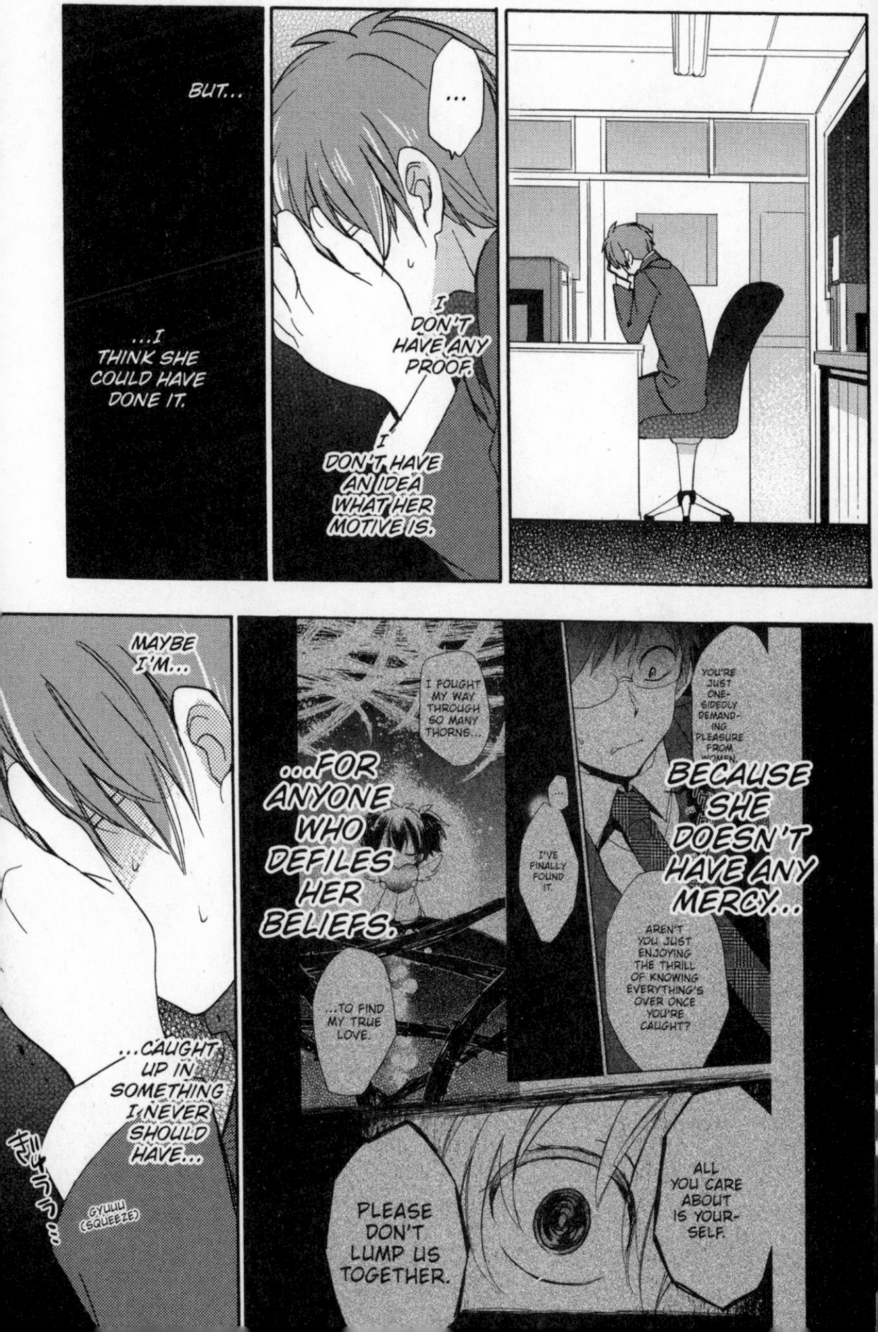
...
I DON'T HAVE ANY PROOF.
I DON'T HAVE AN IDEA WHAT HER MOTIVE IS.
BUT...
...I THINK SHE COULD HAVE DONE IT.
YOU'RE JUST ONE-SIDEDLY DEMANDING PLEASURE FROM
BECAUSE SHE DOESN'T HAVE ANY MERCY...
...
I'VE FINALLY FOUND IT.
AREN'T YOU JUST ENJOYING THE THRILL OF KNOWING EVERYTHING'S OVER ONCE YOU'RE CAUGHT?
I FOUGHT MY WAY THROUGH SO MANY THORNS...
...FOR ANYONE WHO DEFILES HER BELIEFS.
...TO FIND MY TRUE LOVE.
ALL YOU CARE ABOUT IS YOUR-SELF.
PLEASE DON'T LUMP US TOGETHER.
MAYBE I'M...
...CAUGHT UP IN SOMETHING I NEVER SHOULD HAVE...
GYUUU (SQUEEZE)

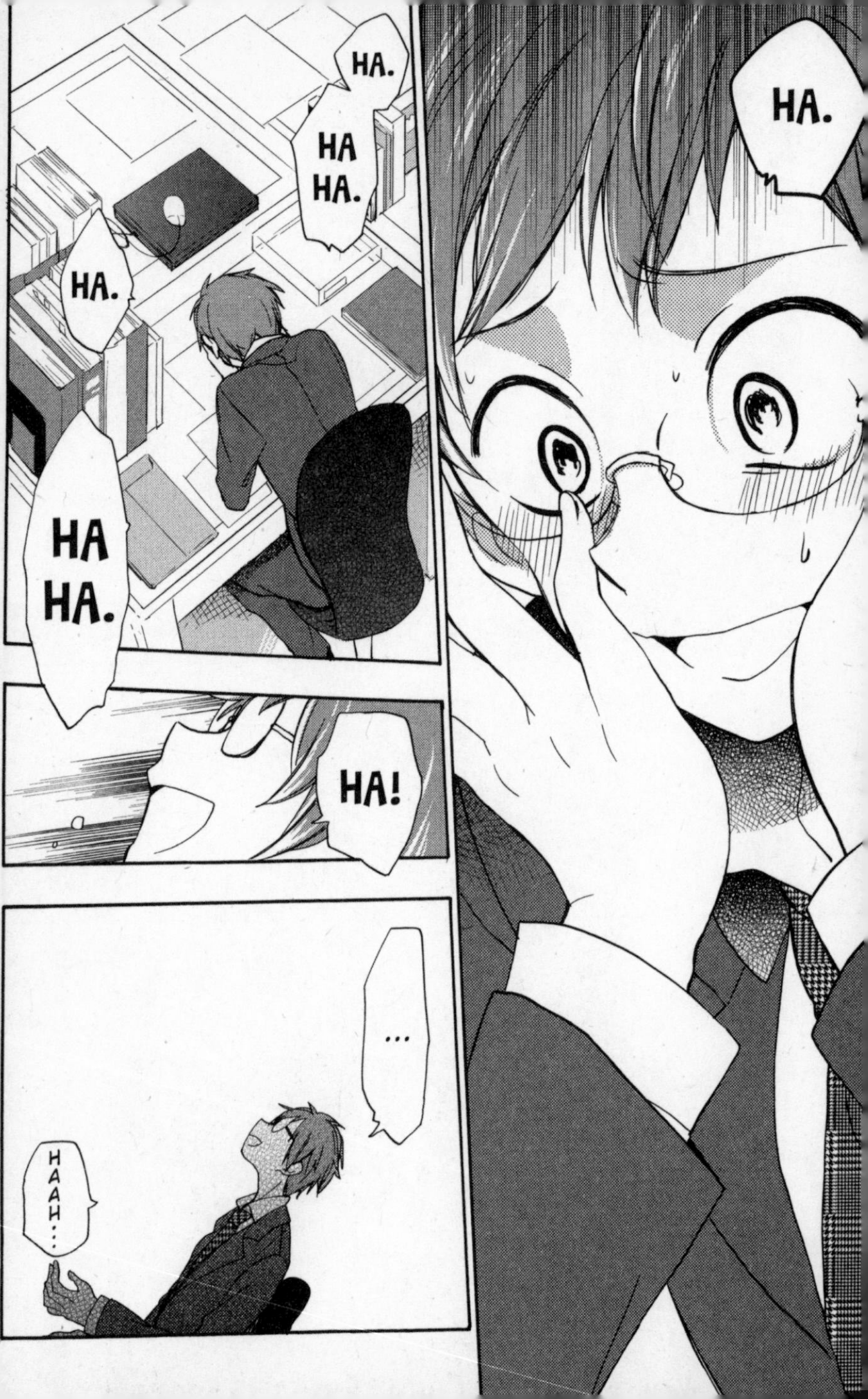
HA.
HA.
HA HA.
HA.
HA HA.
HA!
...
HAAH...

IS IT REAL OR JUST MY IMAGINATION...?

WELL, THEN.

THIS IS JUST SO THRILLING ...

ATRICULATION REC...

1001

MATSUZAKA

SATOU MATSUZAKA

GANA

M. (F)

YEAR 12MONTH 31DAY

...OMES 2

RTMENT 305

(x) xxxx

...ED TO GRADUATE

...ECTED TO GRADUA...

YES

HMM...

WHAT SHALL I DO?

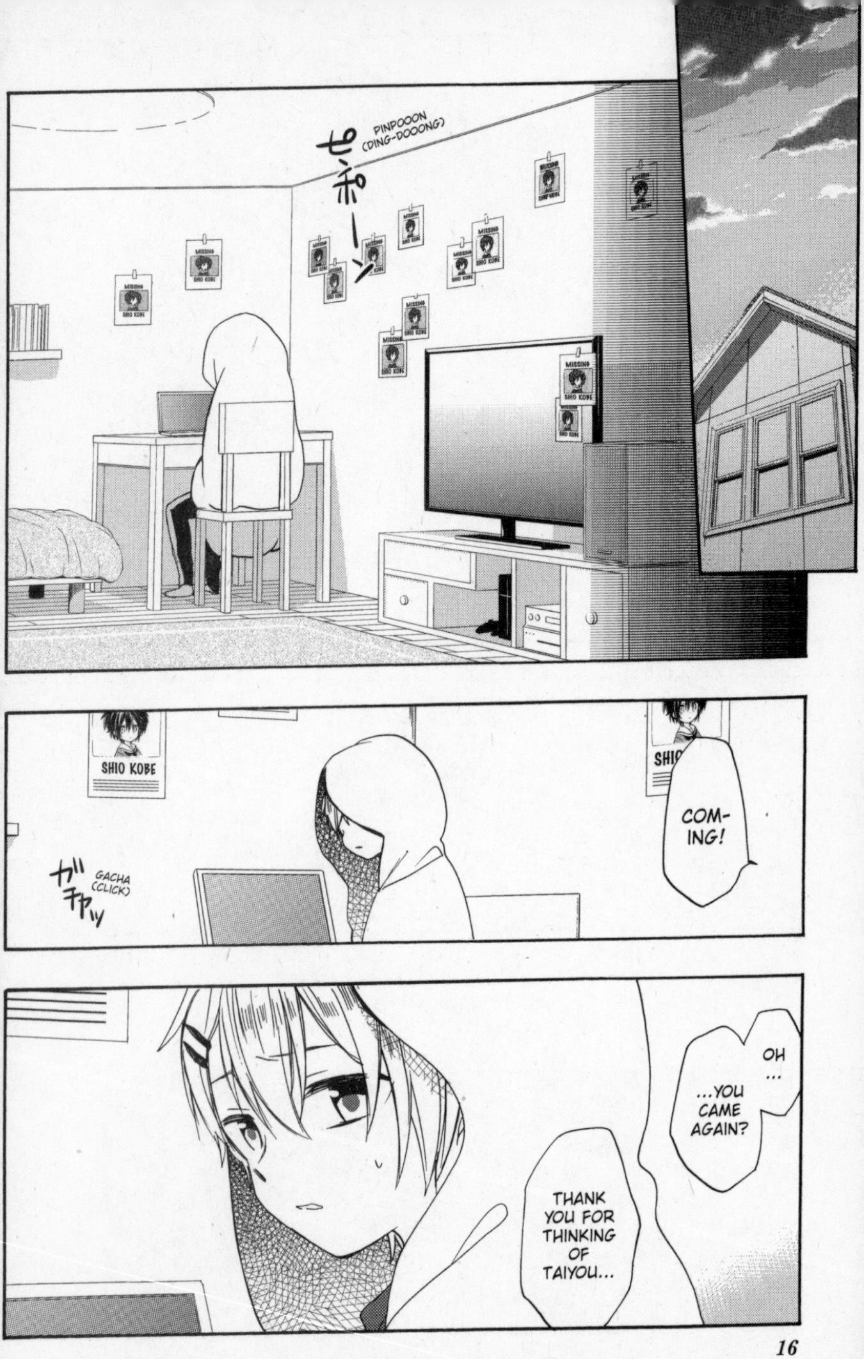
ピンポーン
PINPOOON (DING-DOOONG)
MISSING
SHIO KOBE
SHIO KOBE
COM-ING!
ガチャッ
GACHA (CLICK)
OH ...
...YOU CAME AGAIN?
THANK YOU FOR THINKING OF TAIYOU...

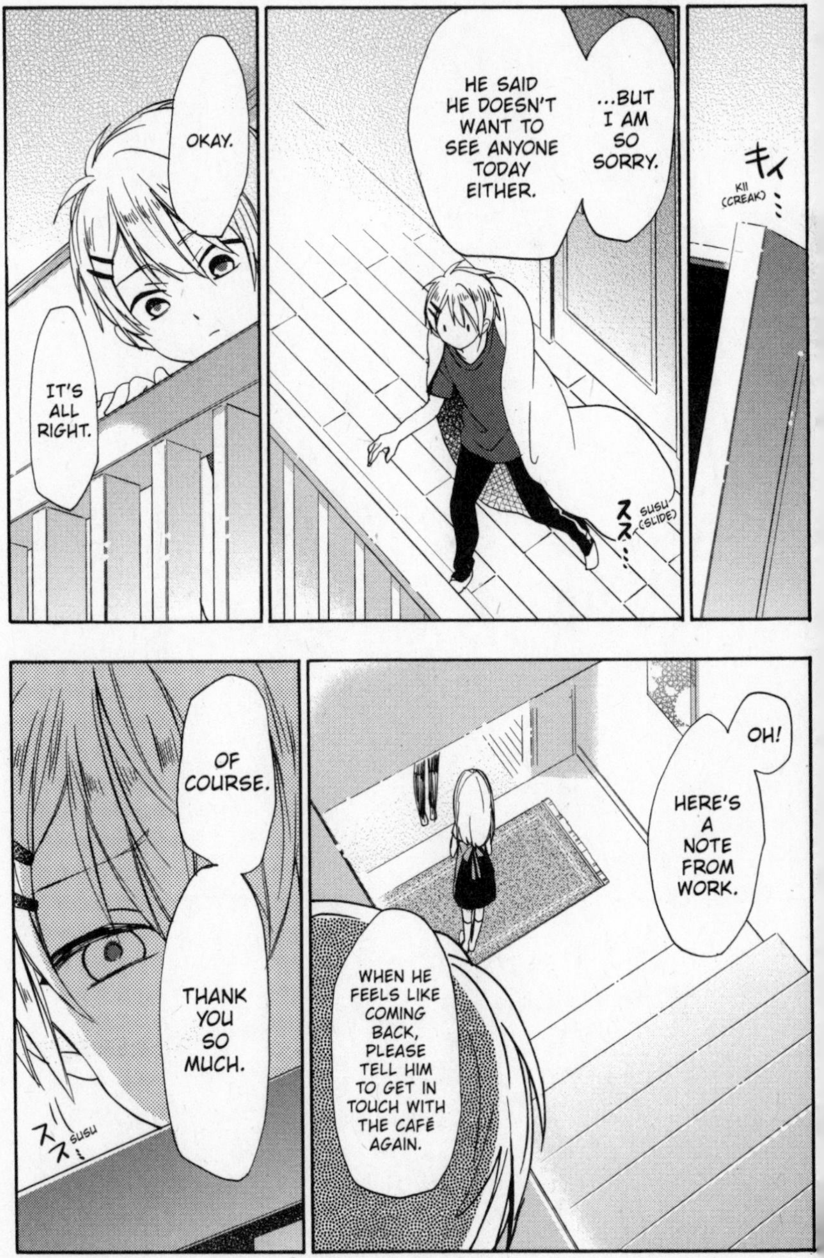
キィ
KII (CREAK)
HE SAID HE DOESN'T WANT TO SEE ANYONE TODAY EITHER.
...BUT I AM SO SORRY.
スス
SUSU (SLIDE)
OKAY.
IT'S ALL RIGHT.
OH!
HERE'S A NOTE FROM WORK.
WHEN HE FEELS LIKE COMING BACK, PLEASE TELL HIM TO GET IN TOUCH WITH THE CAFÉ AGAIN.
OF COURSE.
THANK YOU SO MUCH.
スス
SUSU

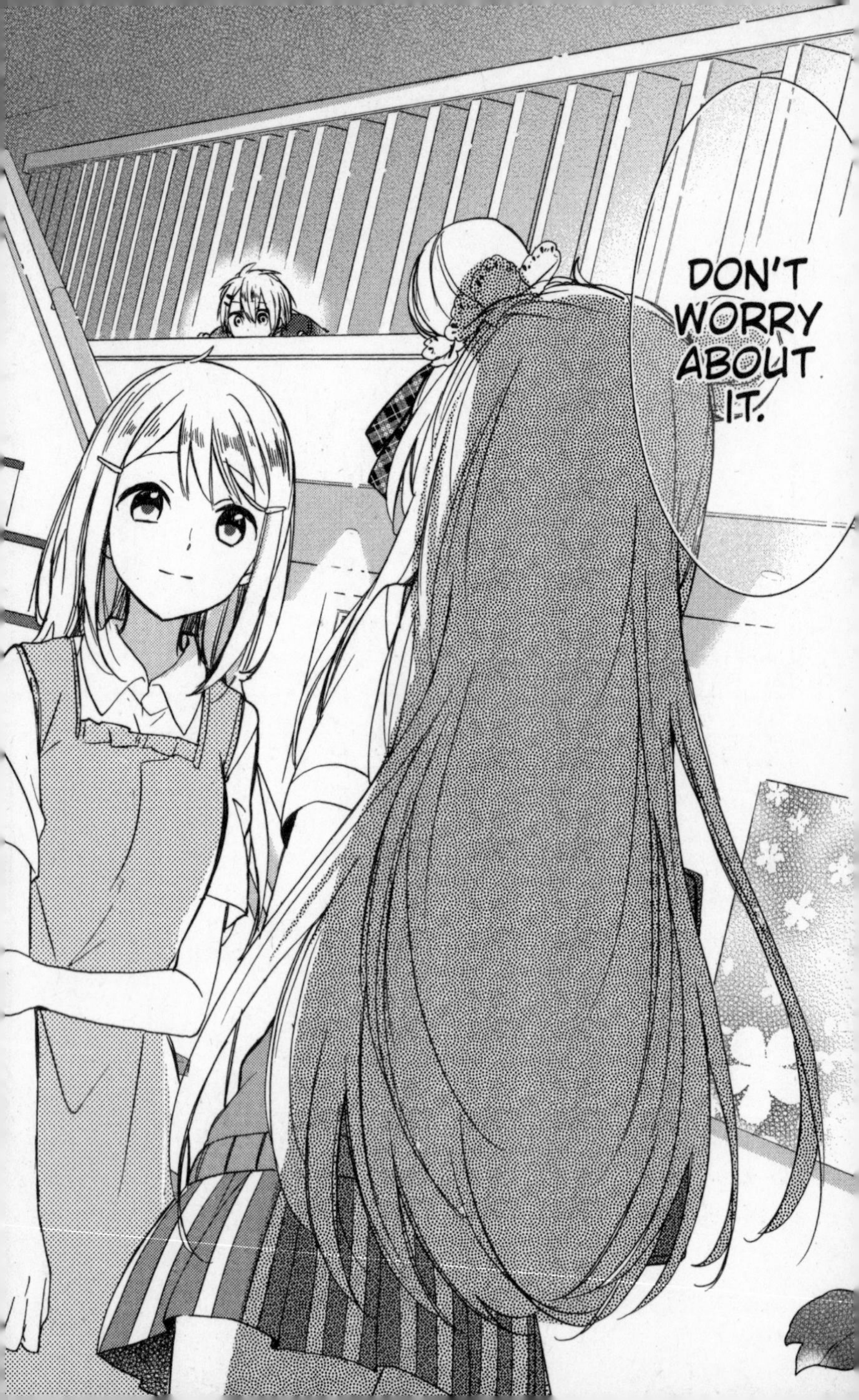
DON'T WORRY ABOUT IT.

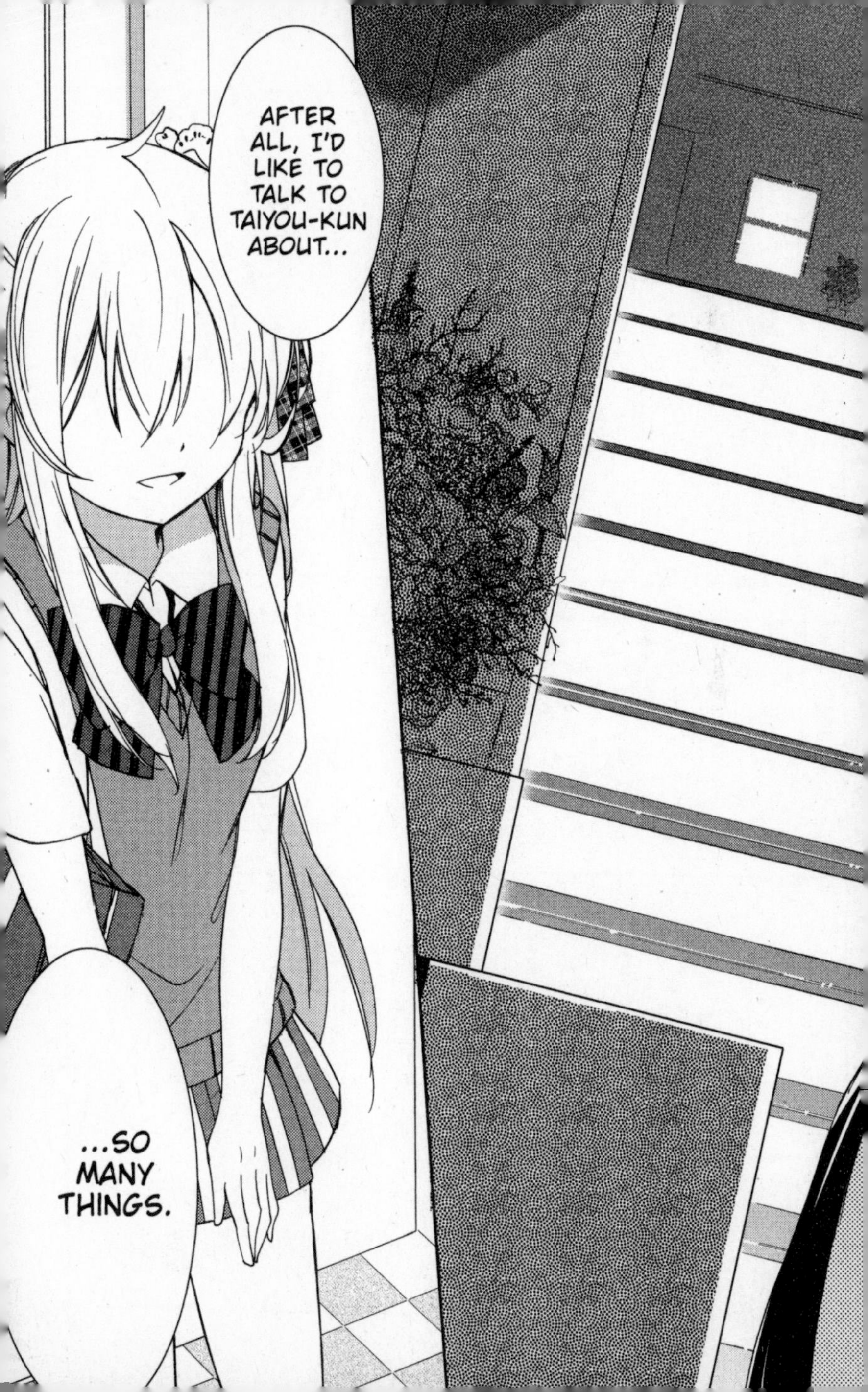
AFTER ALL, I'D LIKE TO TALK TO TAIYOU-KUN ABOUT...
...SO MANY THINGS.

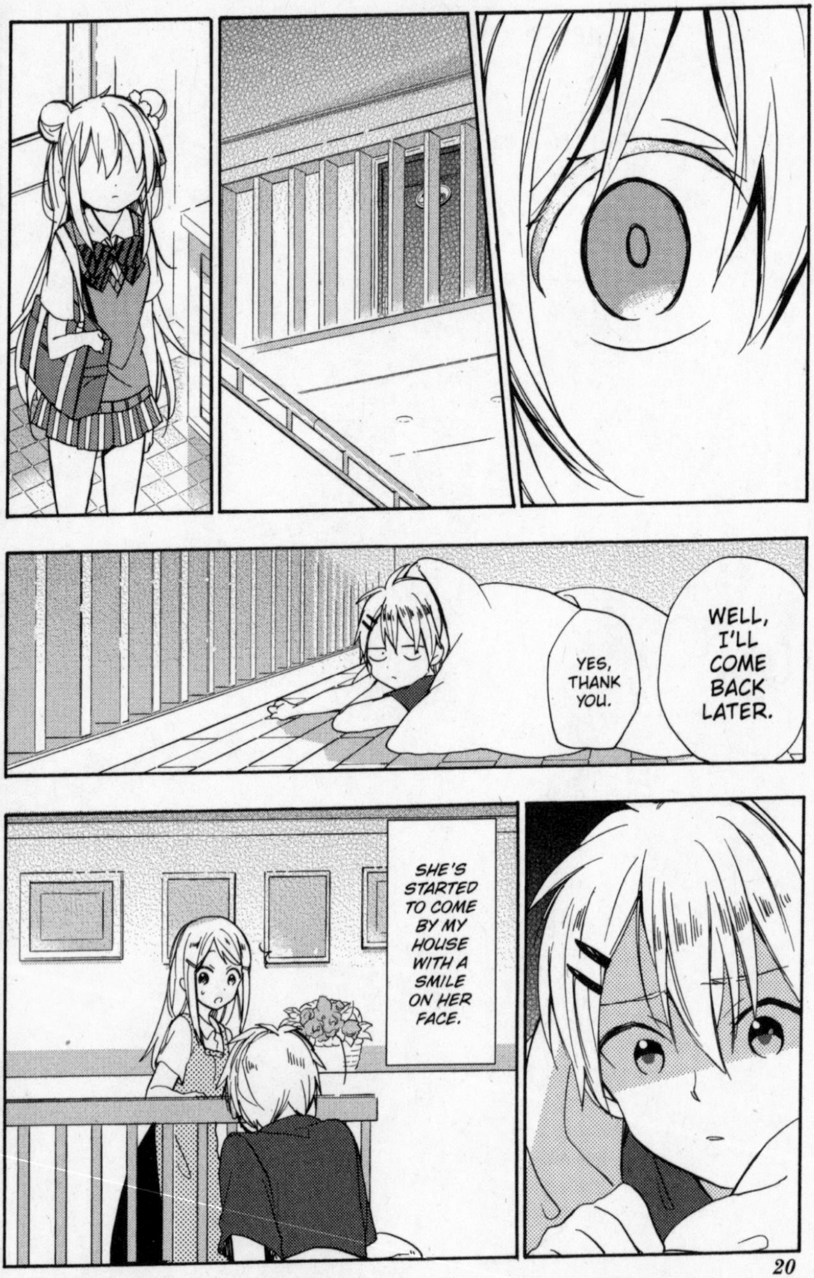
WELL, I'LL COME BACK LATER.
YES, THANK YOU.
SHE'S STARTED TO COME BY MY HOUSE WITH A SMILE ON HER FACE.

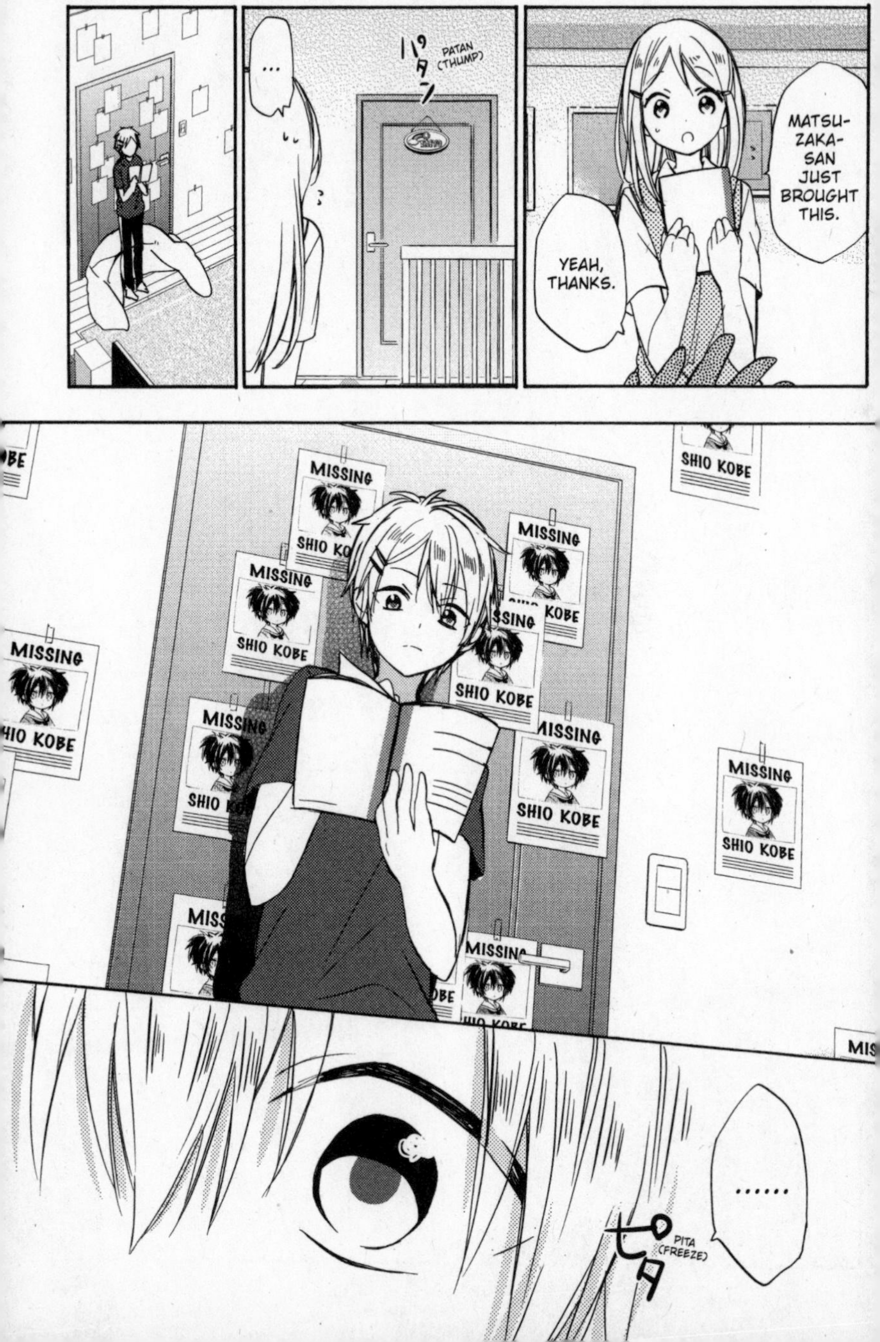

MATSU-ZAKA-SAN JUST BROUGHT THIS.
YEAH, THANKS.
...
パタン
PATAN (THUMP)
MISSING
SHIO KOBE
......
ピタ
PITA (FREEZE)

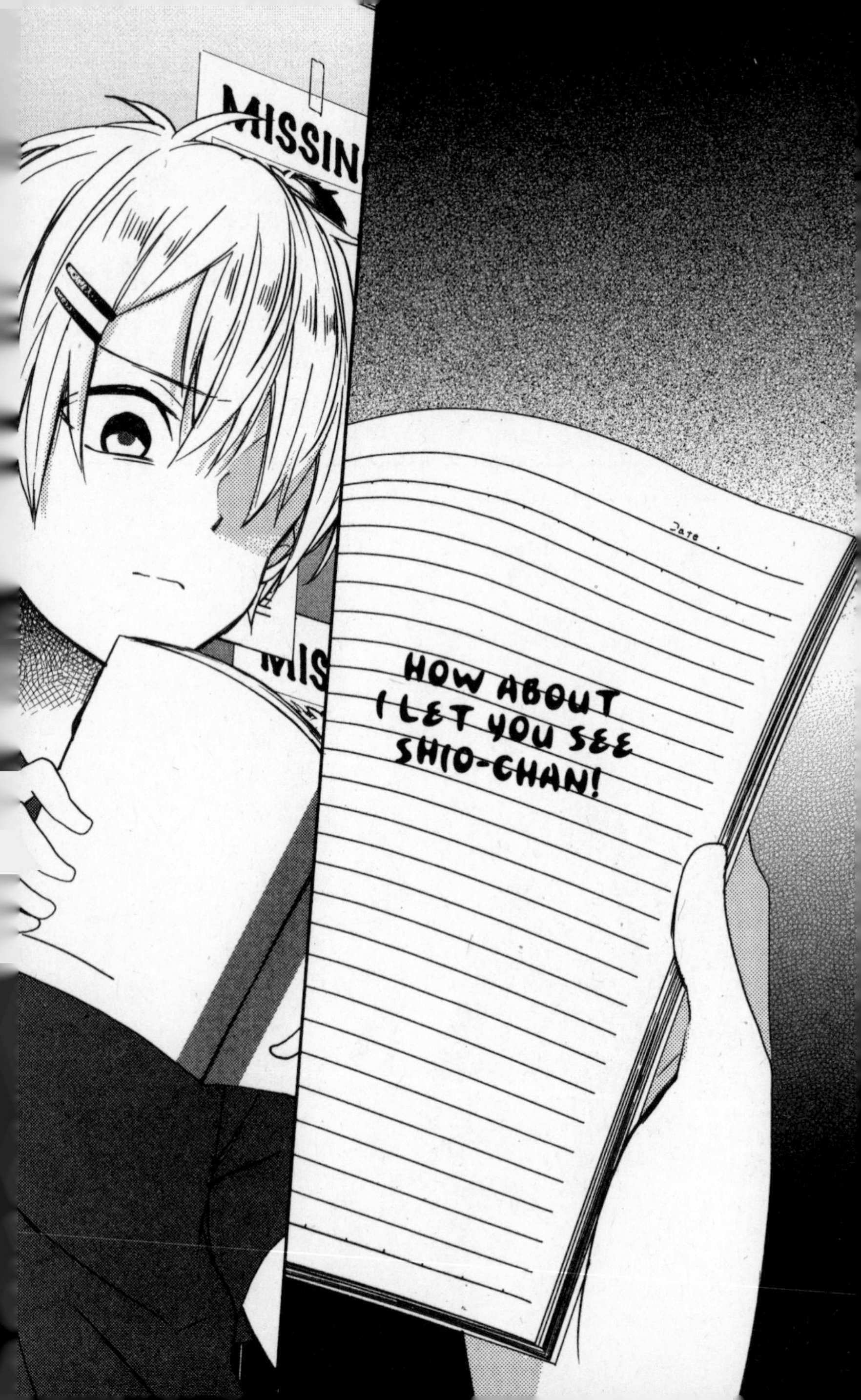
MISSIN
HOW ABOUT I LET YOU SEE SHIO-CHAN!

13TH LIFE: THE STORY OF THE CHANGING GIRL

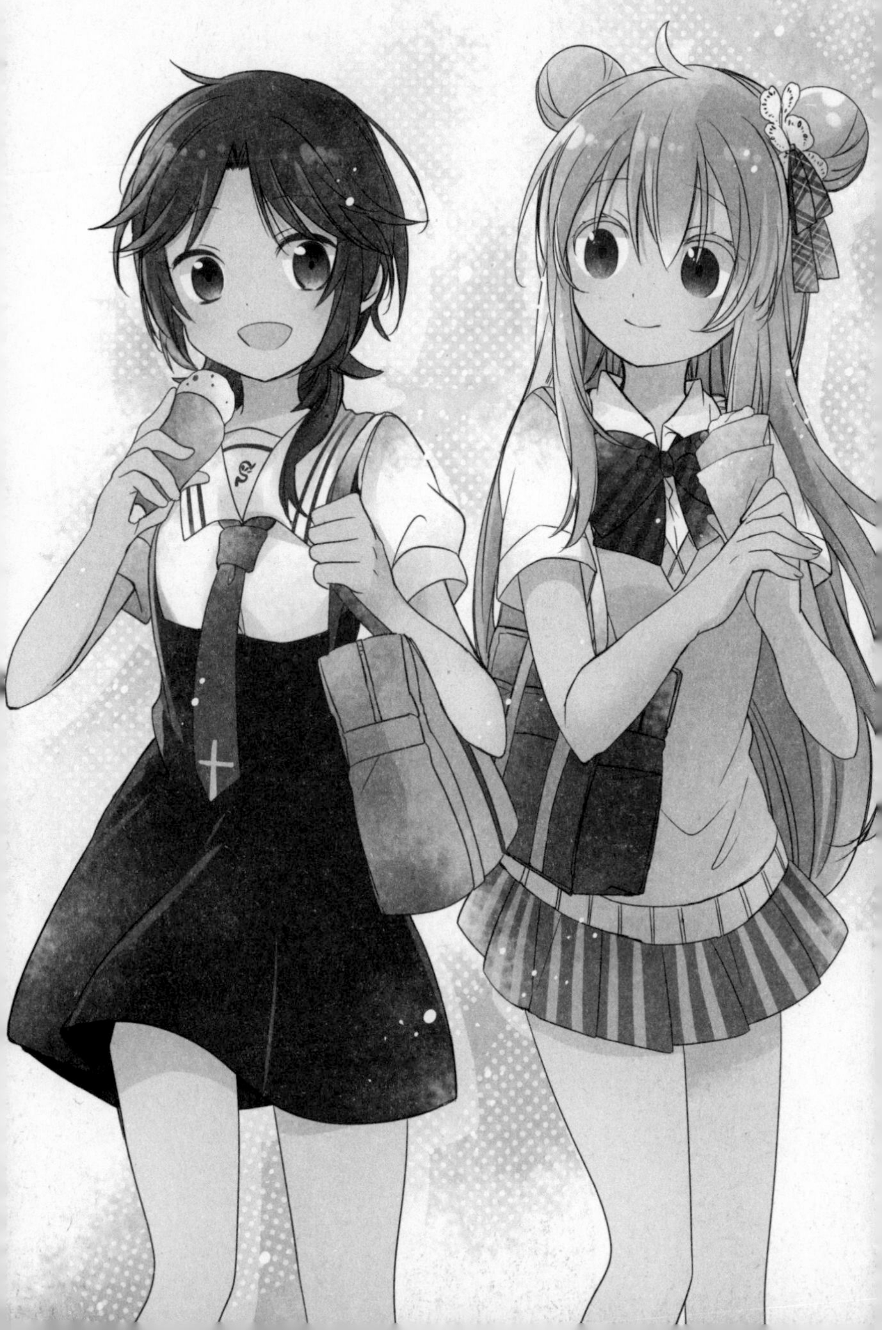

Happy Sugar Life

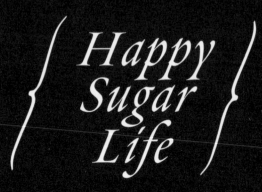

SIGN: CURE A CUTE

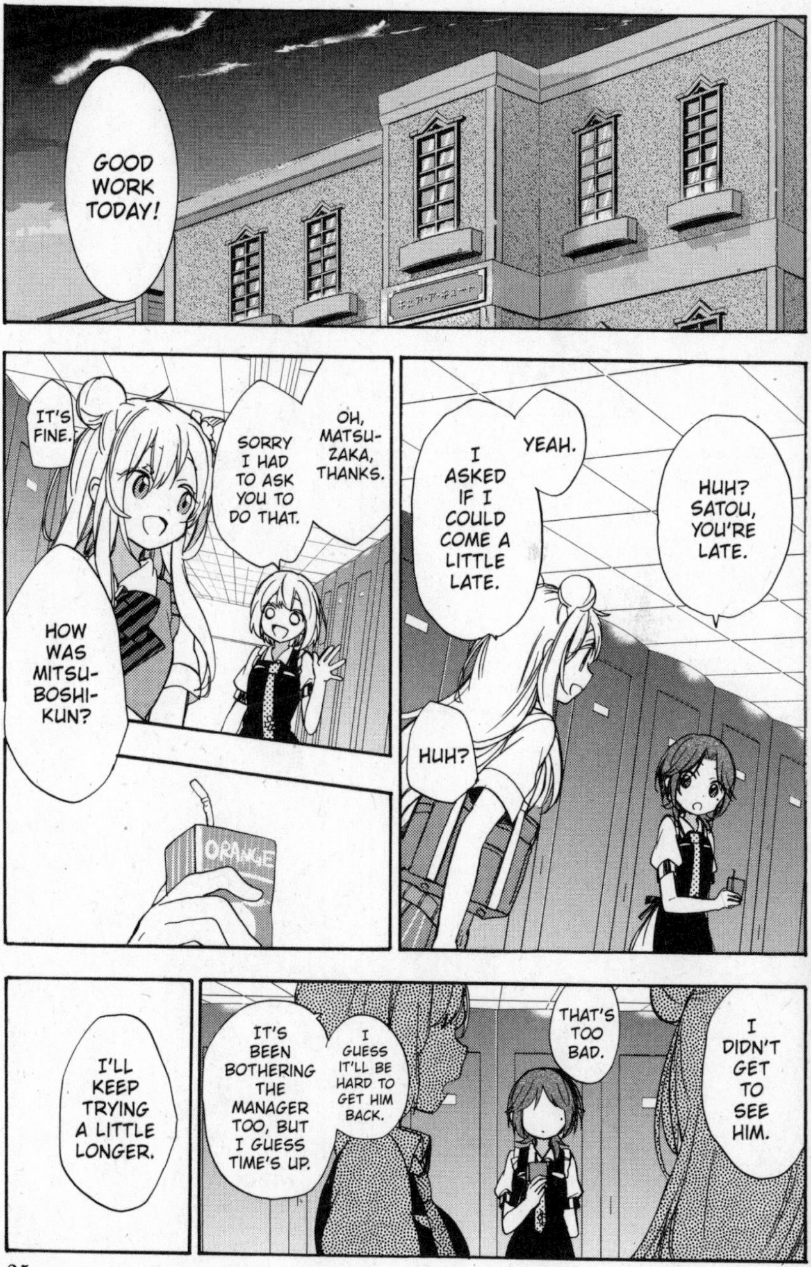
GOOD WORK TODAY!
HUH? SATOU, YOU'RE LATE.
YEAH.
I ASKED IF I COULD COME A LITTLE LATE.
HUH?
OH, MATSU-ZAKA, THANKS.
SORRY I HAD TO ASK YOU TO DO THAT.
IT'S FINE.
HOW WAS MITSU-BOSHI-KUN?
ORANGE
I DIDN'T GET TO SEE HIM.
THAT'S TOO BAD.
I GUESS IT'LL BE HARD TO GET HIM BACK.
IT'S BEEN BOTHERING THE MANAGER TOO, BUT I GUESS TIME'S UP.
I'LL KEEP TRYING A LITTLE LONGER.

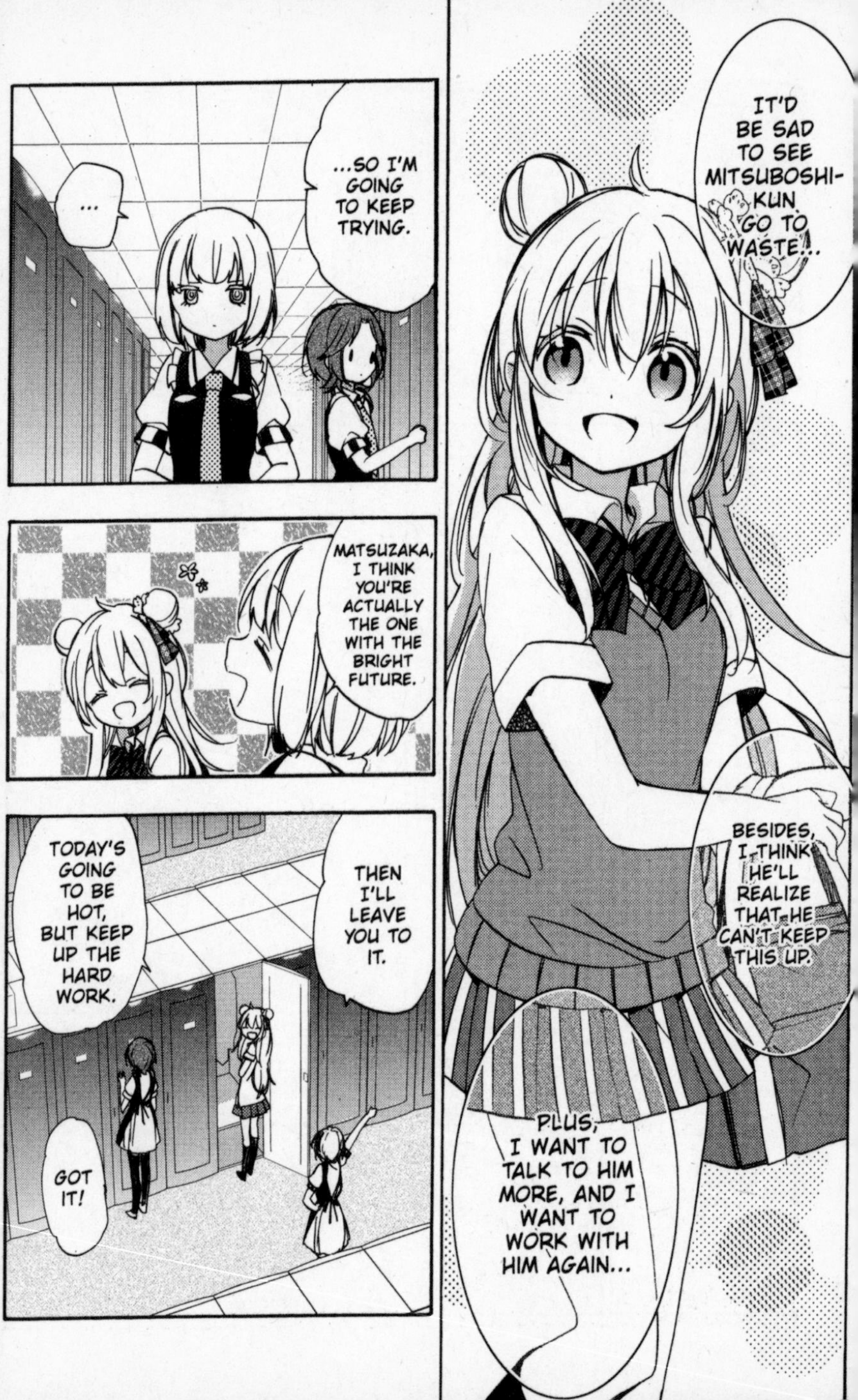
IT'D BE SAD TO SEE MITSUBOSHI-KUN GO TO WASTE...
BESIDES, I THINK HE'LL REALIZE THAT HE CAN'T KEEP THIS UP.
PLUS, I WANT TO TALK TO HIM MORE, AND I WANT TO WORK WITH HIM AGAIN...
...SO I'M GOING TO KEEP TRYING.
...
MATSUZAKA, I THINK YOU'RE ACTUALLY THE ONE WITH THE BRIGHT FUTURE.
THEN I'LL LEAVE YOU TO IT.
TODAY'S GOING TO BE HOT, BUT KEEP UP THE HARD WORK.
GOT IT!

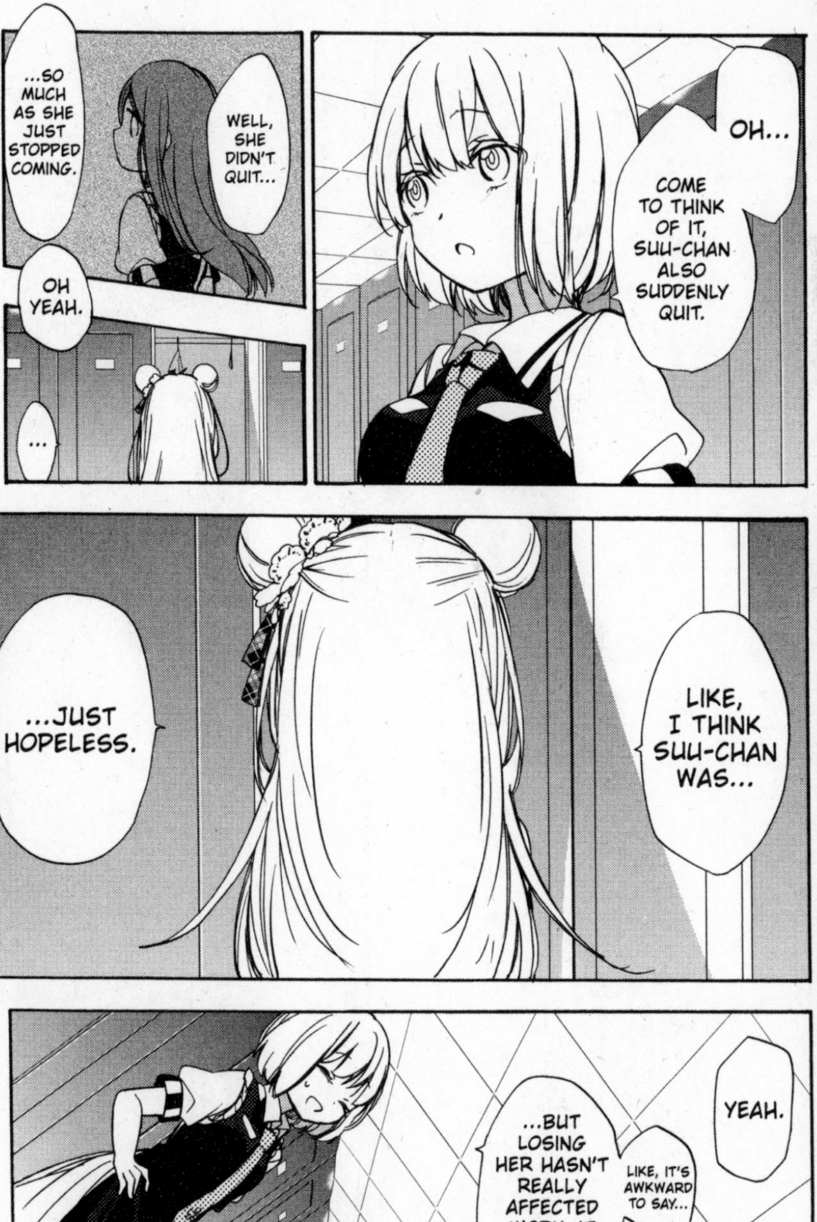
OH...
COME TO THINK OF IT, SUU-CHAN ALSO SUDDENLY QUIT.
WELL, SHE DIDN'T QUIT...
...SO MUCH AS SHE JUST STOPPED COMING.
OH YEAH.
...
LIKE, I THINK SUU-CHAN WAS...
...JUST HOPELESS.
YEAH.
LIKE, IT'S AWKWARD TO SAY...
...BUT LOSING HER HASN'T REALLY AFFECTED WORK AT ALL.

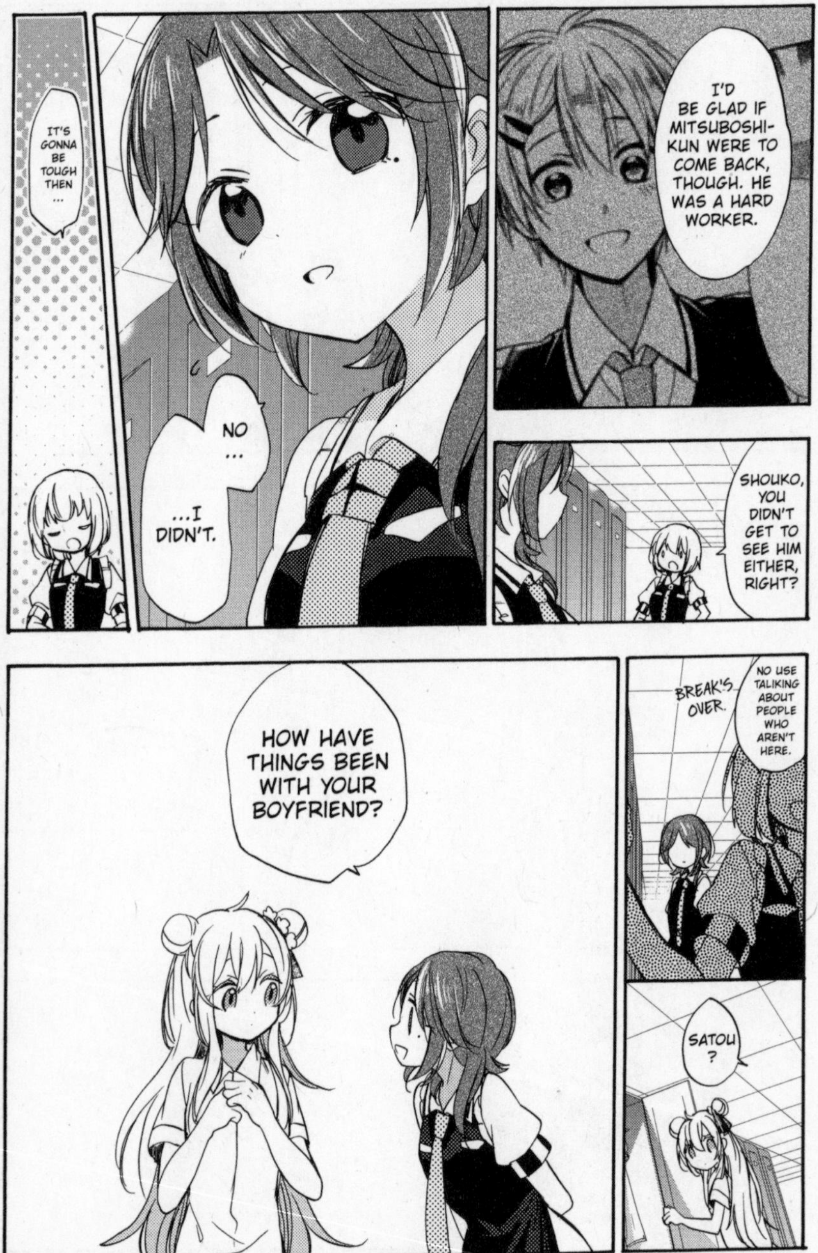
I'D BE GLAD IF MITSUBOSHI-KUN WERE TO COME BACK, THOUGH. HE WAS A HARD WORKER.
SHOUKO, YOU DIDN'T GET TO SEE HIM EITHER, RIGHT?
NO ...
...I DIDN'T.
IT'S GONNA BE TOUGH THEN ...
NO USE TALIKING ABOUT PEOPLE WHO AREN'T HERE.
BREAK'S OVER.
SATOU ?
HOW HAVE THINGS BEEN WITH YOUR BOYFRIEND?

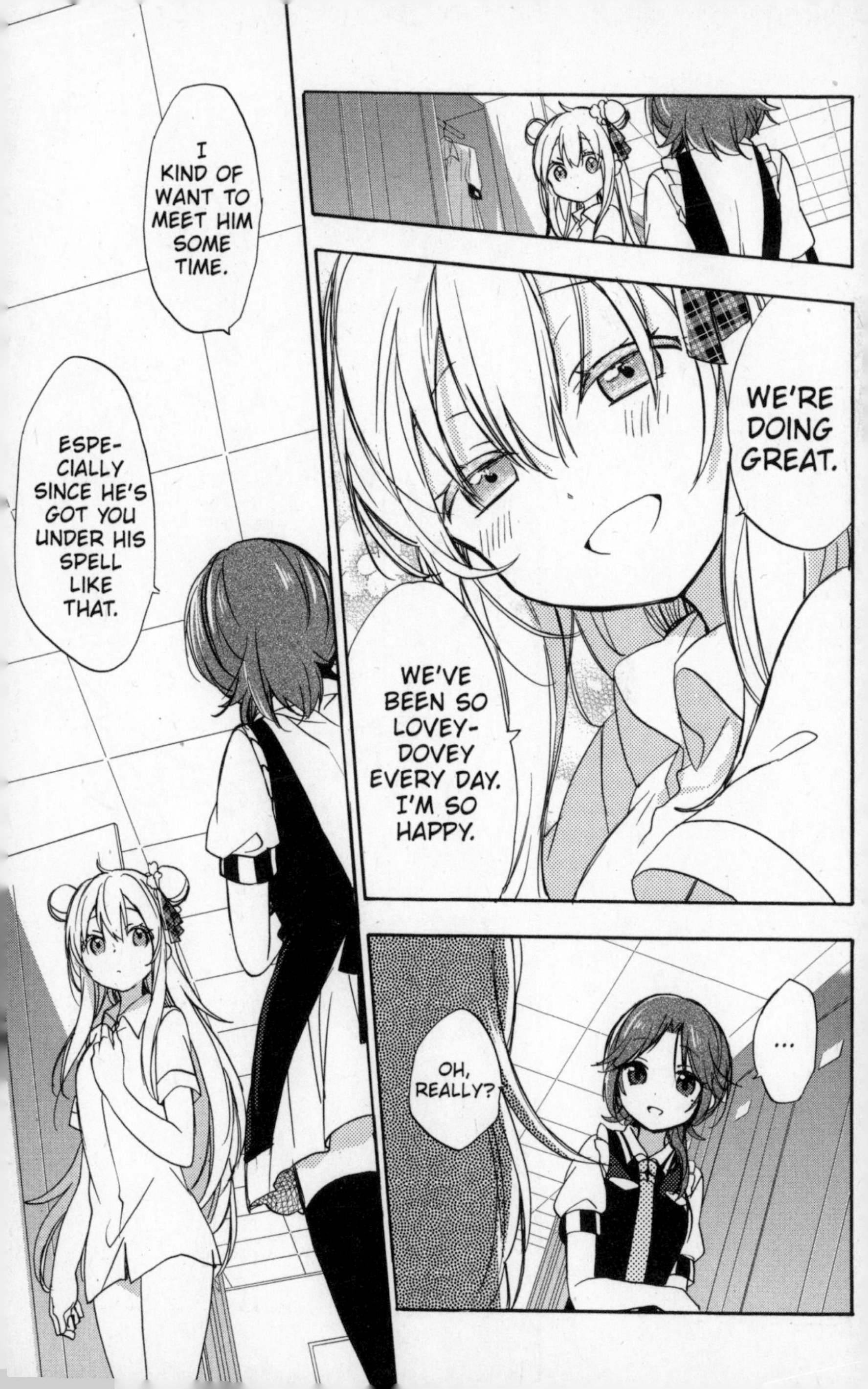
WE'RE DOING GREAT.
WE'VE BEEN SO LOVEY-DOVEY EVERY DAY. I'M SO HAPPY.
...
OH, REALLY?
I KIND OF WANT TO MEET HIM SOME TIME.
ESPE-CIALLY SINCE HE'S GOT YOU UNDER HIS SPELL LIKE THAT.

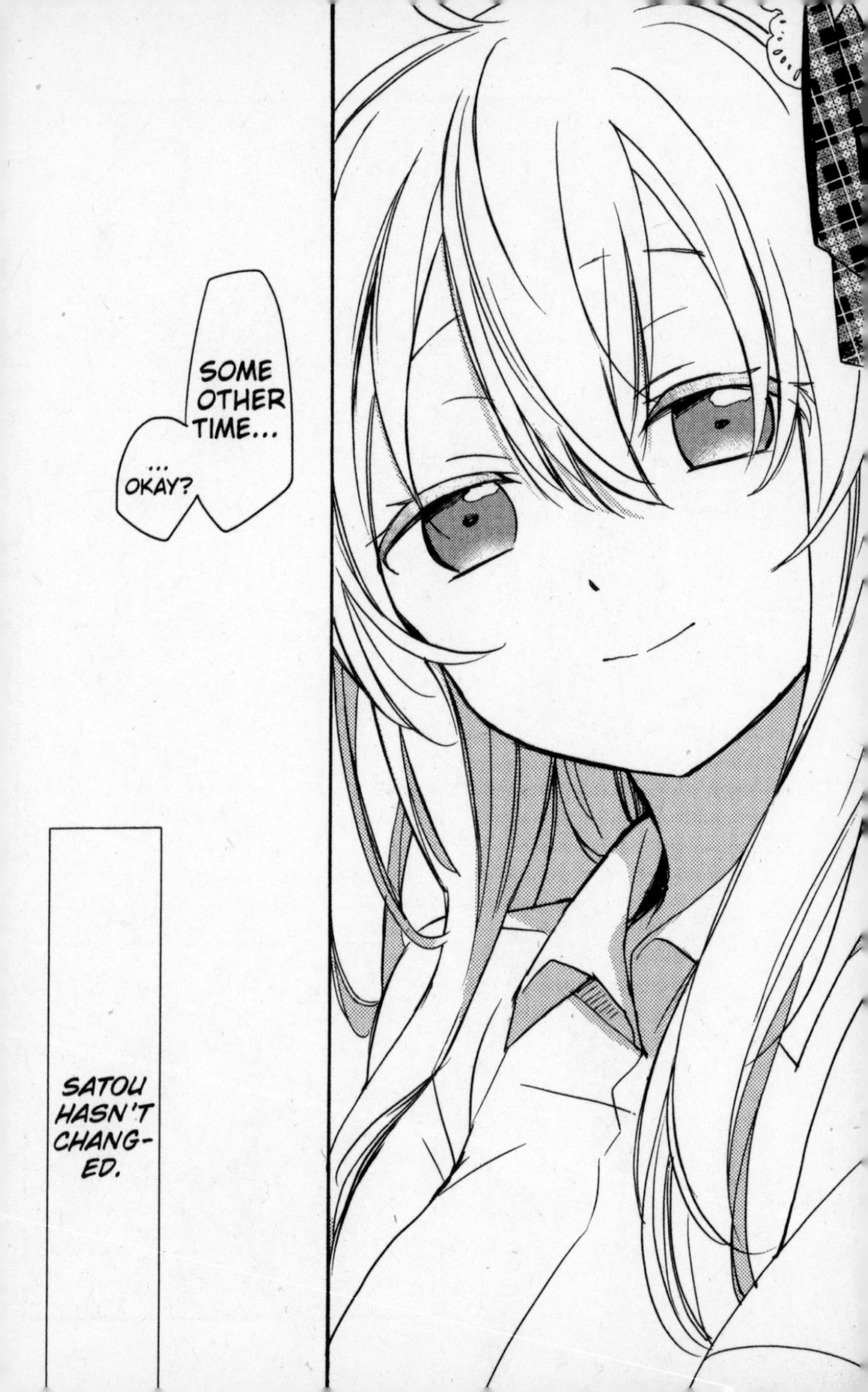
SOME OTHER TIME...
...OKAY?
SATOU HASN'T CHANG-ED.

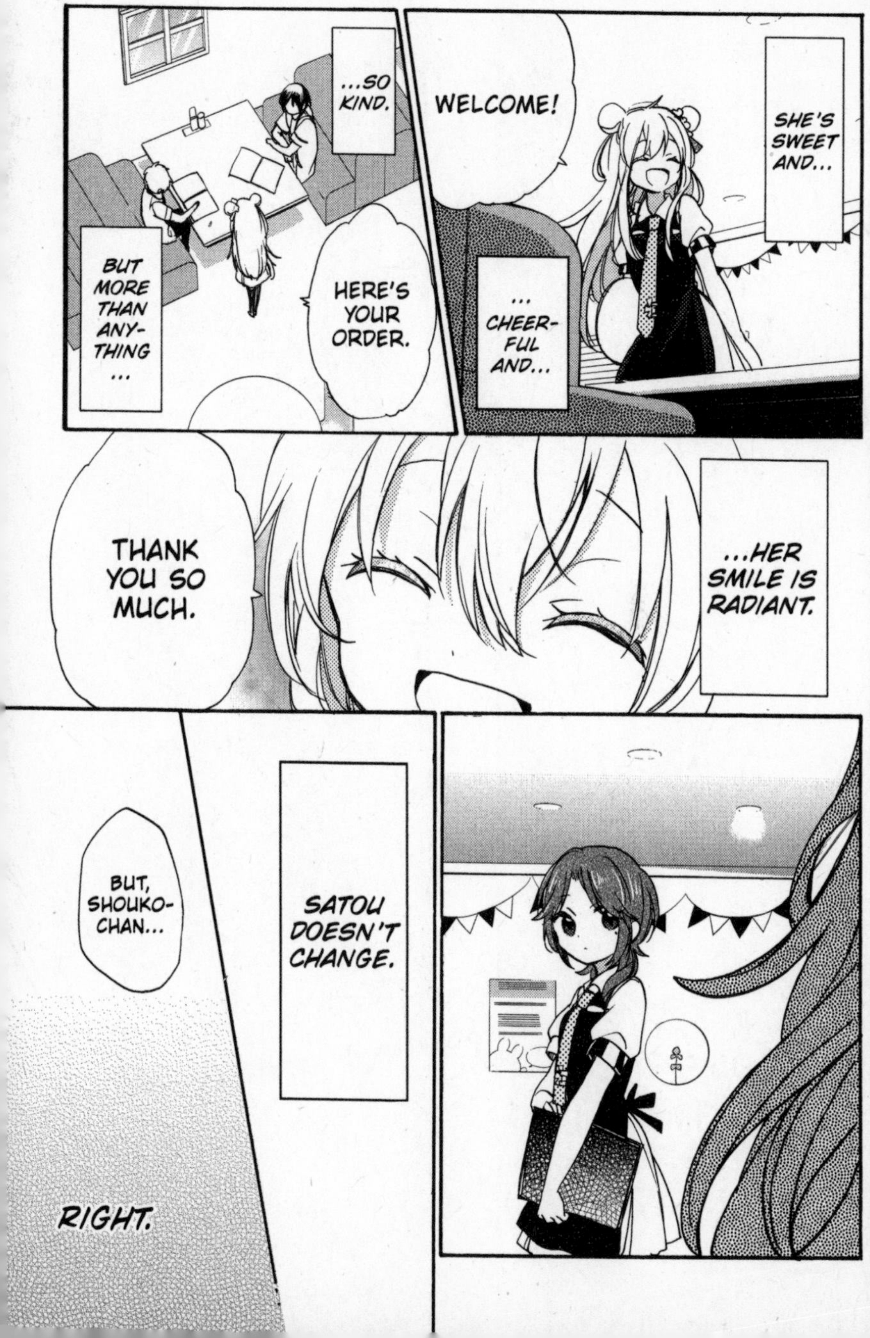
SHE'S SWEET AND...
WELCOME!
...CHEERFUL AND...
...SO KIND.
HERE'S YOUR ORDER.
BUT MORE THAN ANYTHING...
...HER SMILE IS RADIANT.
THANK YOU SO MUCH.
SATOU DOESN'T CHANGE.
BUT, SHOUKO-CHAN...
RIGHT.

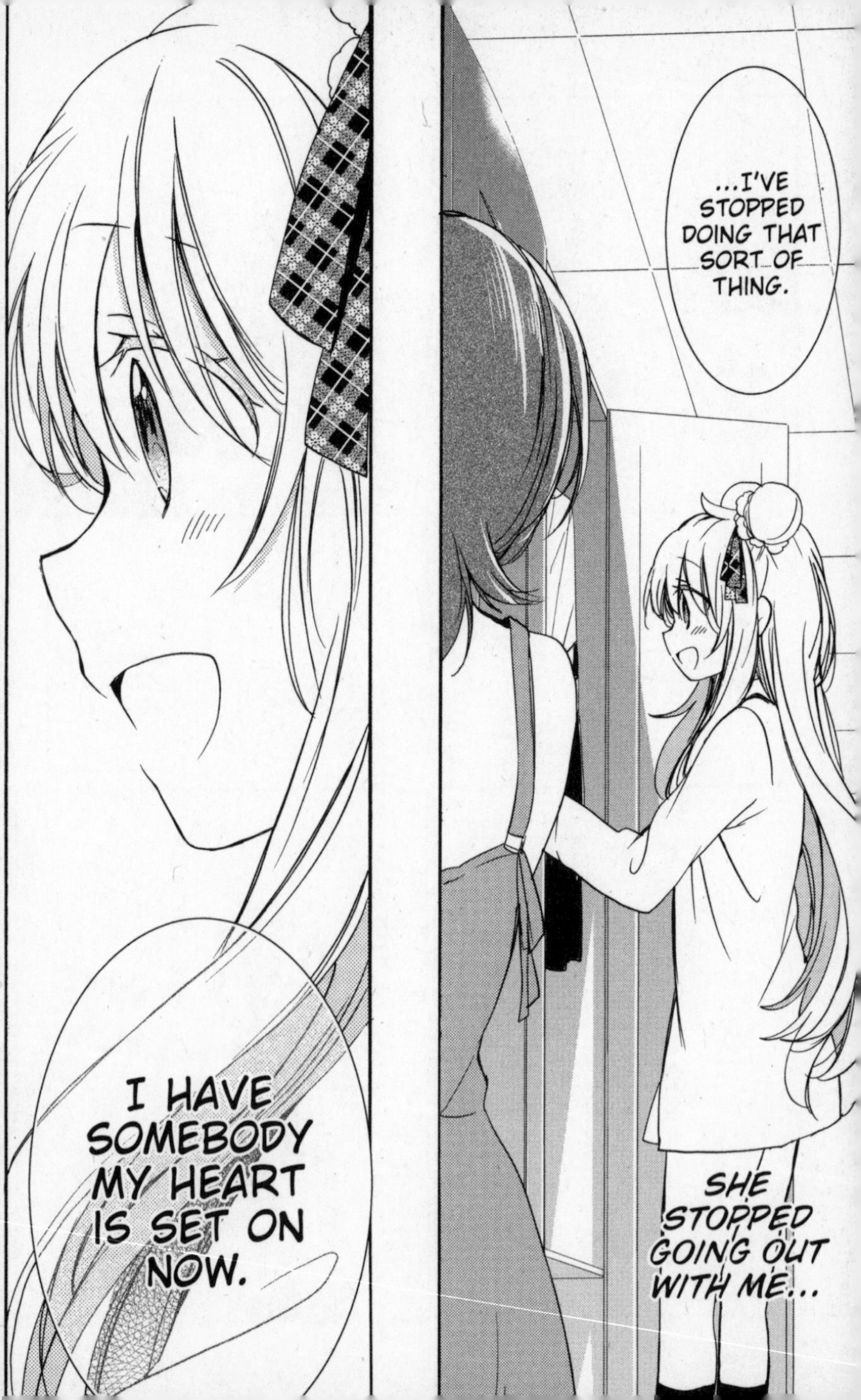
...I'VE STOPPED DOING THAT SORT OF THING.
SHE STOPPED GOING OUT WITH ME...
I HAVE SOMEBODY MY HEART IS SET ON NOW.

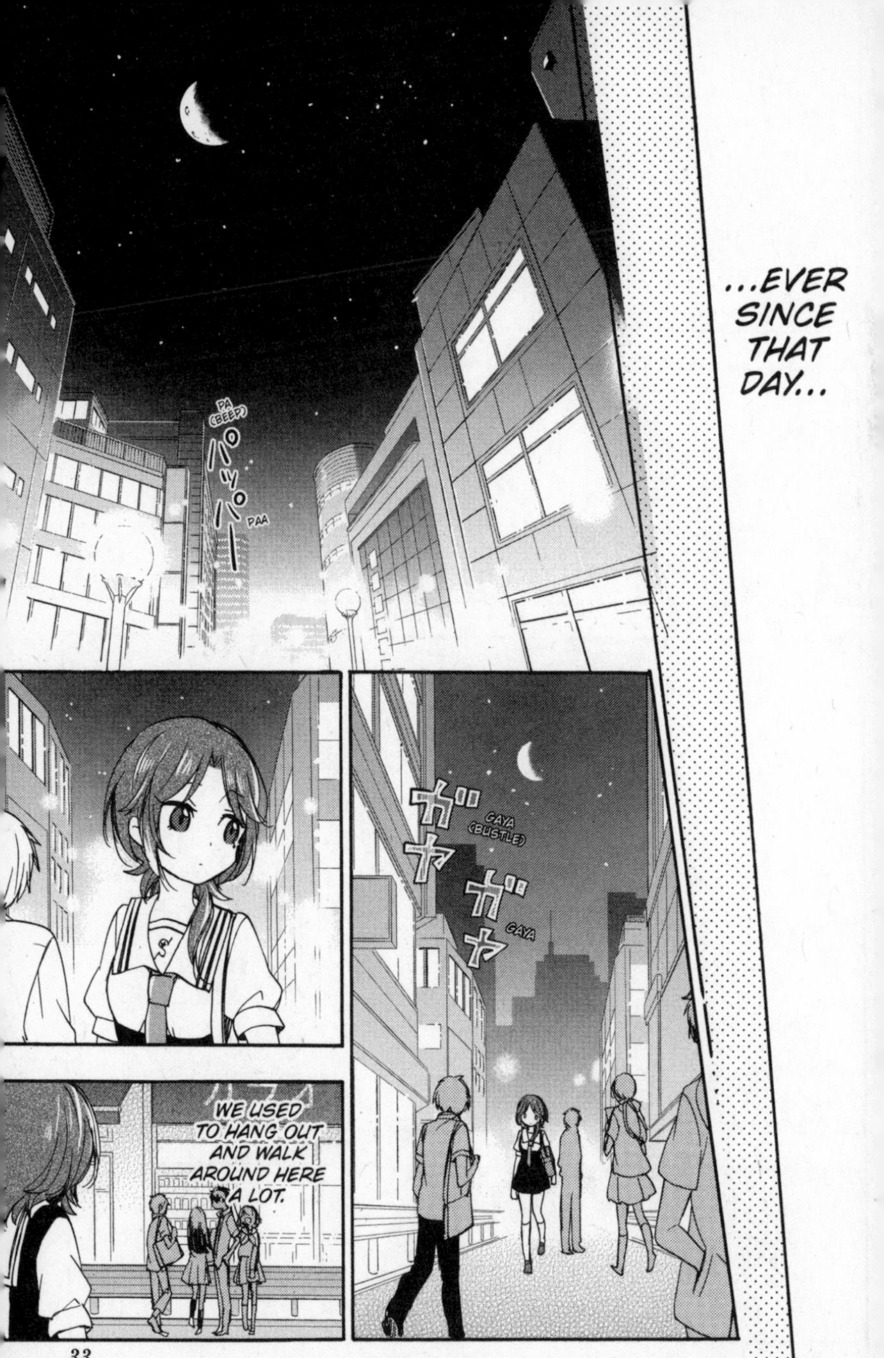
...EVER SINCE THAT DAY...
パッパー
PA (BEEP)
PAA
ガヤガヤ
GAYA (BUSTLE)
GAYA
WE USED TO HANG OUT AND WALK AROUND HERE A LOT.

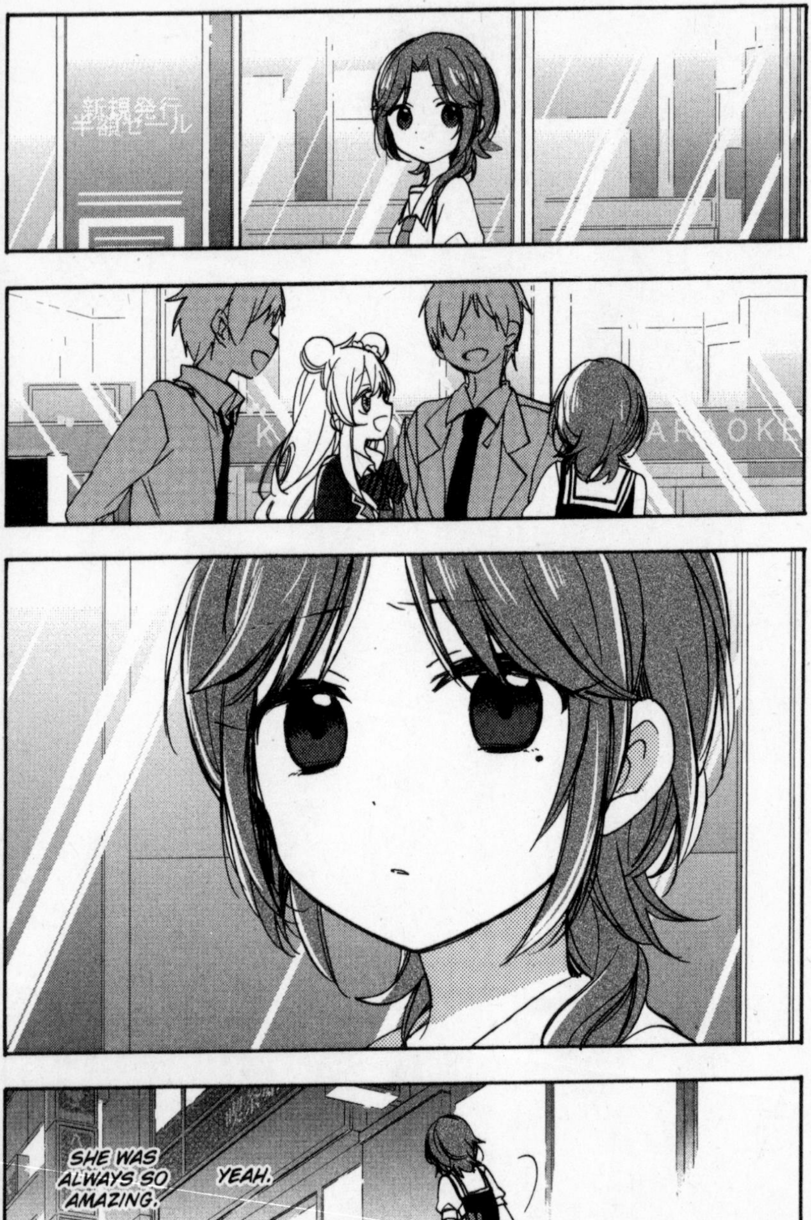
新規発行
半額セール
YEAH.
SHE WAS ALWAYS SO AMAZING.

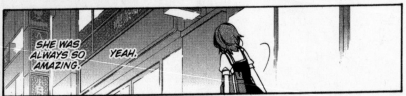

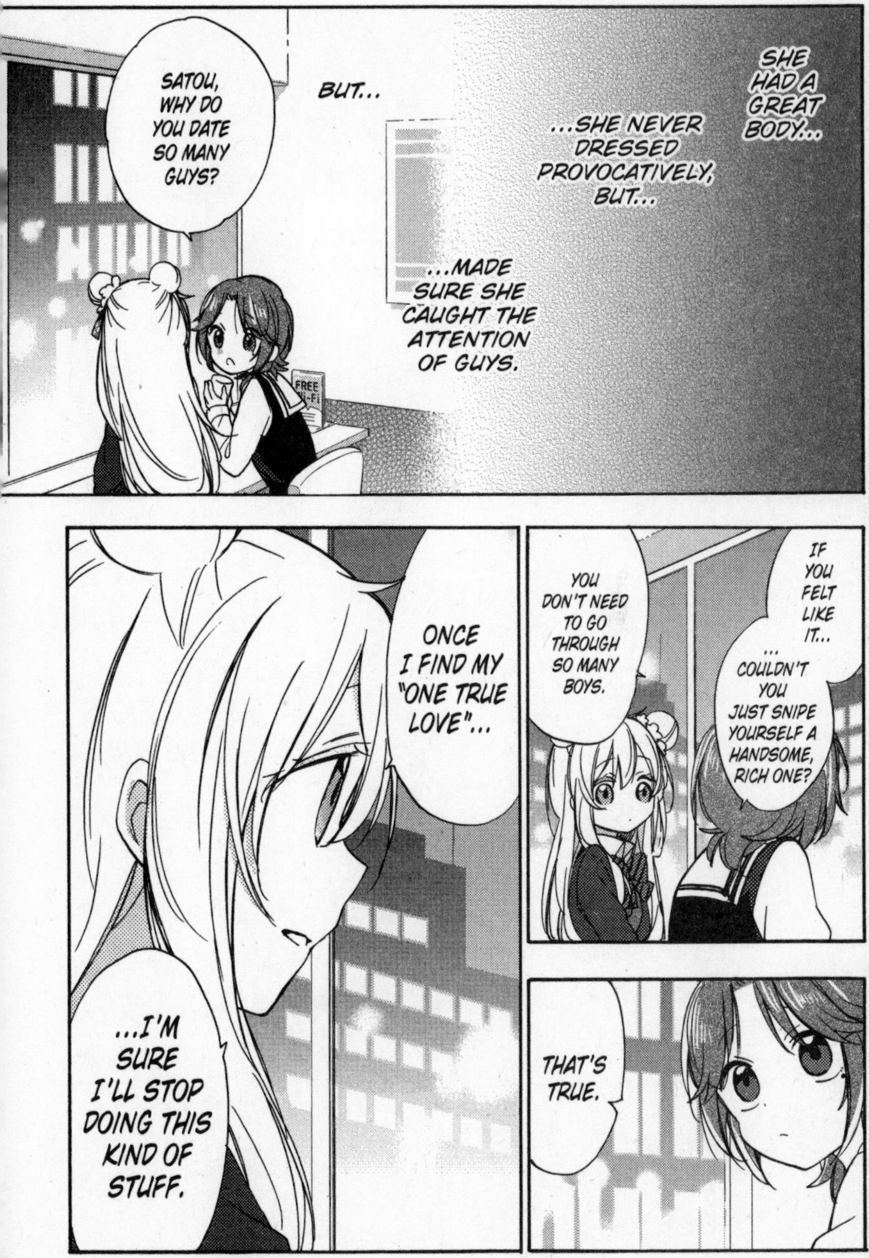
SHE HAD A GREAT BODY...
...SHE NEVER DRESSED PROVOCATIVELY, BUT...
...MADE SURE SHE CAUGHT THE ATTENTION OF GUYS.
BUT...
SATOU, WHY DO YOU DATE SO MANY GUYS?
IF YOU FELT LIKE IT... ...COULDN'T YOU JUST SNIPE YOURSELF A HANDSOME, RICH ONE?
YOU DON'T NEED TO GO THROUGH SO MANY BOYS.
THAT'S TRUE.
ONCE I FIND MY "ONE TRUE LOVE"...
...I'M SURE I'LL STOP DOING THIS KIND OF STUFF.

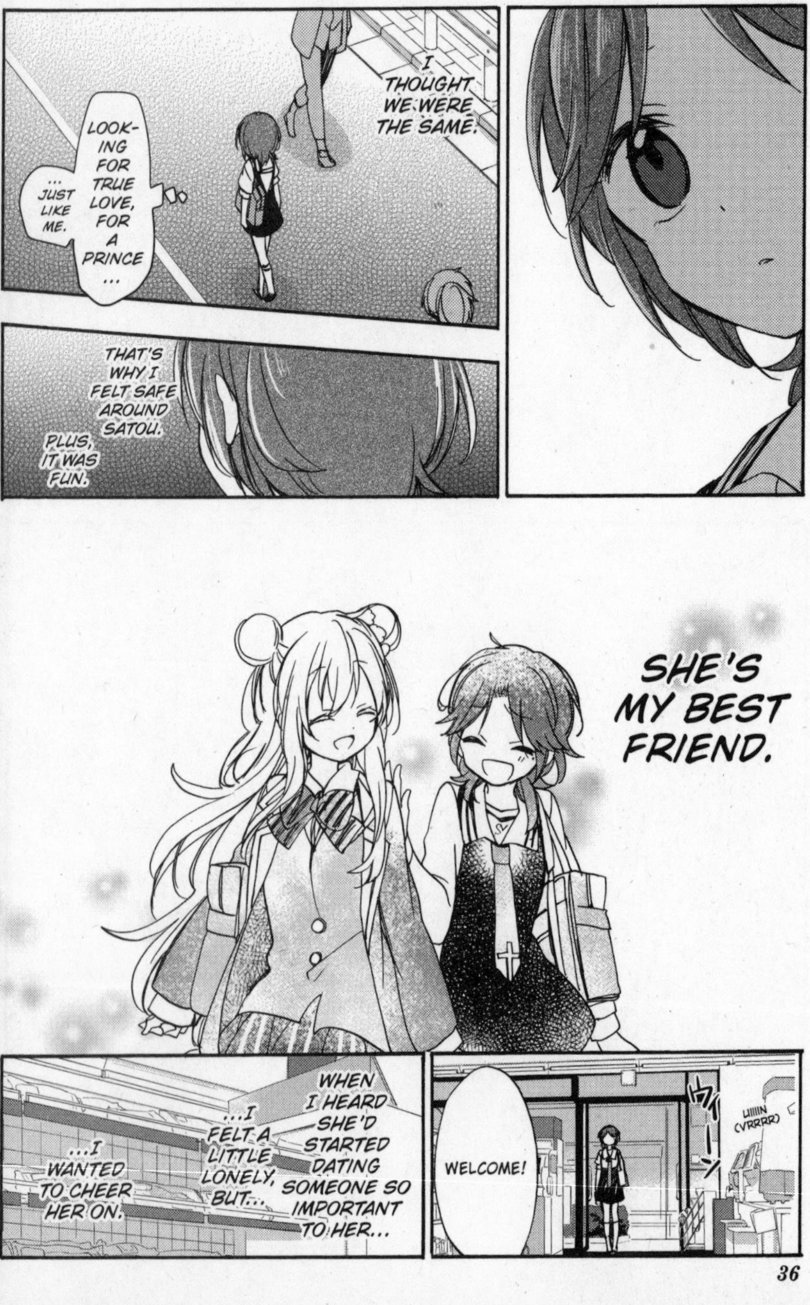
I THOUGHT WE WERE THE SAME.
LOOKING FOR TRUE LOVE, FOR A PRINCE...
...JUST LIKE ME.
THAT'S WHY I FELT SAFE AROUND SATOU.
PLUS, IT WAS FUN.
SHE'S MY BEST FRIEND.
UIIIIN (VRRRR)
WELCOME!
WHEN I HEARD SHE'D STARTED DATING SOMEONE SO IMPORTANT TO HER...
...I FELT A LITTLE LONELY, BUT...
...I WANTED TO CHEER HER ON.

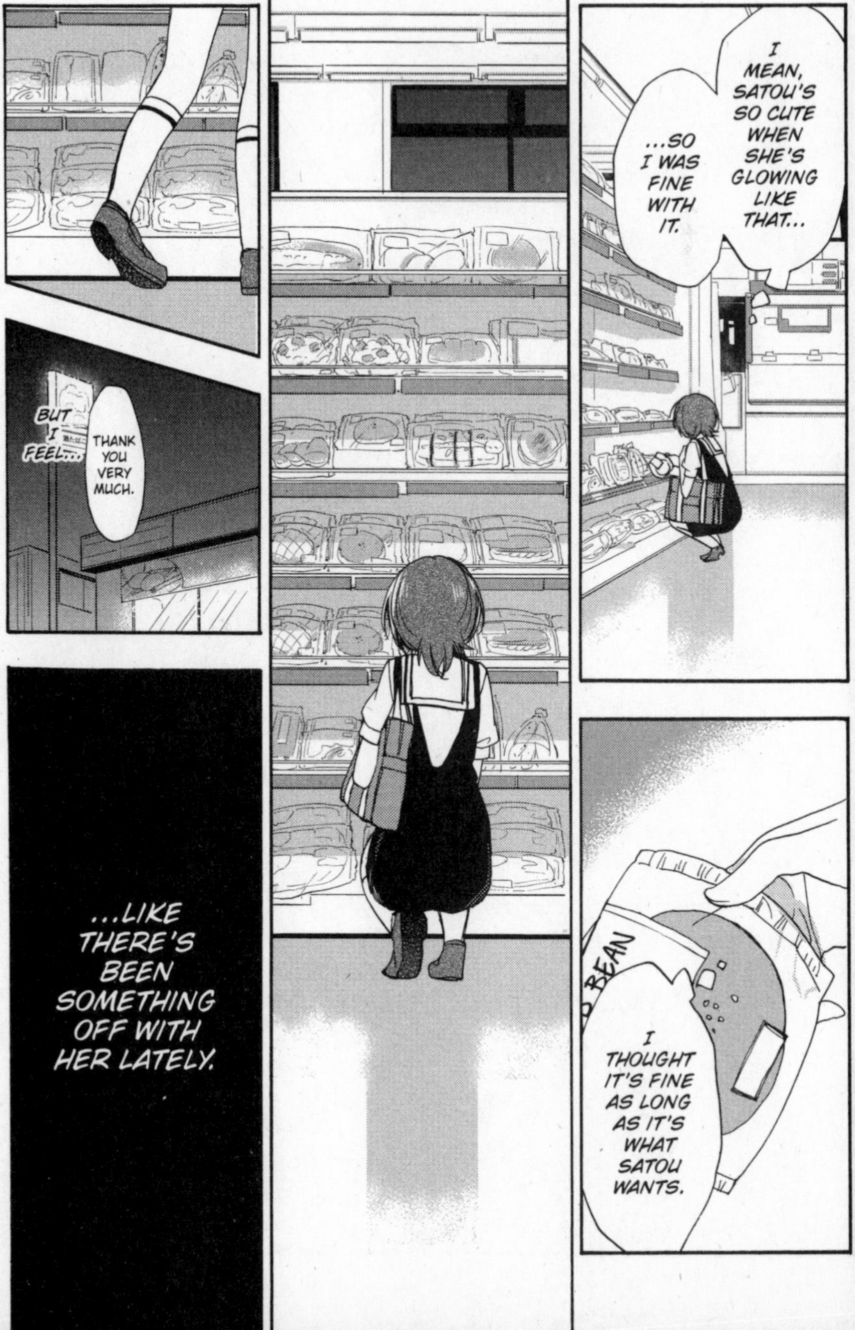
I MEAN, SATOU'S SO CUTE WHEN SHE'S GLOWING LIKE THAT...
...SO I WAS FINE WITH IT.
BEAN
I THOUGHT IT'S FINE AS LONG AS IT'S WHAT SATOU WANTS.
THANK YOU VERY MUCH.
BUT I FEEL...
...LIKE THERE'S BEEN SOMETHING OFF WITH HER LATELY.

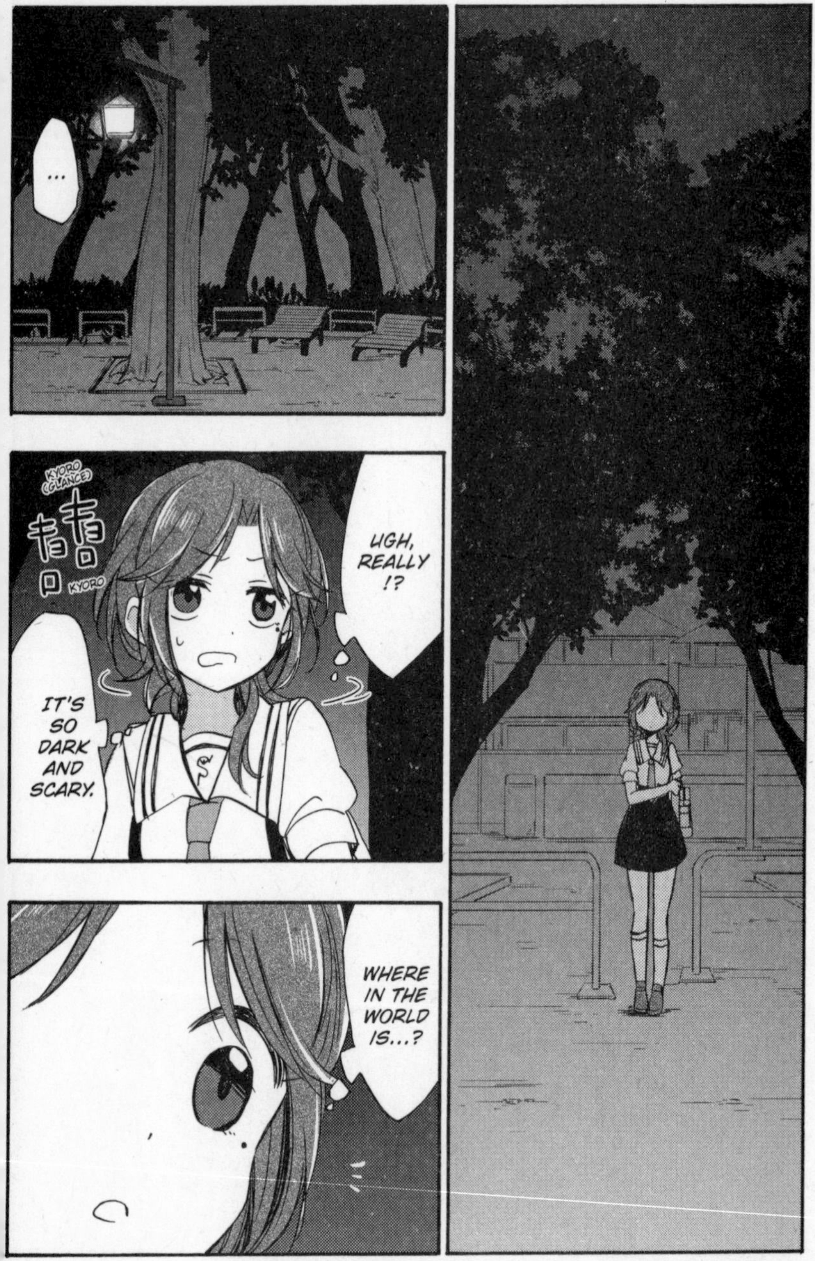
...
UGH, REALLY!?
KYORO (GLANCE) KYORO
IT'S SO DARK AND SCARY.
WHERE IN THE WORLD IS...?

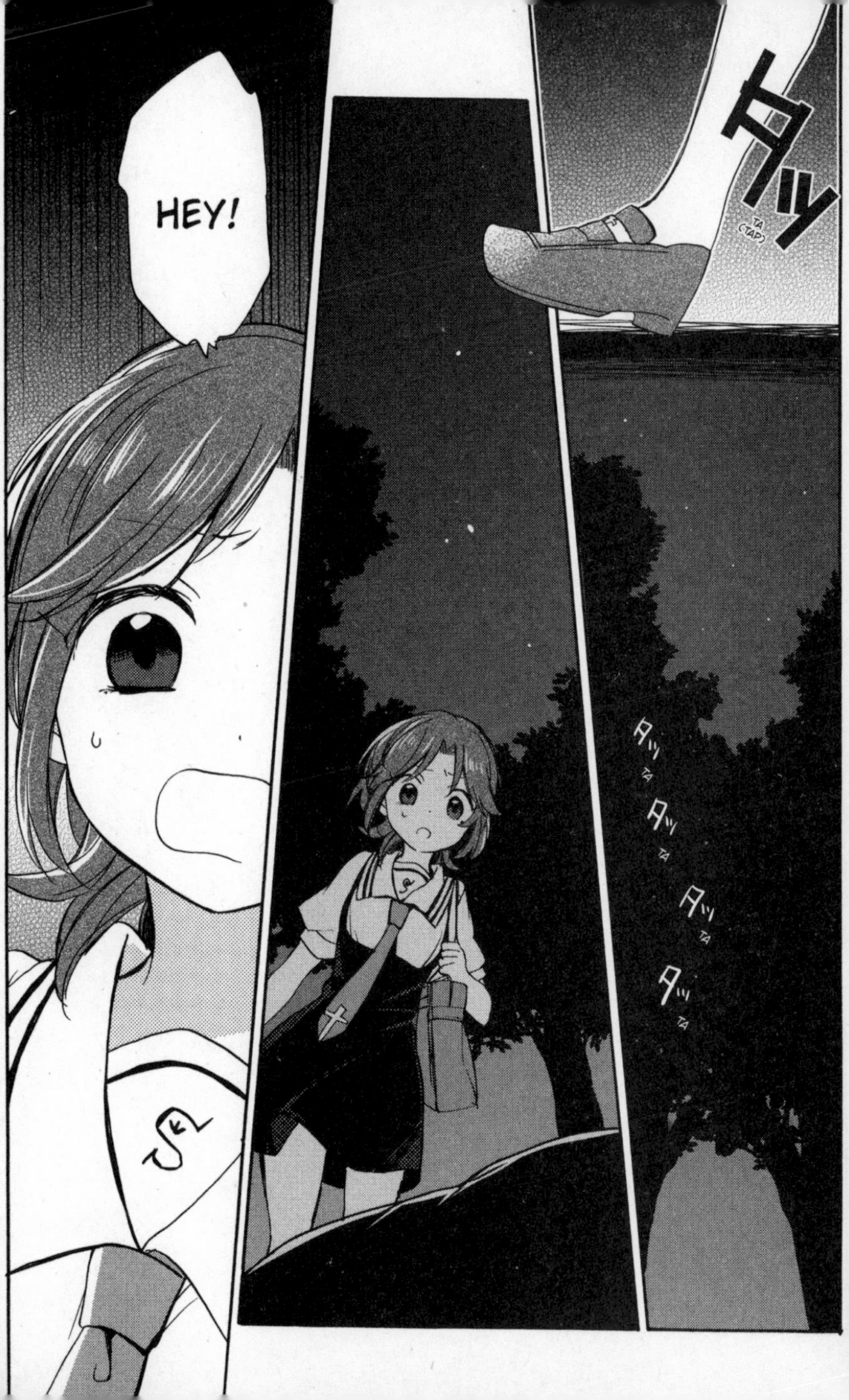
タッ
TA (TAP)
タッ TA
タッ TA
タッ TA
タッ TA
HEY!

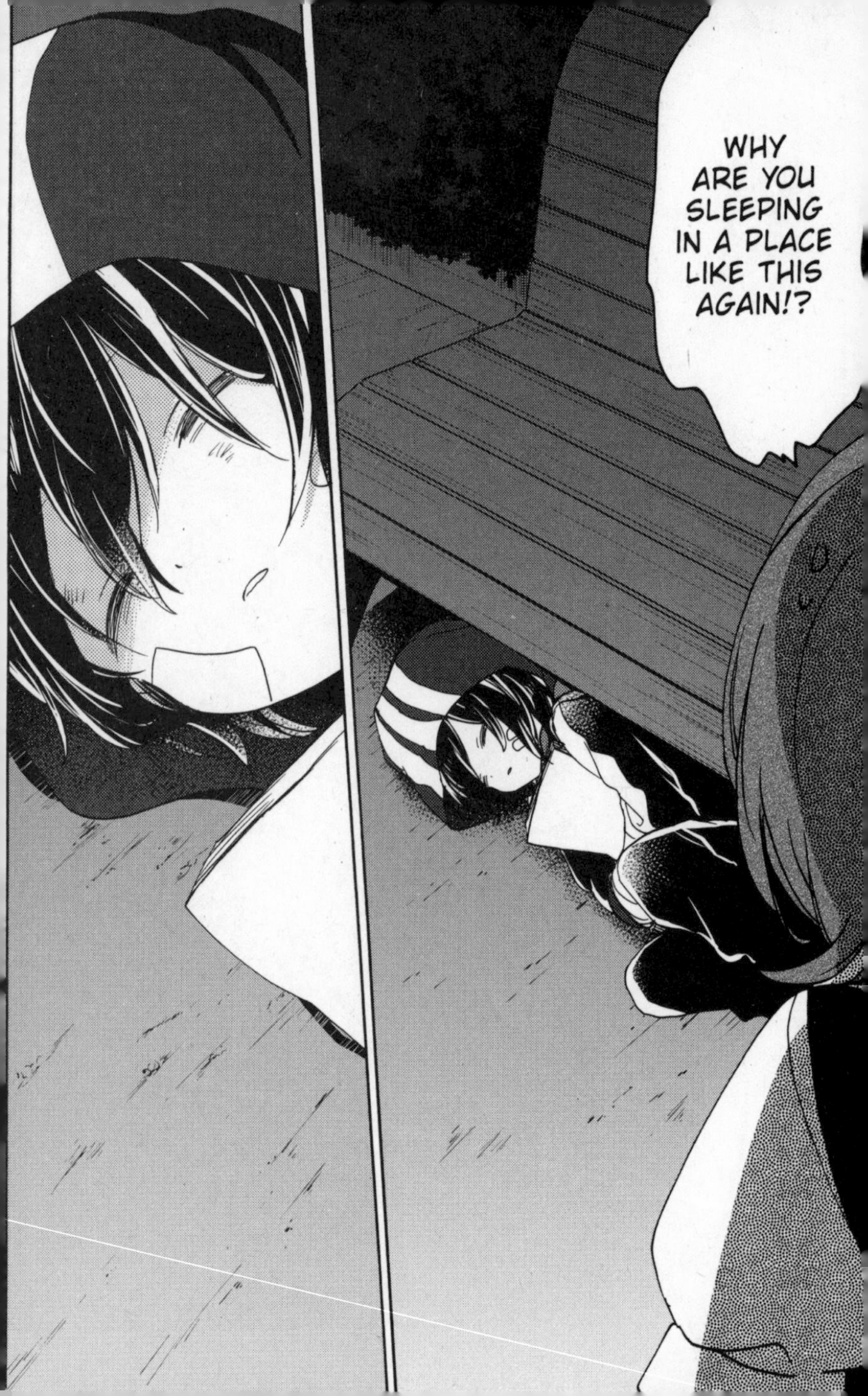
WHY ARE YOU SLEEPING IN A PLACE LIKE THIS AGAIN!?

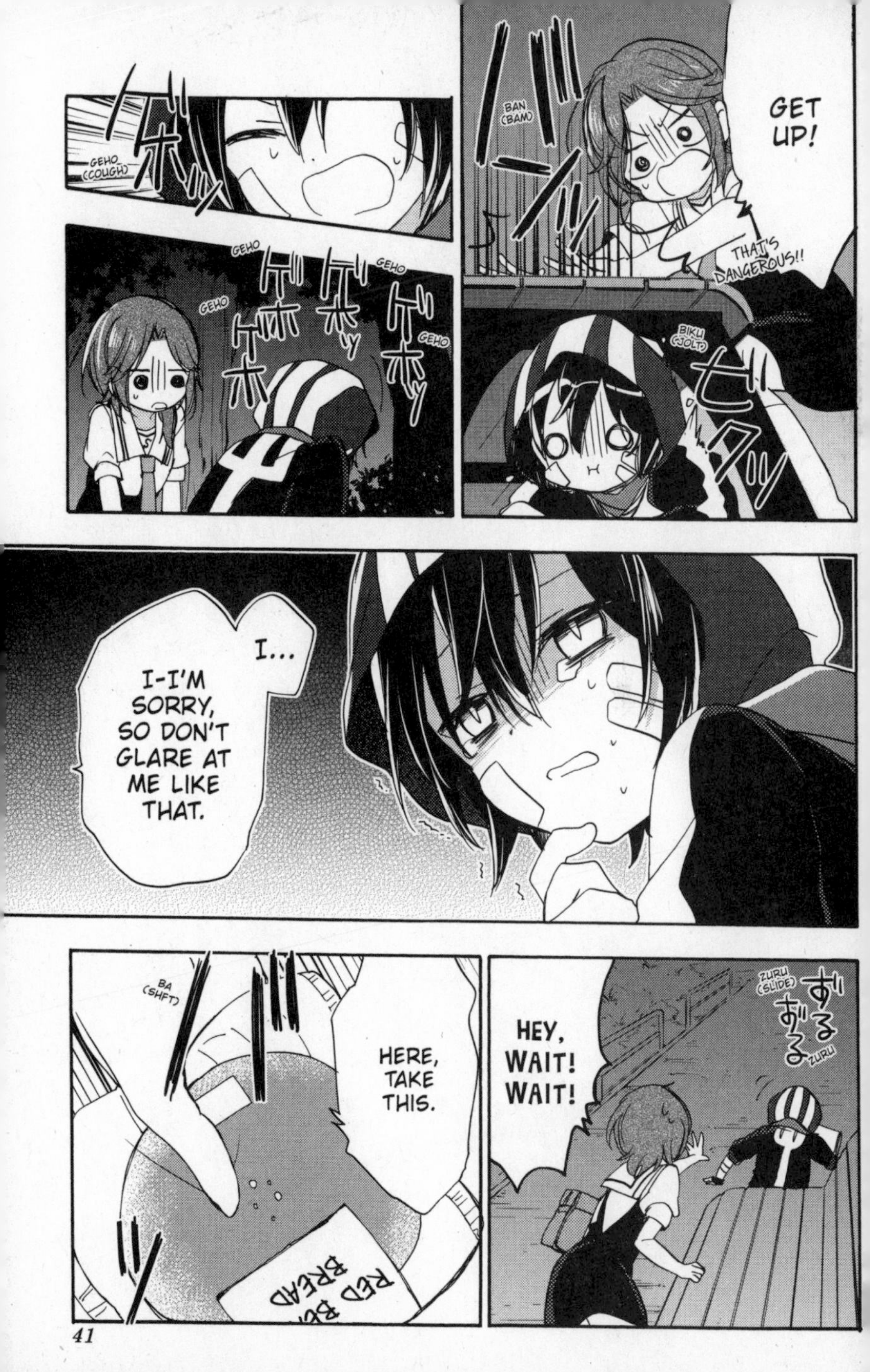
BAN (BAM)
GET UP!
THAT'S DANGEROUS!!
GEHO (COUGH)
BIKU (JOLT)
GEHO
GEHO
GEHO
GEHO
I...
I-I'M SORRY, SO DON'T GLARE AT ME LIKE THAT.
ZURU (SLIDE)
ZURU
HEY, WAIT! WAIT!
BA (SHFT)
HERE, TAKE THIS.
RED BE BREAD

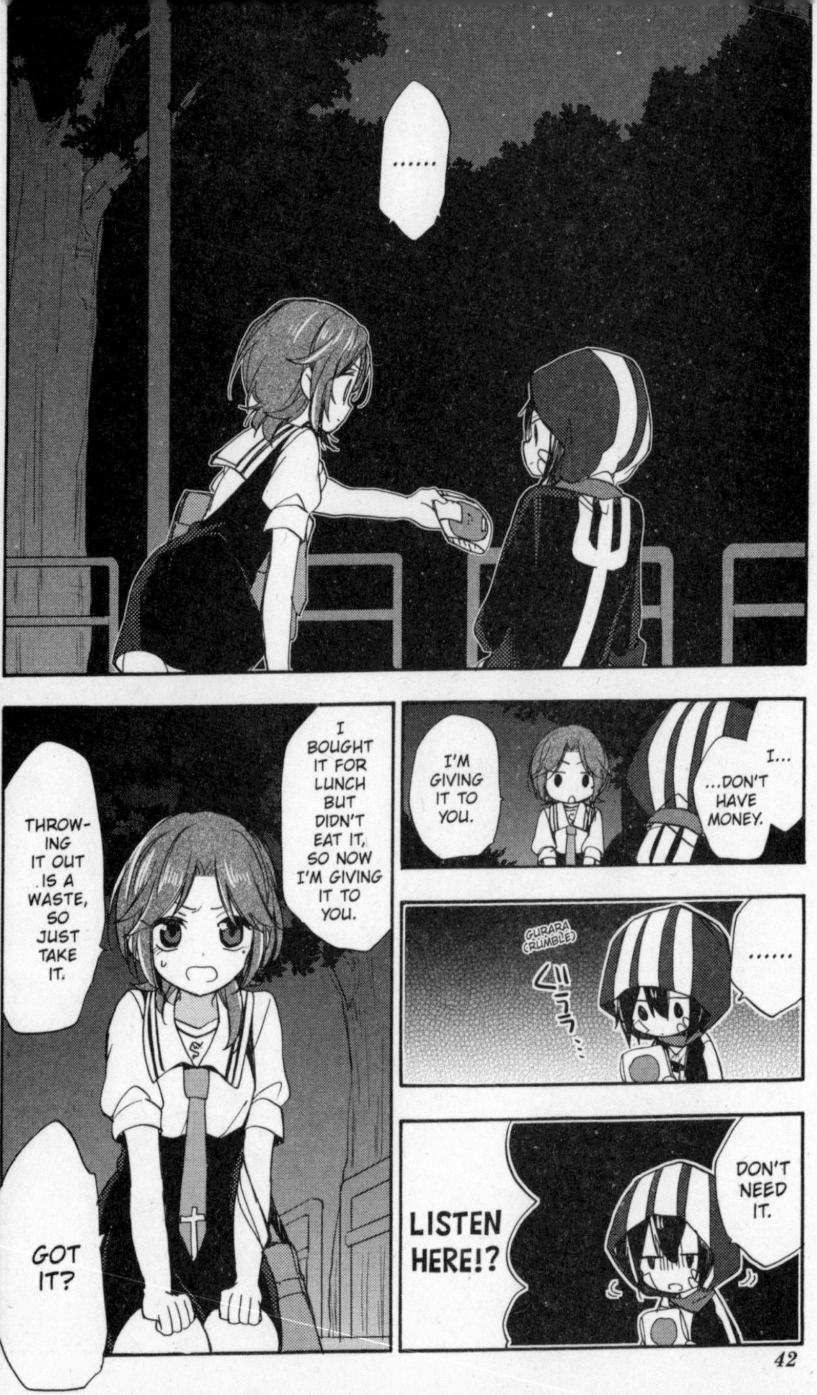
……
I…
…DON'T HAVE MONEY.
I'M GIVING IT TO YOU.
I BOUGHT IT FOR LUNCH BUT DIDN'T EAT IT, SO NOW I'M GIVING IT TO YOU.
THROWING IT OUT IS A WASTE, SO JUST TAKE IT.
GOT IT?
……
GURARA (RUMBLE)
DON'T NEED IT.
LISTEN HERE!?

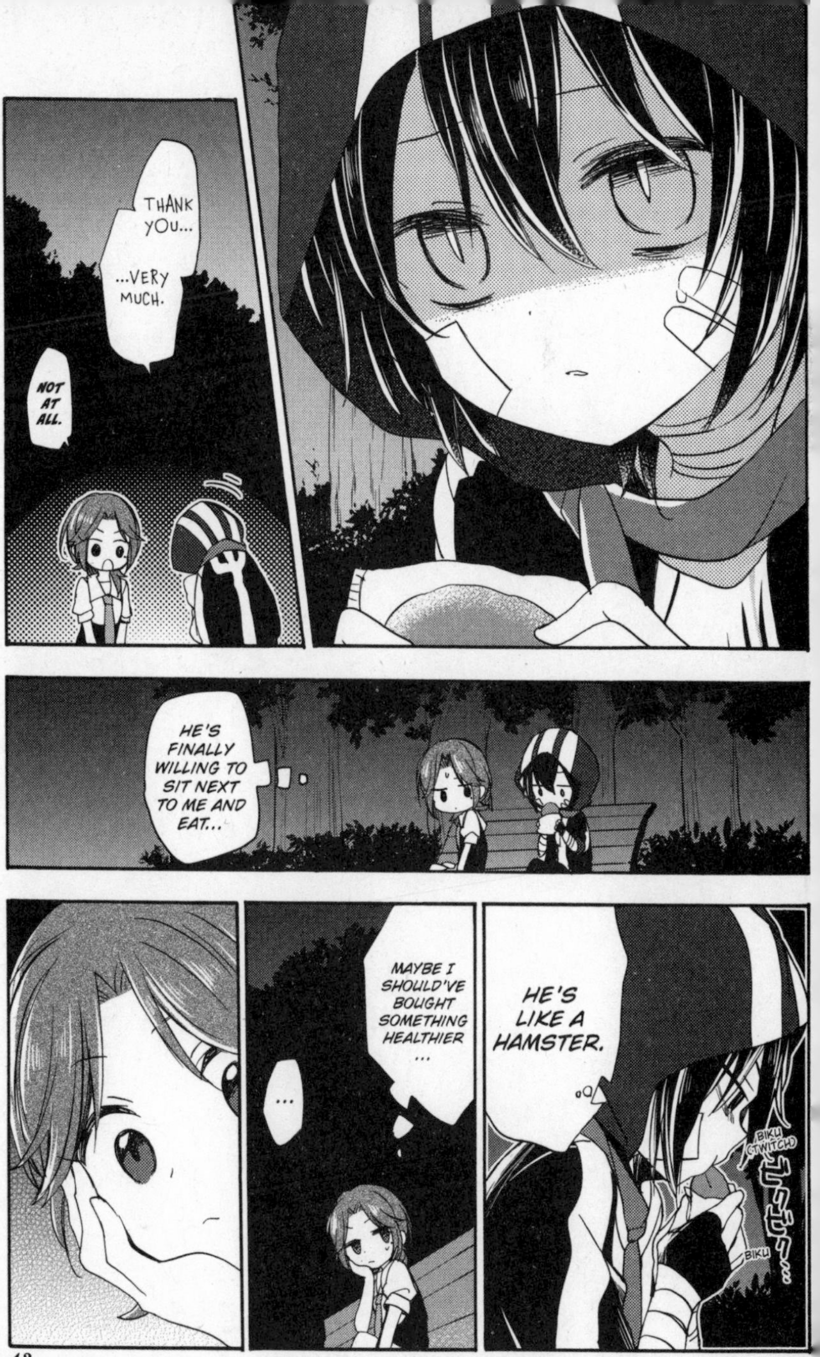
THANK YOU...
...VERY MUCH.
NOT AT ALL.
HE'S FINALLY WILLING TO SIT NEXT TO ME AND EAT...
BIKU (TWITCH)
BIKU
HE'S LIKE A HAMSTER.
MAYBE I SHOULD'VE BOUGHT SOMETHING HEALTHIER...
...

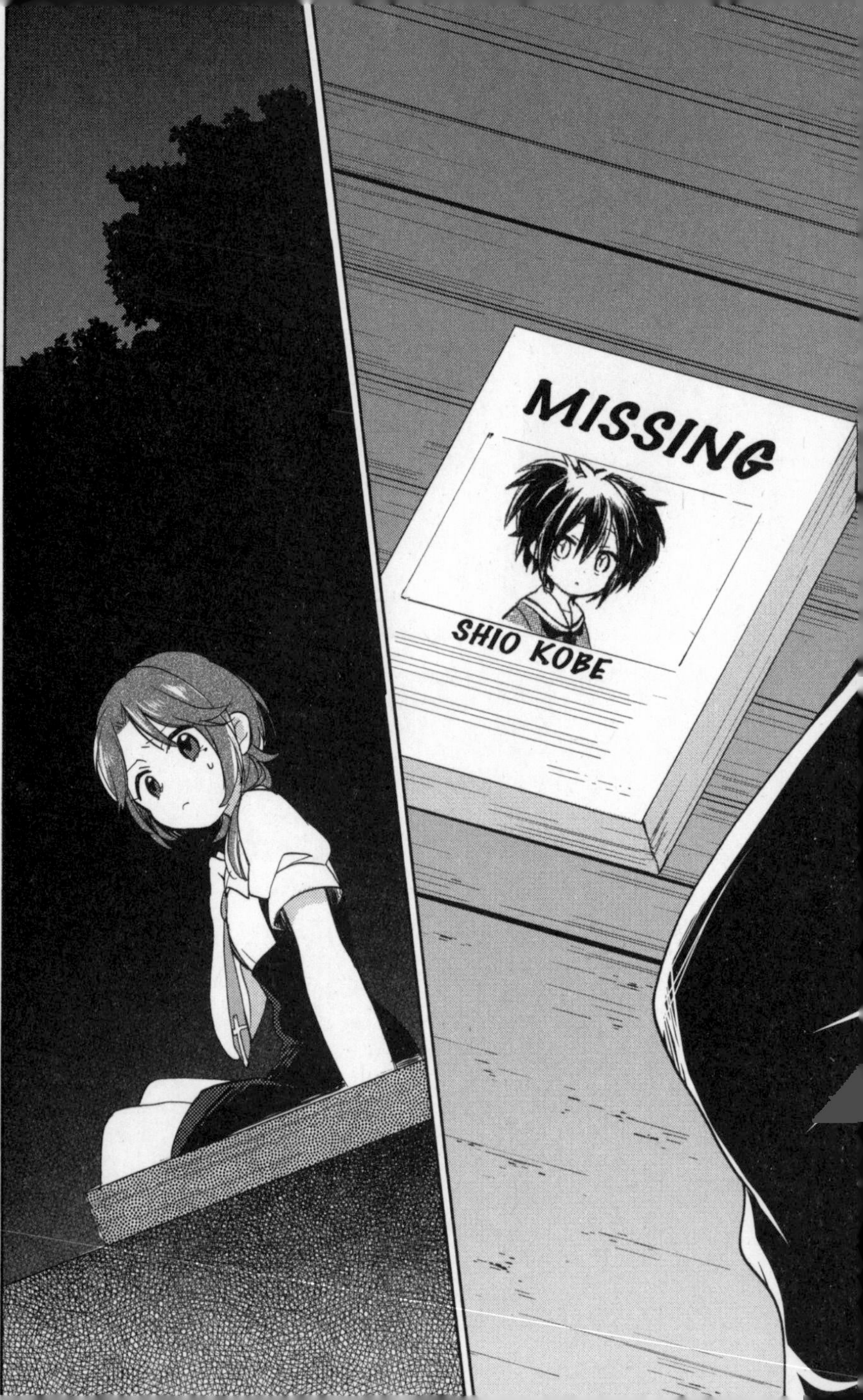
MISSING
SHIO KOBE

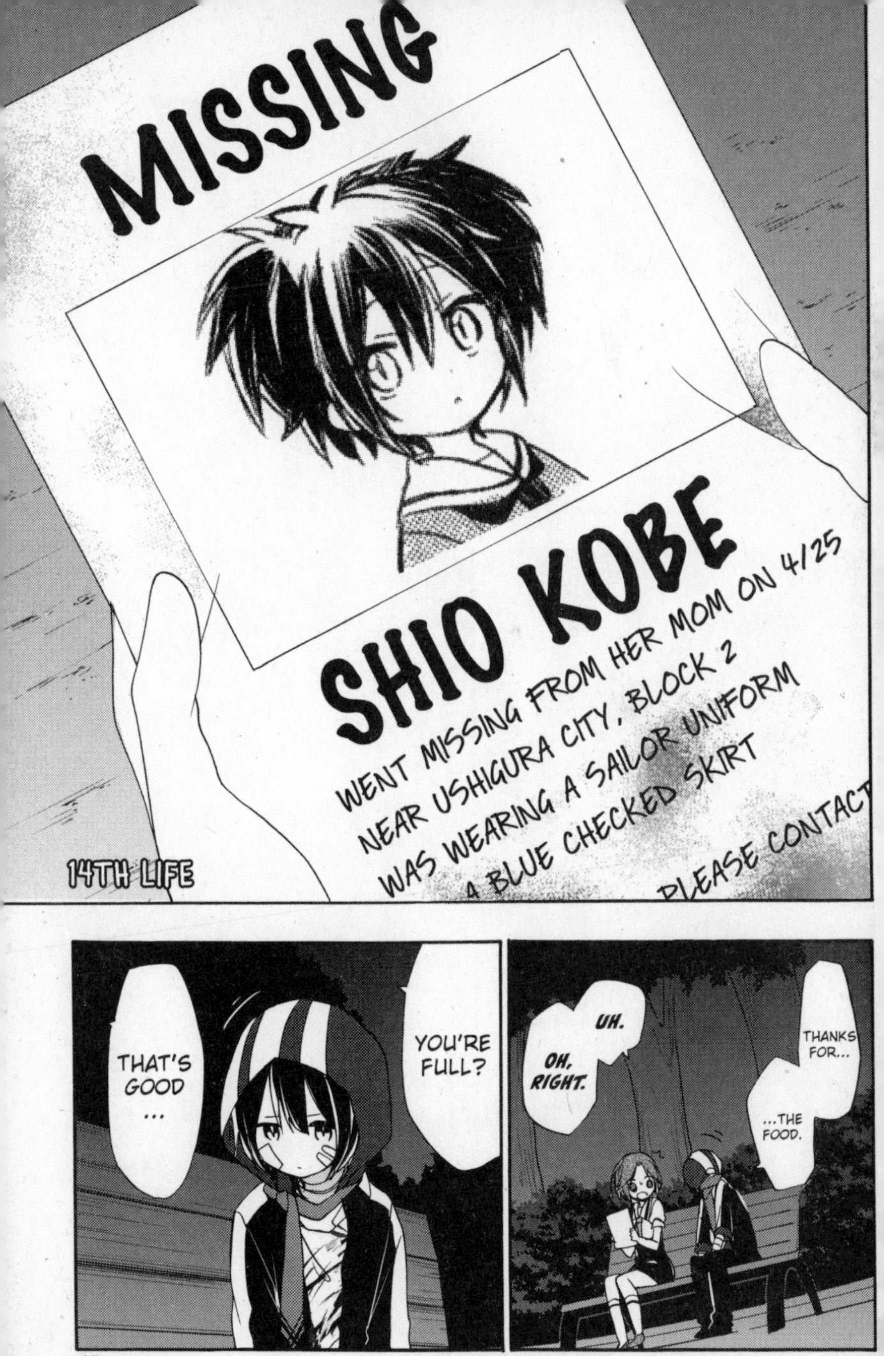
MISSING
SHIO KOBE
WENT MISSING FROM HER MOM ON 4/25
NEAR USHIGURA CITY, BLOCK 2
WAS WEARING A SAILOR UNIFORM
A BLUE CHECKED SKIRT
PLEASE CONTACT
14TH LIFE
THANKS FOR...
...THE FOOD.
UH.
OH, RIGHT.
YOU'RE FULL?
THAT'S GOOD ...

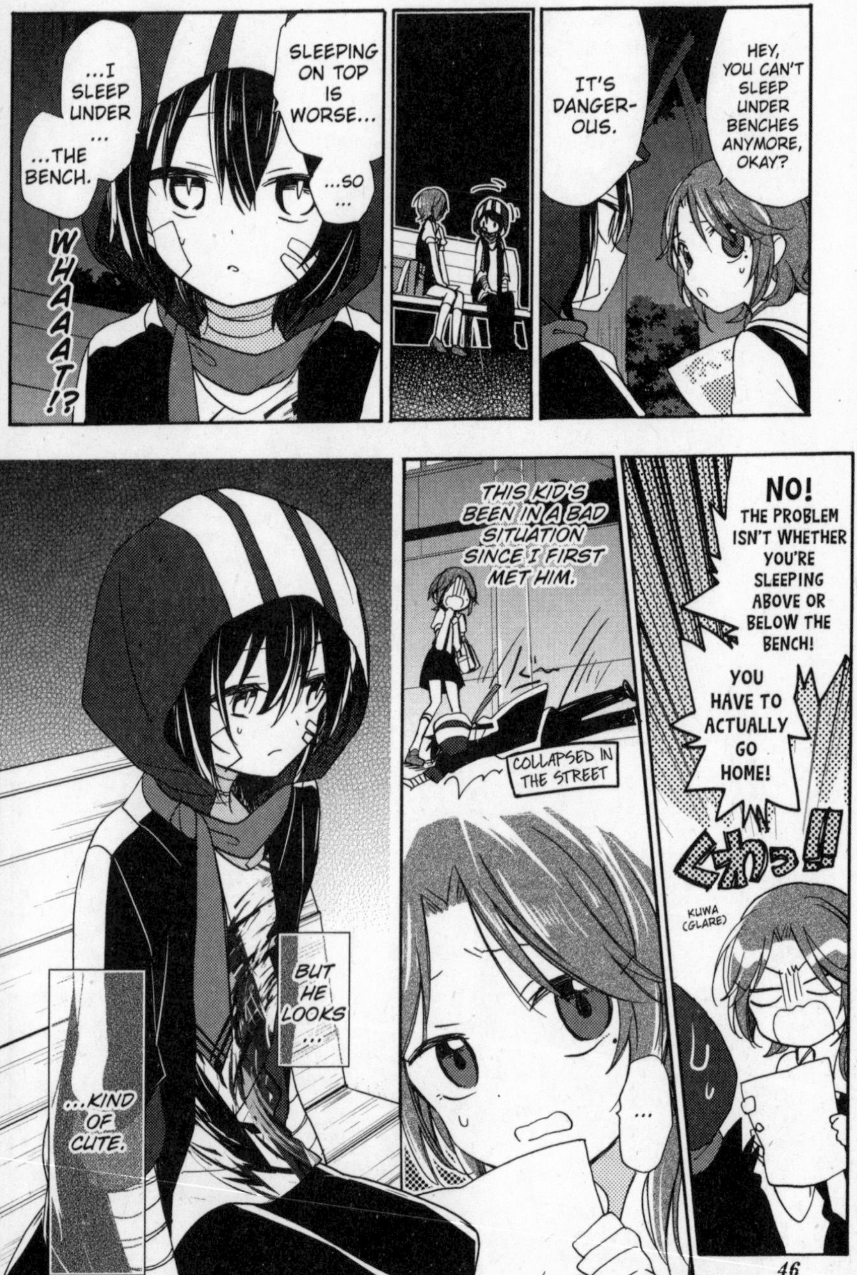
HEY, YOU CAN'T SLEEP UNDER BENCHES ANYMORE, OKAY?
IT'S DANGER-OUS.
SLEEPING ON TOP IS WORSE...
...SO ...
...I SLEEP UNDER ...
...THE BENCH.
WHAAAAT!?
NO! THE PROBLEM ISN'T WHETHER YOU'RE SLEEPING ABOVE OR BELOW THE BENCH!
YOU HAVE TO ACTUALLY GO HOME!
くわっ!!
KUWA (GLARE)
THIS KID'S BEEN IN A BAD SITUATION SINCE I FIRST MET HIM.
COLLAPSED IN THE STREET
...
BUT HE LOOKS ...
...KIND OF CUTE.

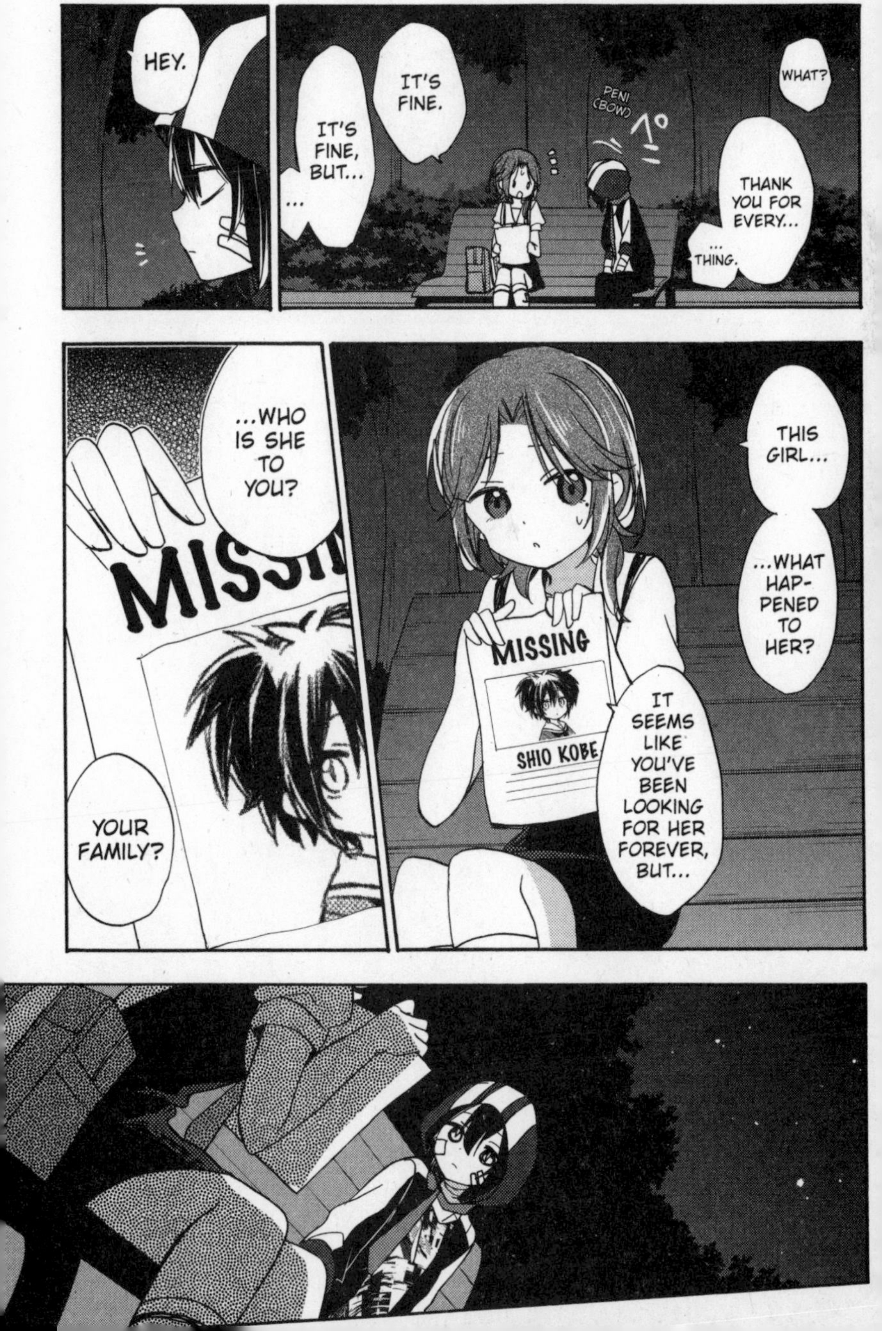
WHAT?
PENI (BOW)
THANK YOU FOR EVERY...
...THING.
IT'S FINE.
IT'S FINE, BUT...
...
HEY.
THIS GIRL...
...WHAT HAP-PENED TO HER?
MISSING
SHIO KOBE
IT SEEMS LIKE YOU'VE BEEN LOOKING FOR HER FOREVER, BUT...
...WHO IS SHE TO YOU?
YOUR FAMILY?

I'M SORRY.

I'M SORRY, ASAHI.

I'M SO SORRY.

THE MOON...

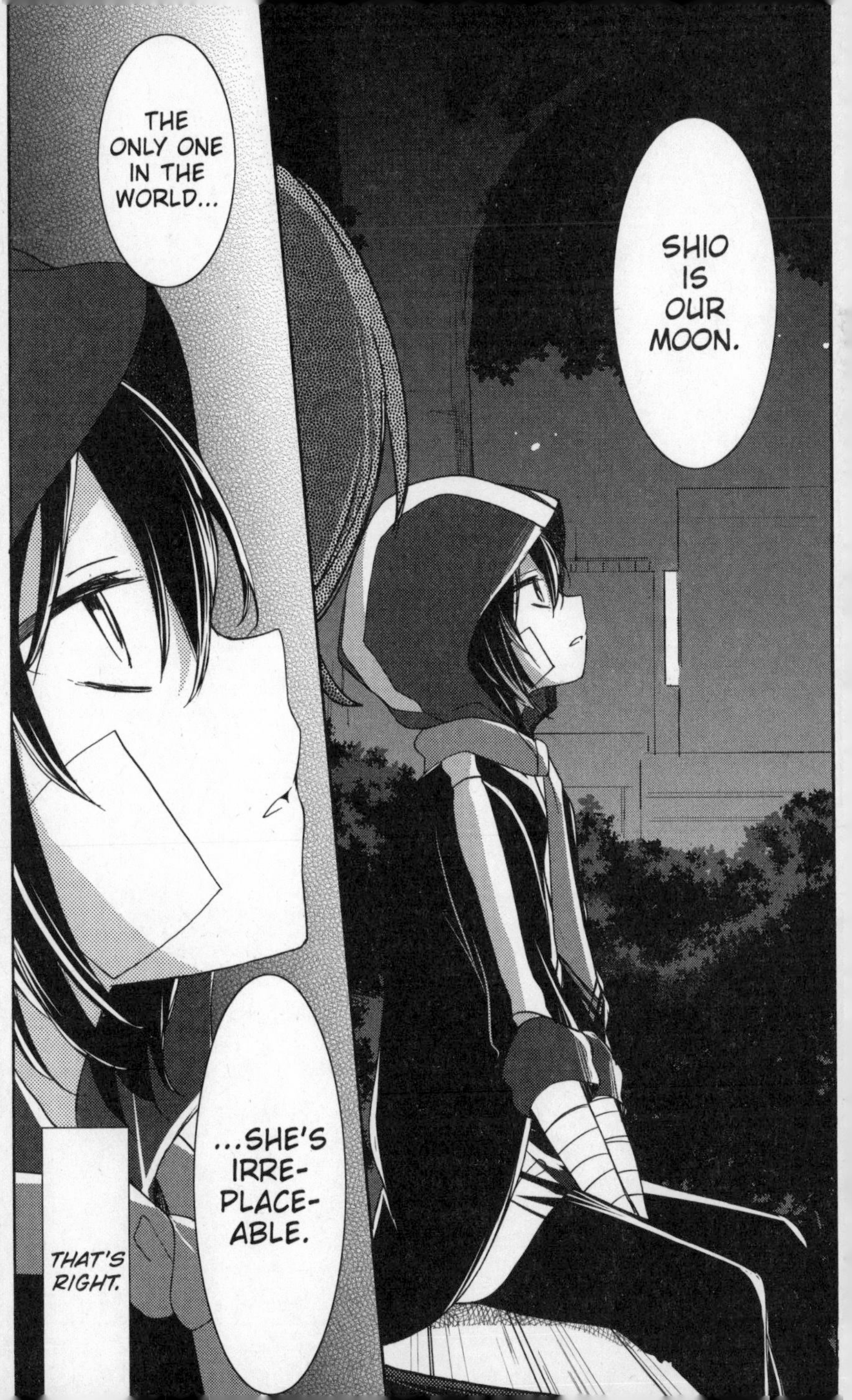
SHIO IS OUR MOON.
THE ONLY ONE IN THE WORLD...
...SHE'S IRRE-PLACE-ABLE.
THAT'S RIGHT.

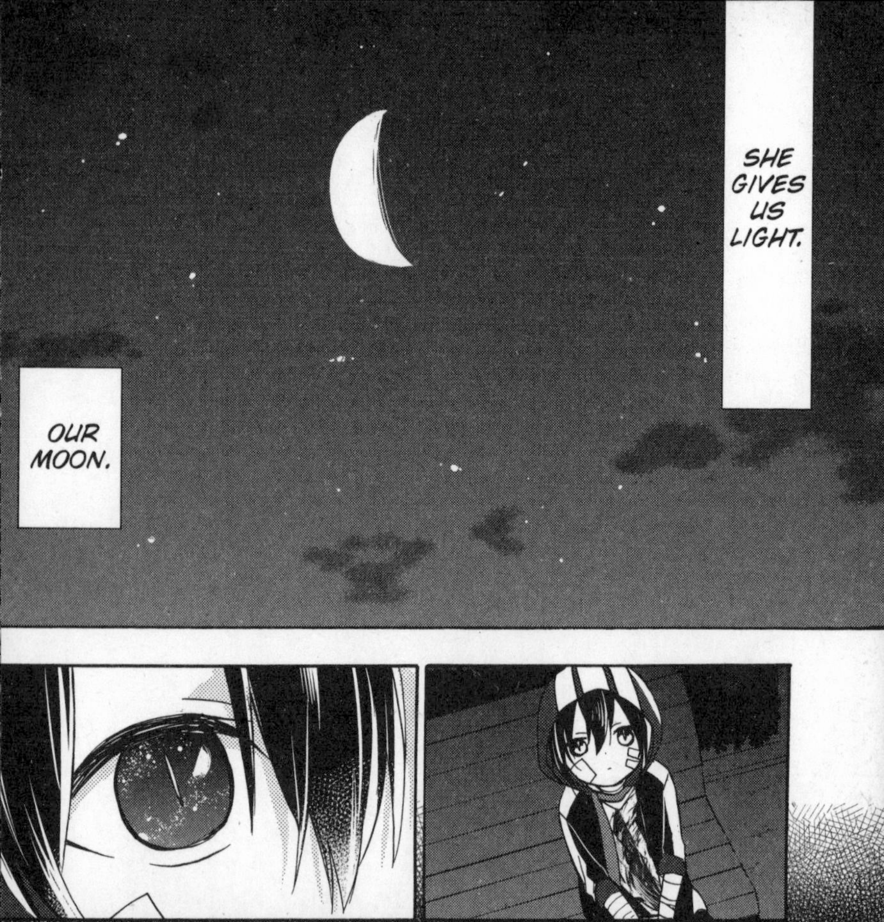
SHE GIVES US LIGHT.
OUR MOON.

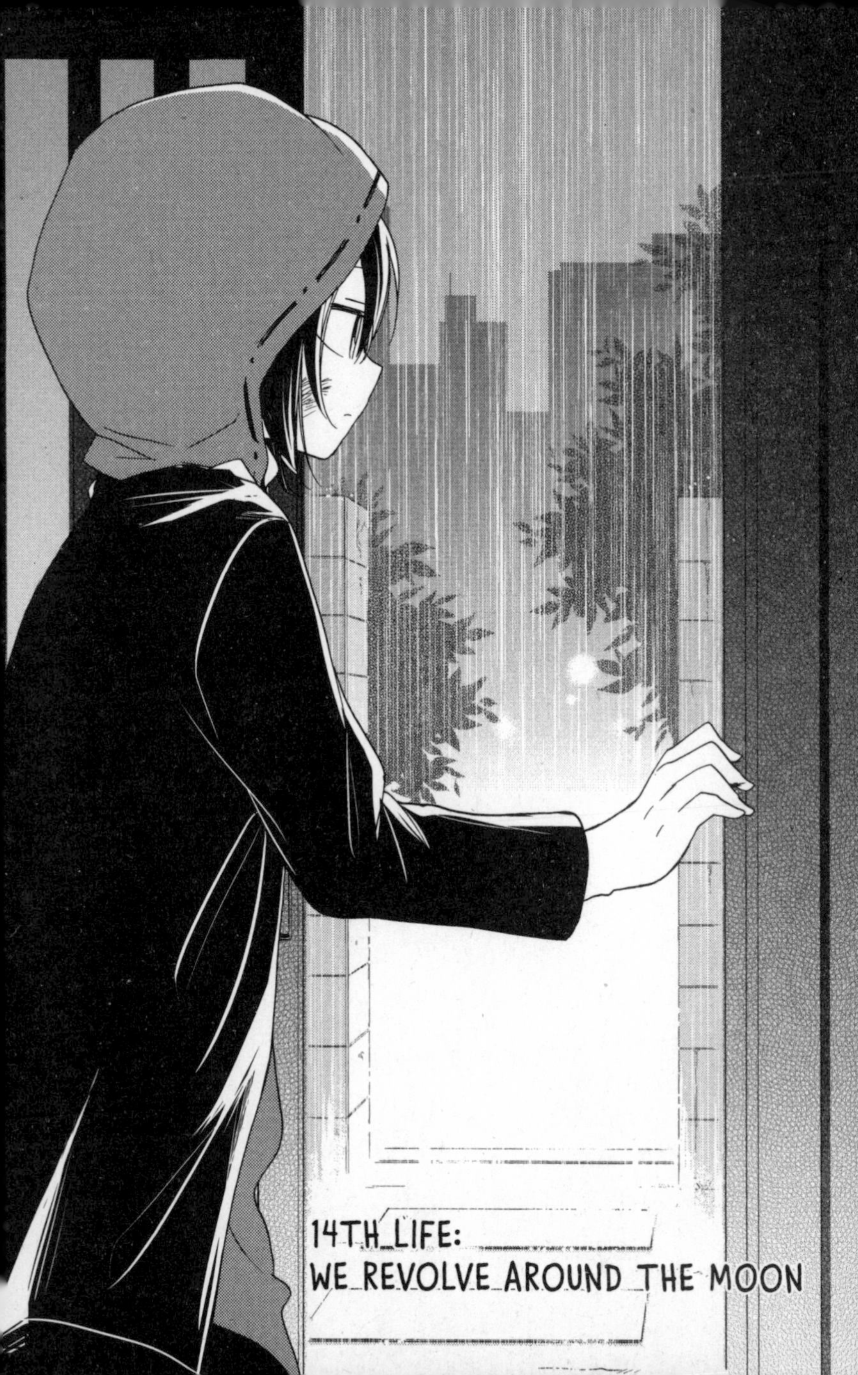
14TH LIFE:
WE REVOLVE AROUND THE MOON

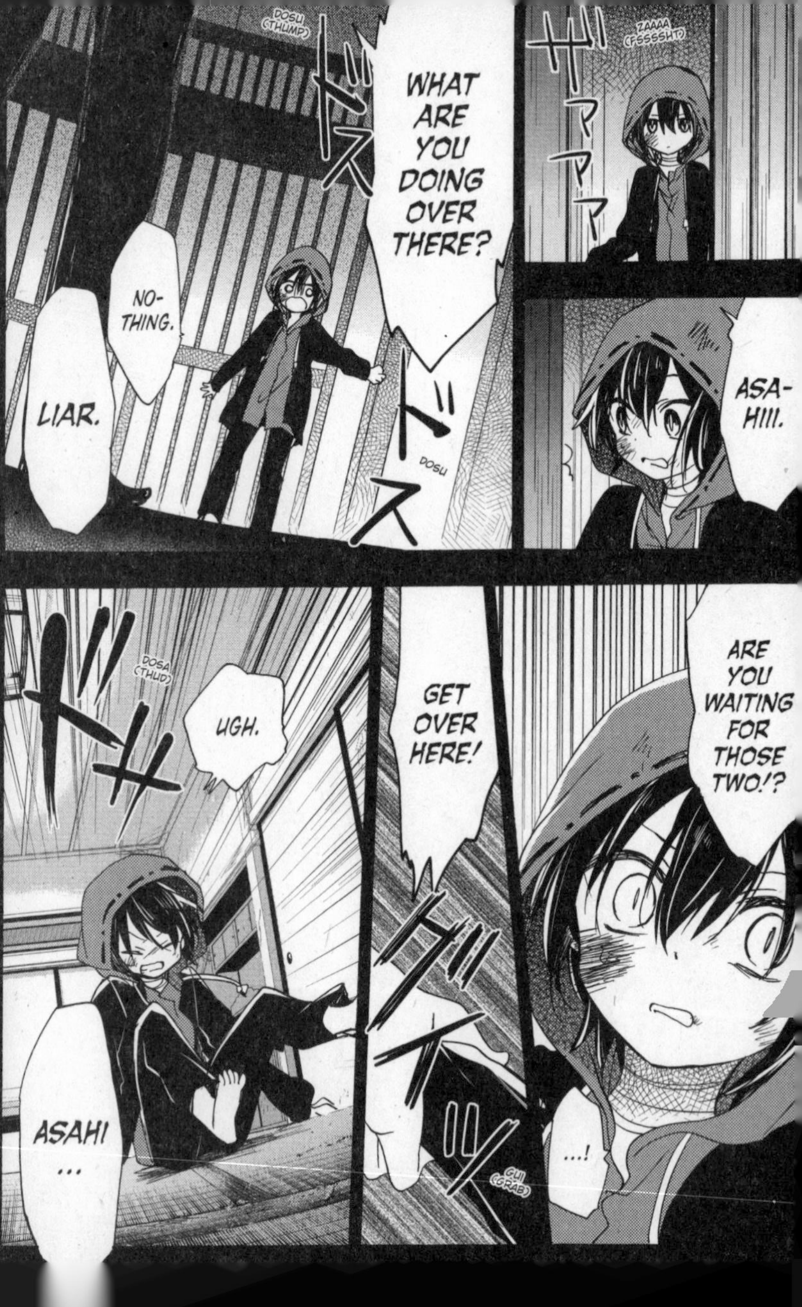
ZAAAA (FSSSHT)
ASA-HIII.
DOSU (THUMP)
WHAT ARE YOU DOING OVER THERE?
NO-THING.
LIAR.
DOSU
ARE YOU WAITING FOR THOSE TWO!?
...!
GET OVER HERE!
GUI (GRAB)
DOSA (THUD)
UGH.
ASAHI...

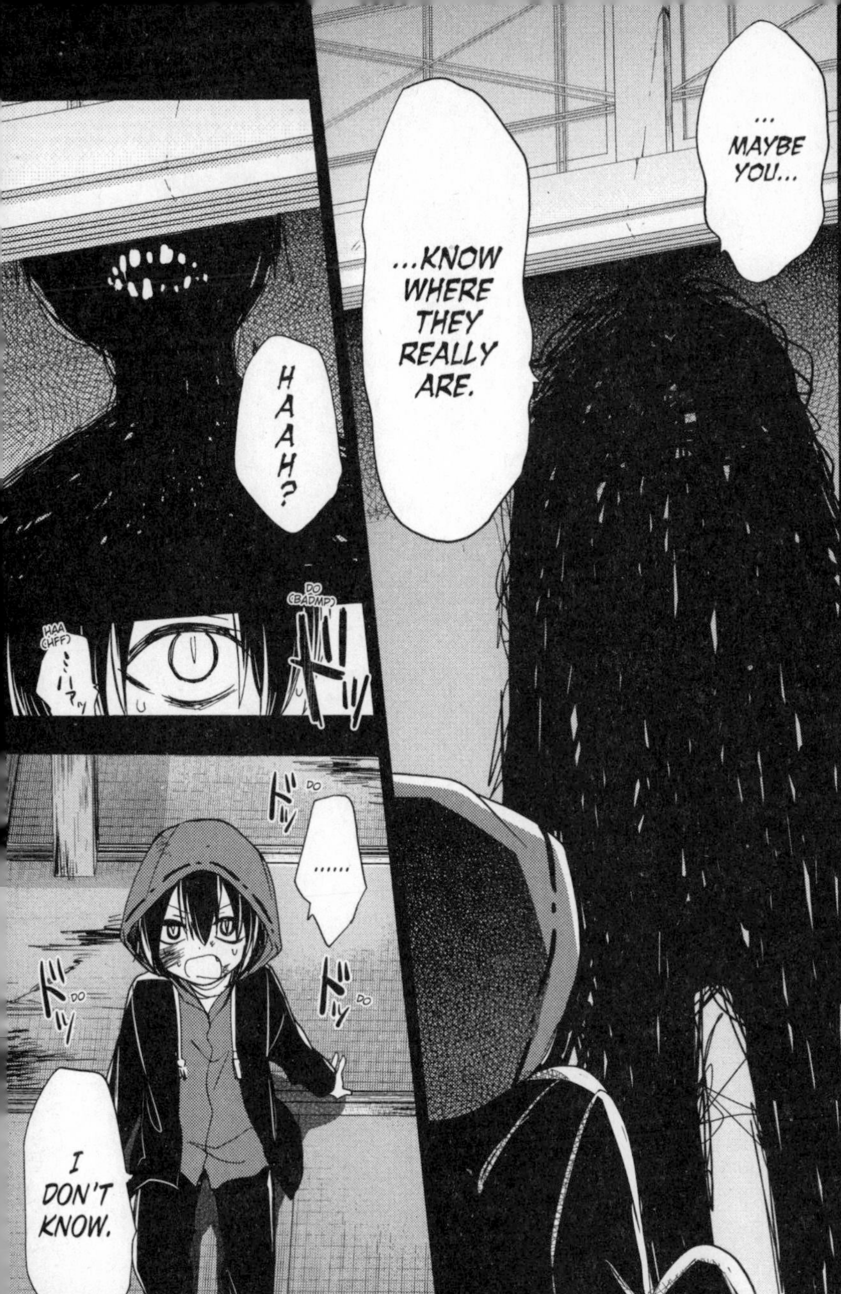

... MAYBE YOU...
...KNOW WHERE THEY REALLY ARE.
HAAAH?
DO (BADMP)
HAA (HFF)
DO
......
DO
DO
I DON'T KNOW.

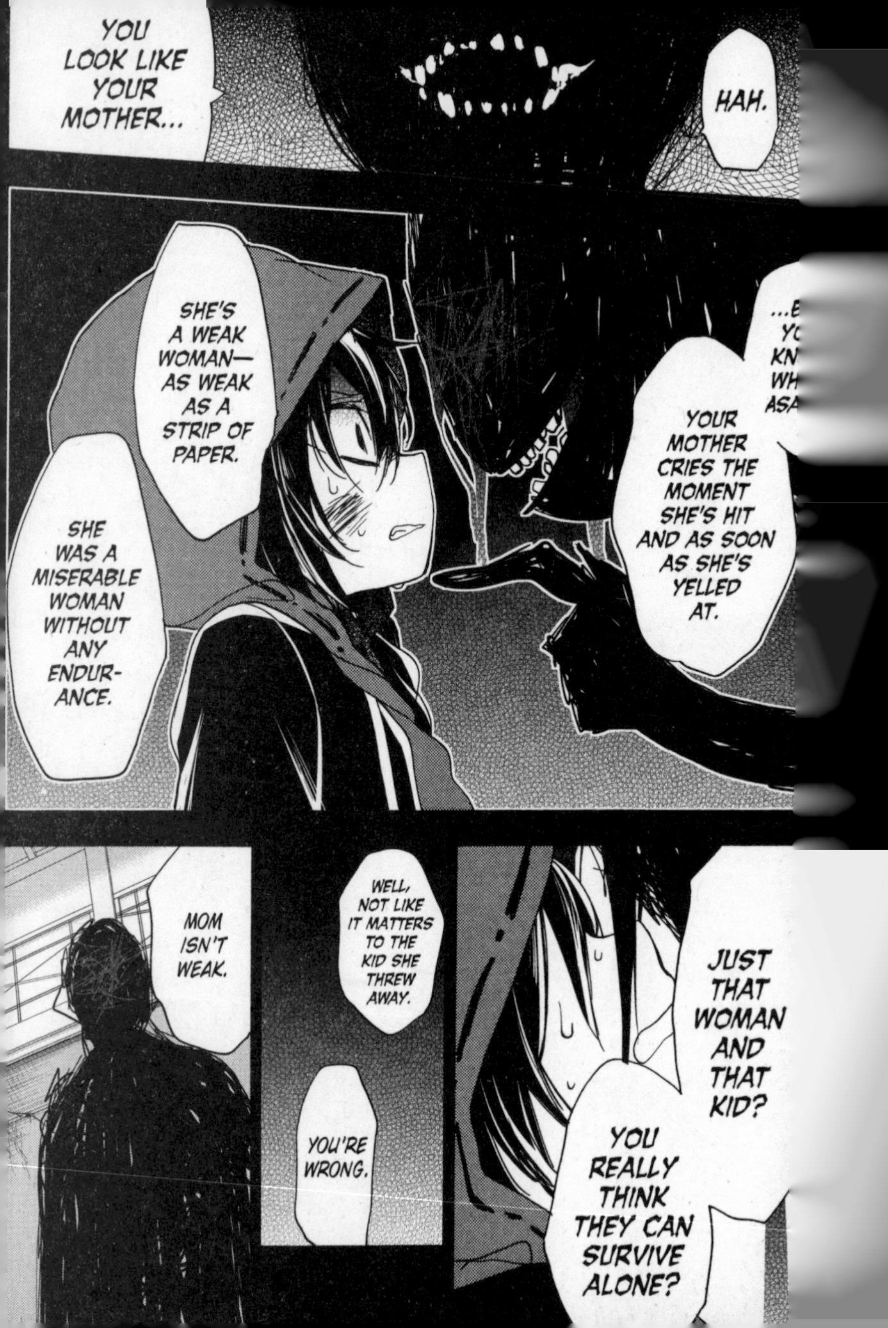
HAH.
YOU LOOK LIKE YOUR MOTHER...
YOUR MOTHER CRIES THE MOMENT SHE'S HIT AND AS SOON AS SHE'S YELLED AT.
SHE'S A WEAK WOMAN— AS WEAK AS A STRIP OF PAPER.
SHE WAS A MISERABLE WOMAN WITHOUT ANY ENDURANCE.
JUST THAT WOMAN AND THAT KID?
YOU REALLY THINK THEY CAN SURVIVE ALONE?
WELL, NOT LIKE IT MATTERS TO THE KID SHE THREW AWAY.
YOU'RE WRONG.
MOM ISN'T WEAK.

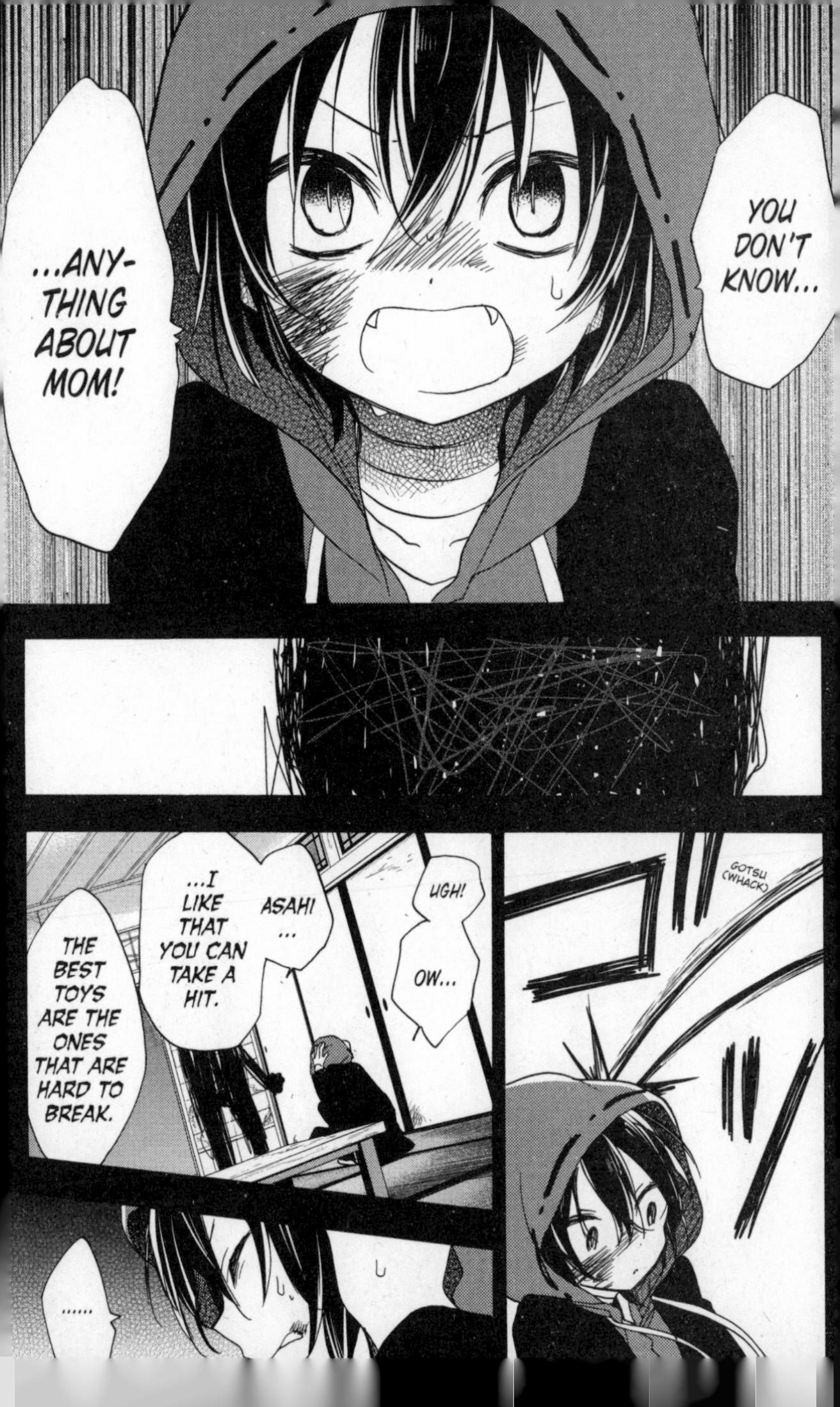
YOU DON'T KNOW...
...ANY-THING ABOUT MOM!
GOTSU (WHACK)
UGH!
OW...
ASAHI...
...I LIKE THAT YOU CAN TAKE A HIT.
THE BEST TOYS ARE THE ONES THAT ARE HARD TO BREAK.
......

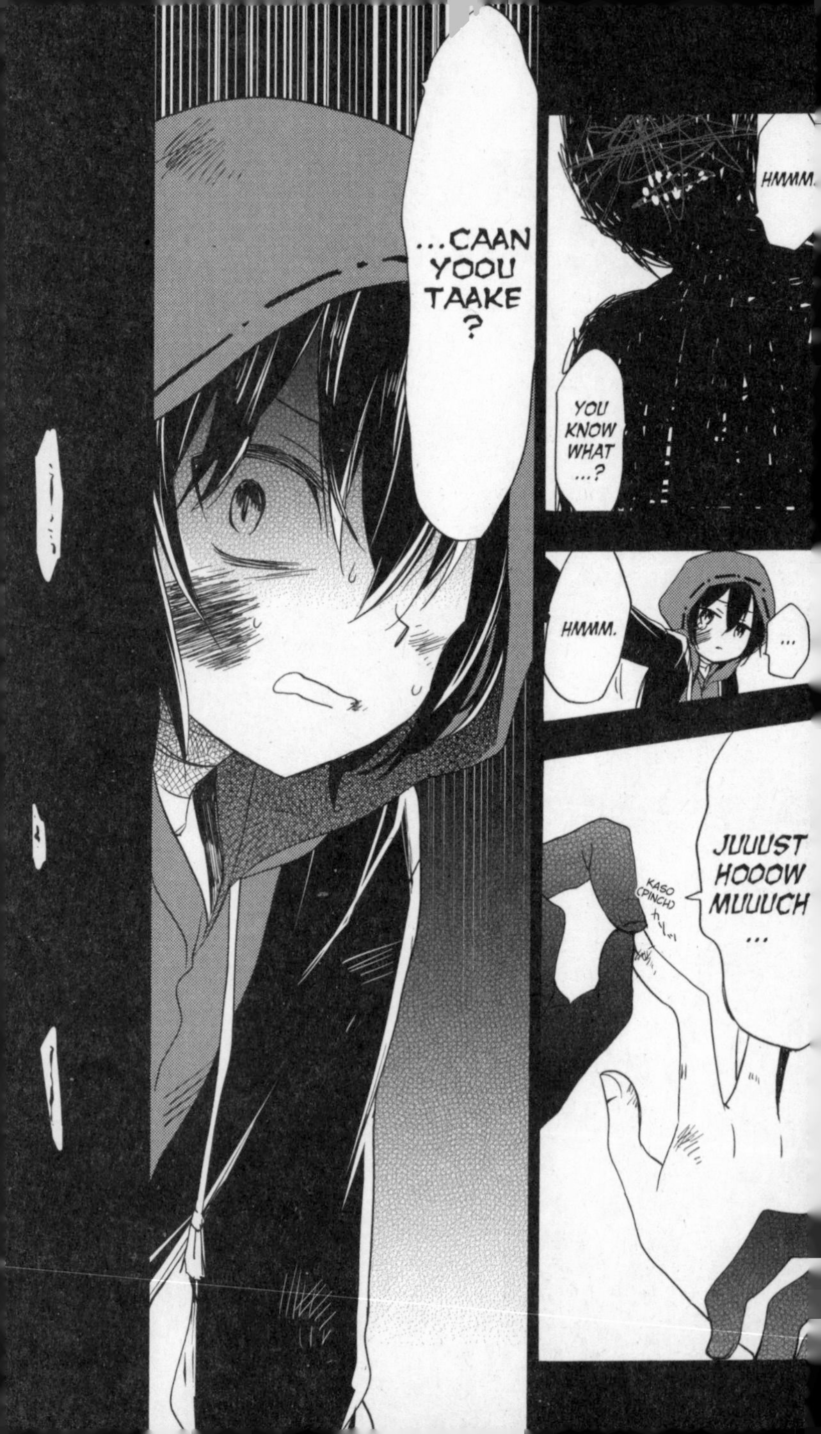
HMMM.
YOU KNOW WHAT ...?
HMMM.
...
JUUUST HOOOW MUUUCH ...
KASO (PINCH)
...CAAN YOOU TAAKE ?

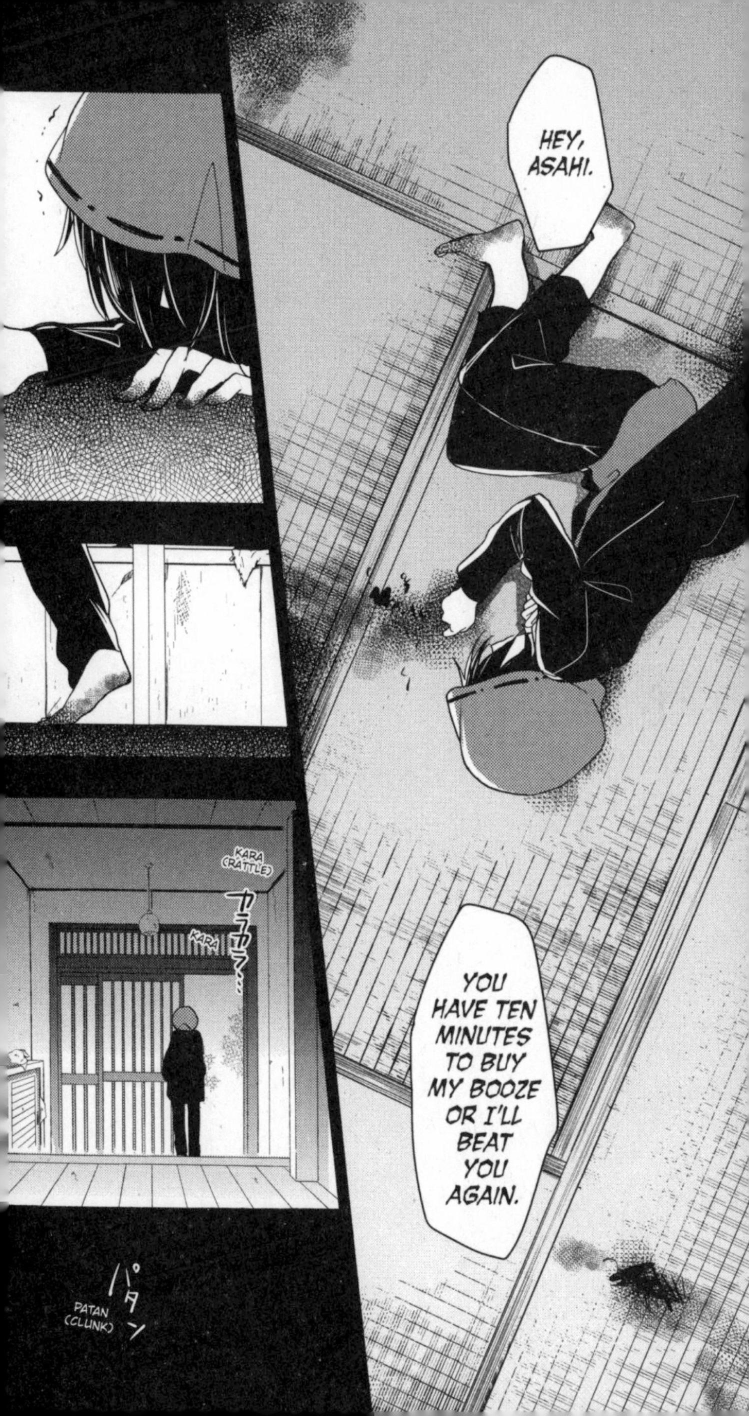
HEY, ASAHI.
YOU HAVE TEN MINUTES TO BUY MY BOOZE OR I'LL BEAT YOU AGAIN.
KARA (RATTLE)
カラカラ…
KARA
パタン
PATAN (CLUNK)

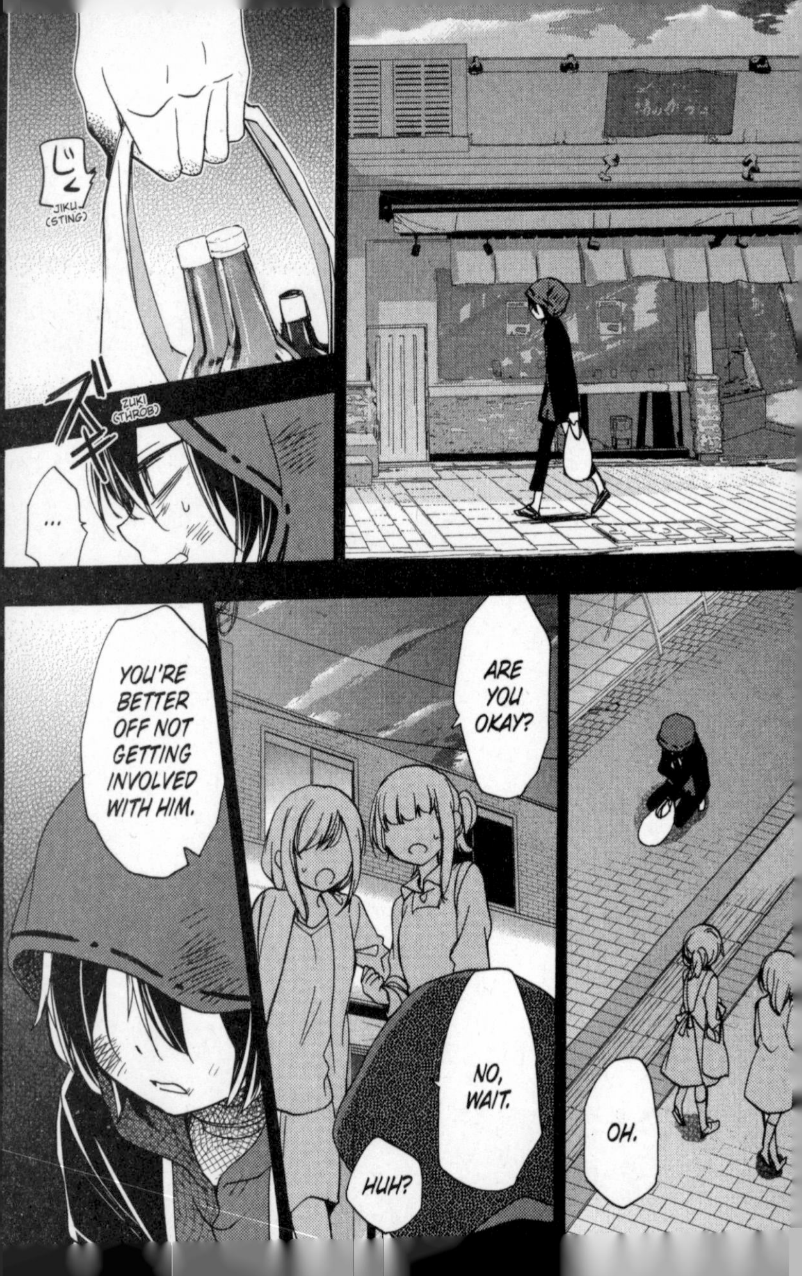

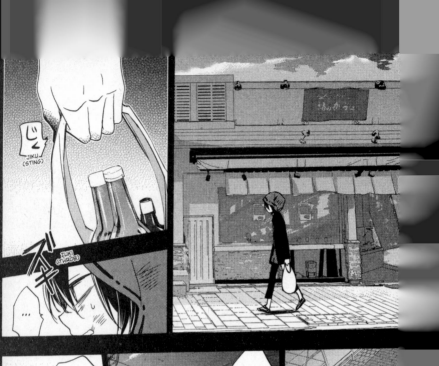

じく
JIKU (STING)
ズキ
ZUKI (THROB)
...
OH.
ARE YOU OKAY?
NO, WAIT.
HUH?
YOU'RE BETTER OFF NOT GETTING INVOLVED WITH HIM.

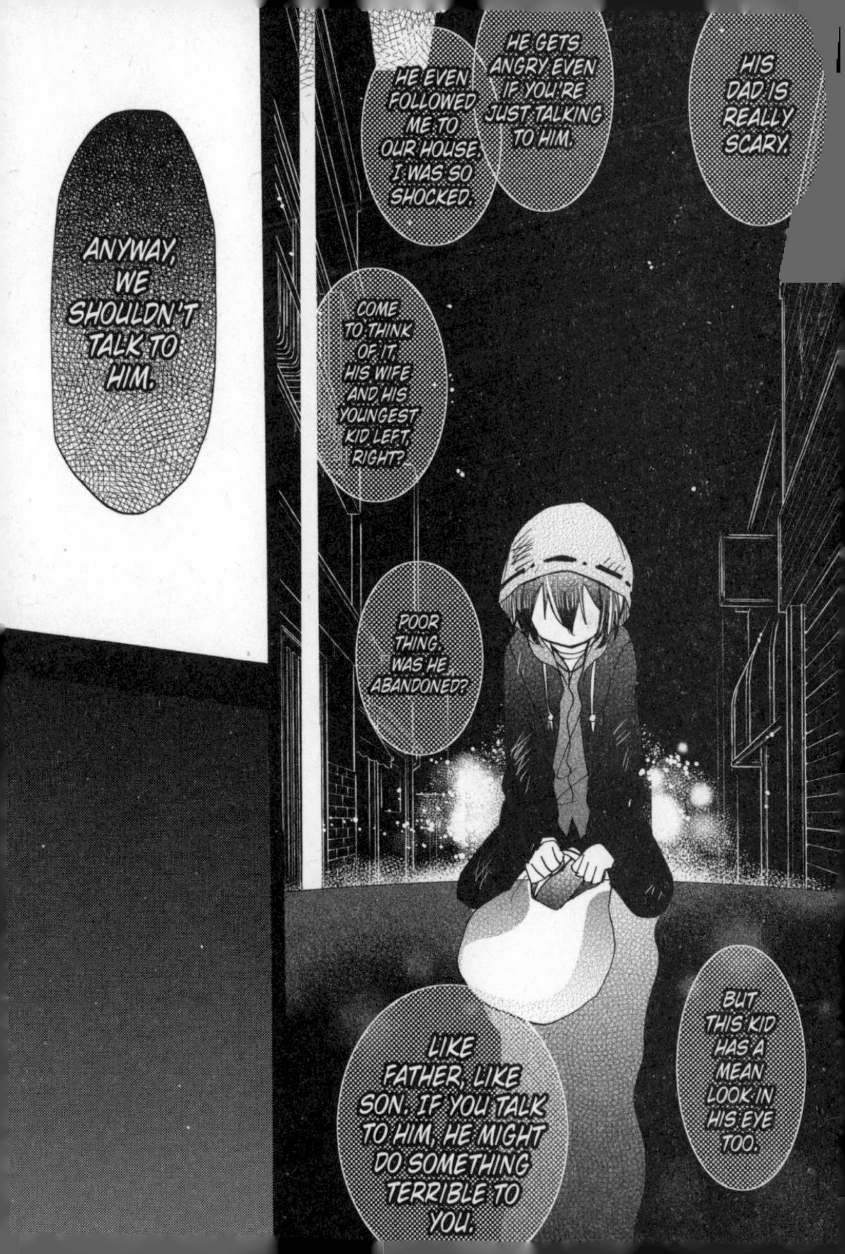
HIS DAD IS REALLY SCARY.
HE GETS ANGRY EVEN IF YOU'RE JUST TALKING TO HIM.
HE EVEN FOLLOWED ME TO OUR HOUSE. I WAS SO SHOCKED.
COME TO THINK OF IT, HIS WIFE AND HIS YOUNGEST KID LEFT, RIGHT?
POOR THING. WAS HE ABANDONED?
BUT THIS KID HAS A MEAN LOOK IN HIS EYE TOO.
LIKE FATHER, LIKE SON. IF YOU TALK TO HIM, HE MIGHT DO SOMETHING TERRIBLE TO YOU.
ANYWAY, WE SHOULDN'T TALK TO HIM.

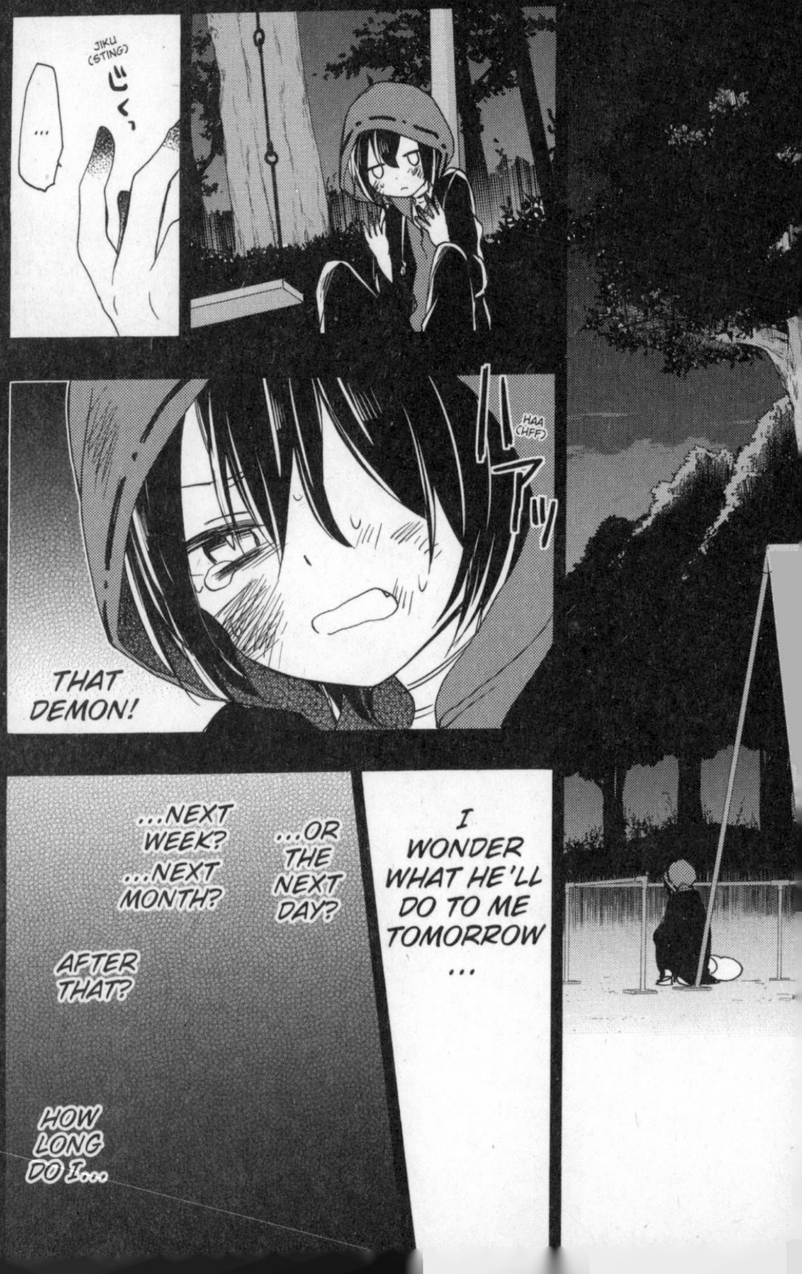
JIKU (STING)
じくっ
...
HAA (HFF)
ハァッ
THAT DEMON!
I WONDER WHAT HE'LL DO TO ME TOMORROW ...
...OR THE NEXT DAY?
...NEXT WEEK? ...NEXT MONTH?
AFTER THAT?
HOW LONG DO I...

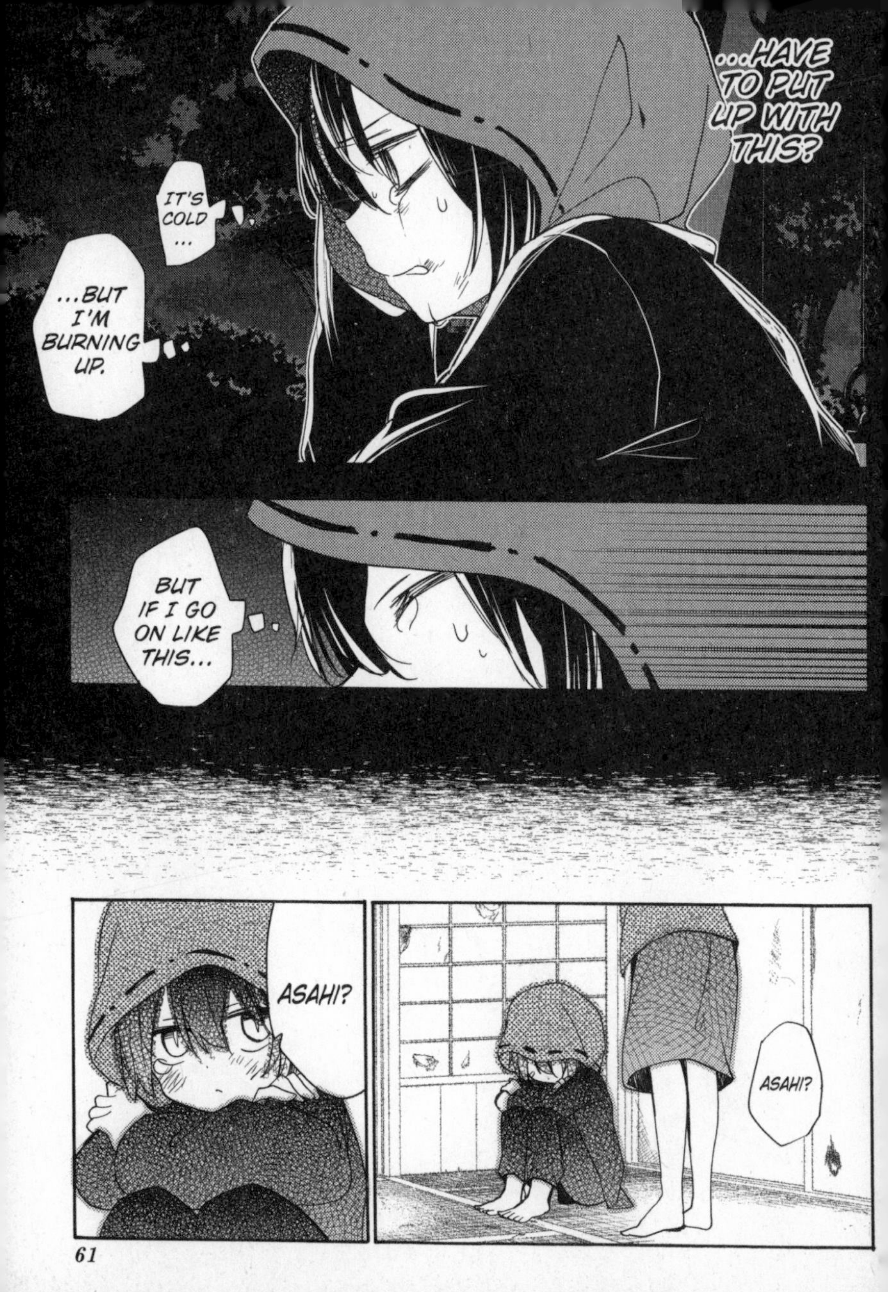
...HAVE TO PUT UP WITH THIS?
IT'S COLD...
...BUT I'M BURNING UP.
BUT IF I GO ON LIKE THIS...
ASAHI?
ASAHI?

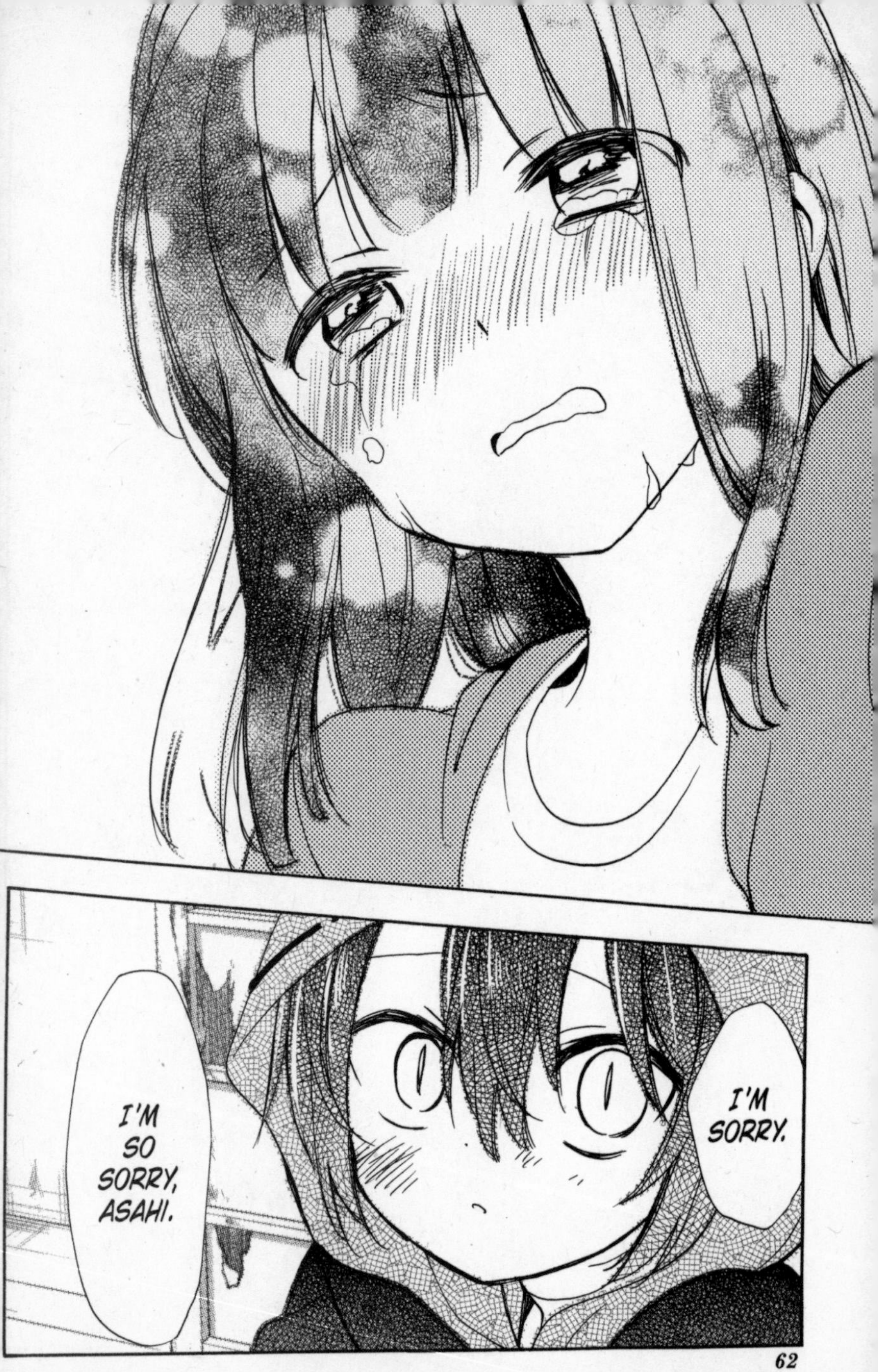
I'M SORRY.
I'M SO SORRY, ASAHI.

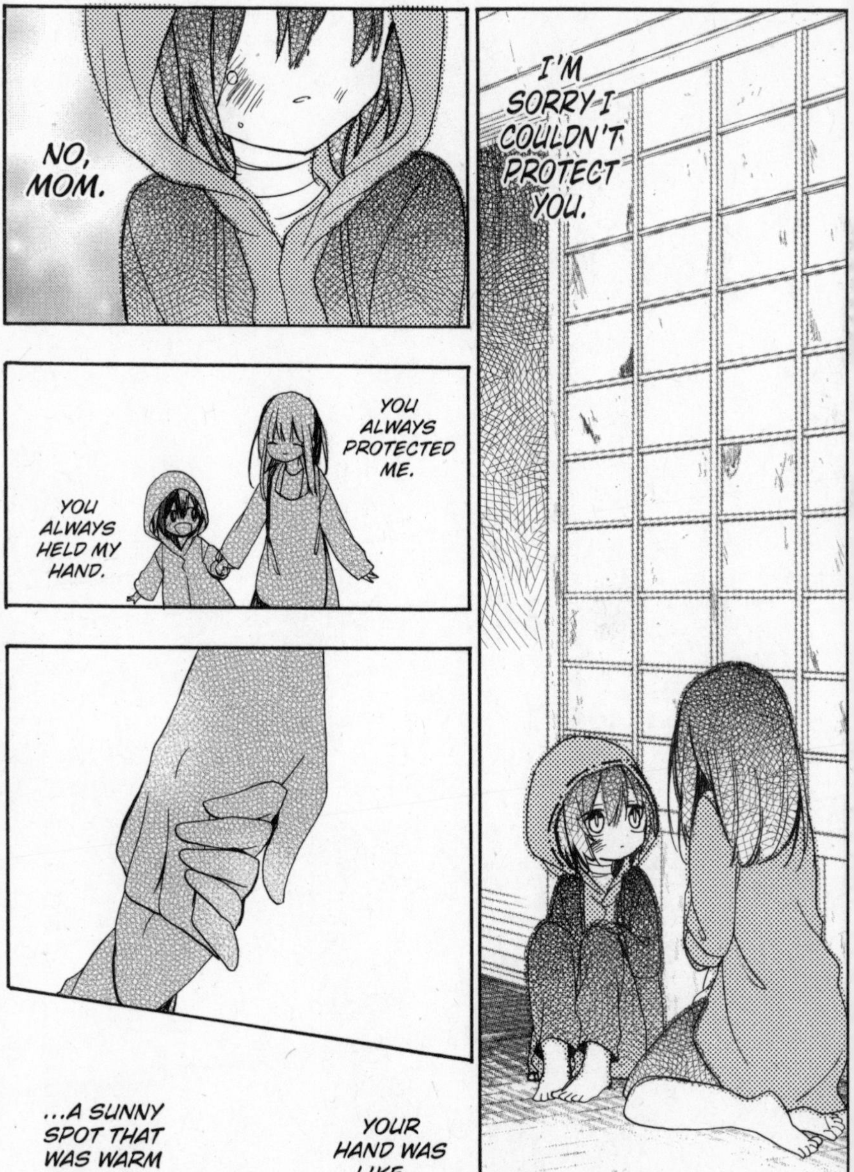
I'M SORRY I COULDN'T PROTECT YOU.
NO, MOM.
YOU ALWAYS PROTECTED ME.
YOU ALWAYS HELD MY HAND.
YOUR HAND WAS LIKE...
...A SUNNY SPOT THAT WAS WARM AND SAFE.

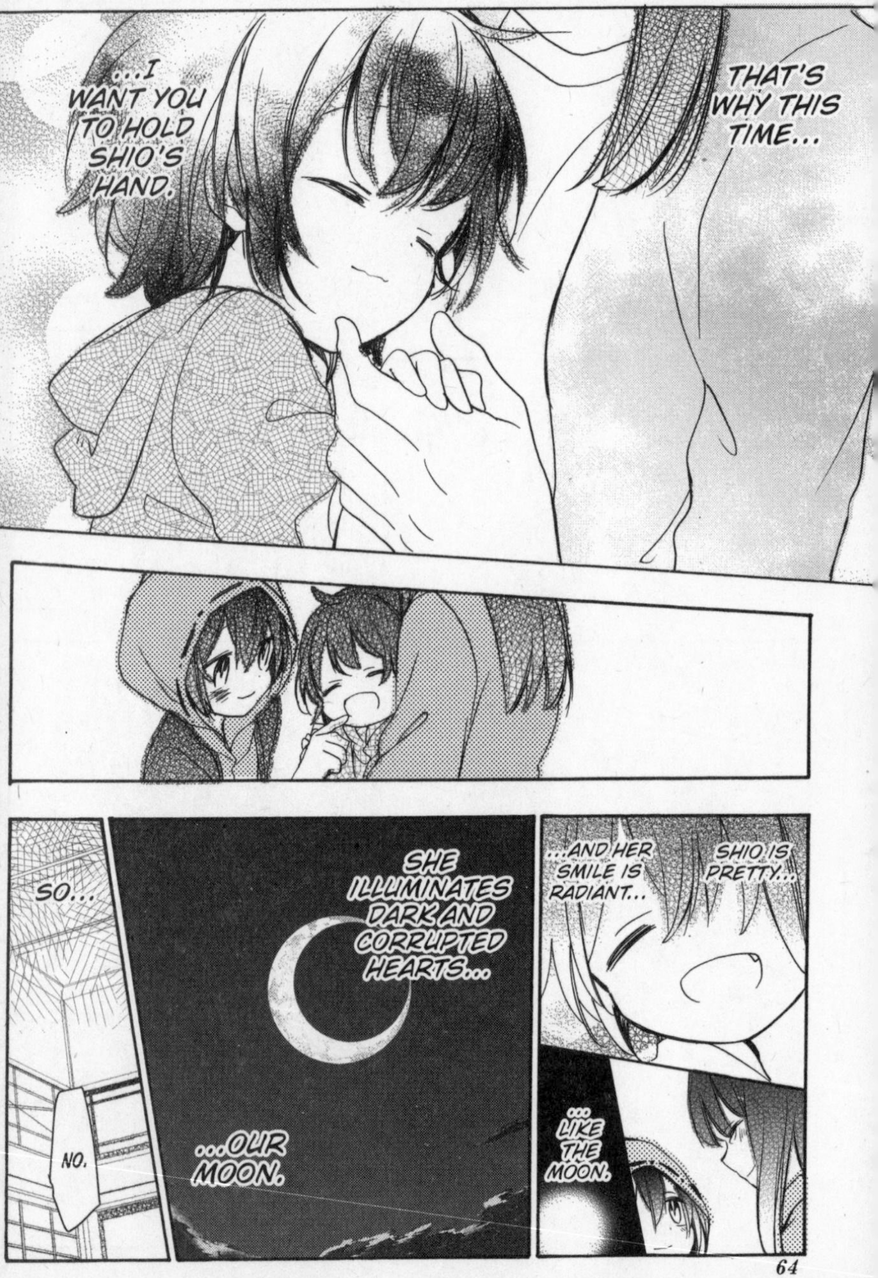
THAT'S WHY THIS TIME...
...I WANT YOU TO HOLD SHIO'S HAND.
SHIO IS PRETTY...
...AND HER SMILE IS RADIANT...
...LIKE THE MOON.
SHE ILLUMINATES DARK AND CORRUPTED HEARTS...
...OUR MOON.
SO...
NO.

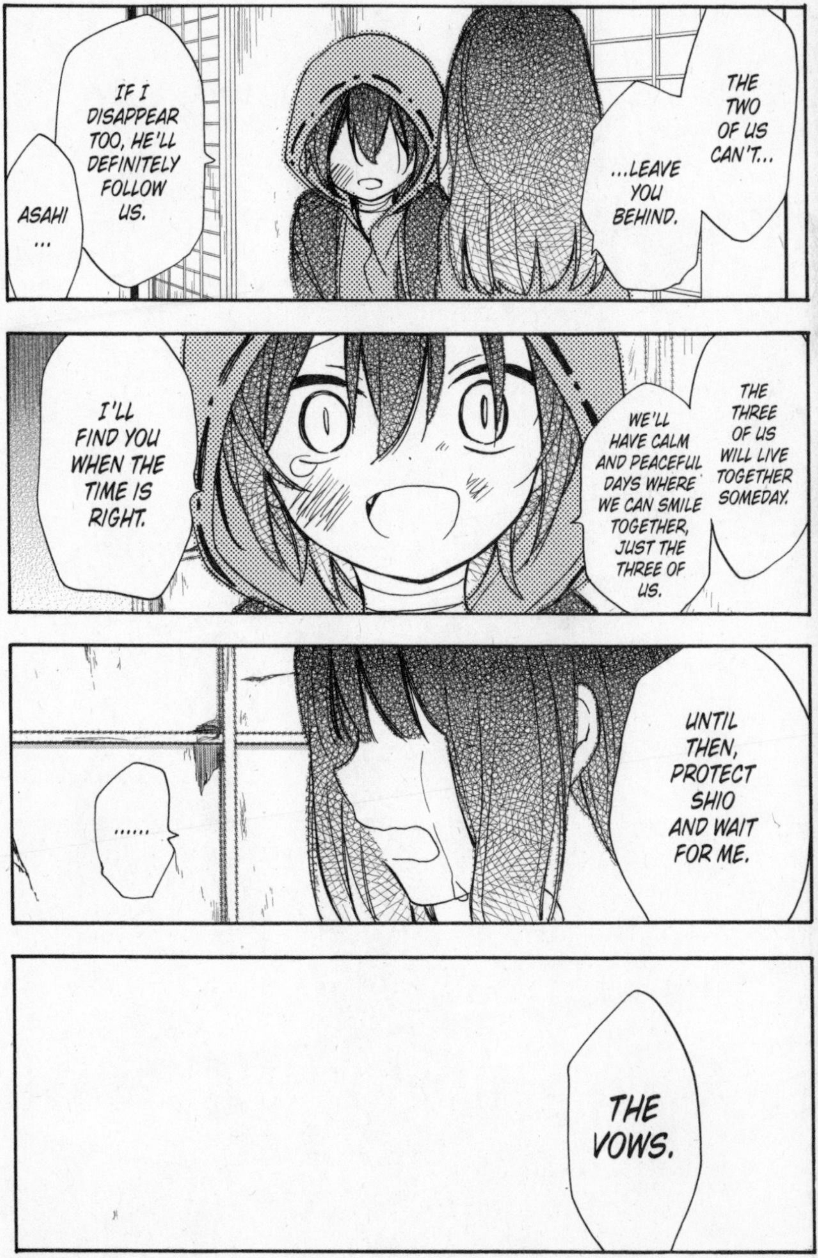
THE TWO OF US CAN'T...
...LEAVE YOU BEHIND.
IF I DISAPPEAR TOO, HE'LL DEFINITELY FOLLOW US.
ASAHI...
THE THREE OF US WILL LIVE TOGETHER SOMEDAY.
WE'LL HAVE CALM AND PEACEFUL DAYS WHERE WE CAN SMILE TOGETHER, JUST THE THREE OF US.
I'LL FIND YOU WHEN THE TIME IS RIGHT.
UNTIL THEN, PROTECT SHIO AND WAIT FOR ME.
......
THE VOWS.

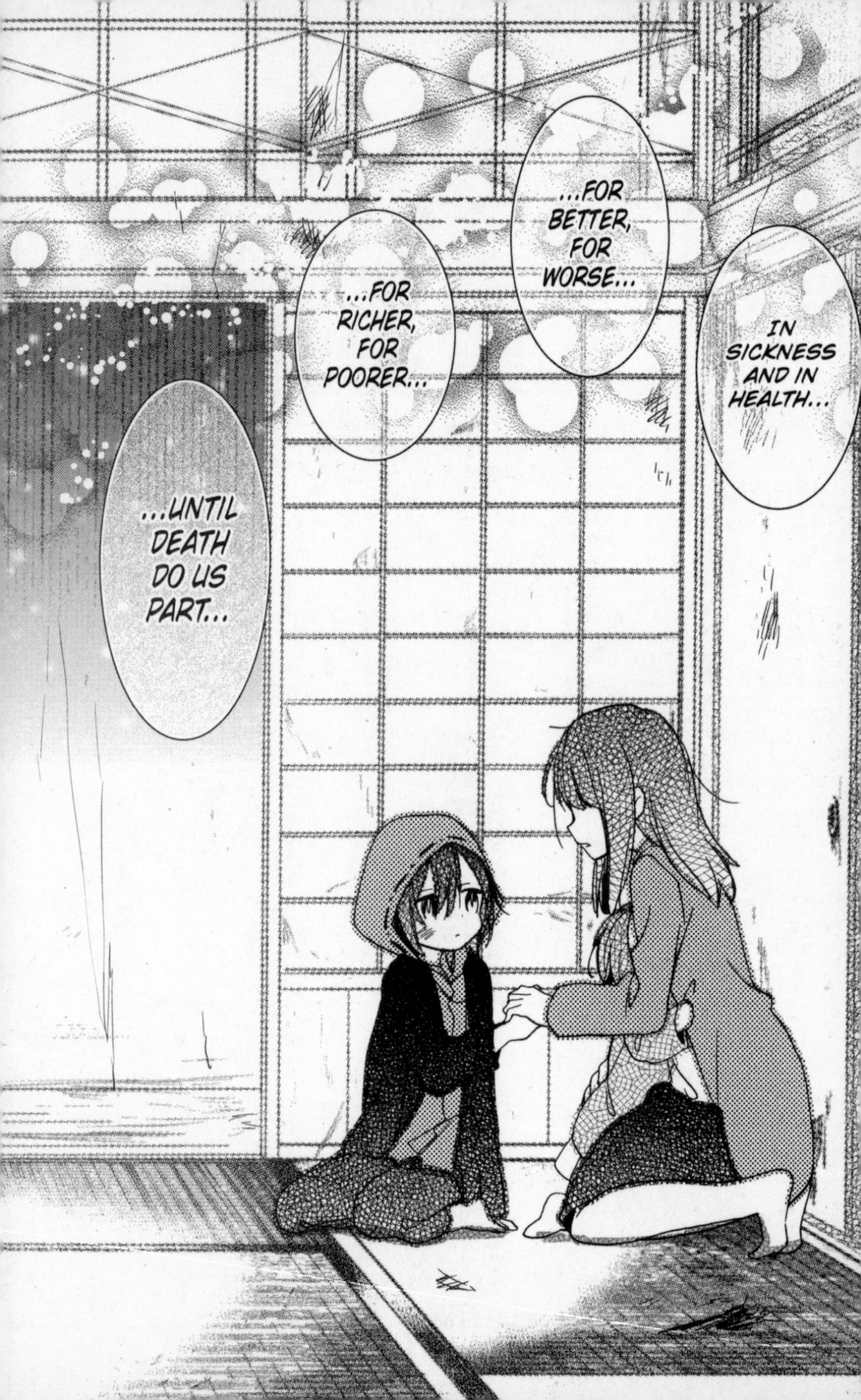
...FOR BETTER, FOR WORSE...
...FOR RICHER, FOR POORER...
IN SICKNESS AND IN HEALTH...
...UNTIL DEATH DO US PART...

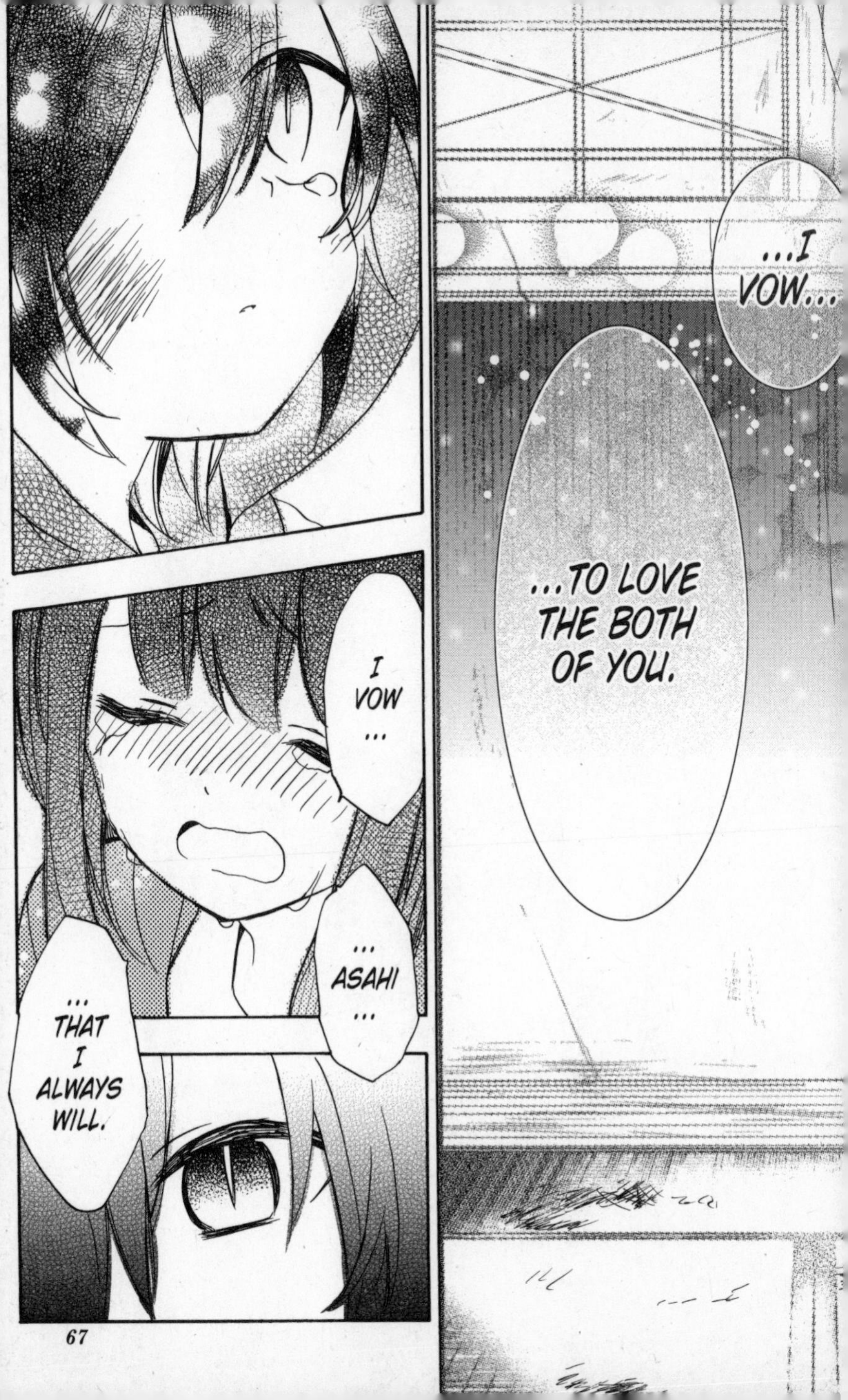
...I VOW...
...TO LOVE THE BOTH OF YOU.
I VOW ...
... ASAHI ...
... THAT I ALWAYS WILL.

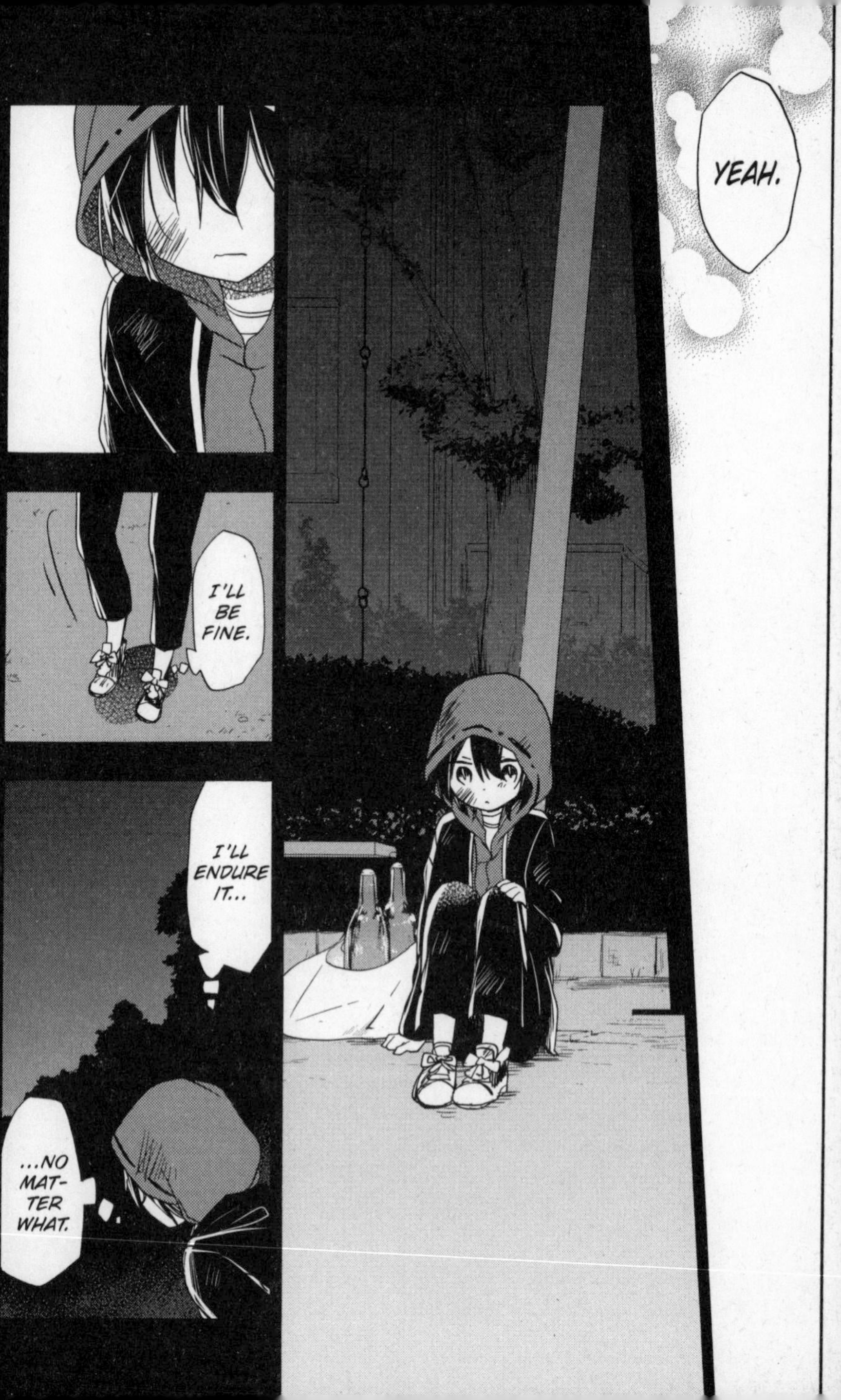
YEAH.
I'LL BE FINE.
I'LL ENDURE IT...
...NO MAT-TER WHAT.

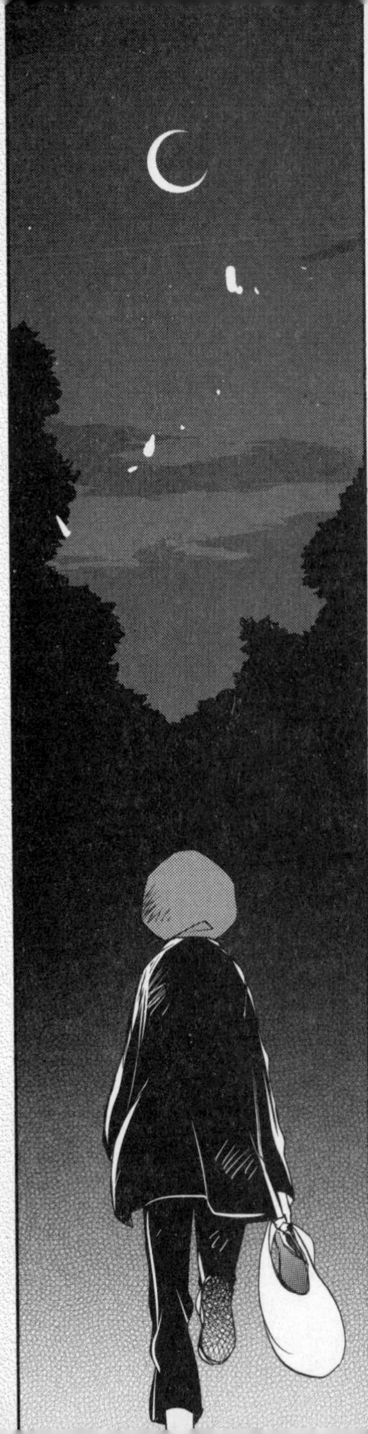
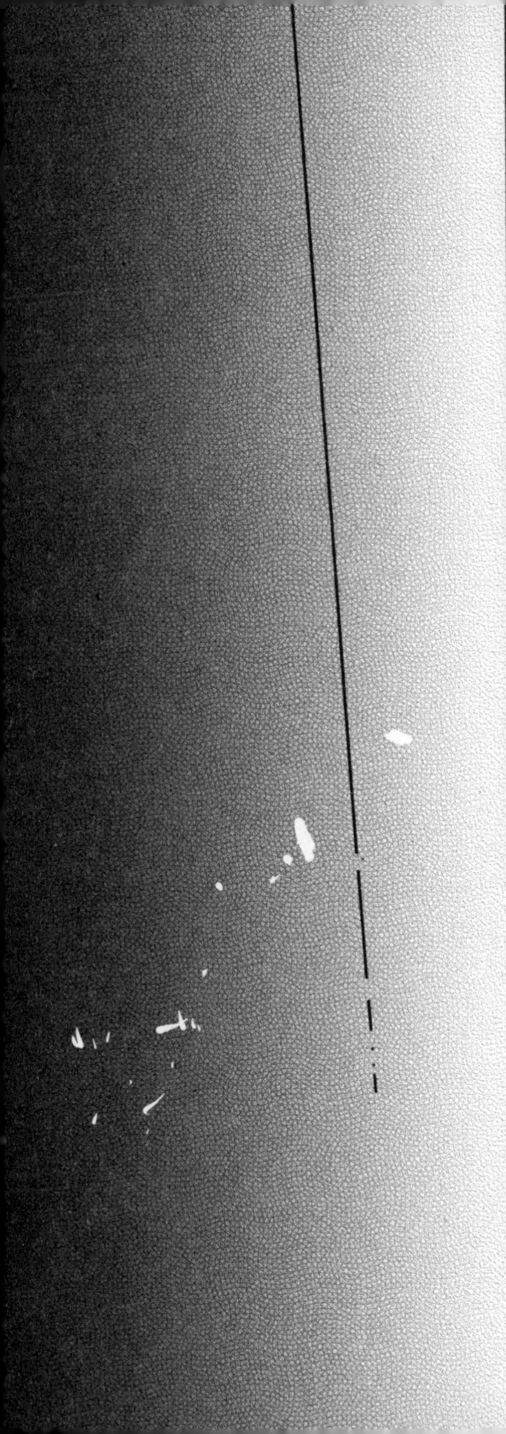

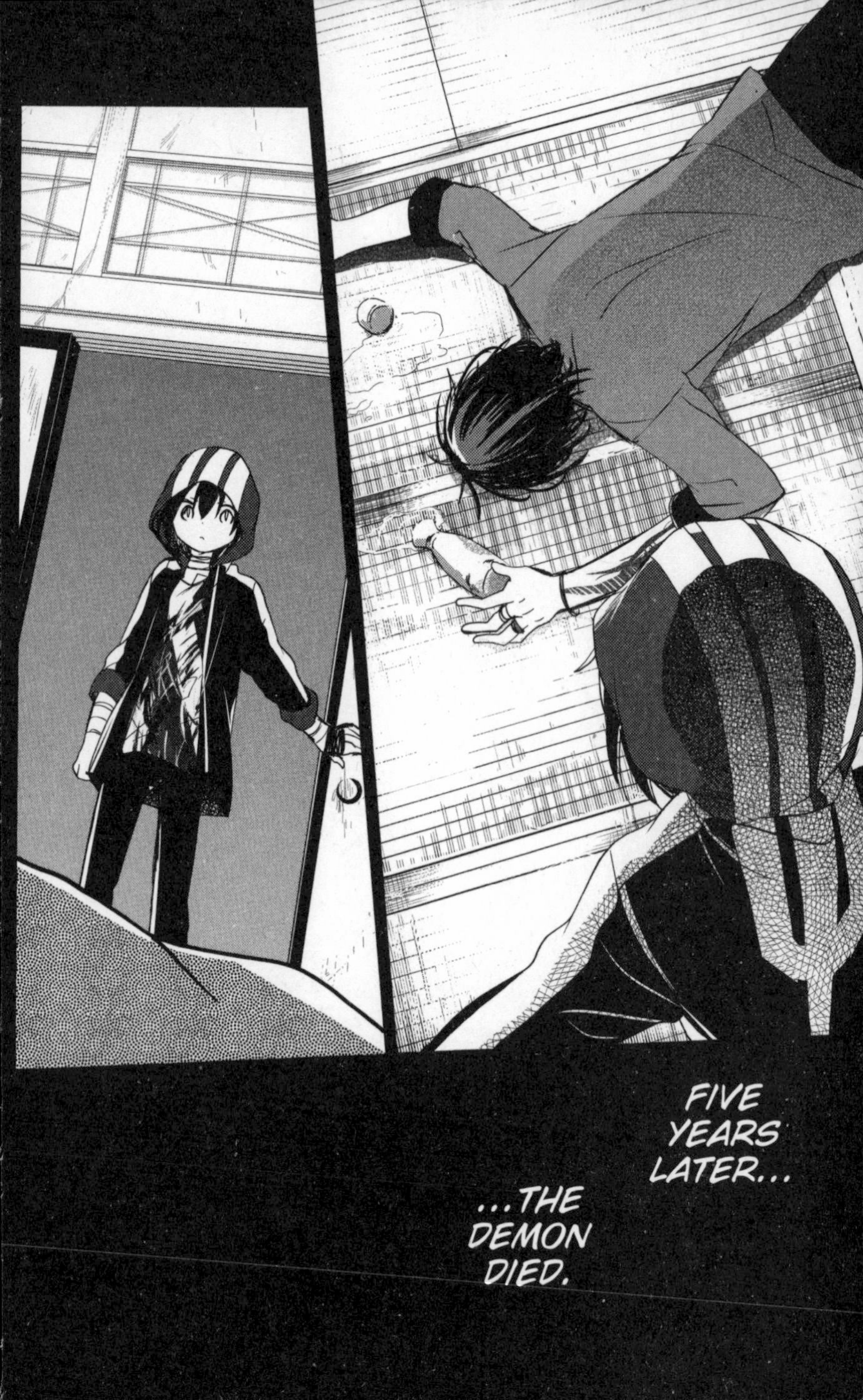
FIVE YEARS LATER...
...THE DEMON DIED.

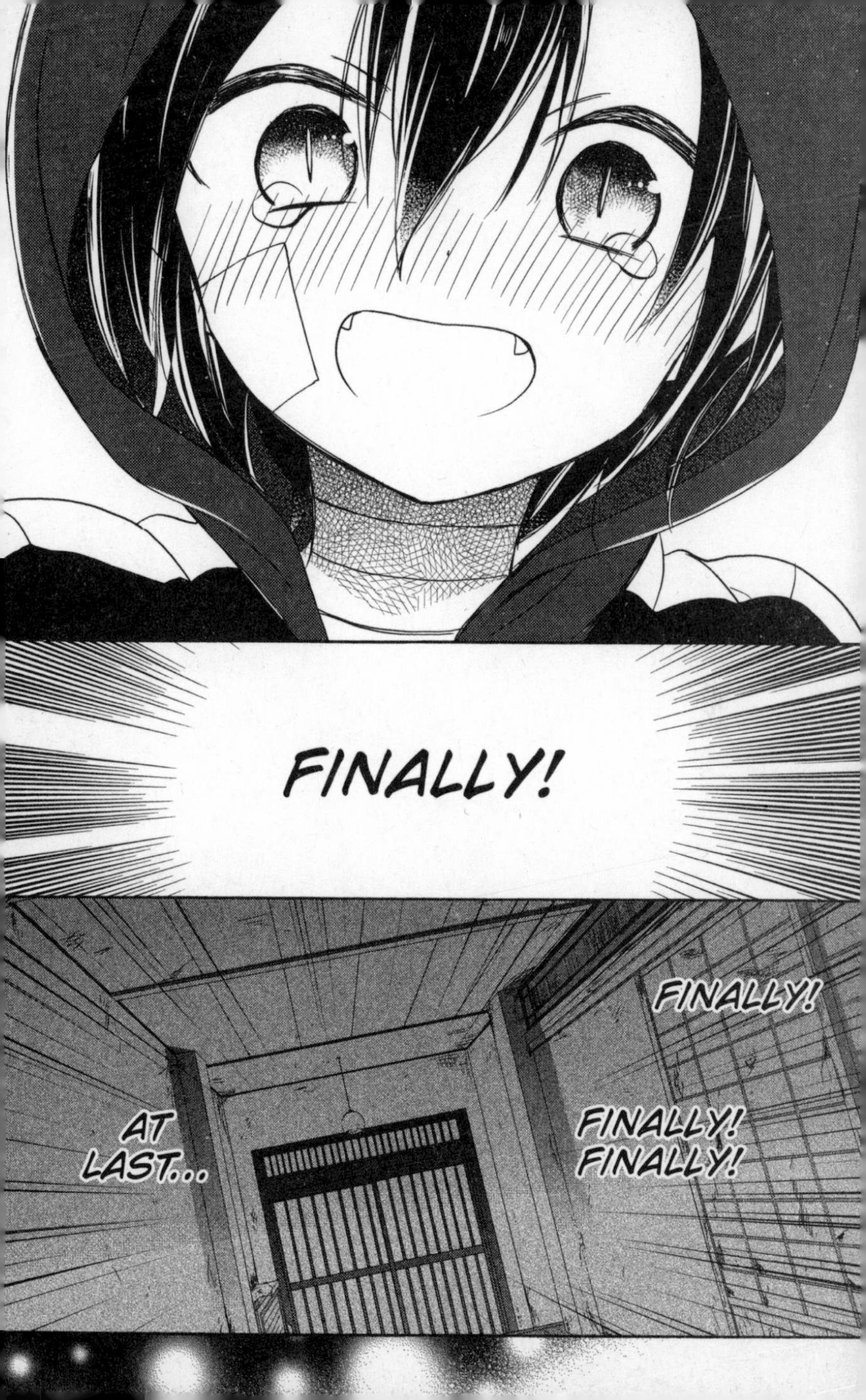
FINALLY!
FINALLY!
FINALLY!
FINALLY!
AT LAST...

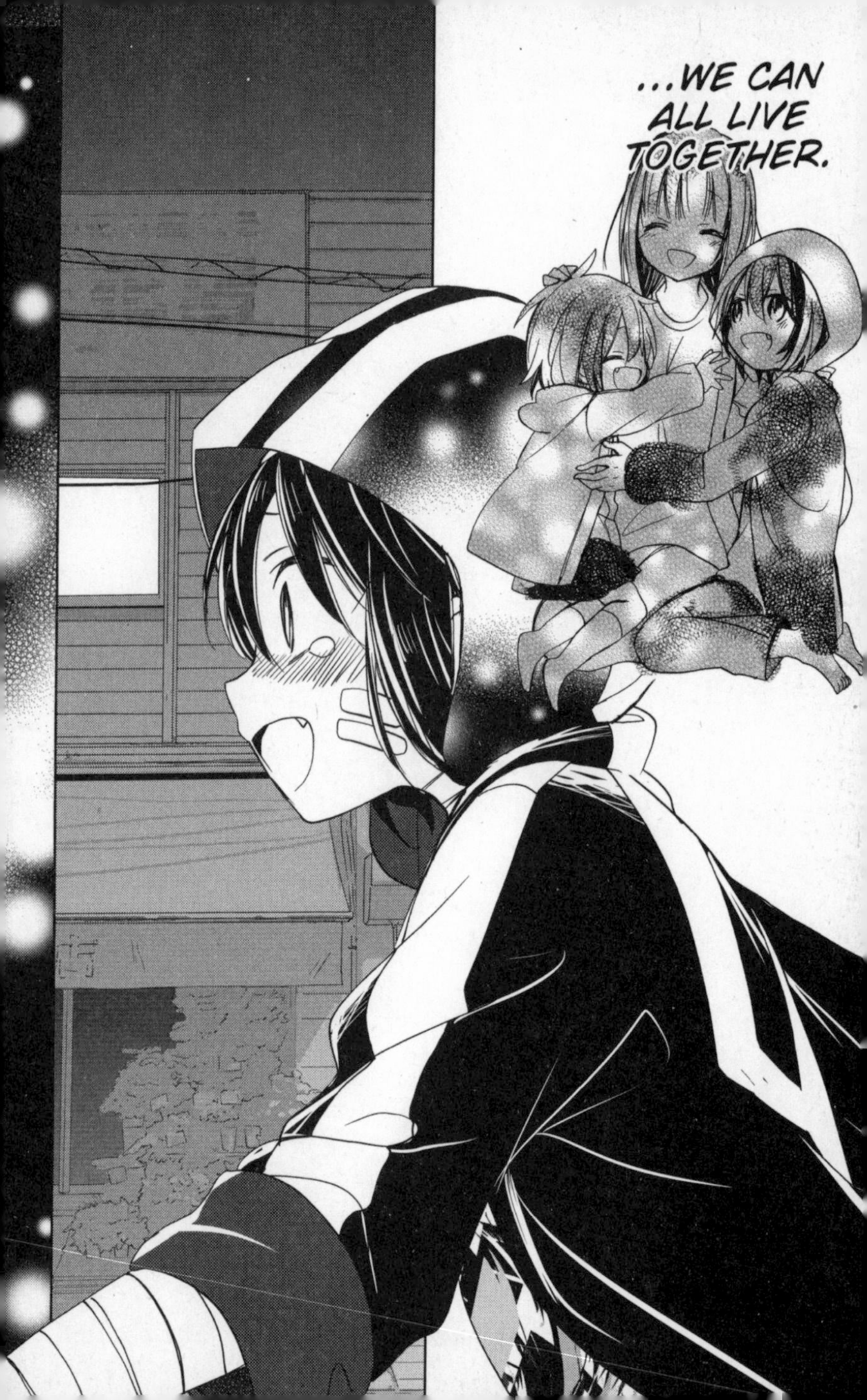
...WE CAN ALL LIVE TOGETHER.

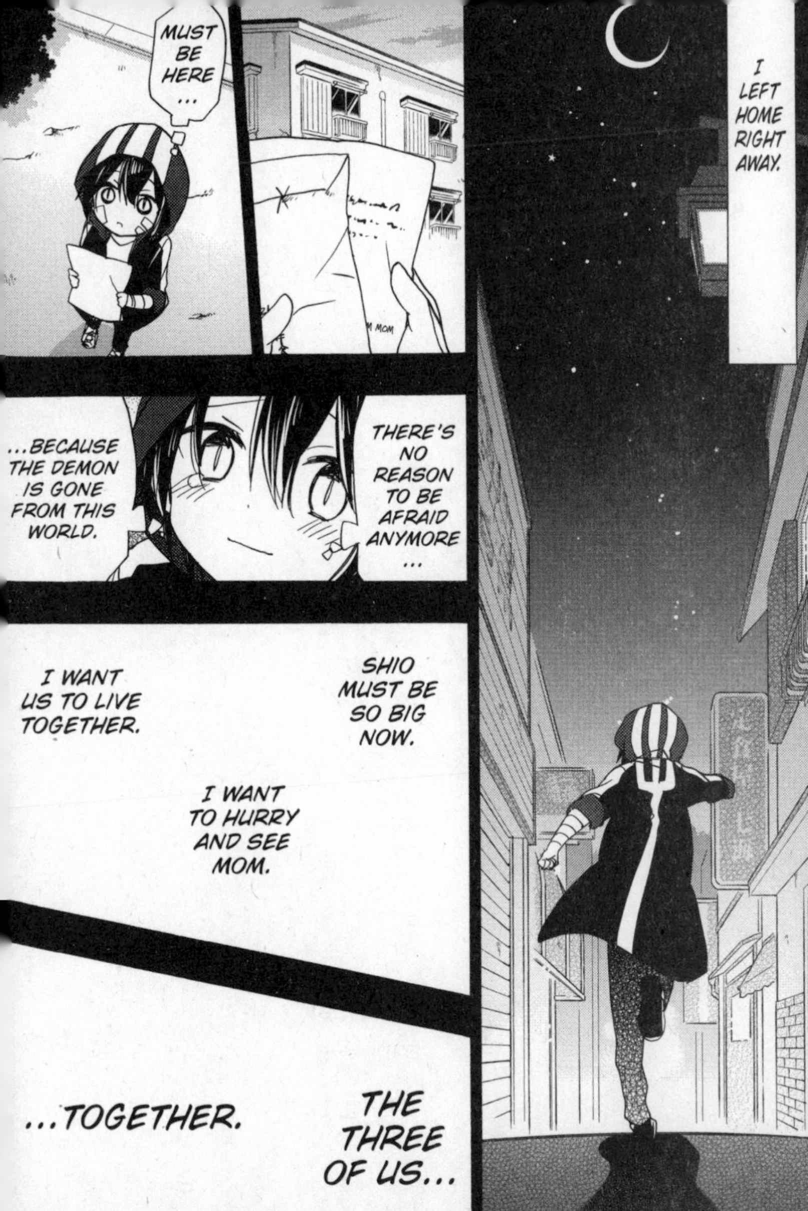
I LEFT HOME RIGHT AWAY.
MUST BE HERE...
THERE'S NO REASON TO BE AFRAID ANYMORE...
...BECAUSE THE DEMON IS GONE FROM THIS WORLD.
SHIO MUST BE SO BIG NOW.
I WANT US TO LIVE TOGETHER.
I WANT TO HURRY AND SEE MOM.
THE THREE OF US...
...TOGETHER.

THAT'S
HOW IT
SHOULD
HAVE
BEEN.

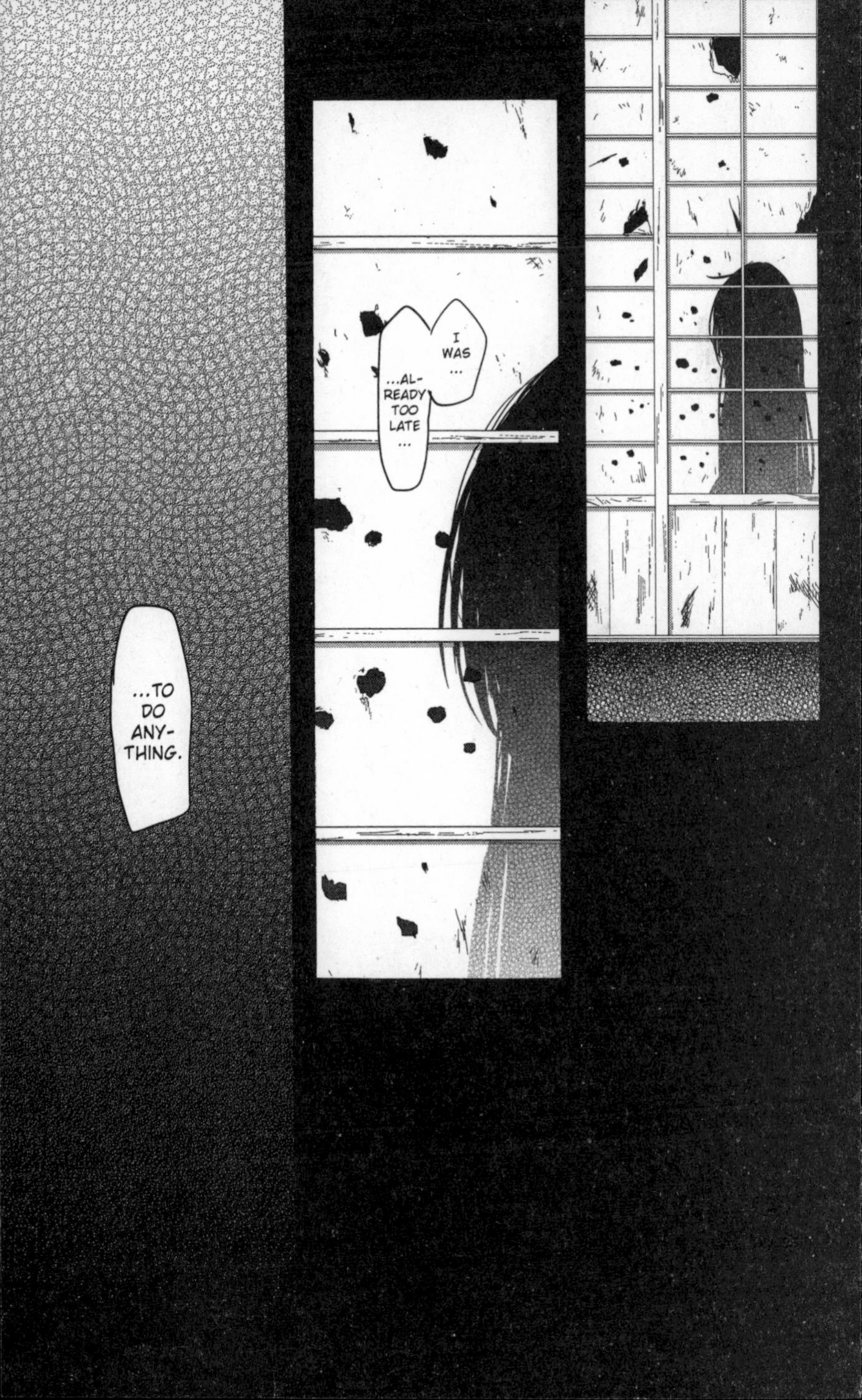
I WAS ...
...AL-READY TOO LATE ...
...TO DO ANY-THING.

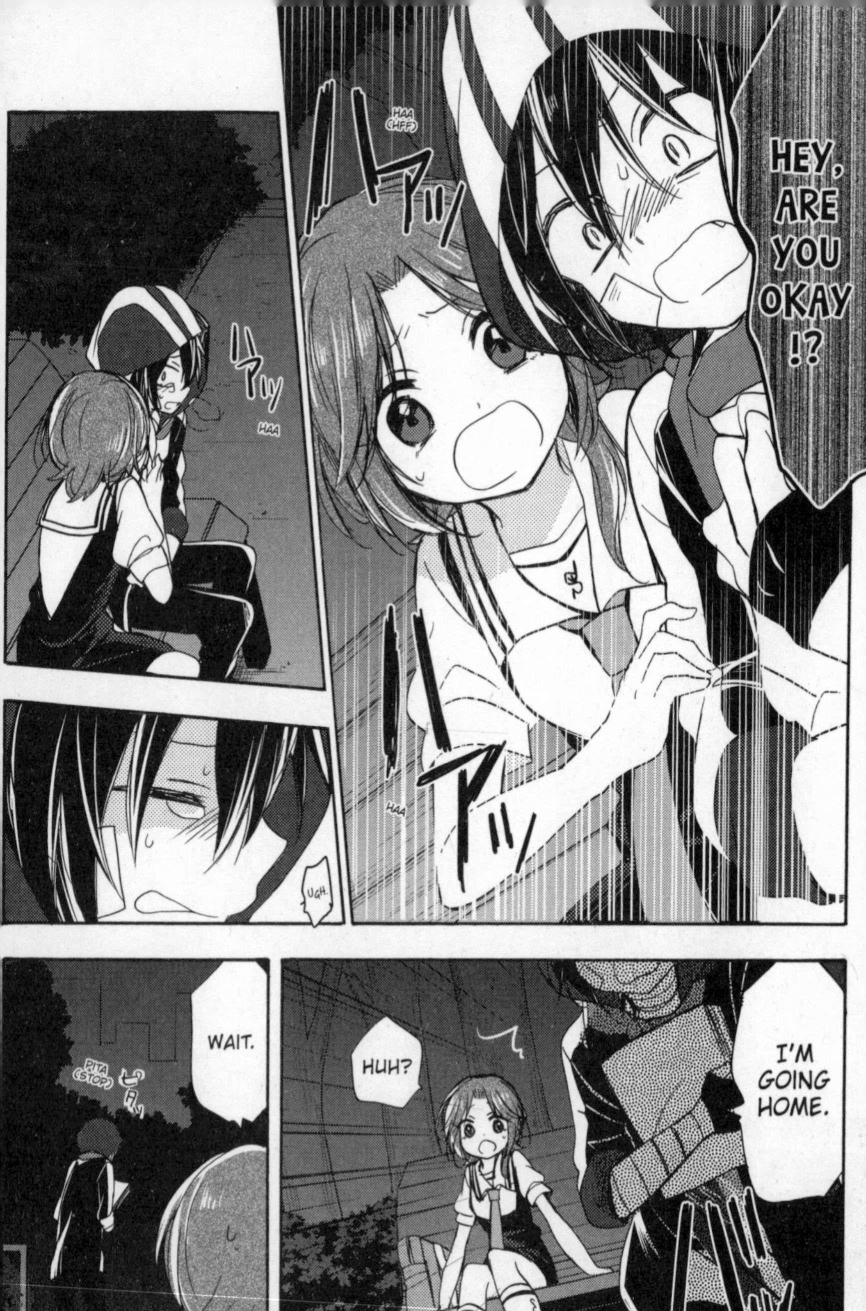
HAA (HFF)
HEY, ARE YOU OKAY!?
HAA
HAA
UGH.
I'M GOING HOME.
HUH?
BA (BAM)
WAIT.
PITA (STOP)

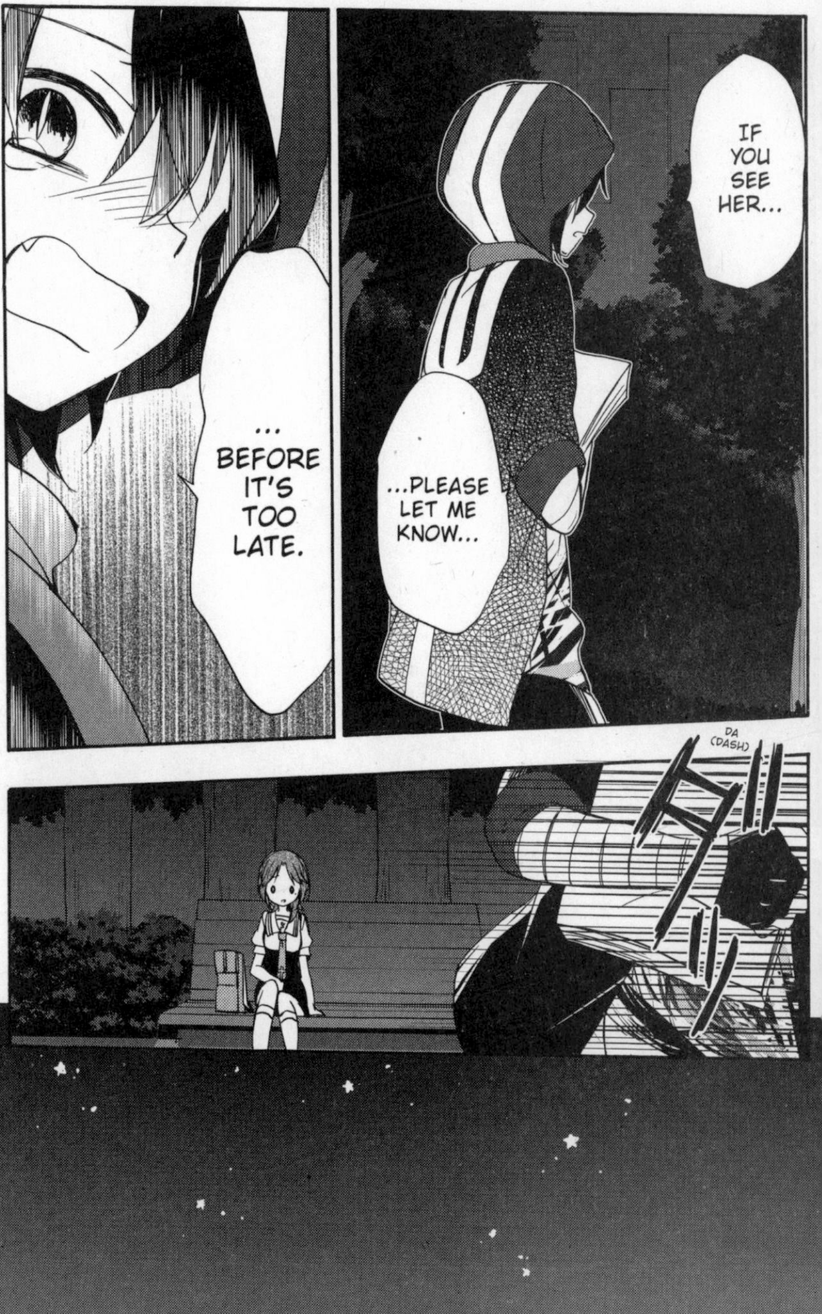
IF YOU SEE HER...
...PLEASE LET ME KNOW...
... BEFORE IT'S TOO LATE.
DA (DASH)

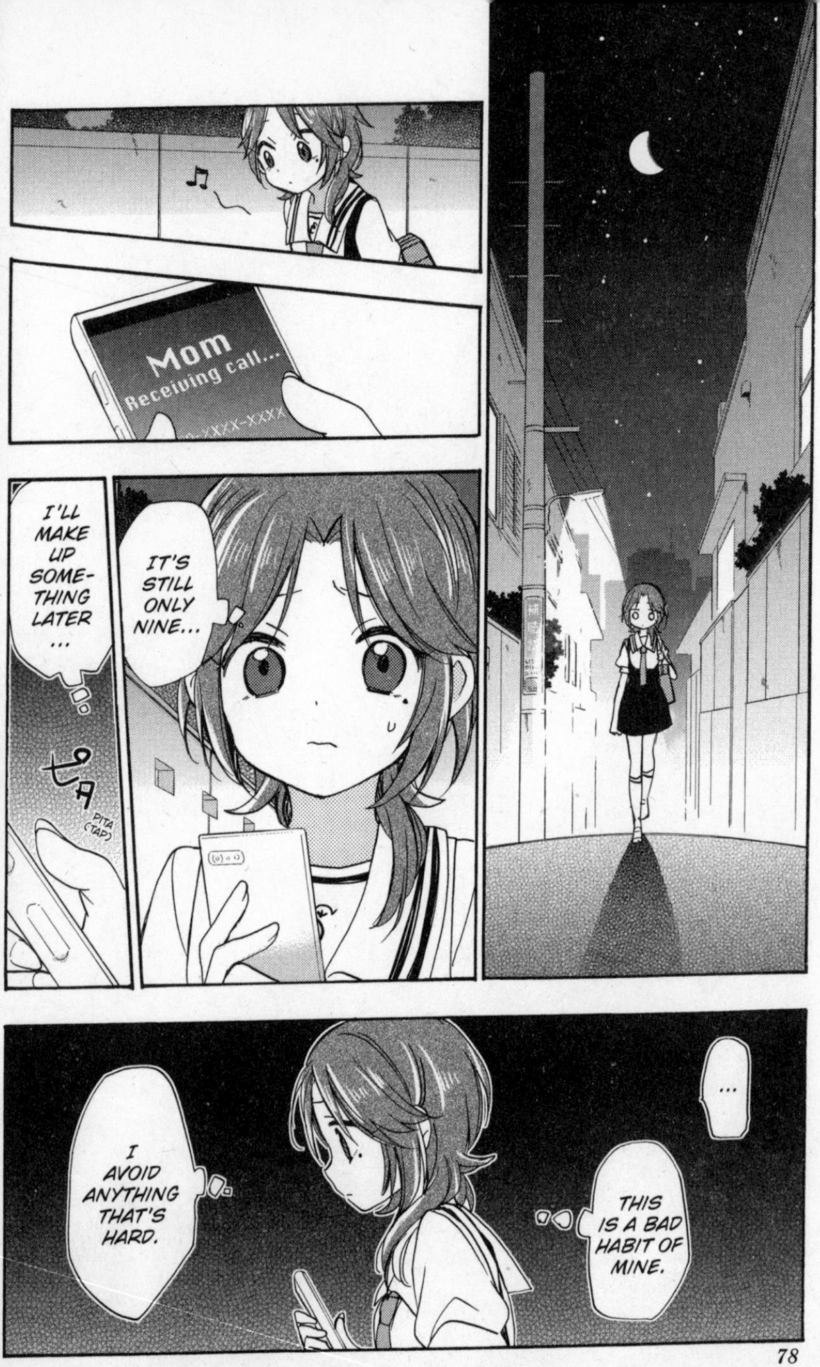
Mom
Receiving call...
IT'S STILL ONLY NINE...
I'LL MAKE UP SOME-THING LATER...
ぴた
PITA (TAP)
...
THIS IS A BAD HABIT OF MINE.
I AVOID ANYTHING THAT'S HARD.

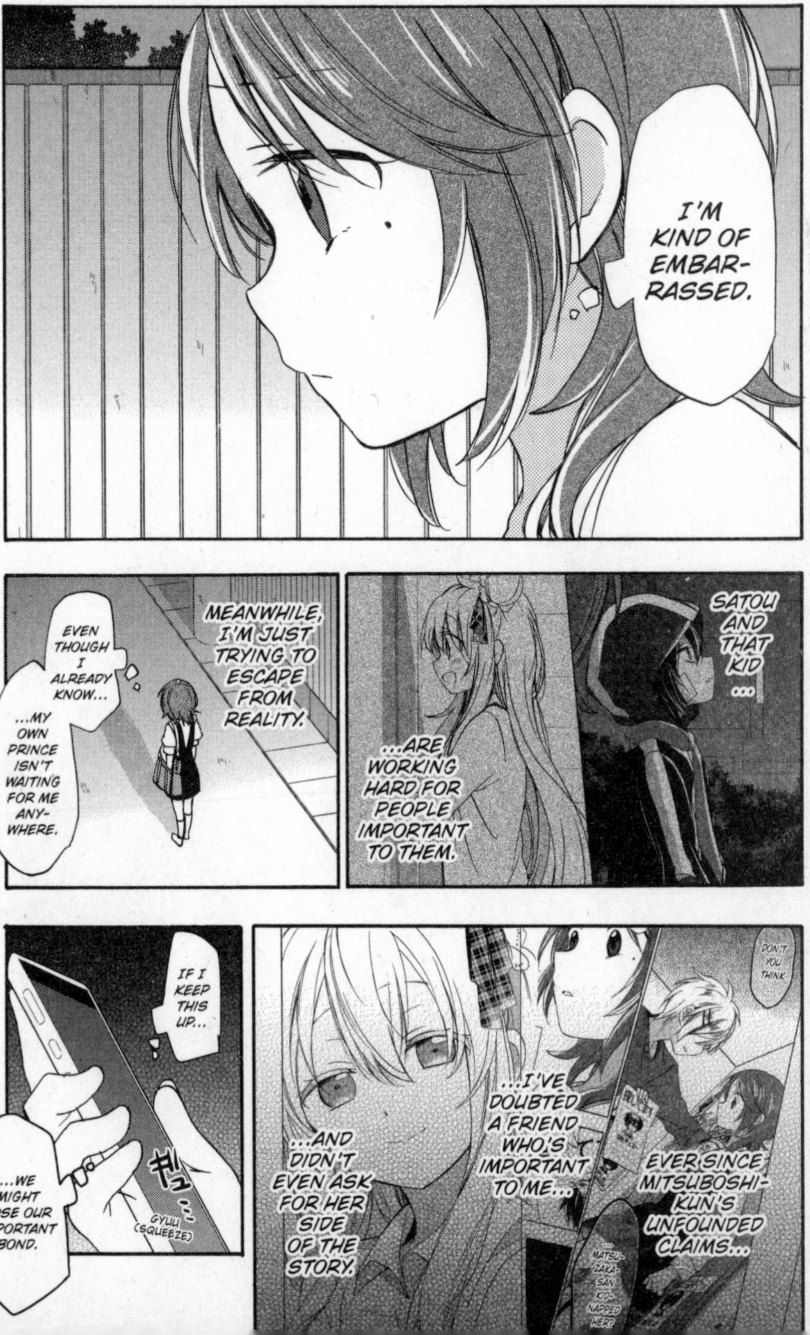
I'M KIND OF EMBAR-RASSED.
SATOU AND THAT KID...
...ARE WORKING HARD FOR PEOPLE IMPORTANT TO THEM.
MEANWHILE, I'M JUST TRYING TO ESCAPE FROM REALITY.
EVEN THOUGH I ALREADY KNOW...
...MY OWN PRINCE ISN'T WAITING FOR ME ANY-WHERE.
DON'T YOU THINK...
...MATSU-ZAKA-SAN KID-NAPPED HER?
EVER SINCE MITSUBOSHI-KUN'S UNFOUNDED CLAIMS...
...I'VE DOUBTED A FRIEND WHO'S IMPORTANT TO ME...
...AND DIDN'T EVEN ASK FOR HER SIDE OF THE STORY.
IF I KEEP THIS UP...
ギュ...
GYUU (SQUEEZE)
...WE MIGHT LOSE OUR IMPORTANT BOND.

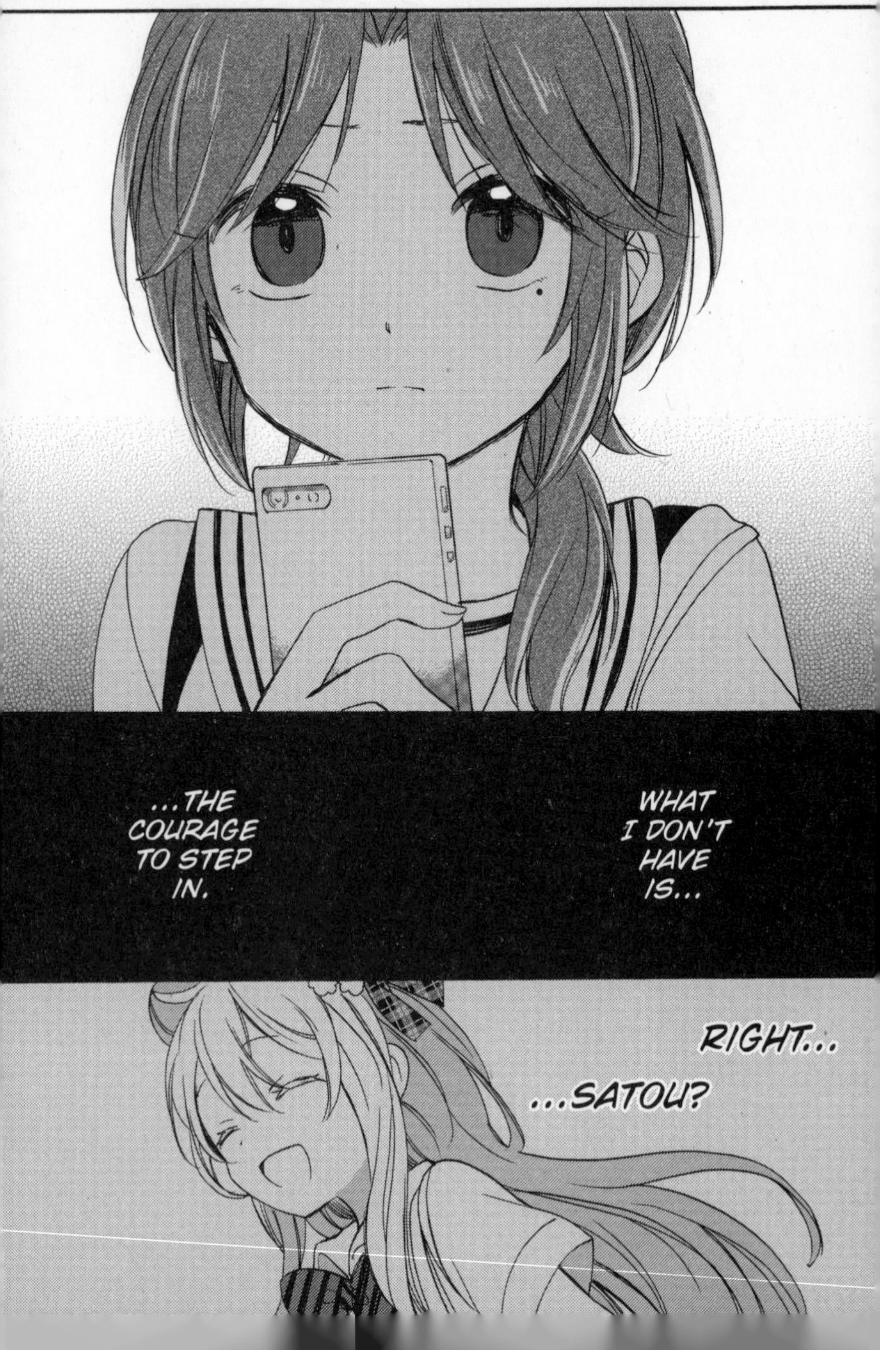
WHAT I DON'T HAVE IS...
...THE COURAGE TO STEP IN.
RIGHT...
...SATOU?

Happy
Sugar
Life

Happy
Sugar
Life

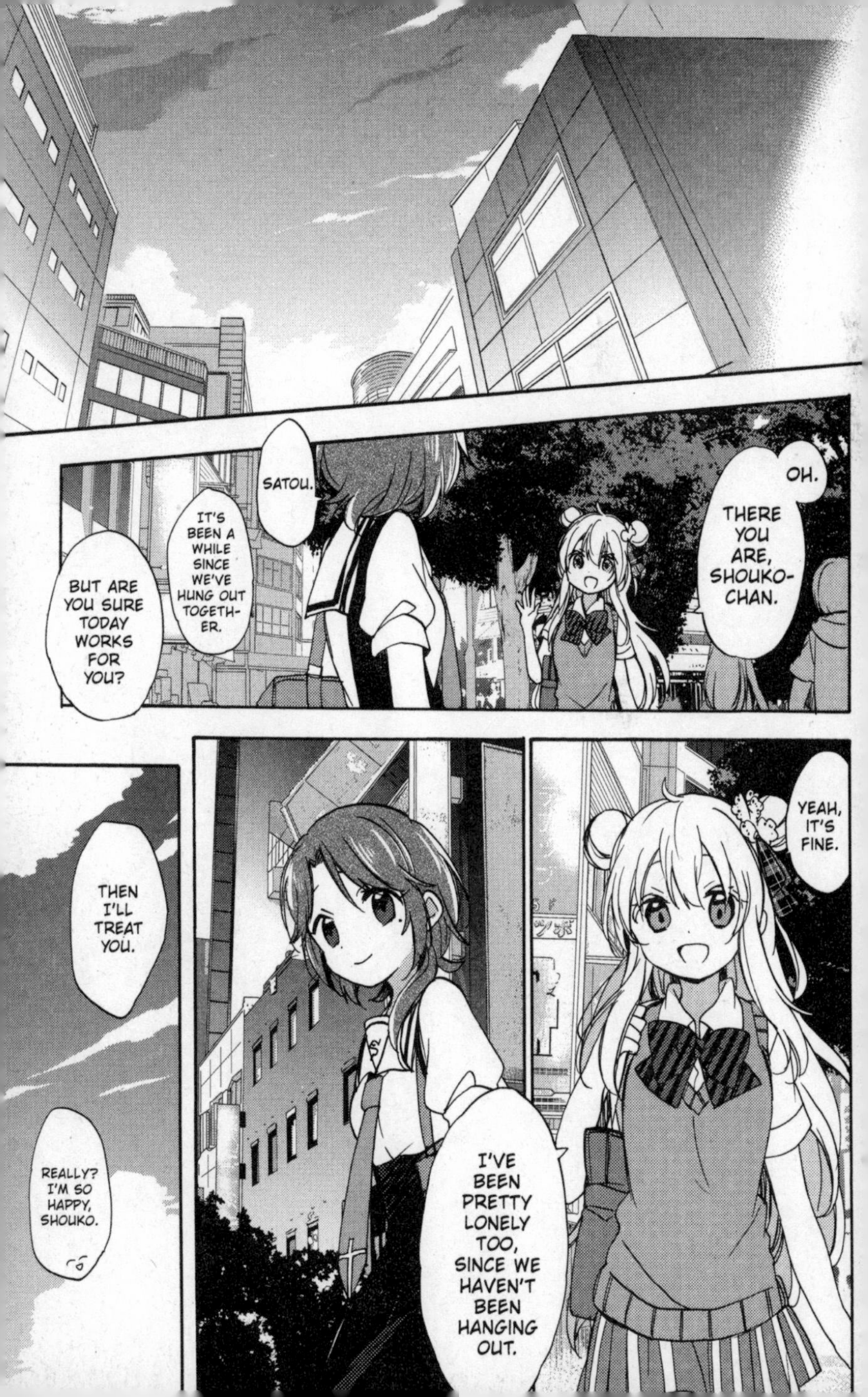
OH.
THERE YOU ARE, SHOUKO-CHAN.
SATOU.
IT'S BEEN A WHILE SINCE WE'VE HUNG OUT TOGETH-ER.
BUT ARE YOU SURE TODAY WORKS FOR YOU?
YEAH, IT'S FINE.
I'VE BEEN PRETTY LONELY TOO, SINCE WE HAVEN'T BEEN HANGING OUT.
THEN I'LL TREAT YOU.
REALLY? I'M SO HAPPY, SHOUKO.

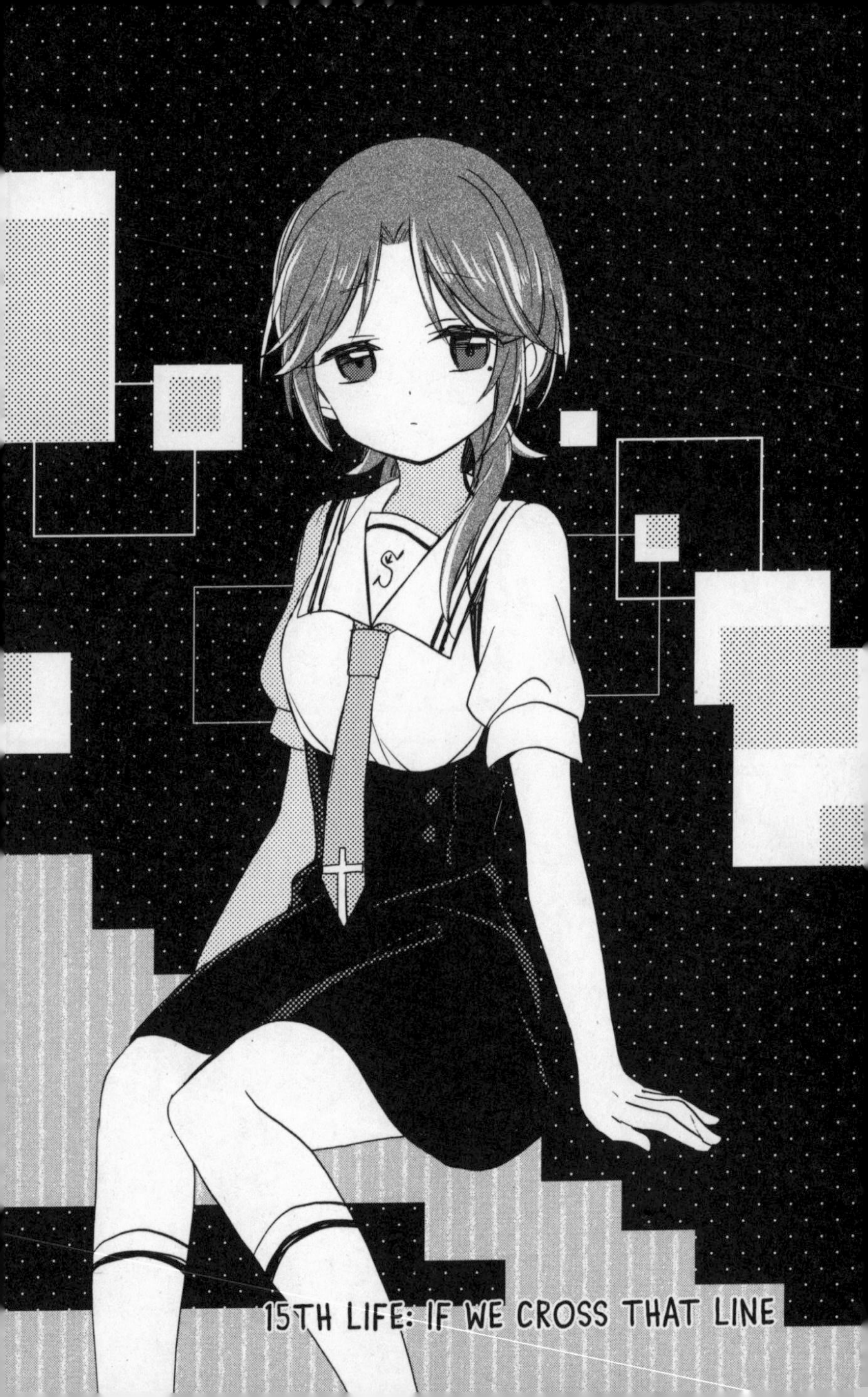
15TH LIFE: IF WE CROSS THAT LINE

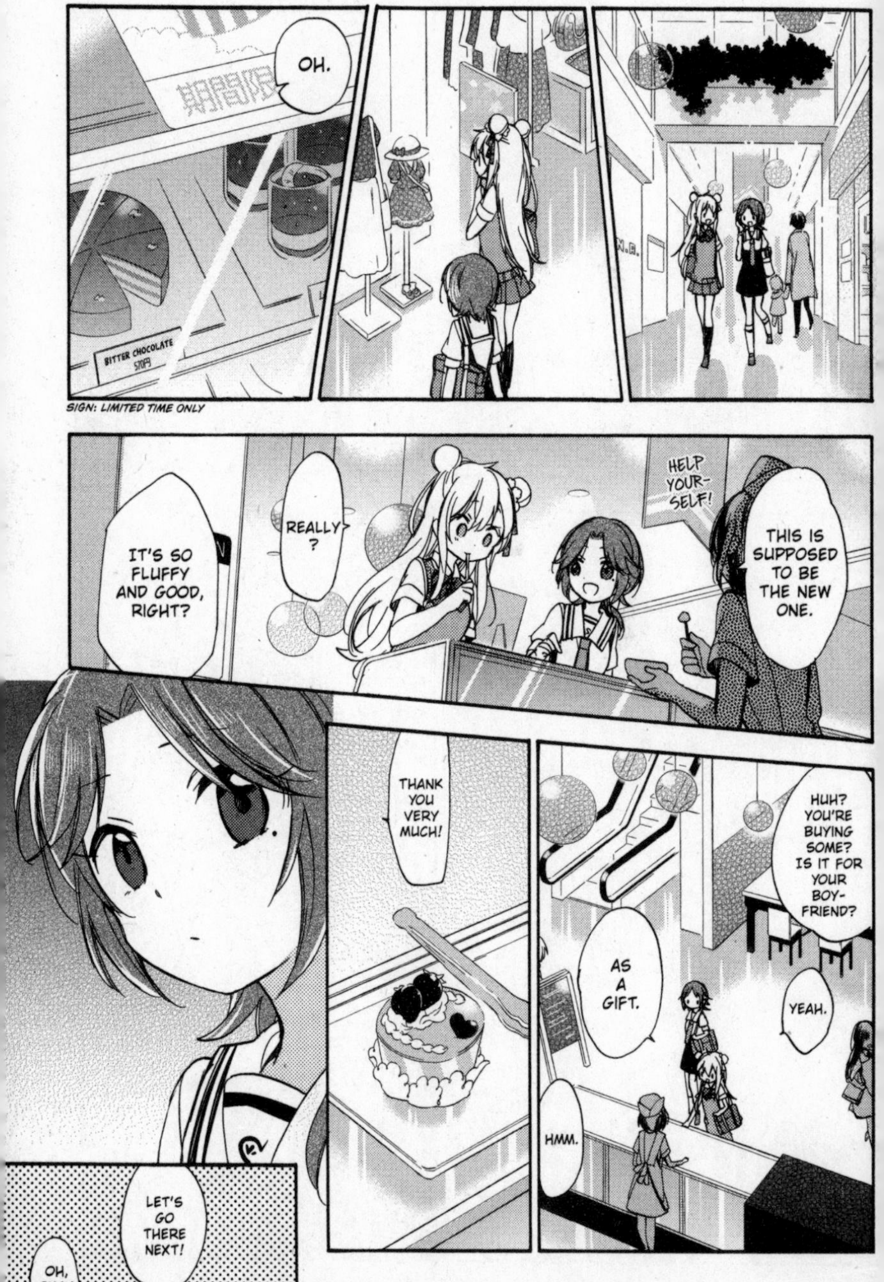
OH.
BITTER CHOCOLATE
570円
HELP YOURSELF!
THIS IS SUPPOSED TO BE THE NEW ONE.
REALLY?
IT'S SO FLUFFY AND GOOD, RIGHT?
HUH? YOU'RE BUYING SOME? IS IT FOR YOUR BOYFRIEND?
YEAH.
AS A GIFT.
HMM.
THANK YOU VERY MUCH!
LET'S GO THERE NEXT!
OH, OKAY.

SIGN: LIMITED TIME ONLY

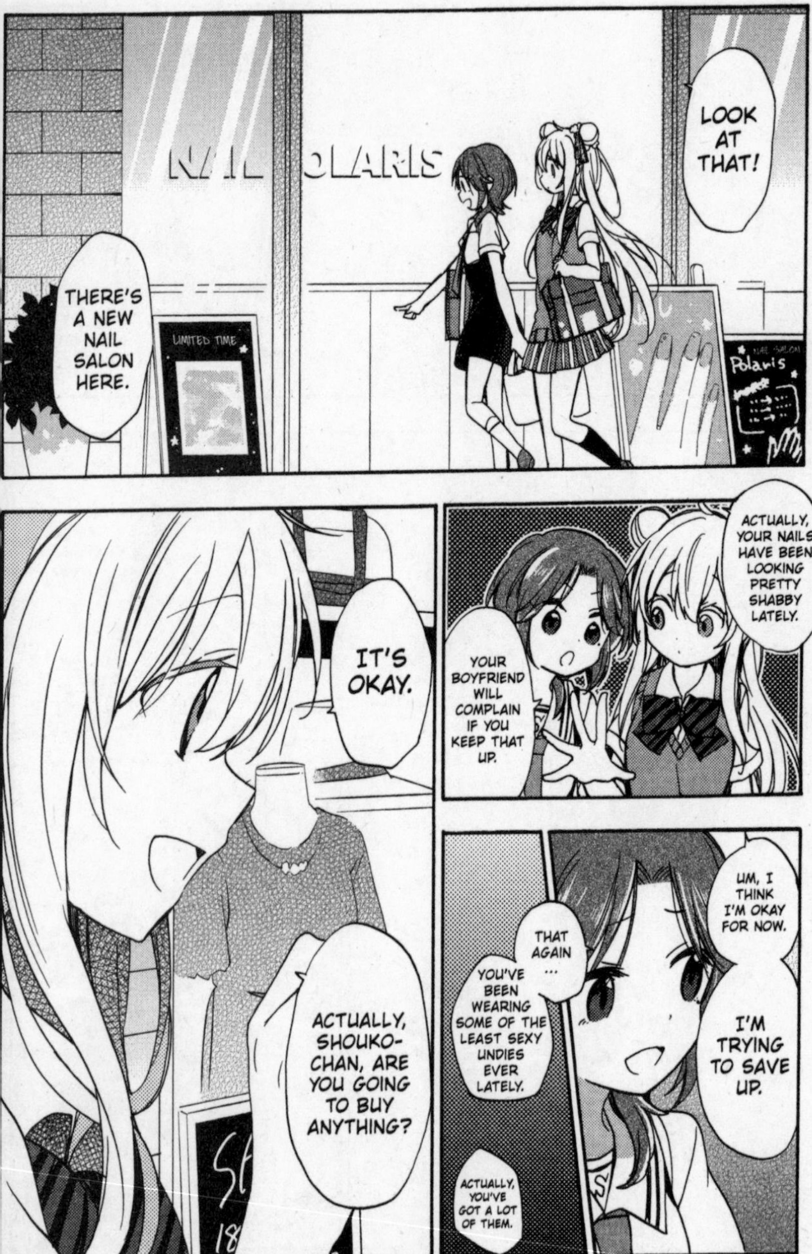
LOOK AT THAT!
THERE'S A NEW NAIL SALON HERE.
LIMITED TIME
NAIL SALON Polaris
ACTUALLY, YOUR NAILS HAVE BEEN LOOKING PRETTY SHABBY LATELY.
YOUR BOYFRIEND WILL COMPLAIN IF YOU KEEP THAT UP.
UM, I THINK I'M OKAY FOR NOW.
I'M TRYING TO SAVE UP.
THAT AGAIN ...
YOU'VE BEEN WEARING SOME OF THE LEAST SEXY UNDIES EVER LATELY.
ACTUALLY, YOU'VE GOT A LOT OF THEM.
IT'S OKAY.
ACTUALLY, SHOUKO-CHAN, ARE YOU GOING TO BUY ANYTHING?

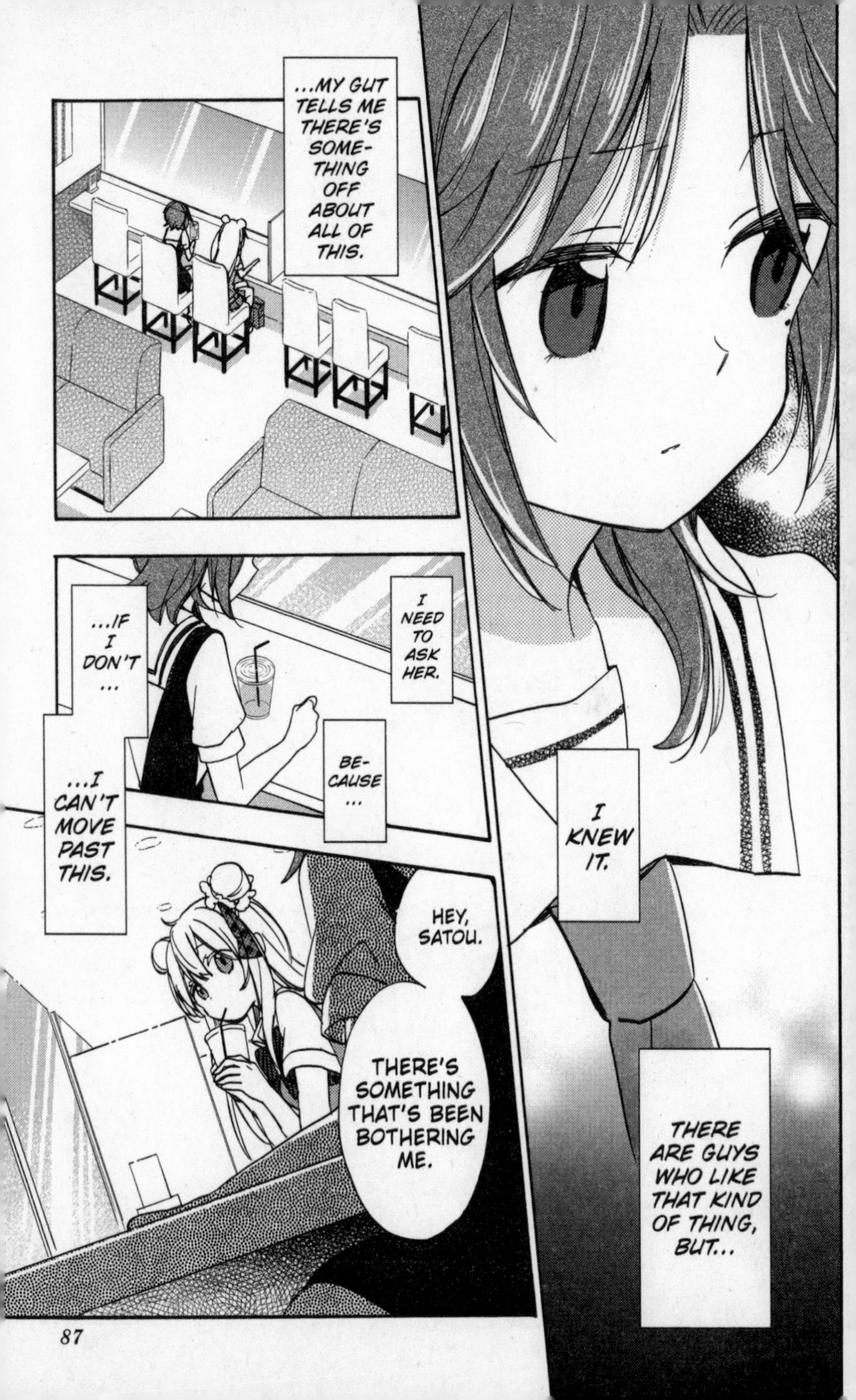
I KNEW IT.
THERE ARE GUYS WHO LIKE THAT KIND OF THING, BUT...
...MY GUT TELLS ME THERE'S SOMETHING OFF ABOUT ALL OF THIS.
I NEED TO ASK HER.
BECAUSE...
...IF I DON'T...
...I CAN'T MOVE PAST THIS.
HEY, SATOU.
THERE'S SOMETHING THAT'S BEEN BOTHERING ME.

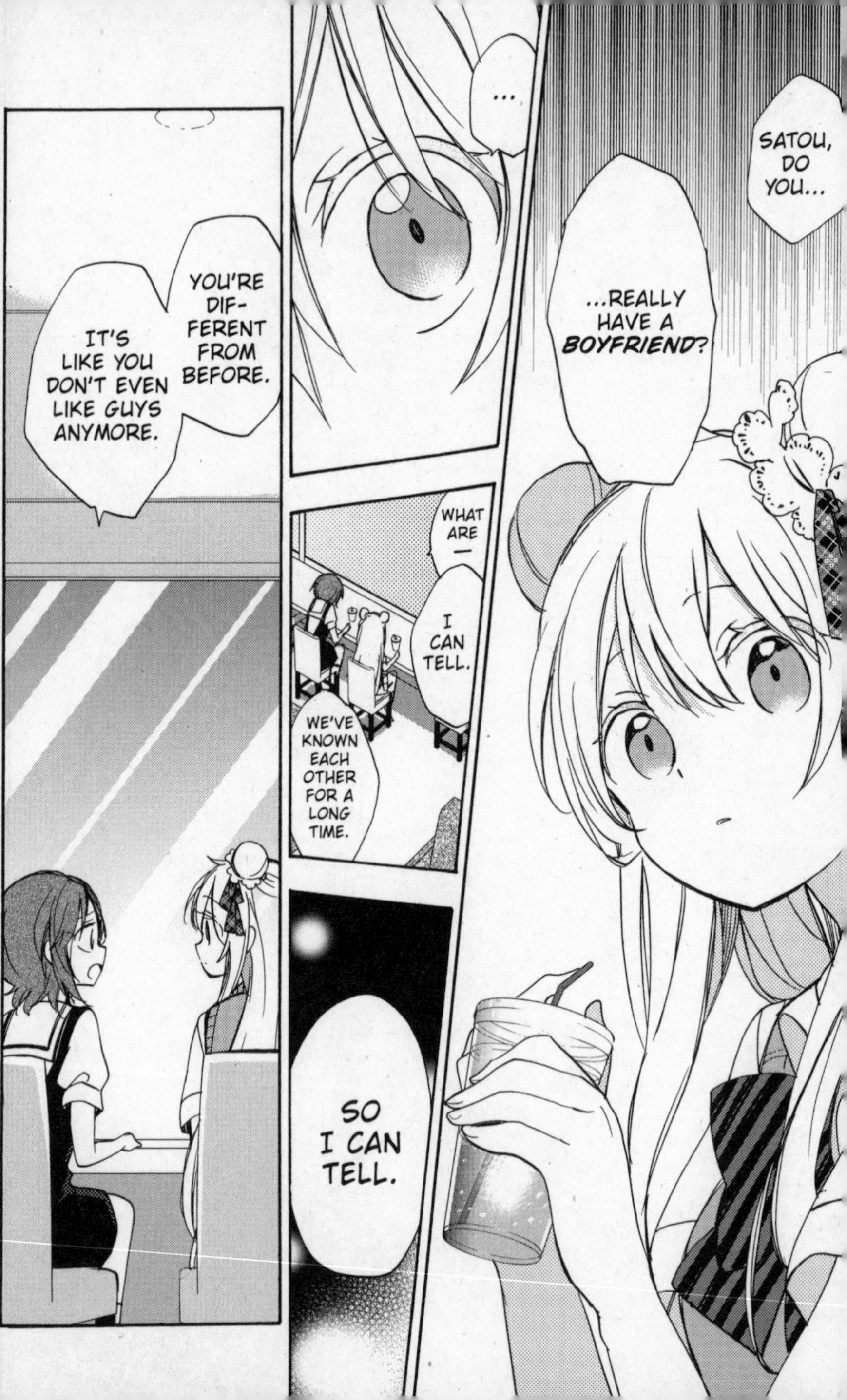
SATOU, DO YOU...
...REALLY HAVE A *BOYFRIEND*?
...
WHAT ARE—
I CAN TELL.
WE'VE KNOWN EACH OTHER FOR A LONG TIME.
SO I CAN TELL.
YOU'RE DIF-FERENT FROM BEFORE.
IT'S LIKE YOU DON'T EVEN LIKE GUYS ANYMORE.

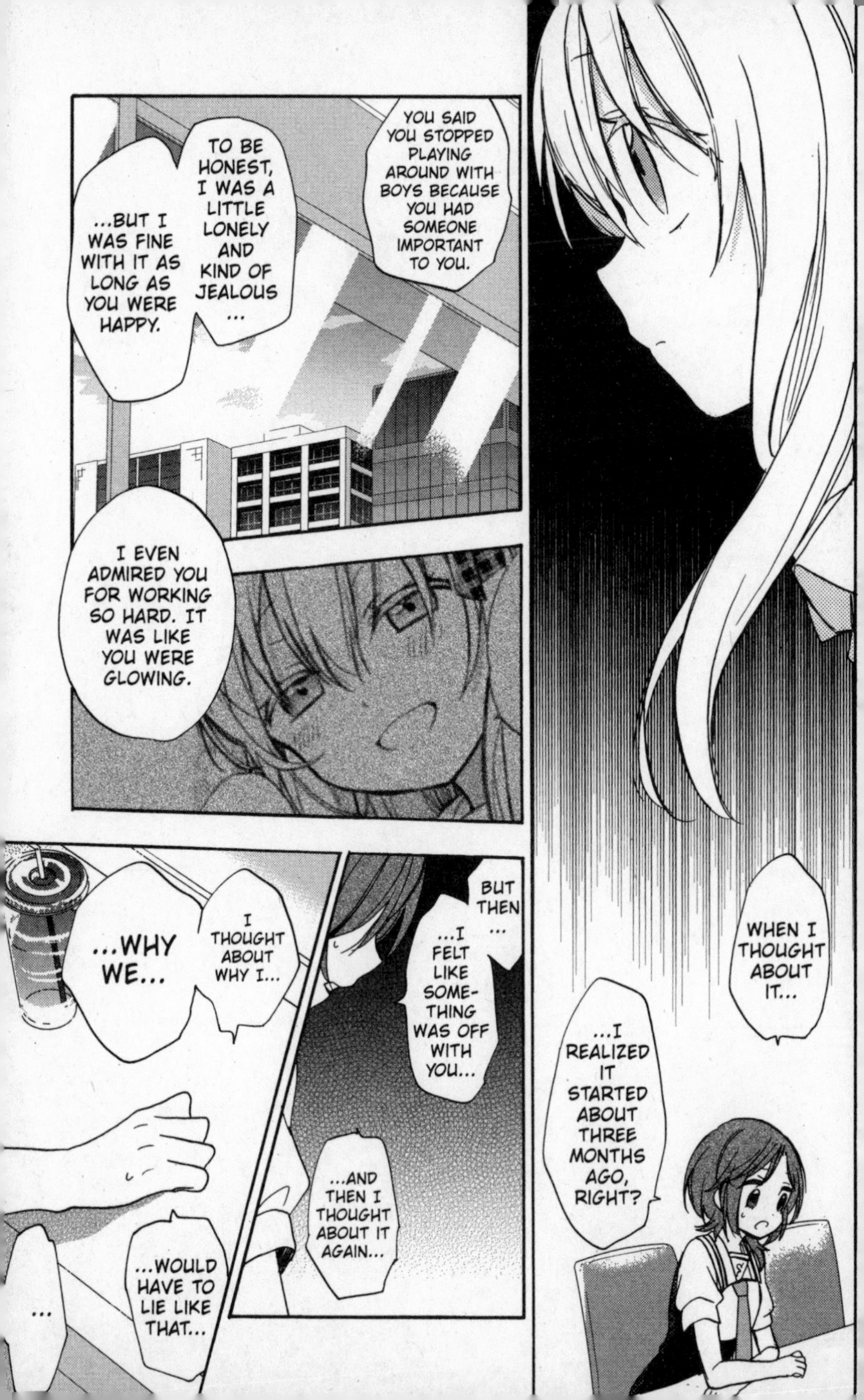
WHEN I THOUGHT ABOUT IT...
...I REALIZED IT STARTED ABOUT THREE MONTHS AGO, RIGHT?
YOU SAID YOU STOPPED PLAYING AROUND WITH BOYS BECAUSE YOU HAD SOMEONE IMPORTANT TO YOU.
TO BE HONEST, I WAS A LITTLE LONELY AND KIND OF JEALOUS...
...BUT I WAS FINE WITH IT AS LONG AS YOU WERE HAPPY.
I EVEN ADMIRED YOU FOR WORKING SO HARD. IT WAS LIKE YOU WERE GLOWING.
BUT THEN...
...I FELT LIKE SOME-THING WAS OFF WITH YOU...
...AND THEN I THOUGHT ABOUT IT AGAIN...
I THOUGHT ABOUT WHY I...
...WHY WE...
...WOULD HAVE TO LIE LIKE THAT...
...

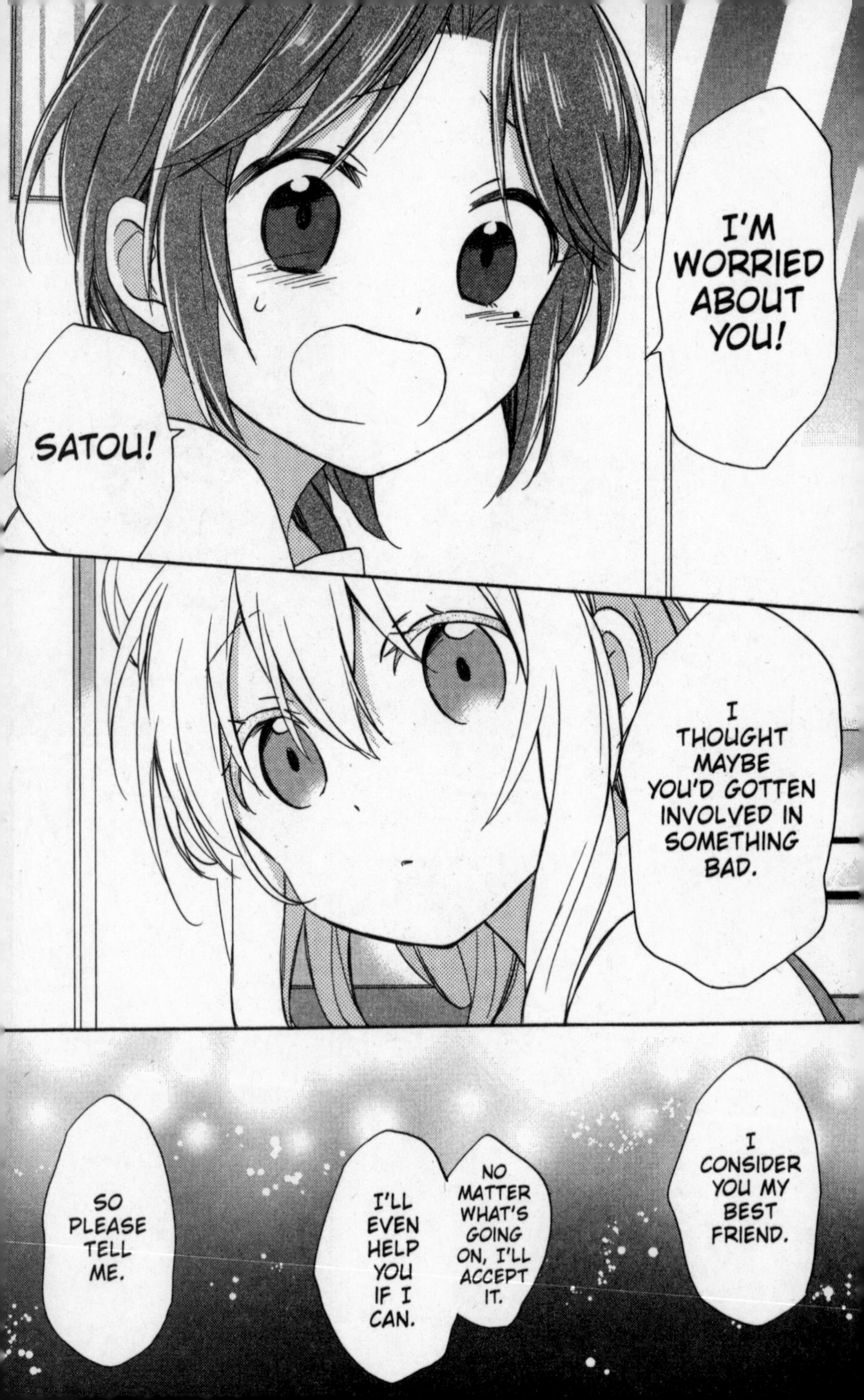
I'M WORRIED ABOUT YOU!
SATOU!
I THOUGHT MAYBE YOU'D GOTTEN INVOLVED IN SOMETHING BAD.
I CONSIDER YOU MY BEST FRIEND.
NO MATTER WHAT'S GOING ON, I'LL ACCEPT IT.
I'LL EVEN HELP YOU IF I CAN.
SO PLEASE TELL ME.

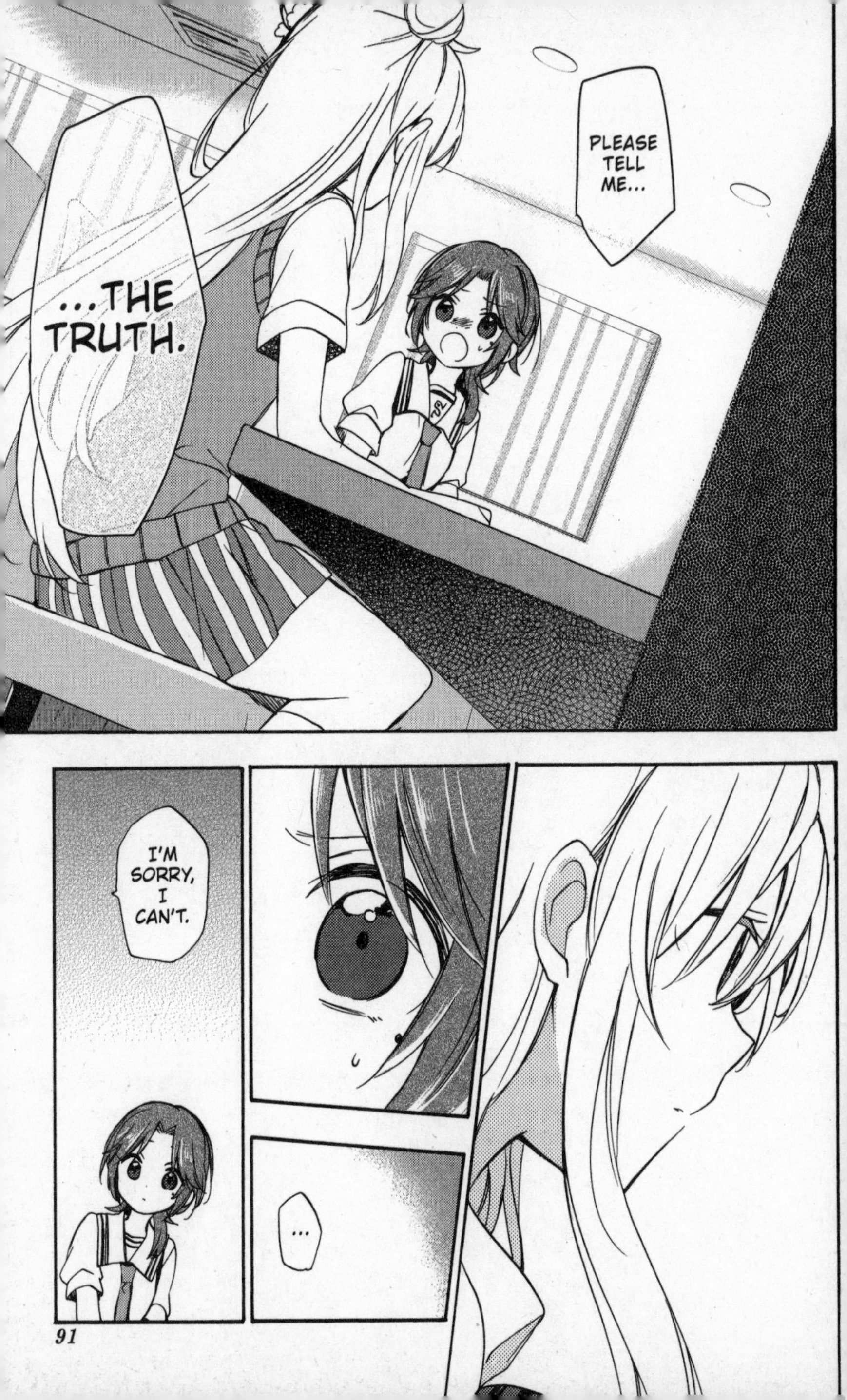
PLEASE TELL ME...
...THE TRUTH.
...
I'M SORRY, I CAN'T.

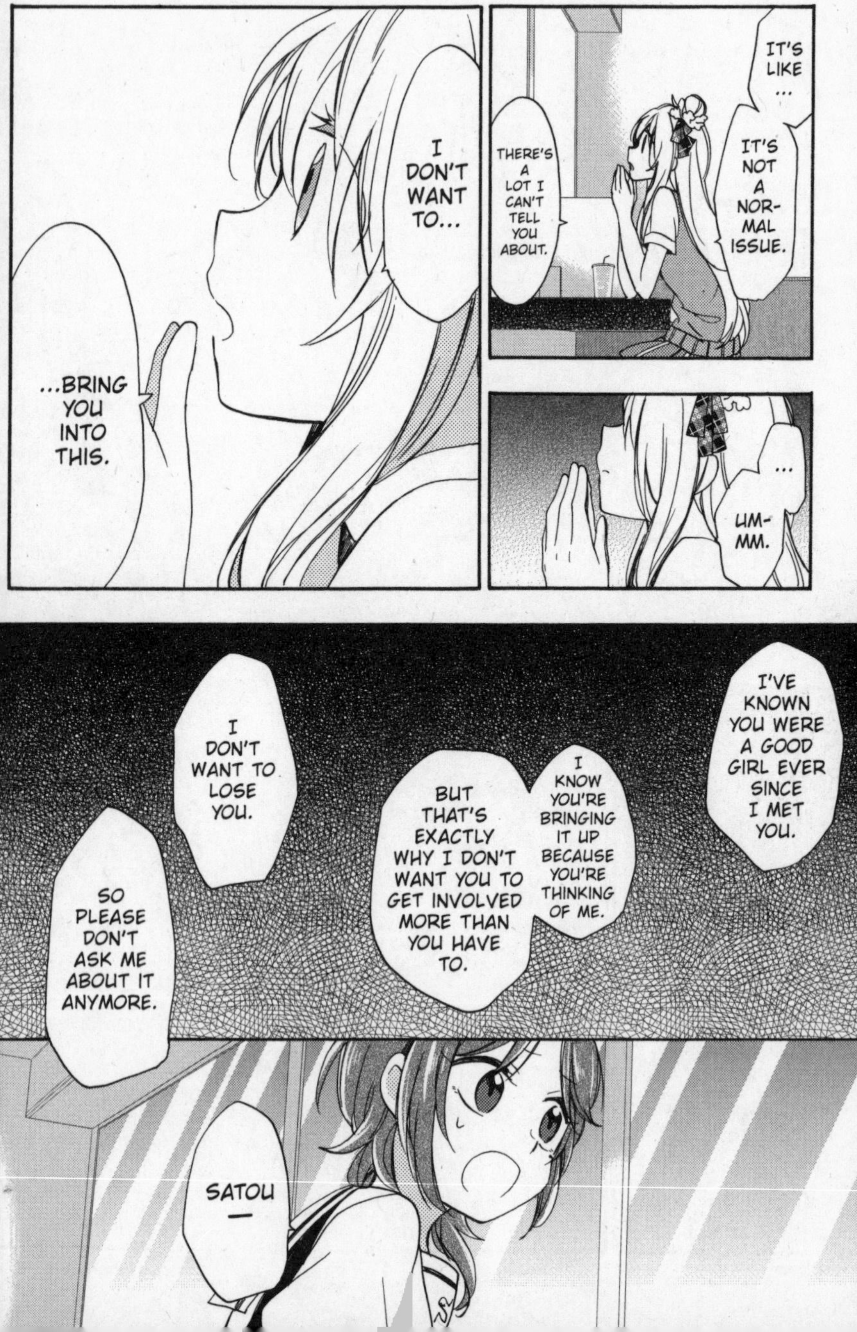
IT'S LIKE...
IT'S NOT A NORMAL ISSUE.
THERE'S A LOT I CAN'T TELL YOU ABOUT.
...
UMM.
I DON'T WANT TO...
...BRING YOU INTO THIS.
I'VE KNOWN YOU WERE A GOOD GIRL EVER SINCE I MET YOU.
I KNOW YOU'RE BRINGING IT UP BECAUSE YOU'RE THINKING OF ME.
BUT THAT'S EXACTLY WHY I DON'T WANT YOU TO GET INVOLVED MORE THAN YOU HAVE TO.
I DON'T WANT TO LOSE YOU.
SO PLEASE DON'T ASK ME ABOUT IT ANYMORE.
SATOU—

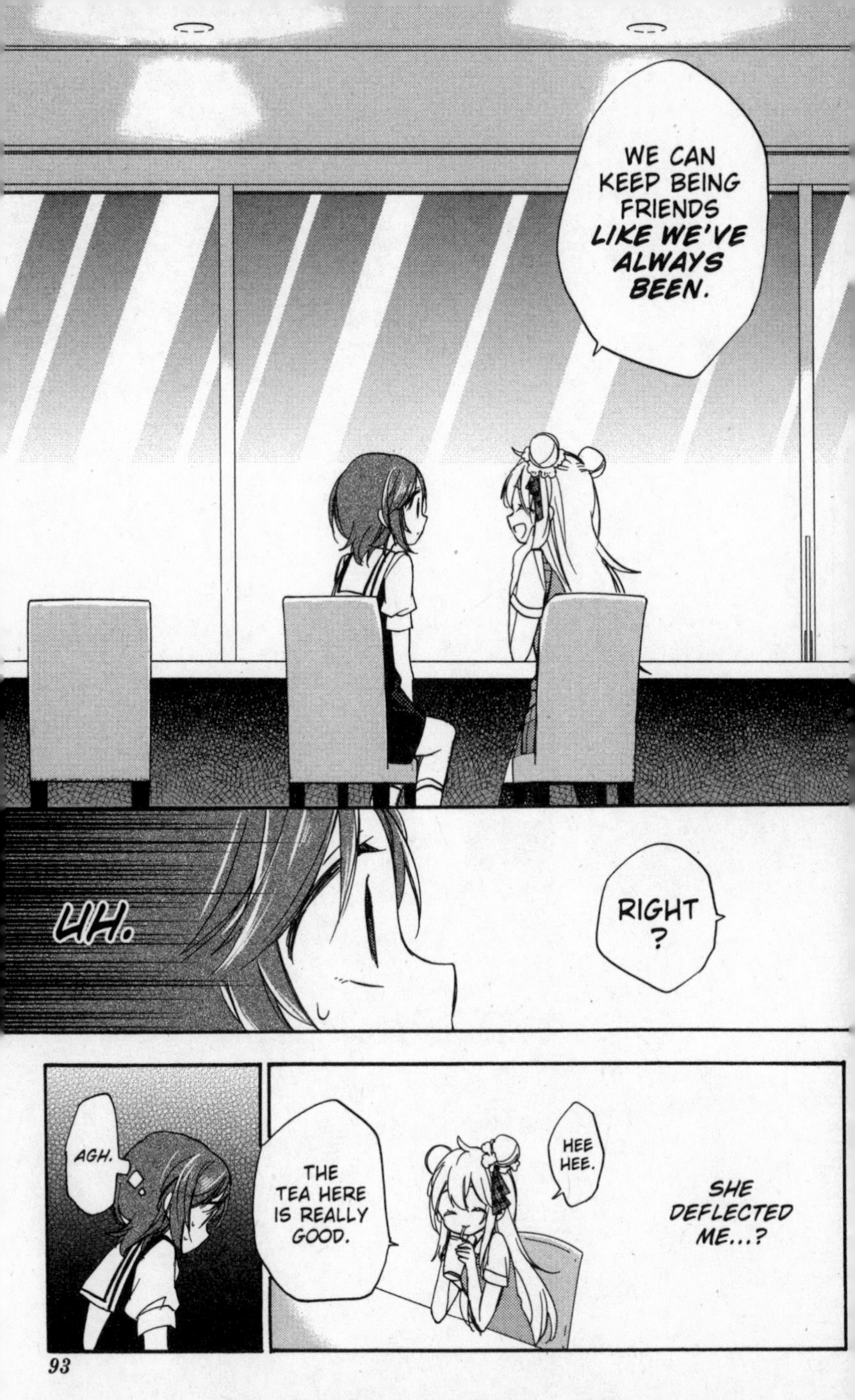

WE CAN KEEP BEING FRIENDS LIKE WE'VE ALWAYS BEEN.
RIGHT?
UH.
HEE HEE.
THE TEA HERE IS REALLY GOOD.
SHE DEFLECTED ME...?
AGH.

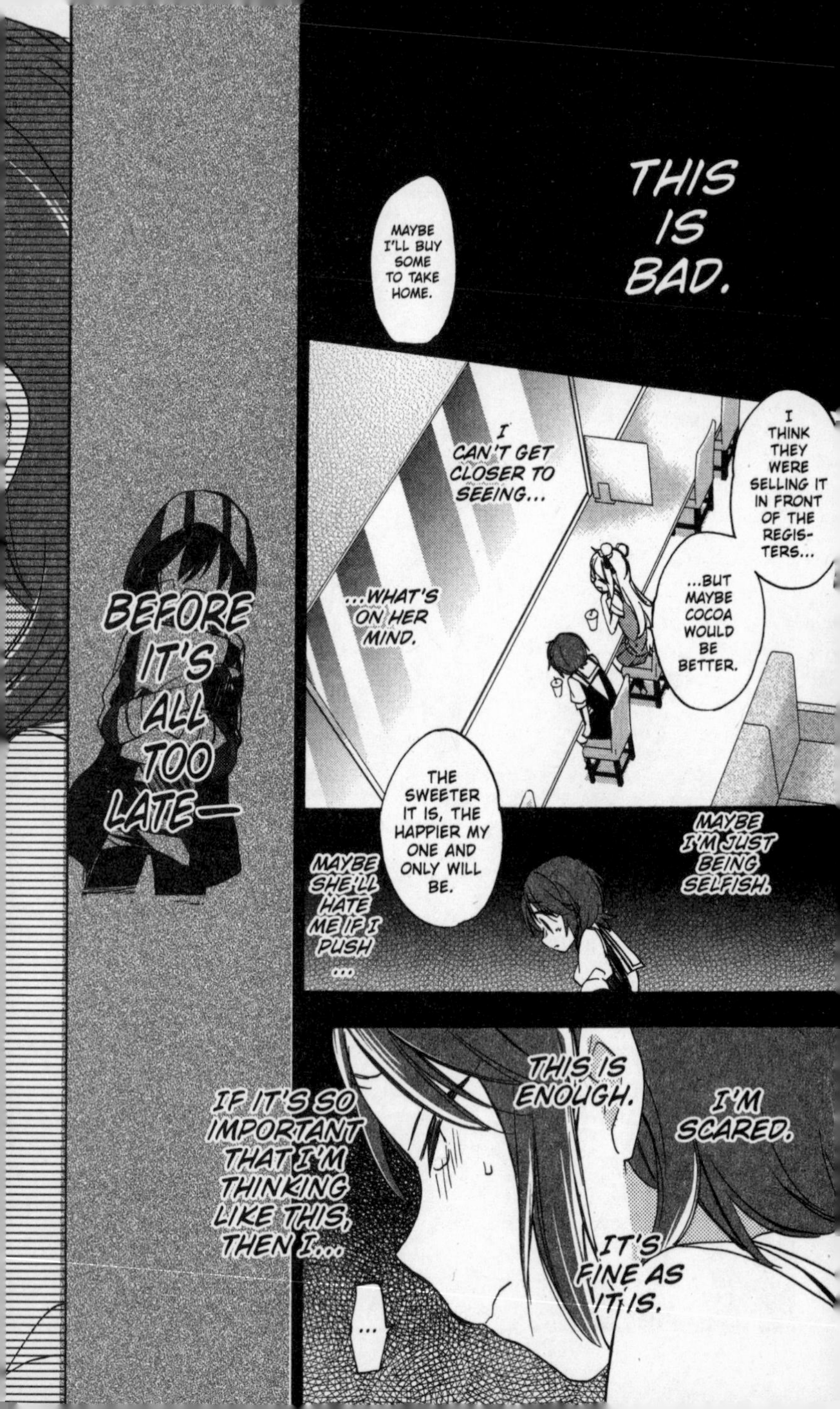
THIS IS BAD.
MAYBE I'LL BUY SOME TO TAKE HOME.
I THINK THEY WERE SELLING IT IN FRONT OF THE REGIS-TERS...
...BUT MAYBE COCOA WOULD BE BETTER.
I CAN'T GET CLOSER TO SEEING...
...WHAT'S ON HER MIND.
MAYBE I'M JUST BEING SELFISH.
THE SWEETER IT IS, THE HAPPIER MY ONE AND ONLY WILL BE.
MAYBE SHE'LL HATE ME IF I PUSH...
I'M SCARED.
THIS IS ENOUGH.
IT'S FINE AS IT IS.
IF IT'S SO IMPORTANT THAT I'M THINKING LIKE THIS, THEN I...
...
BEFORE IT'S ALL TOO LATE—

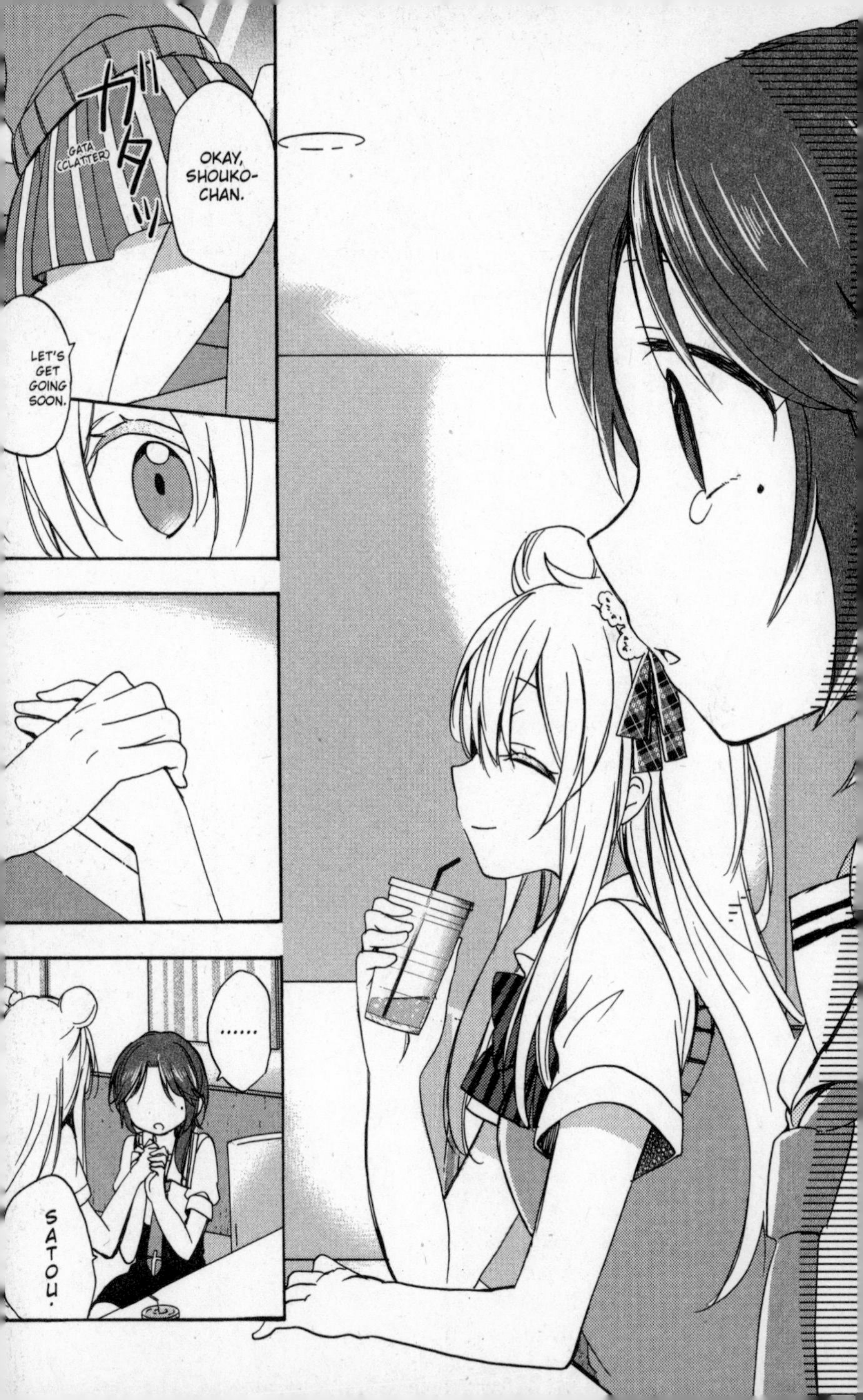
———
OKAY, SHOUKO-CHAN.
GATA (CLATTER)
LET'S GET GOING SOON.
......
SATOU.

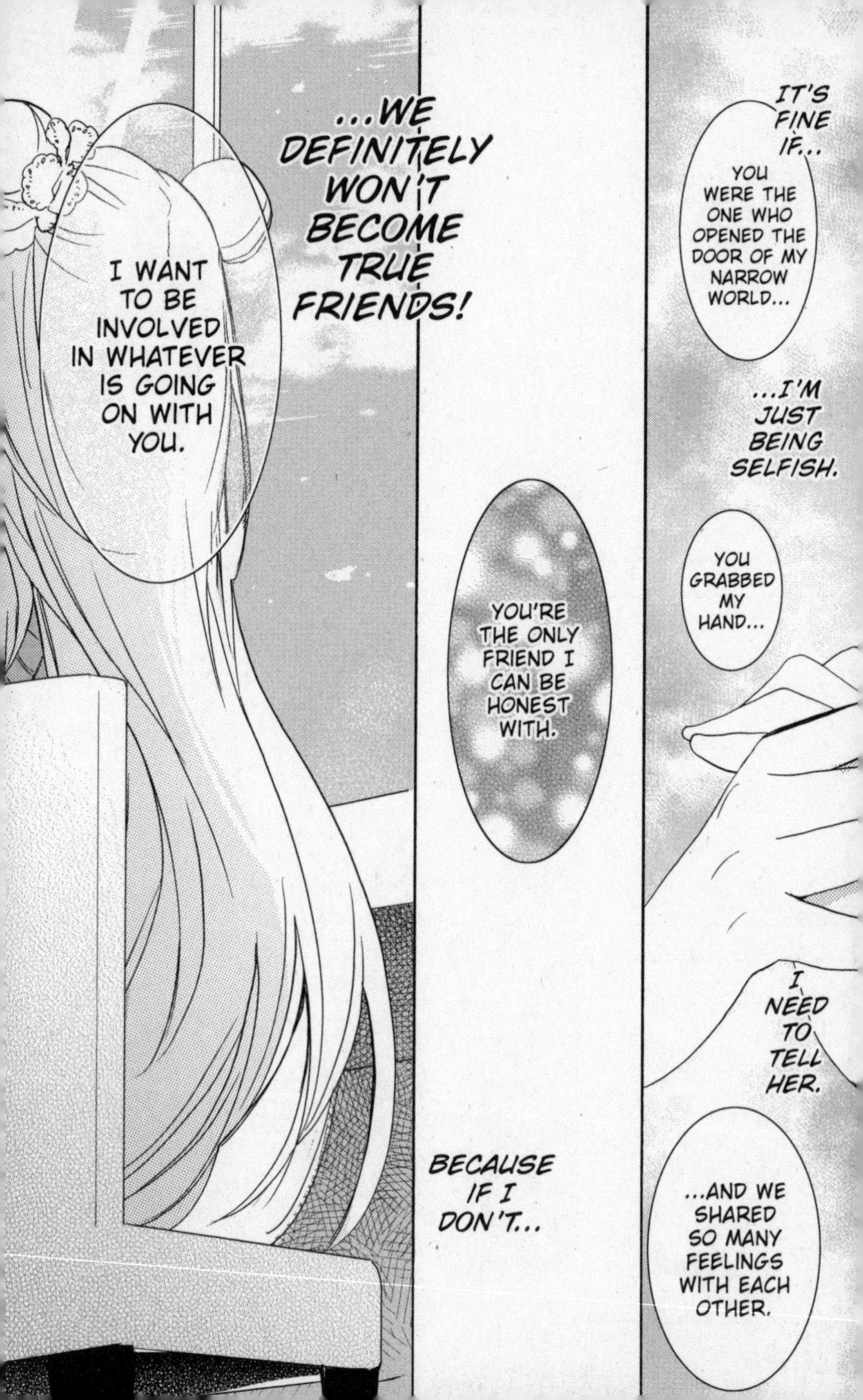
IT'S FINE IF...
YOU WERE THE ONE WHO OPENED THE DOOR OF MY NARROW WORLD...
...I'M JUST BEING SELFISH.
YOU GRABBED MY HAND...
I NEED TO TELL HER.
...AND WE SHARED SO MANY FEELINGS WITH EACH OTHER.
YOU'RE THE ONLY FRIEND I CAN BE HONEST WITH.
BECAUSE IF I DON'T...
...WE DEFINITELY WON'T BECOME TRUE FRIENDS!
I WANT TO BE INVOLVED IN WHATEVER IS GOING ON WITH YOU.

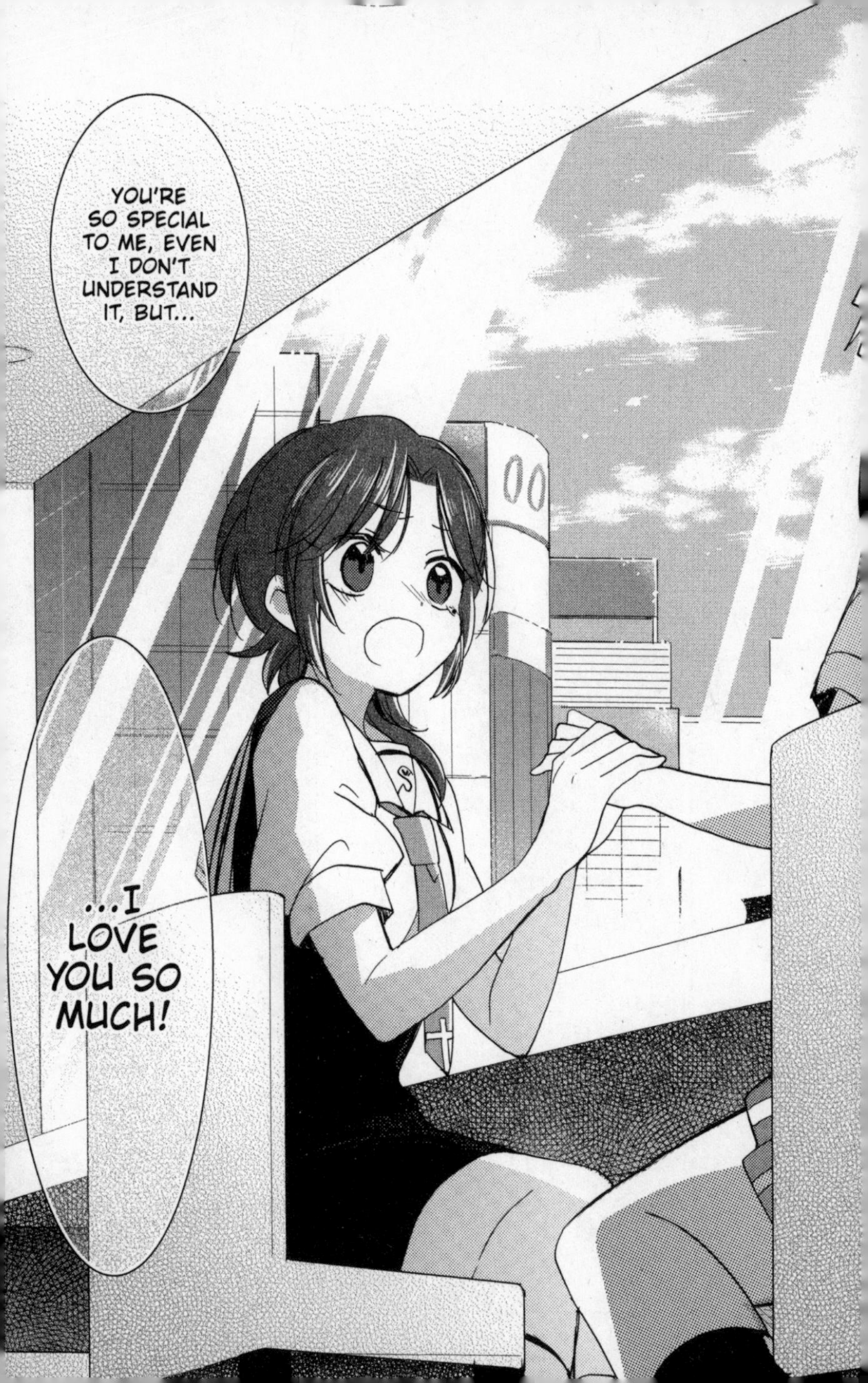
YOU'RE SO SPECIAL TO ME, EVEN I DON'T UNDERSTAND IT, BUT...
...I LOVE YOU SO MUCH!

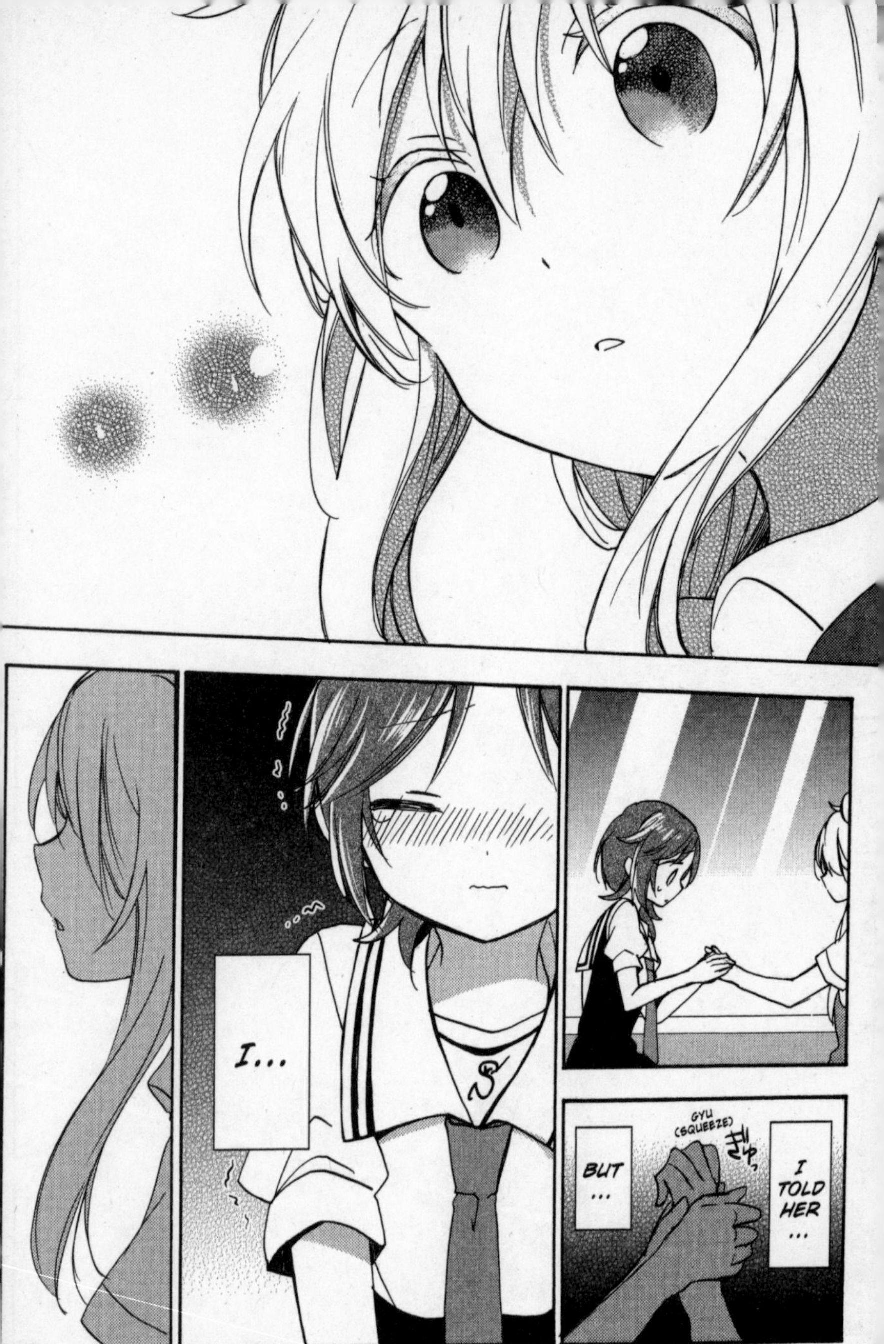
I TOLD HER...
GYU (SQUEEZE)
ぎゅっ
BUT...
I...

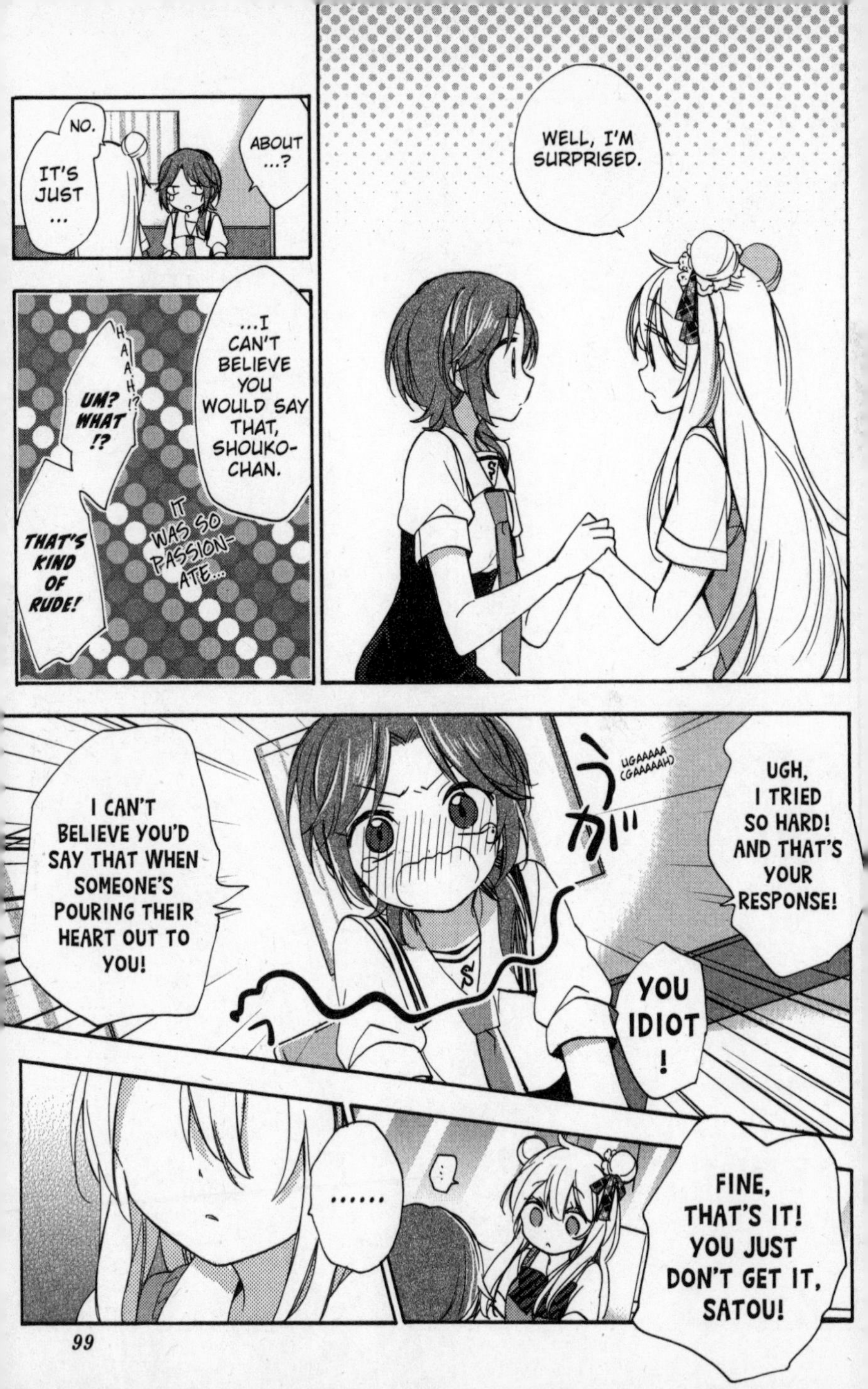
WELL, I'M SURPRISED.
ABOUT ...?
NO.
IT'S JUST ...
...I CAN'T BELIEVE YOU WOULD SAY THAT, SHOUKO-CHAN.
IT WAS SO PASSION-ATE...
HAAH!?
UM? WHAT!?
THAT'S KIND OF RUDE!
UGH, I TRIED SO HARD! AND THAT'S YOUR RESPONSE!
うがぁ
UGAAAAA (GAAAAAH)
YOU IDIOT!
I CAN'T BELIEVE YOU'D SAY THAT WHEN SOMEONE'S POURING THEIR HEART OUT TO YOU!
FINE, THAT'S IT! YOU JUST DON'T GET IT, SATOU!
...
......

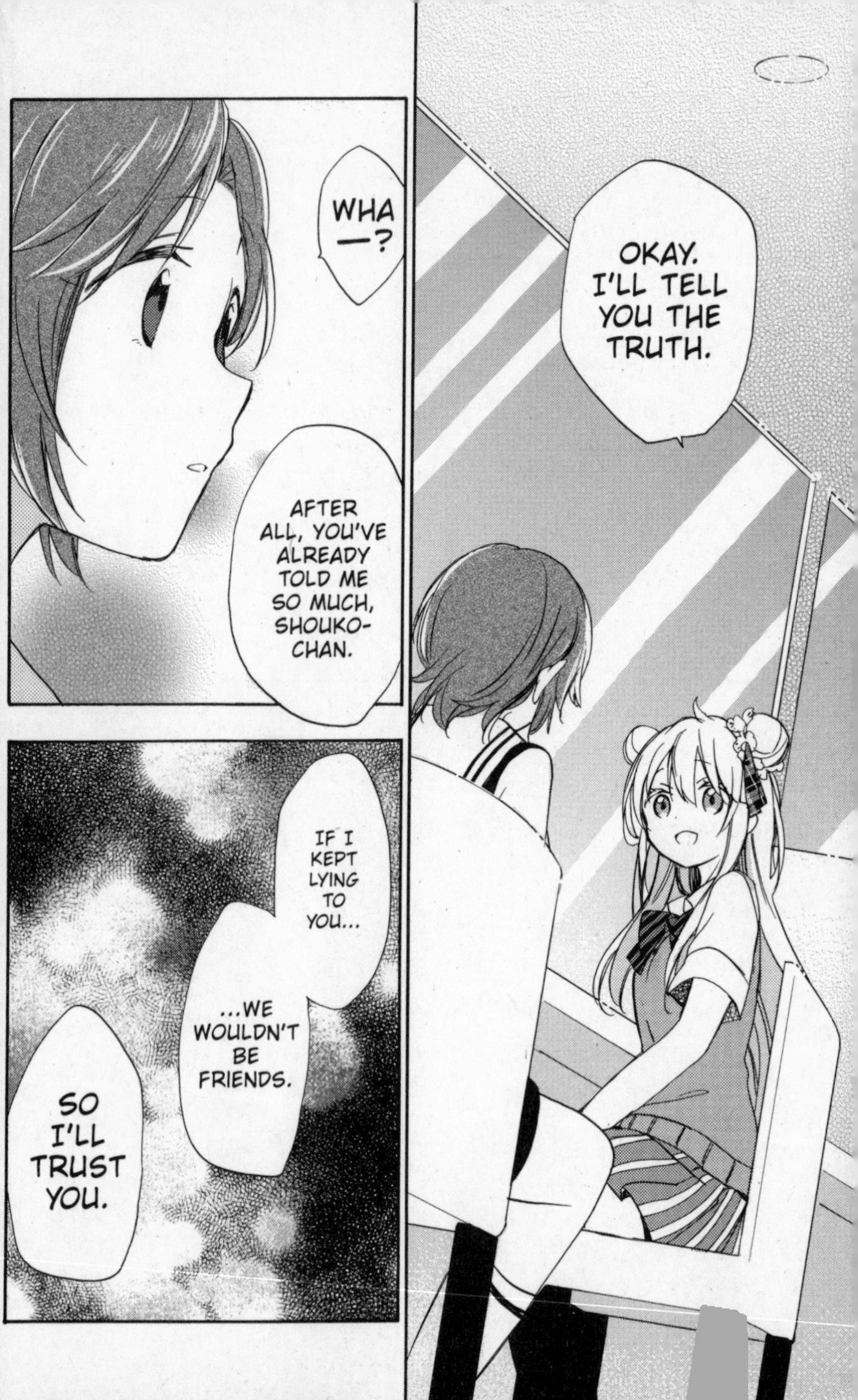
OKAY. I'LL TELL YOU THE TRUTH.
WHA—?
AFTER ALL, YOU'VE ALREADY TOLD ME SO MUCH, SHOUKO-CHAN.
IF I KEPT LYING TO YOU...
...WE WOULDN'T BE FRIENDS.
SO I'LL TRUST YOU.

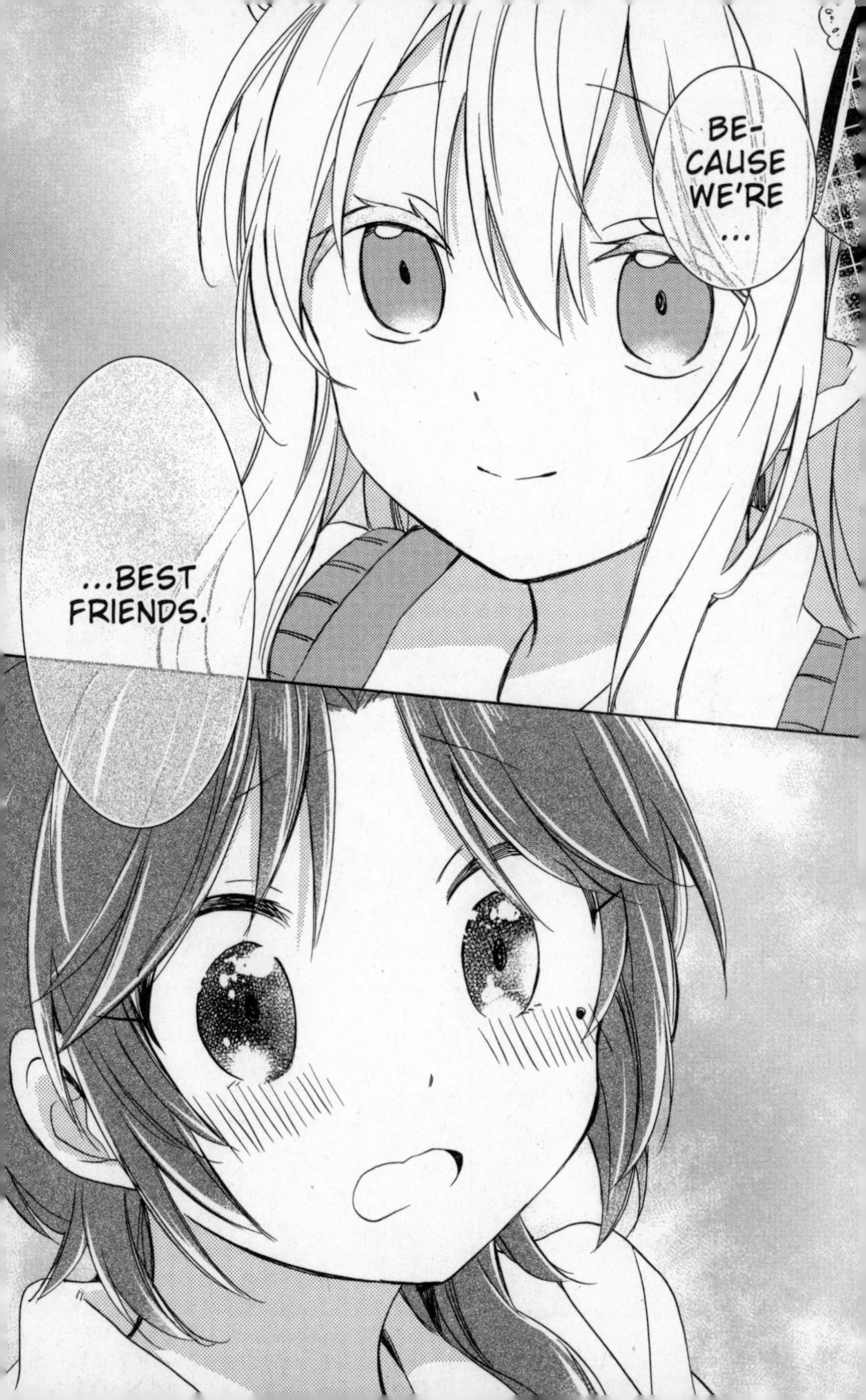
BE-CAUSE WE'RE ...
...BEST FRIENDS.

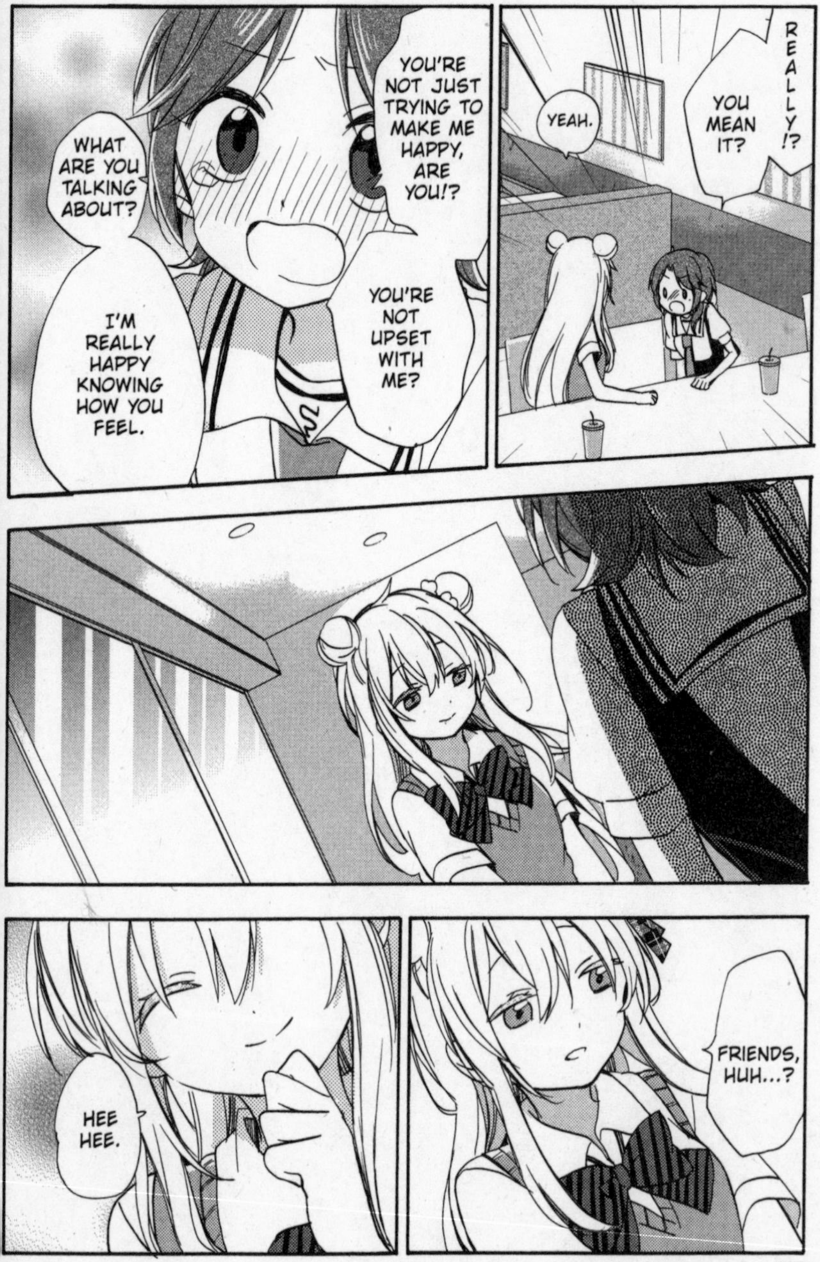
REALLY!?
YOU MEAN IT?
YEAH.
YOU'RE NOT JUST TRYING TO MAKE ME HAPPY, ARE YOU!?
YOU'RE NOT UPSET WITH ME?
WHAT ARE YOU TALKING ABOUT?
I'M REALLY HAPPY KNOWING HOW YOU FEEL.
FRIENDS, HUH...?
HEE HEE.

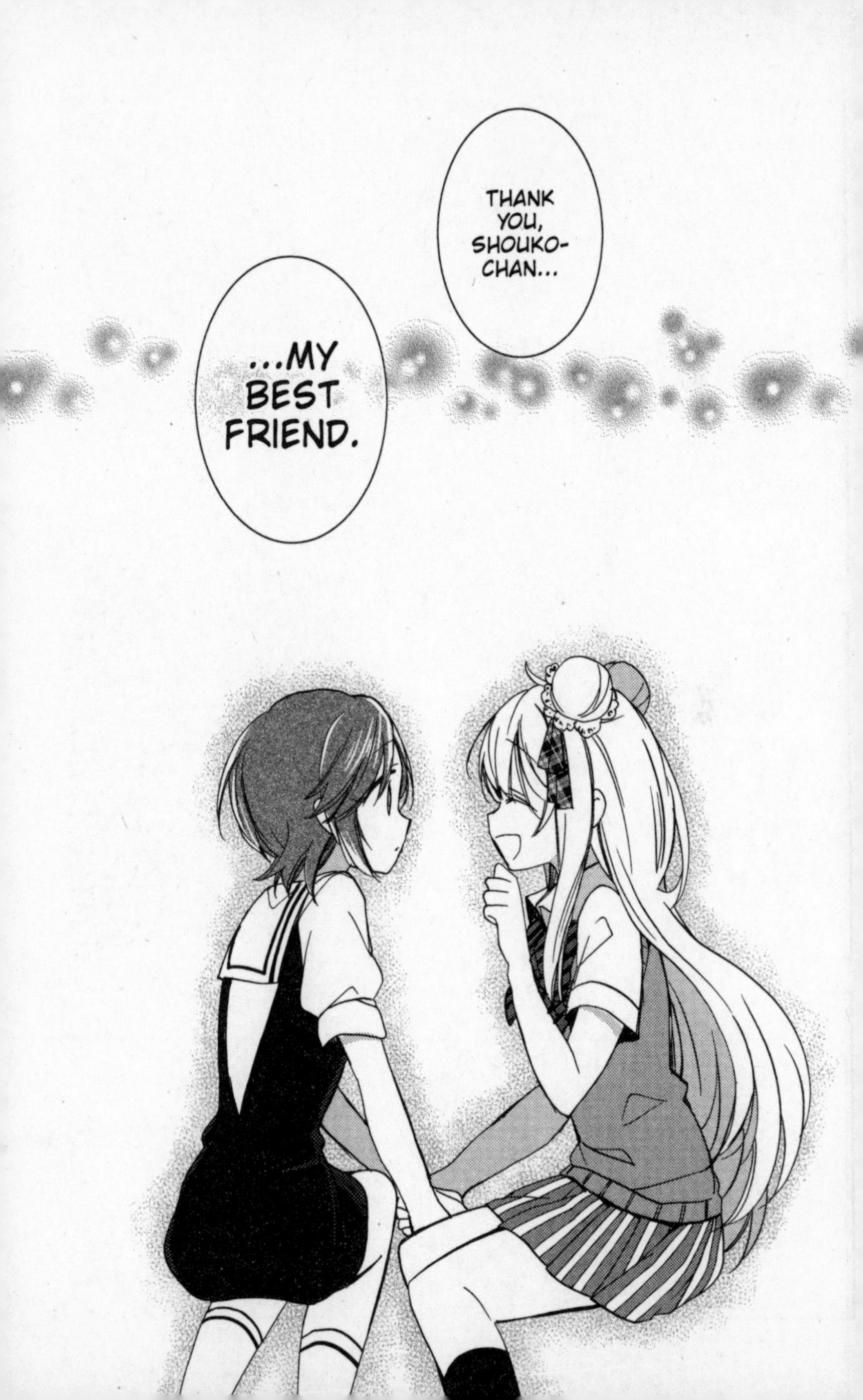
THANK YOU, SHOUKO-CHAN...
...MY BEST FRIEND.

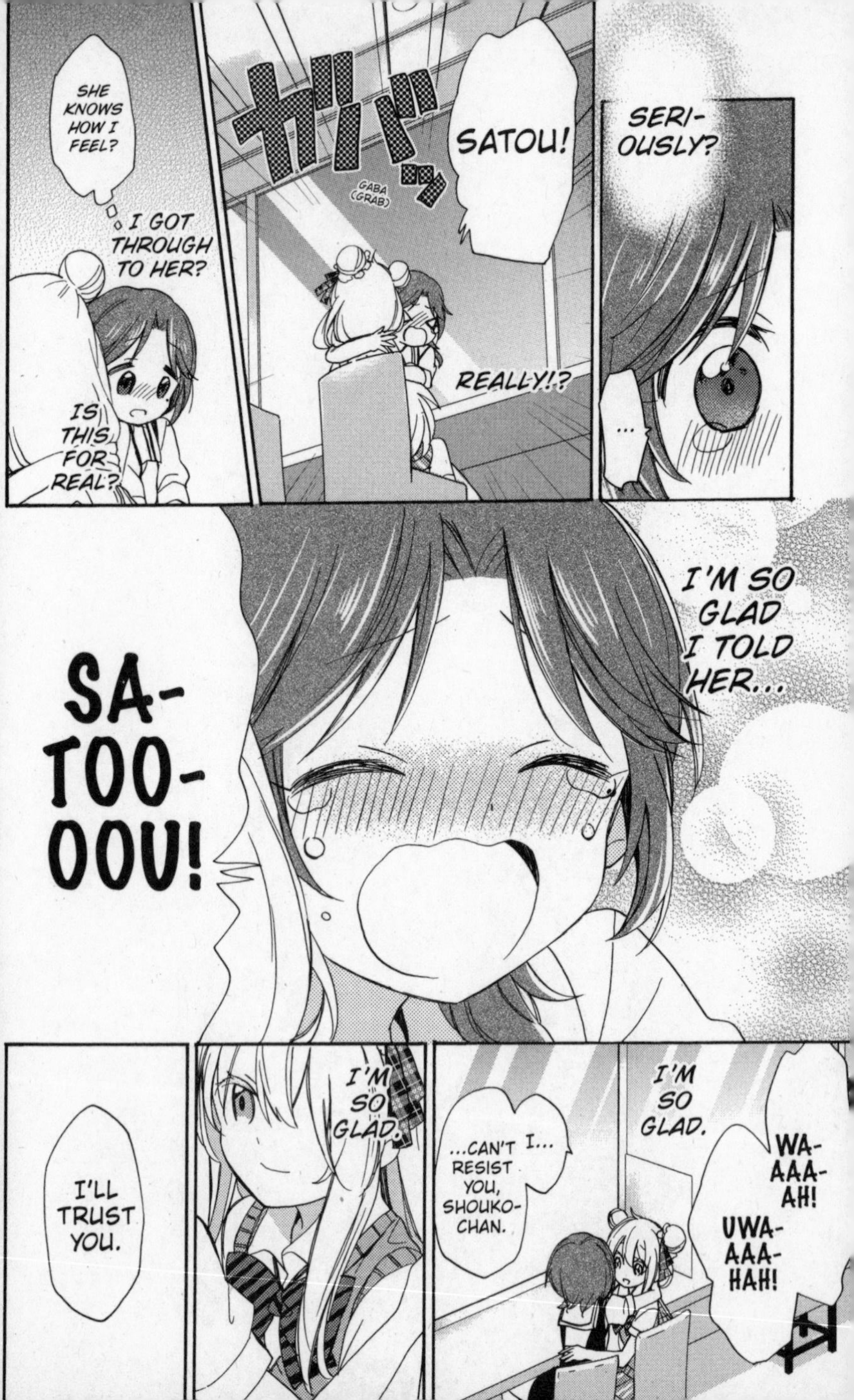
SERI-OUSLY?
...
SATOU!
ガバッ
GABA (GRAB)
REALLY!?
SHE KNOWS HOW I FEEL?
I GOT THROUGH TO HER?
IS THIS FOR REAL?
I'M SO GLAD I TOLD HER...
SA-TOO-OOU!
WA-AAA-AH!
UWA-AAA-HAH!
I'M SO GLAD.
I...
...CAN'T RESIST YOU, SHOUKO-CHAN.
I'M SO GLAD.
I'LL TRUST YOU.

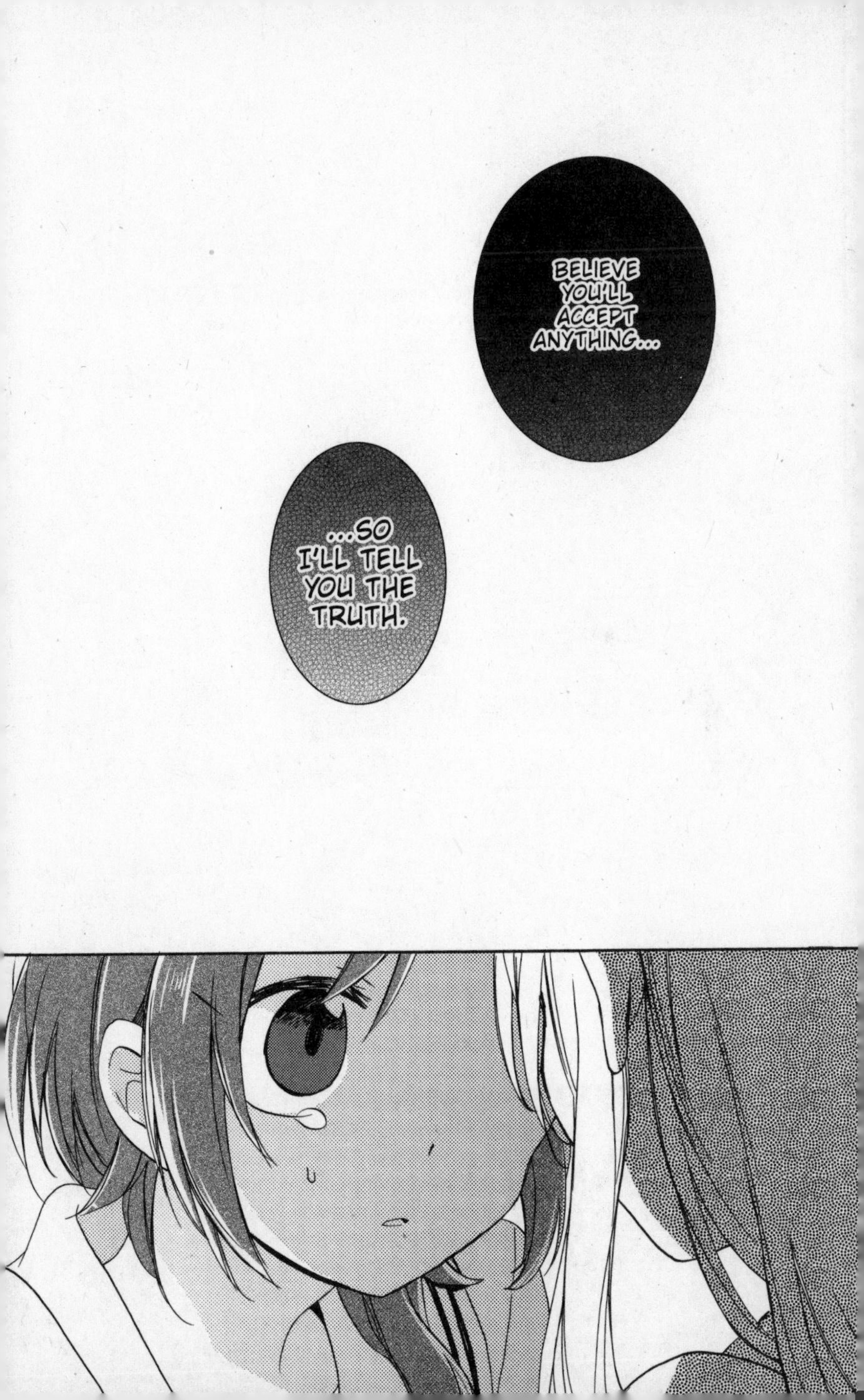
BELIEVE YOU'LL ACCEPT ANYTHING...
...SO I'LL TELL YOU THE TRUTH.

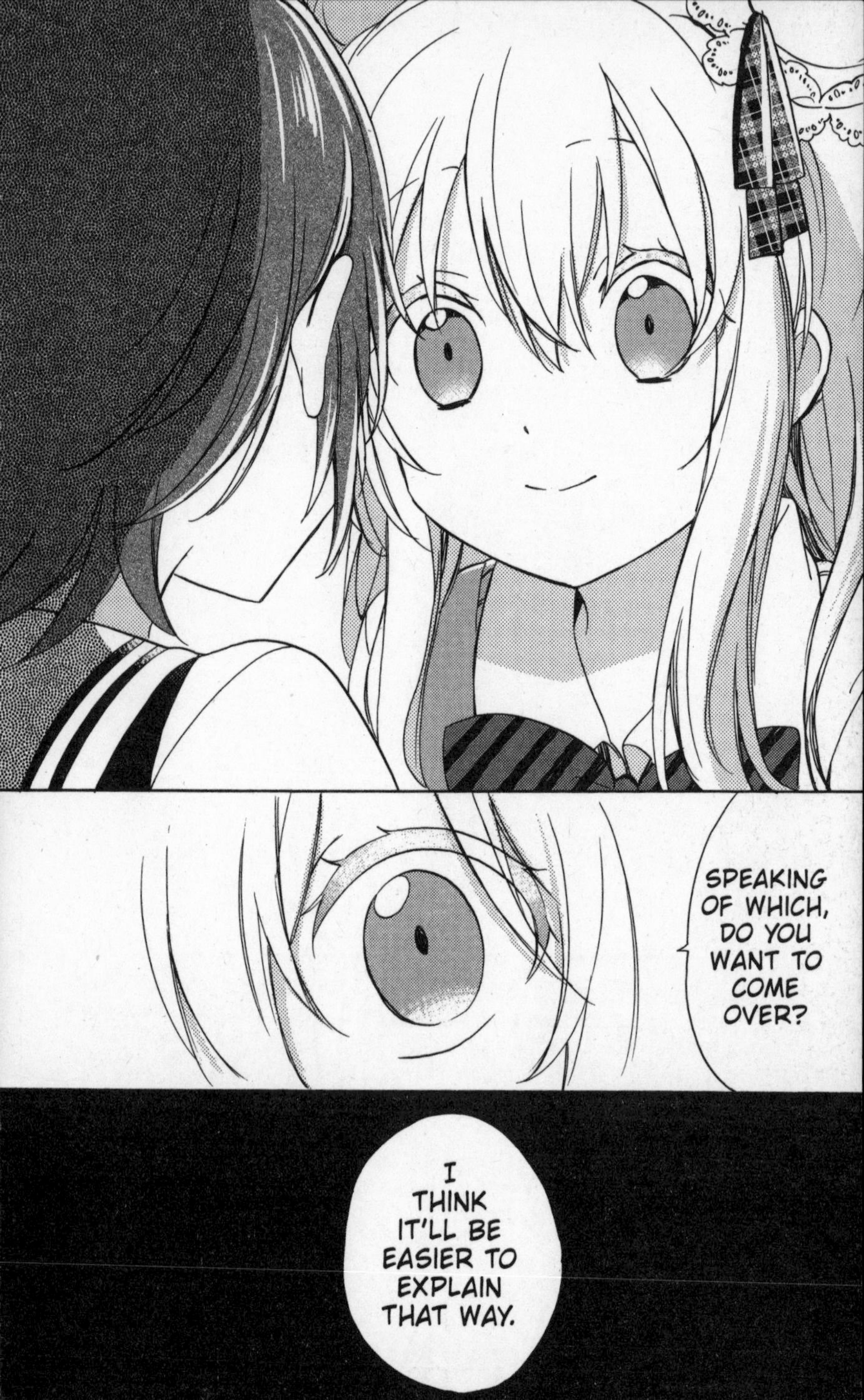
SPEAKING OF WHICH, DO YOU WANT TO COME OVER?
I THINK IT'LL BE EASIER TO EXPLAIN THAT WAY.

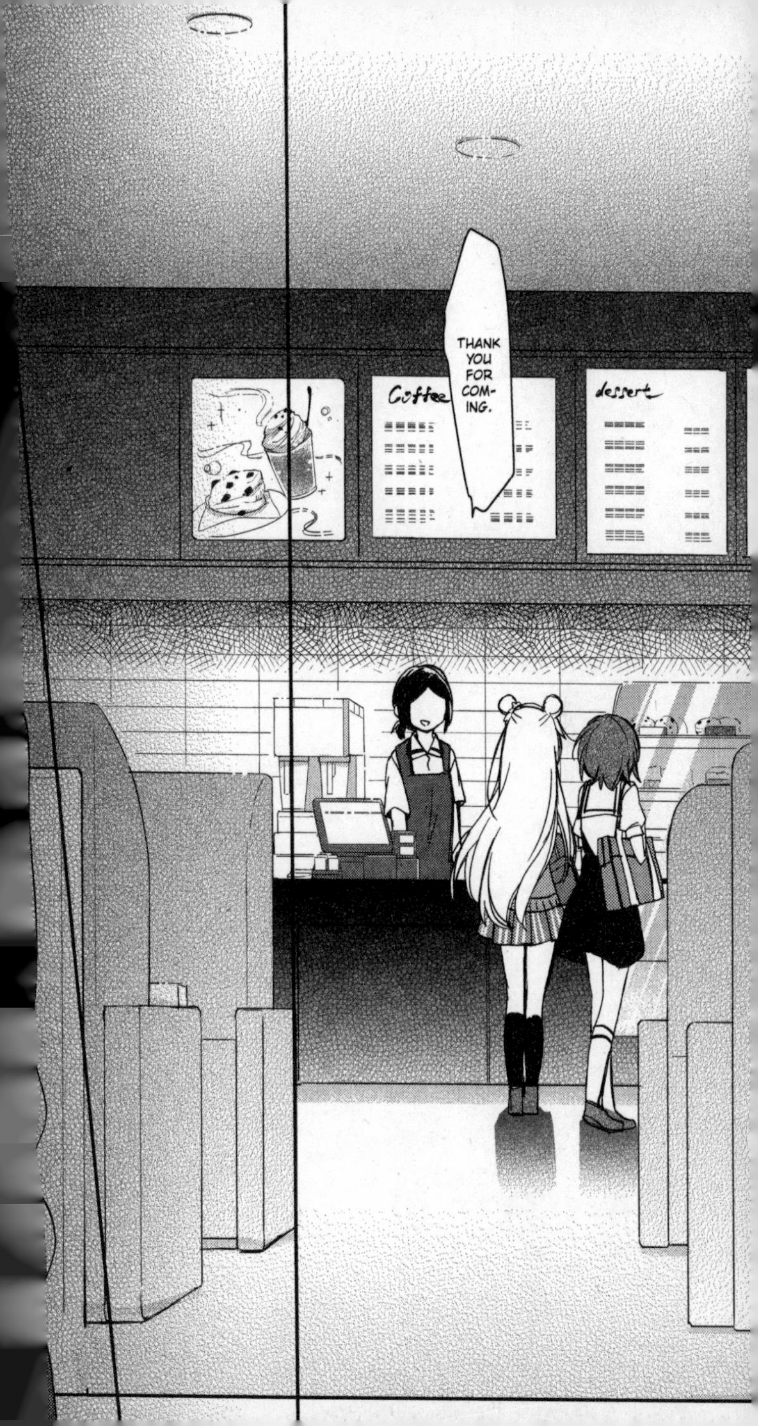
THANK YOU FOR COM-ING.
Coffee
dessert

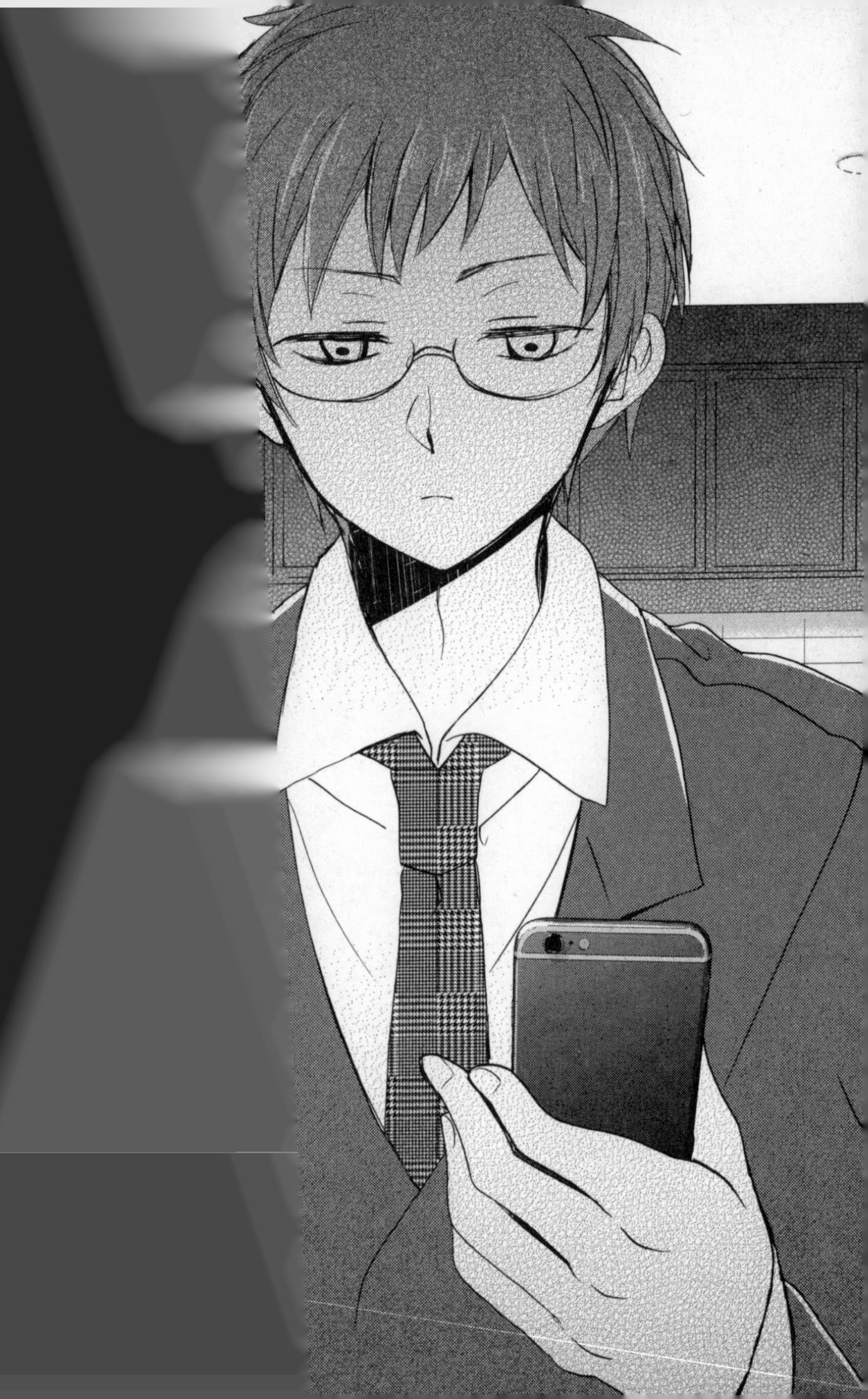

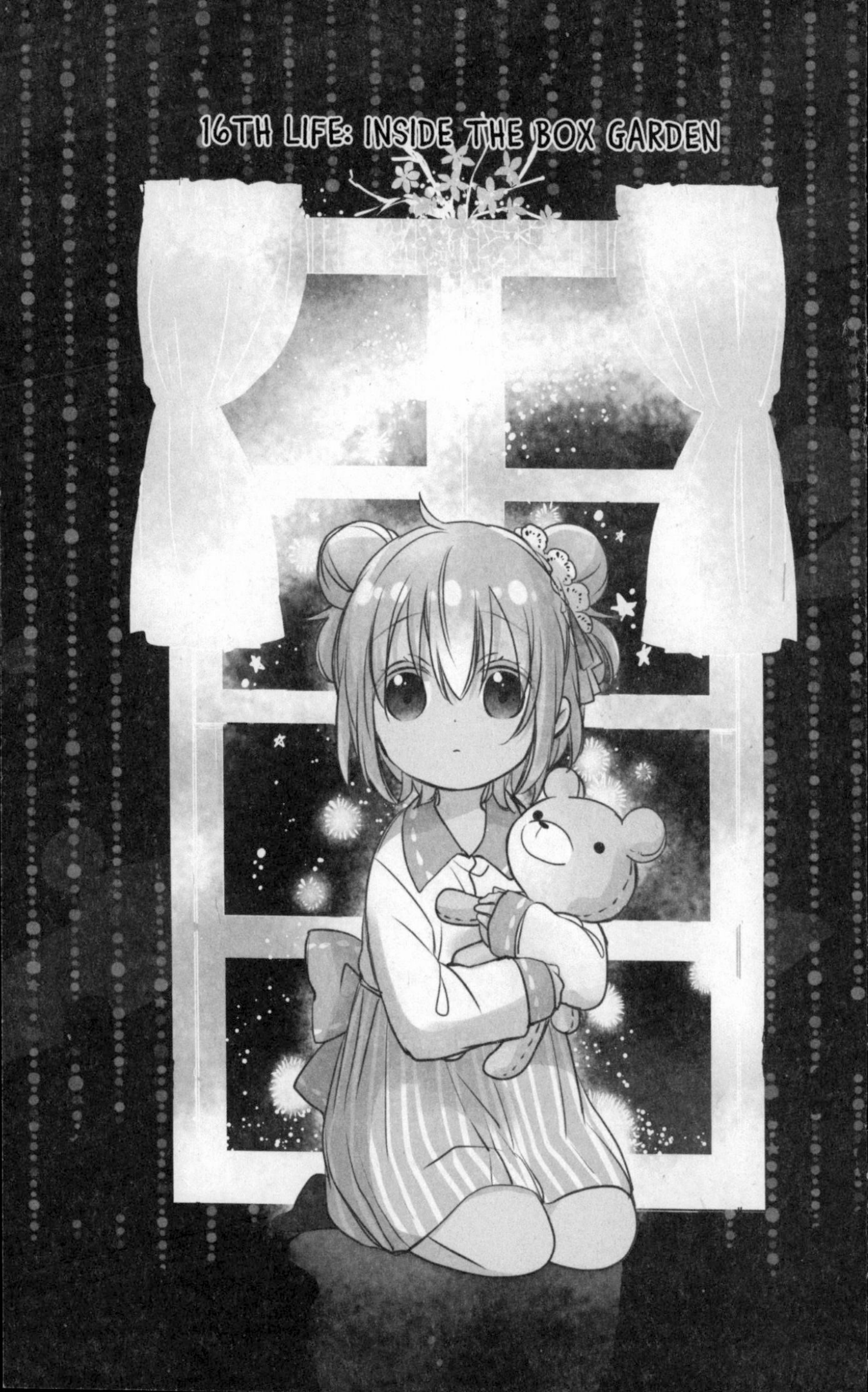
16TH LIFE: INSIDE THE BOX GARDEN

Happy
Sugar
Life

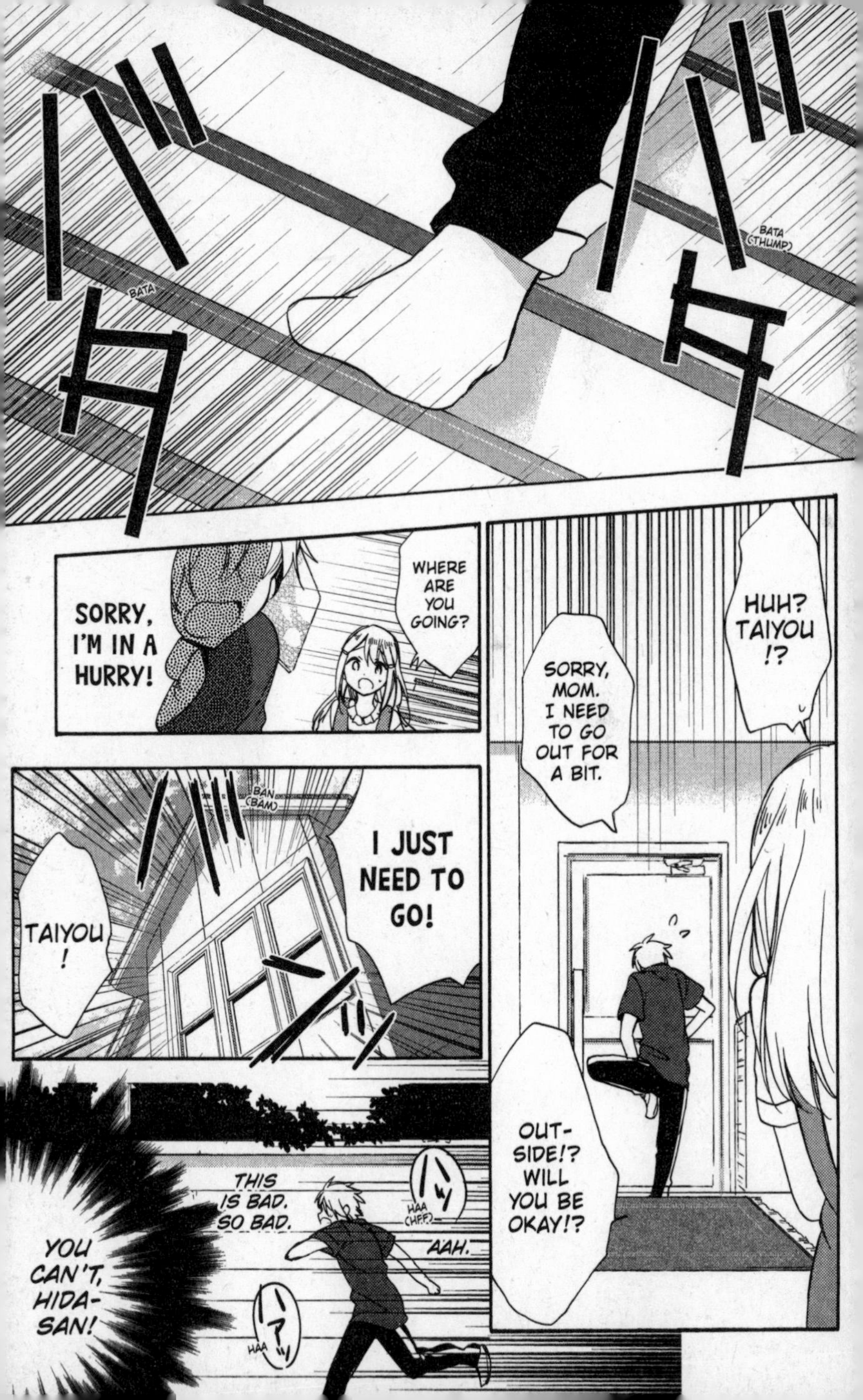
BATA (THUMP)
BATA
HUH? TAIYOU!?
SORRY, MOM. I NEED TO GO OUT FOR A BIT.
OUT-SIDE!? WILL YOU BE OKAY!?
WHERE ARE YOU GOING?
SORRY, I'M IN A HURRY!
BAN (BAM)
I JUST NEED TO GO!
TAIYOU!
HAA (CHFF)
THIS IS BAD. SO BAD.
AAH.
HAA
YOU CAN'T, HIDA-SAN!

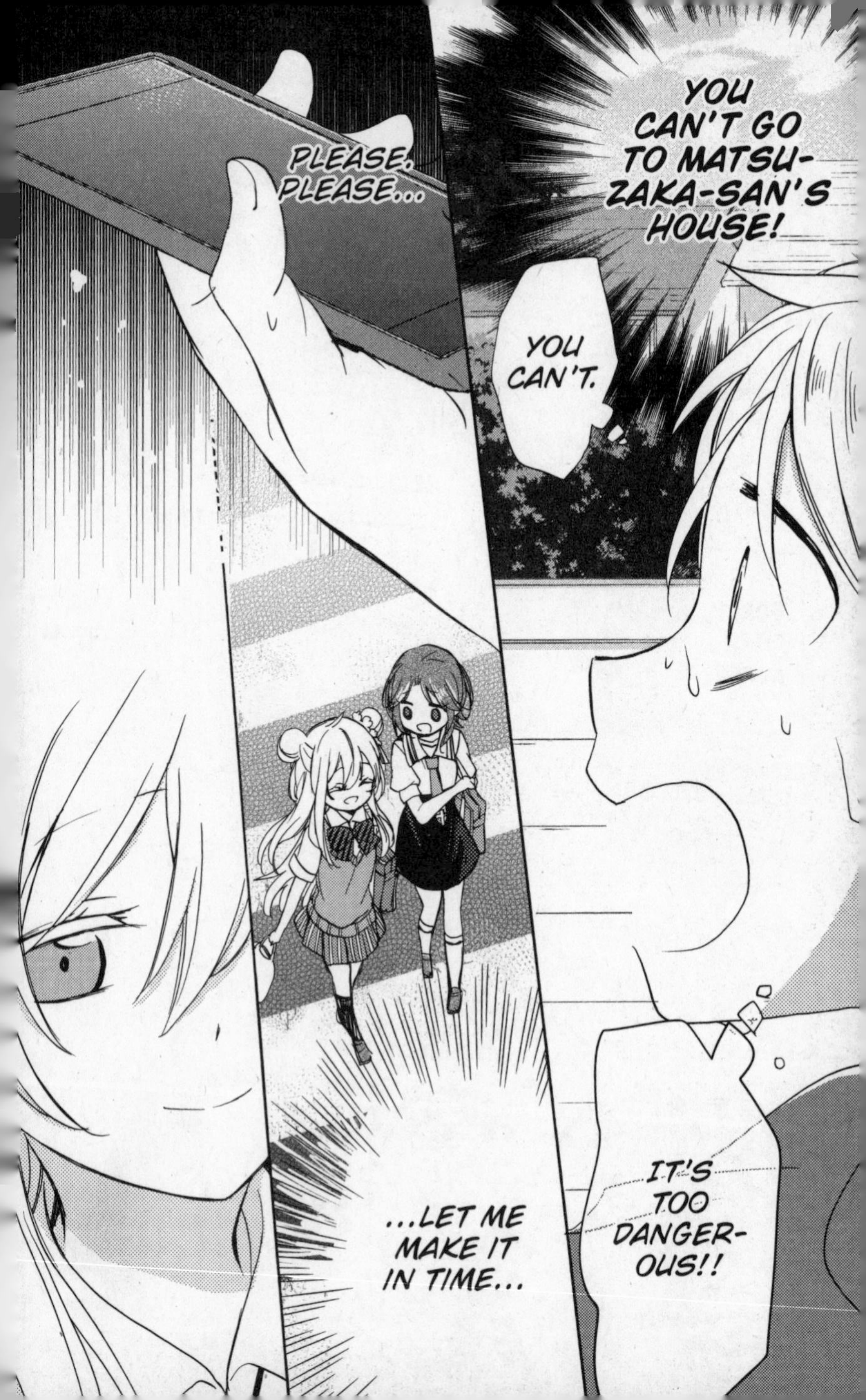
YOU CAN'T GO TO MATSU-ZAKA-SAN'S HOUSE!
YOU CAN'T.
IT'S TOO DANGER-OUS!!
PLEASE. PLEASE...
...LET ME MAKE IT IN TIME...

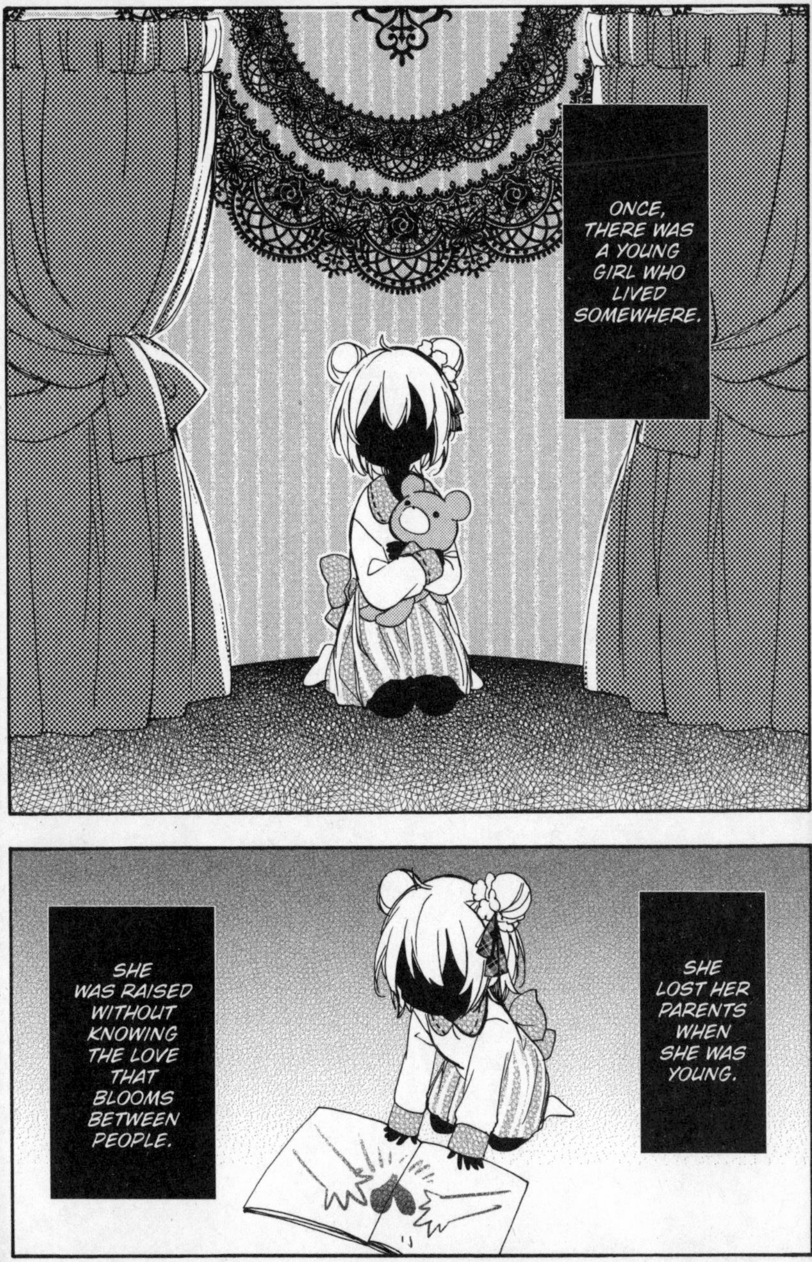
ONCE, THERE WAS A YOUNG GIRL WHO LIVED SOMEWHERE.
SHE LOST HER PARENTS WHEN SHE WAS YOUNG.
SHE WAS RAISED WITHOUT KNOWING THE LOVE THAT BLOOMS BETWEEN PEOPLE.

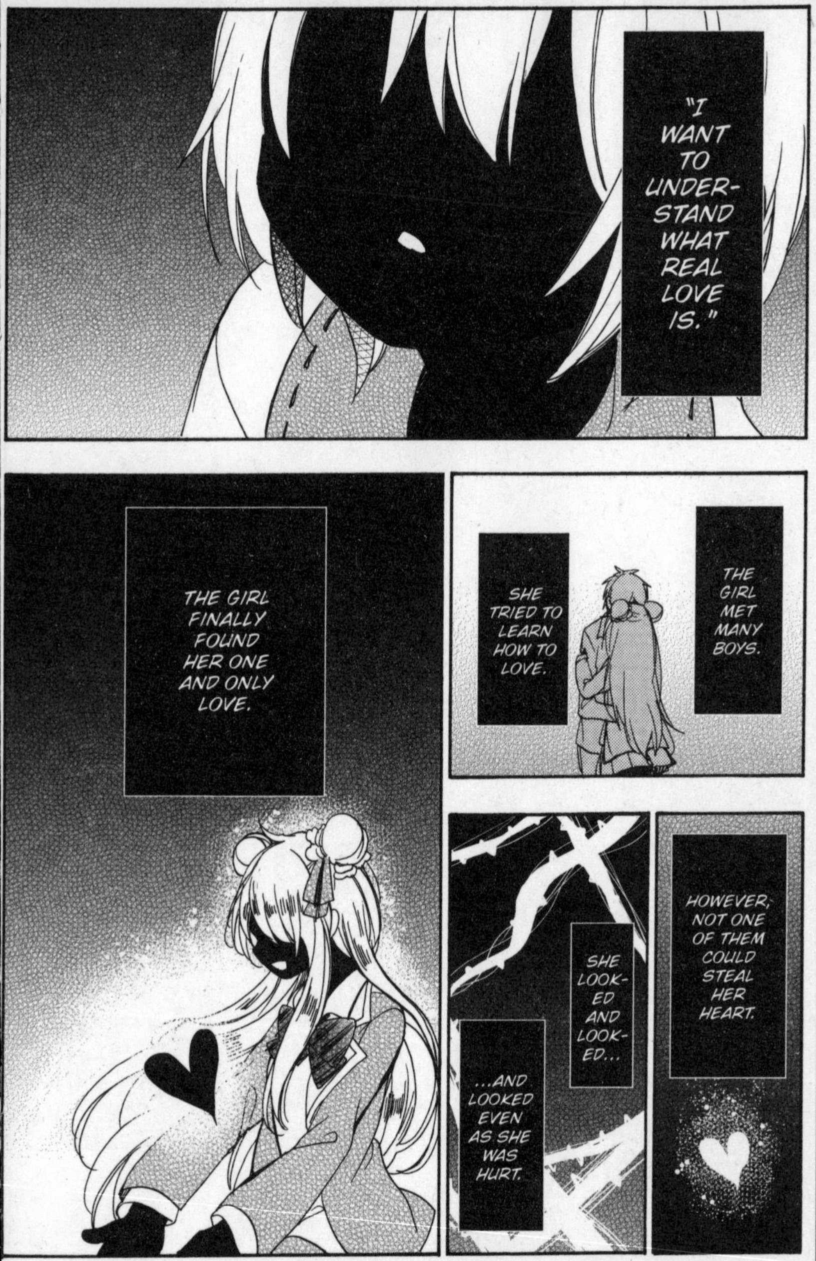
"I WANT TO UNDER-STAND WHAT REAL LOVE IS."
THE GIRL MET MANY BOYS.
SHE TRIED TO LEARN HOW TO LOVE.
HOWEVER, NOT ONE OF THEM COULD STEAL HER HEART.
SHE LOOKED AND LOOKED...
...AND LOOKED EVEN AS SHE WAS HURT.
THE GIRL FINALLY FOUND HER ONE AND ONLY LOVE.

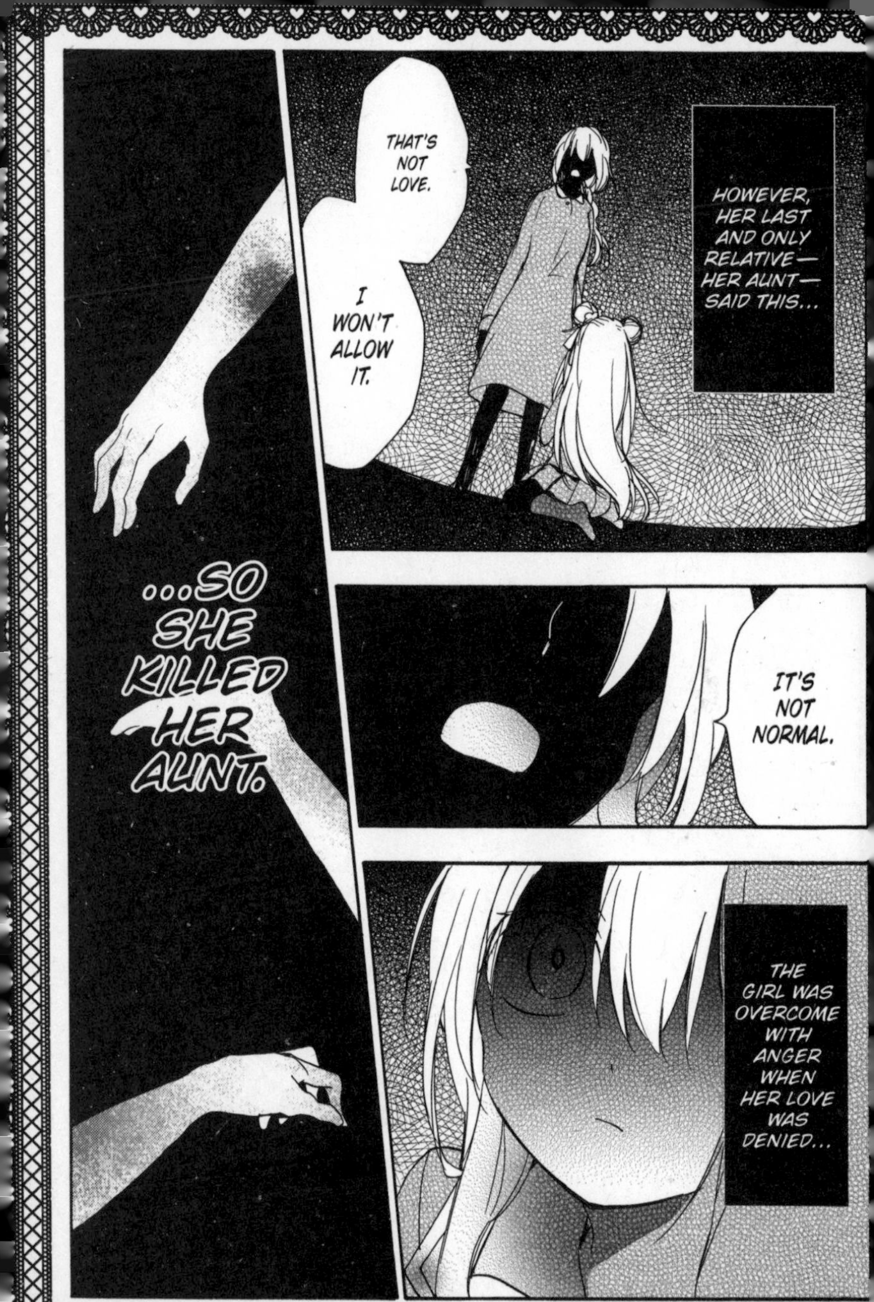

HOWEVER, HER LAST AND ONLY RELATIVE—HER AUNT—SAID THIS...
THAT'S NOT LOVE.
I WON'T ALLOW IT.
IT'S NOT NORMAL.
THE GIRL WAS OVERCOME WITH ANGER WHEN HER LOVE WAS DENIED...
...SO SHE KILLED HER AUNT.

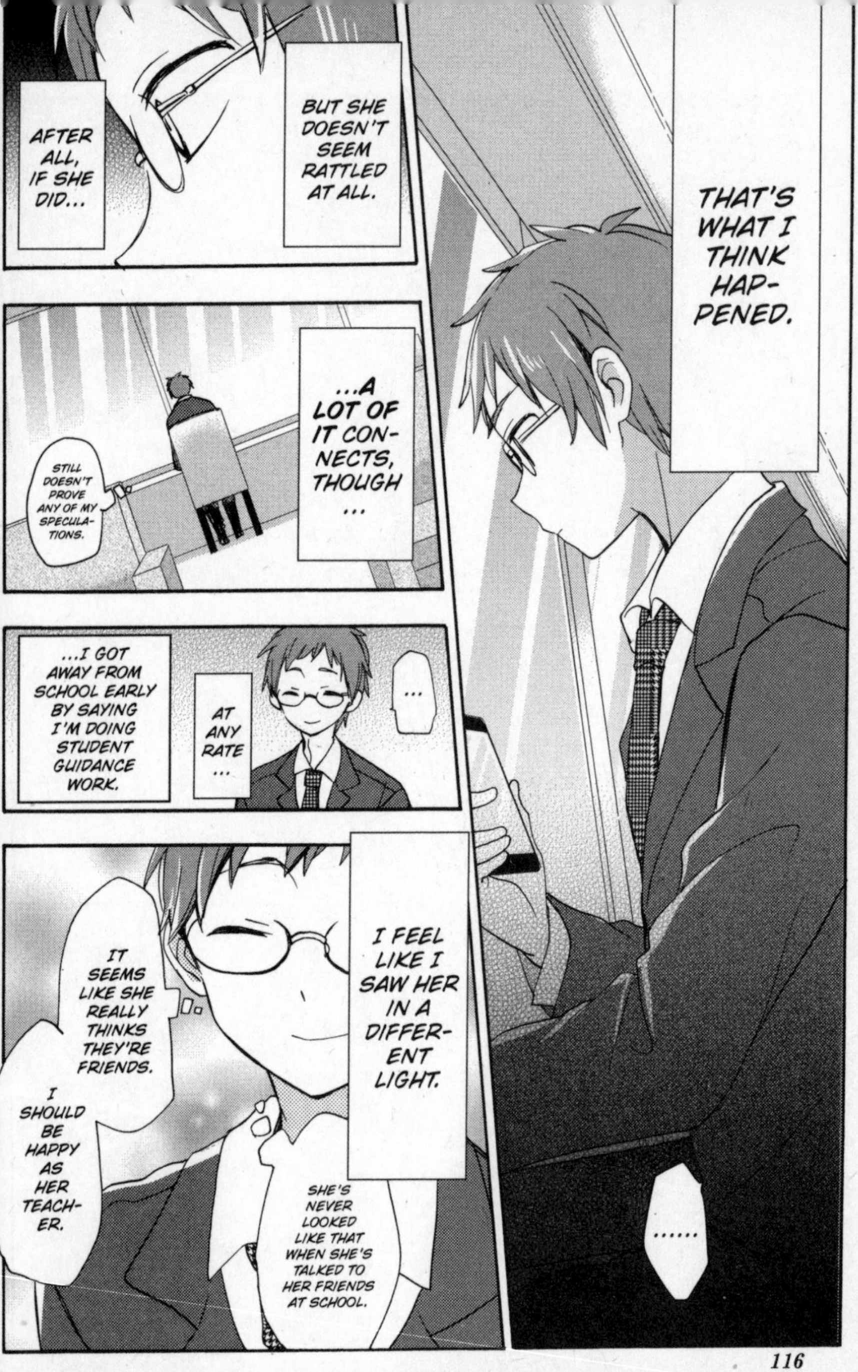
THAT'S WHAT I THINK HAPPENED.
......
BUT SHE DOESN'T SEEM RATTLED AT ALL.
AFTER ALL, IF SHE DID...
...A LOT OF IT CONNECTS, THOUGH...
STILL DOESN'T PROVE ANY OF MY SPECULATIONS.
...
AT ANY RATE...
...I GOT AWAY FROM SCHOOL EARLY BY SAYING I'M DOING STUDENT GUIDANCE WORK.
I FEEL LIKE I SAW HER IN A DIFFERENT LIGHT.
SHE'S NEVER LOOKED LIKE THAT WHEN SHE'S TALKED TO HER FRIENDS AT SCHOOL.
IT SEEMS LIKE SHE REALLY THINKS THEY'RE FRIENDS.
I SHOULD BE HAPPY AS HER TEACHER.

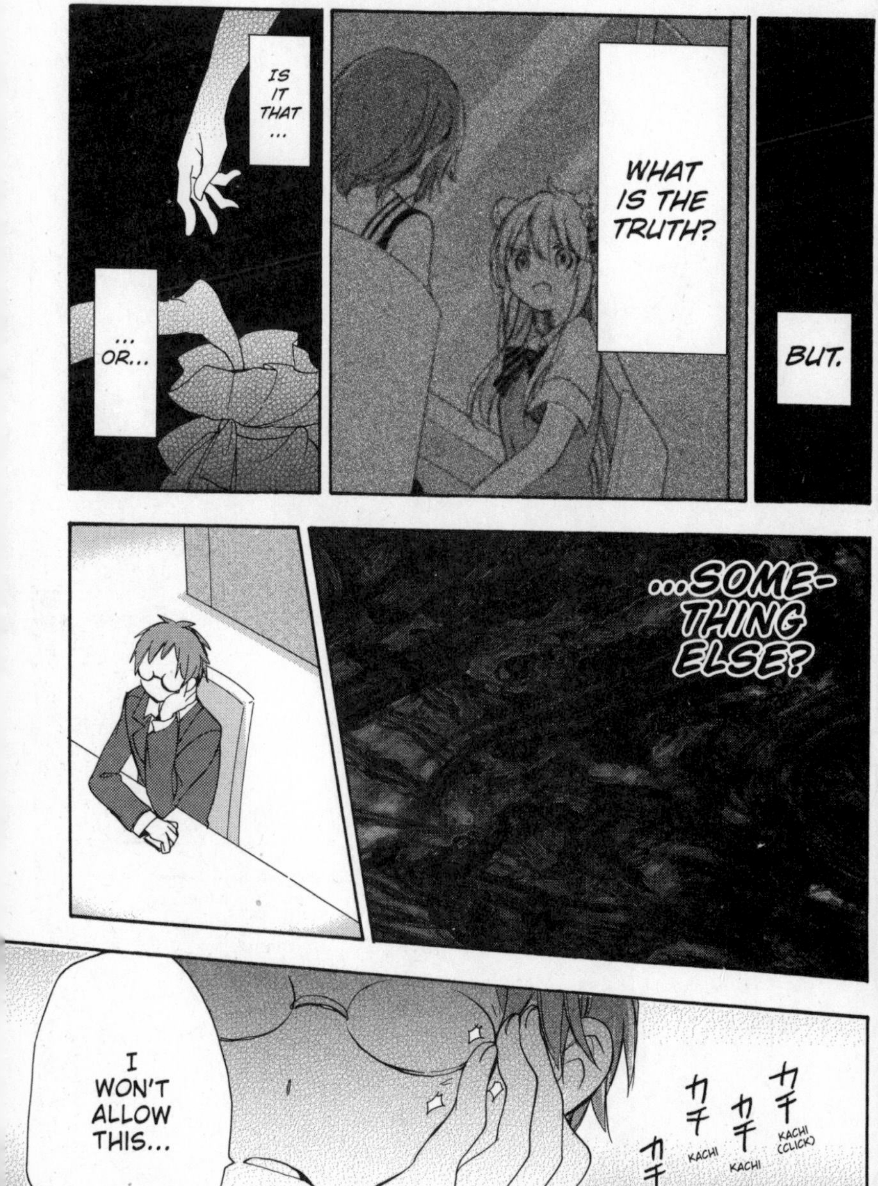
BUT.
WHAT IS THE TRUTH?
IS IT THAT...
... OR...
...SOME-THING ELSE?
カチ KACHI (CLICK)
カチ KACHI
カチ KACHI
カチ KACHI
I WON'T ALLOW THIS...

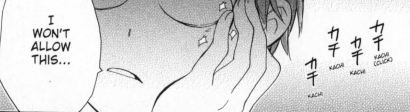

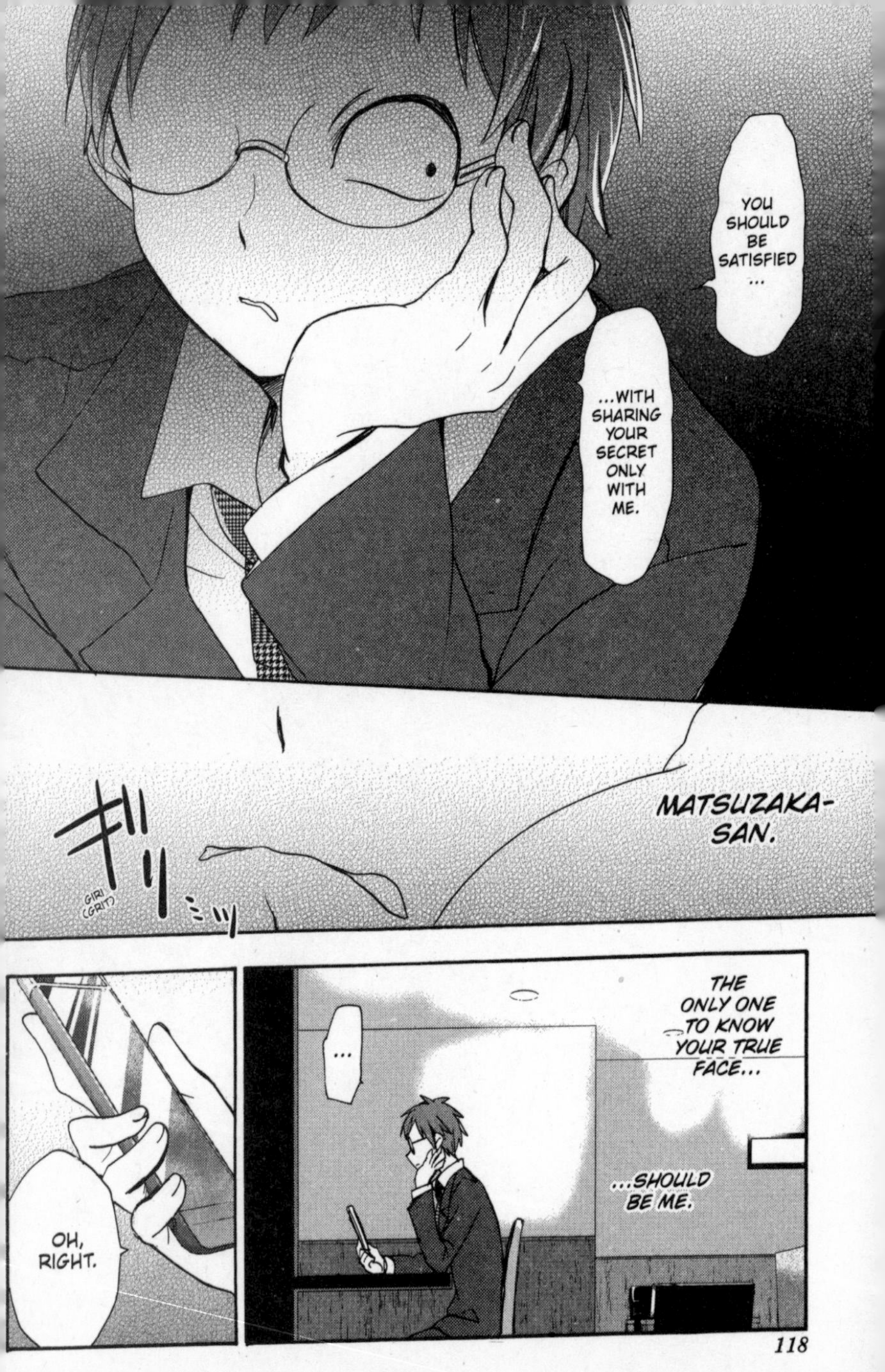
YOU SHOULD BE SATISFIED ...
...WITH SHARING YOUR SECRET ONLY WITH ME.
MATSUZAKA-SAN.
ギリッ
GIRI (GRIT)
THE ONLY ONE TO KNOW YOUR TRUE FACE...
...SHOULD BE ME.
...
OH, RIGHT.

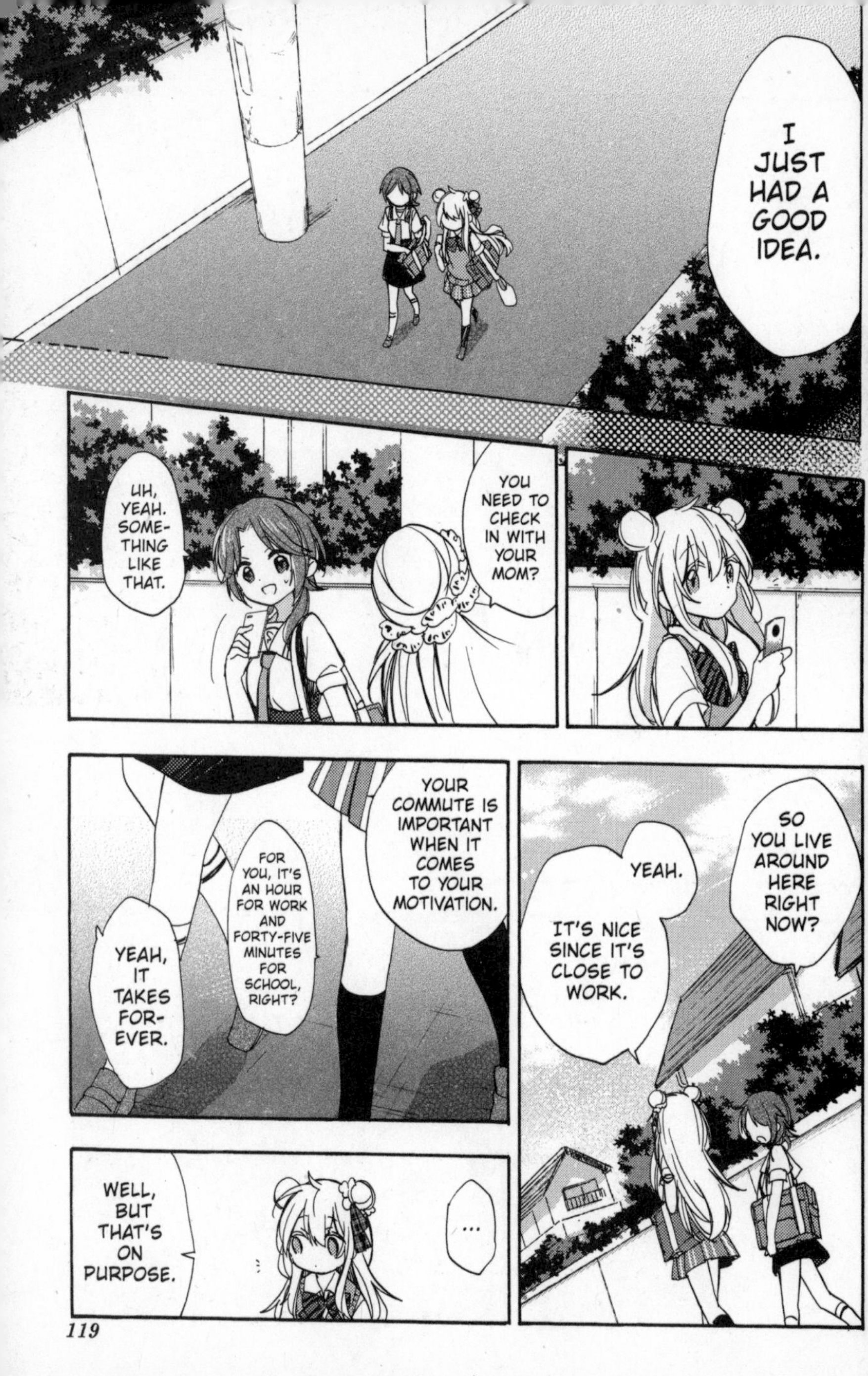
I JUST HAD A GOOD IDEA.
YOU NEED TO CHECK IN WITH YOUR MOM?
UH, YEAH. SOME-THING LIKE THAT.
SO YOU LIVE AROUND HERE RIGHT NOW?
YEAH.
IT'S NICE SINCE IT'S CLOSE TO WORK.
YOUR COMMUTE IS IMPORTANT WHEN IT COMES TO YOUR MOTIVATION.
FOR YOU, IT'S AN HOUR FOR WORK AND FORTY-FIVE MINUTES FOR SCHOOL, RIGHT?
YEAH, IT TAKES FOR-EVER.
...
WELL, BUT THAT'S ON PURPOSE.

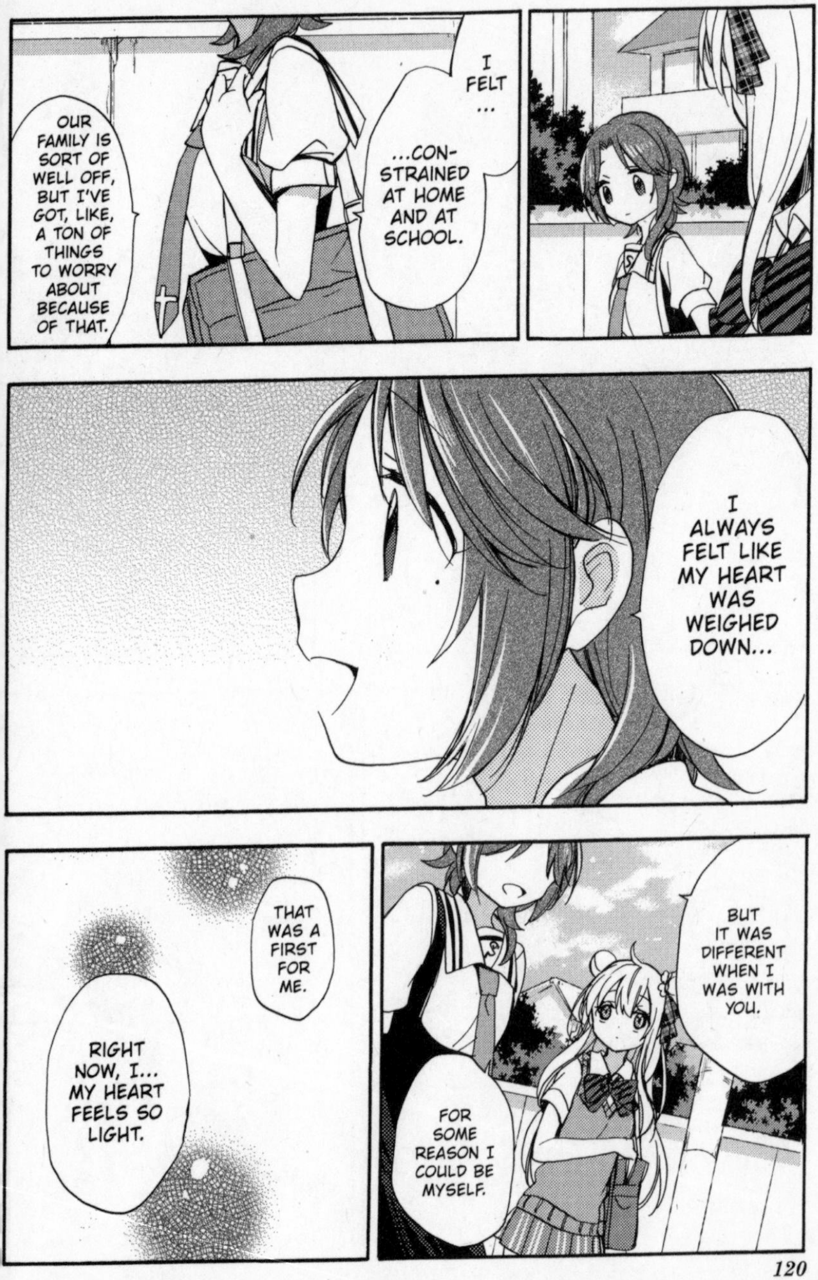
I FELT ...
...CON-STRAINED AT HOME AND AT SCHOOL.
OUR FAMILY IS SORT OF WELL OFF, BUT I'VE GOT, LIKE, A TON OF THINGS TO WORRY ABOUT BECAUSE OF THAT.
I ALWAYS FELT LIKE MY HEART WAS WEIGHED DOWN...
BUT IT WAS DIFFERENT WHEN I WAS WITH YOU.
FOR SOME REASON I COULD BE MYSELF.
THAT WAS A FIRST FOR ME.
RIGHT NOW, I... MY HEART FEELS SO LIGHT.

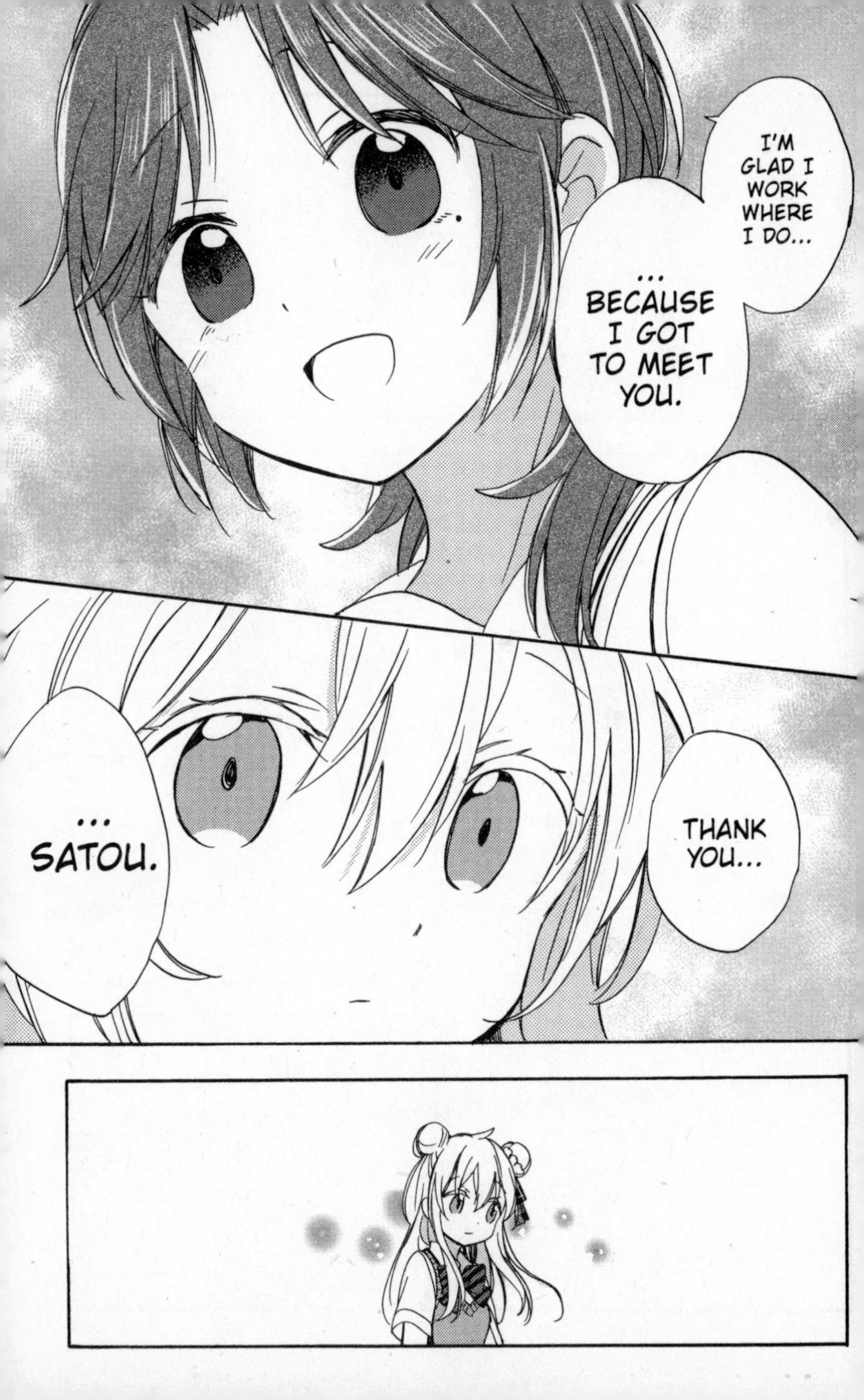
I'M GLAD I WORK WHERE I DO...
...BECAUSE I GOT TO MEET YOU.
THANK YOU...
...SATOU.

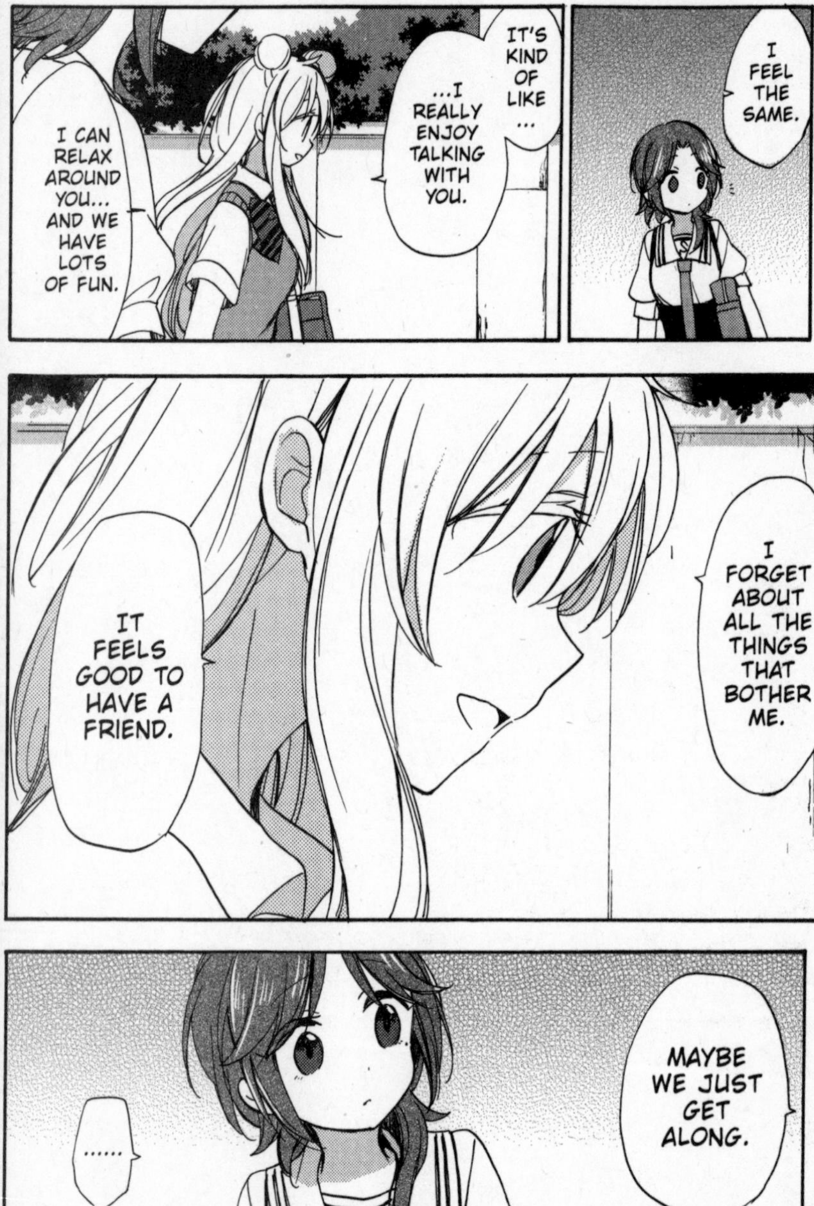
I FEEL THE SAME.
IT'S KIND OF LIKE ...
...I REALLY ENJOY TALKING WITH YOU.
I CAN RELAX AROUND YOU... AND WE HAVE LOTS OF FUN.
I FORGET ABOUT ALL THE THINGS THAT BOTHER ME.
IT FEELS GOOD TO HAVE A FRIEND.
MAYBE WE JUST GET ALONG.
......

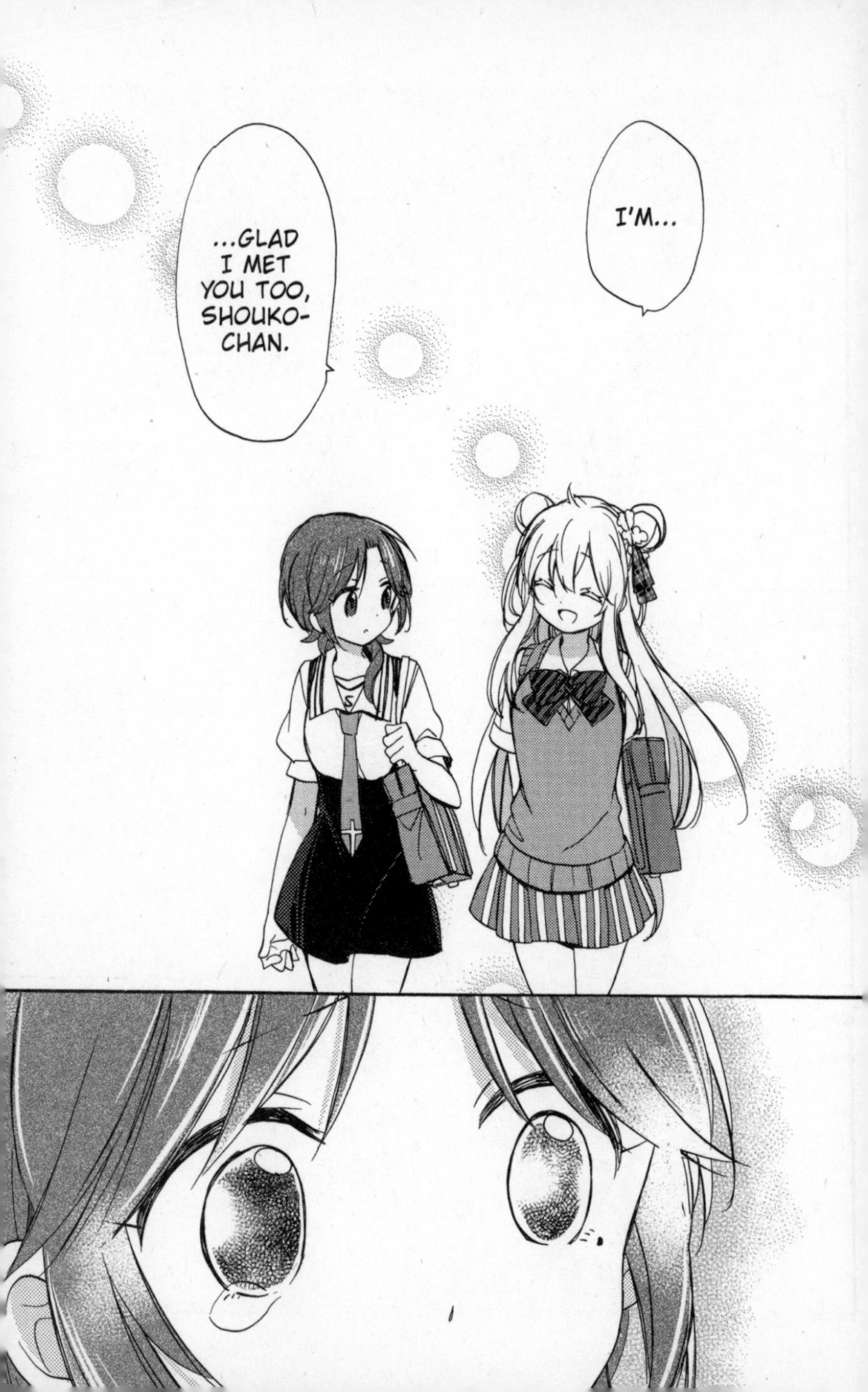
I'M...
...GLAD I MET YOU TOO, SHOUKO-CHAN.

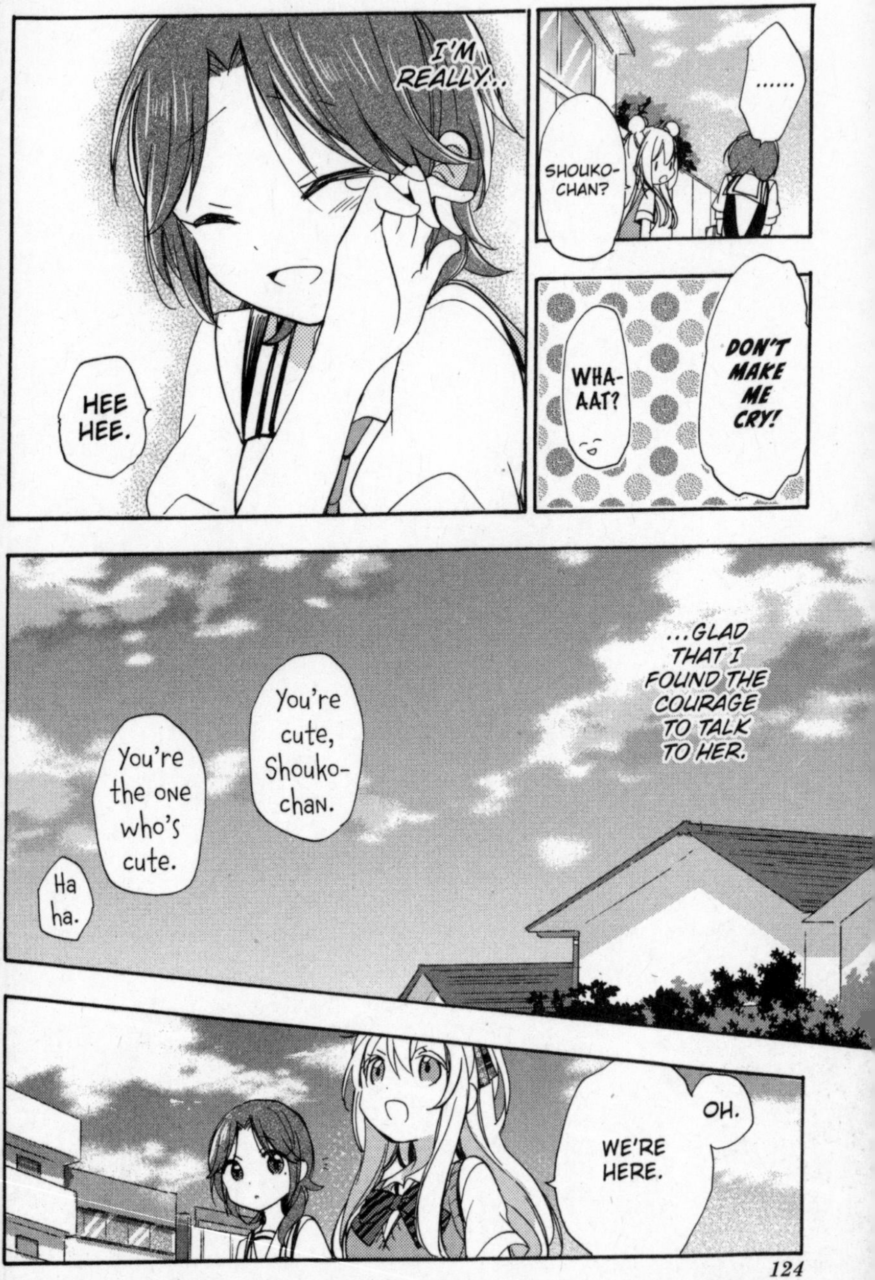
......
SHOUKO-CHAN?
DON'T MAKE ME CRY!
WHA-AAT?
I'M REALLY...
HEE HEE.
...GLAD THAT I FOUND THE COURAGE TO TALK TO HER.
You're cute, Shouko-chan.
You're the one who's cute.
Ha ha.
OH.
WE'RE HERE.

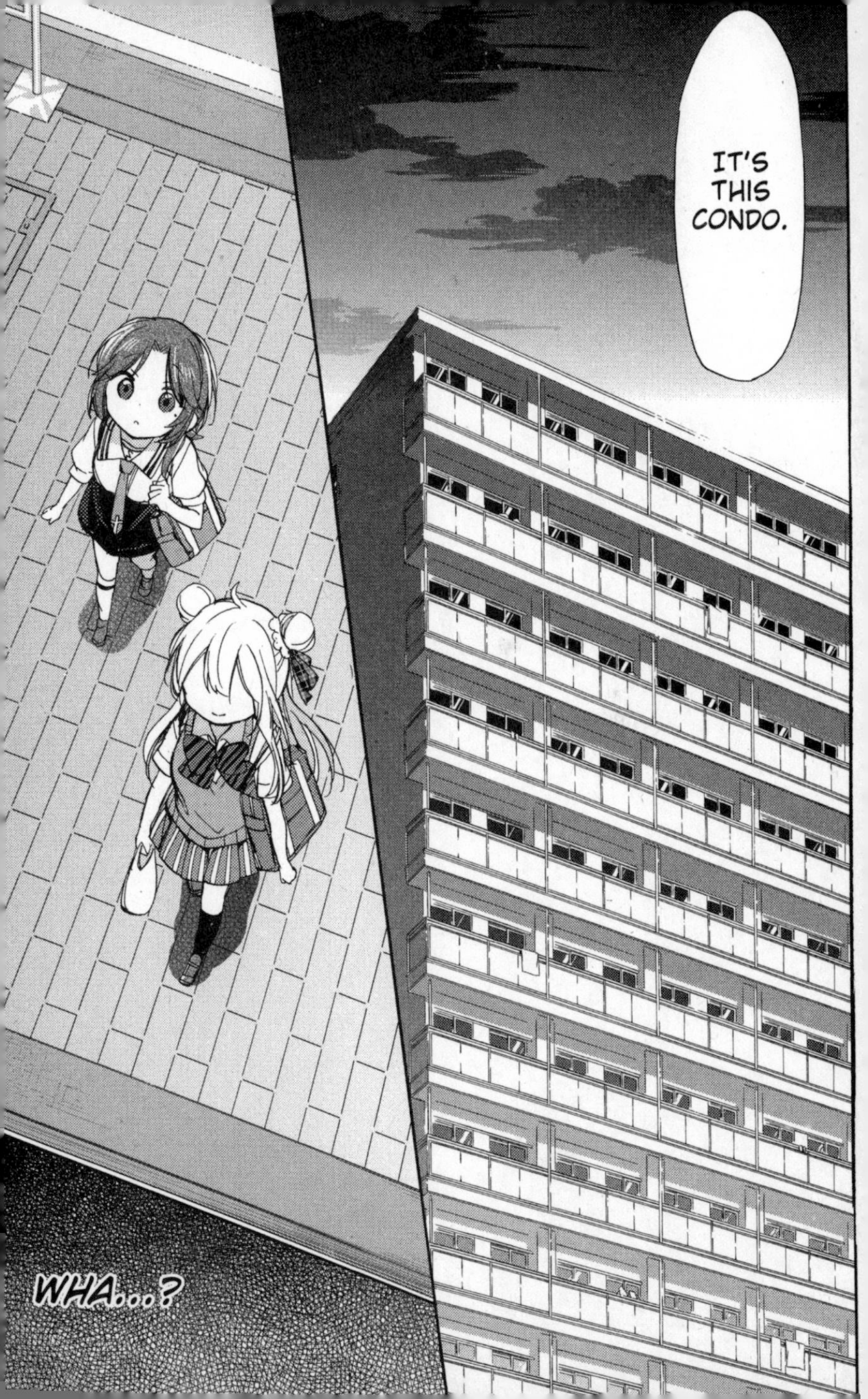
IT'S THIS CONDO.
WHA...?

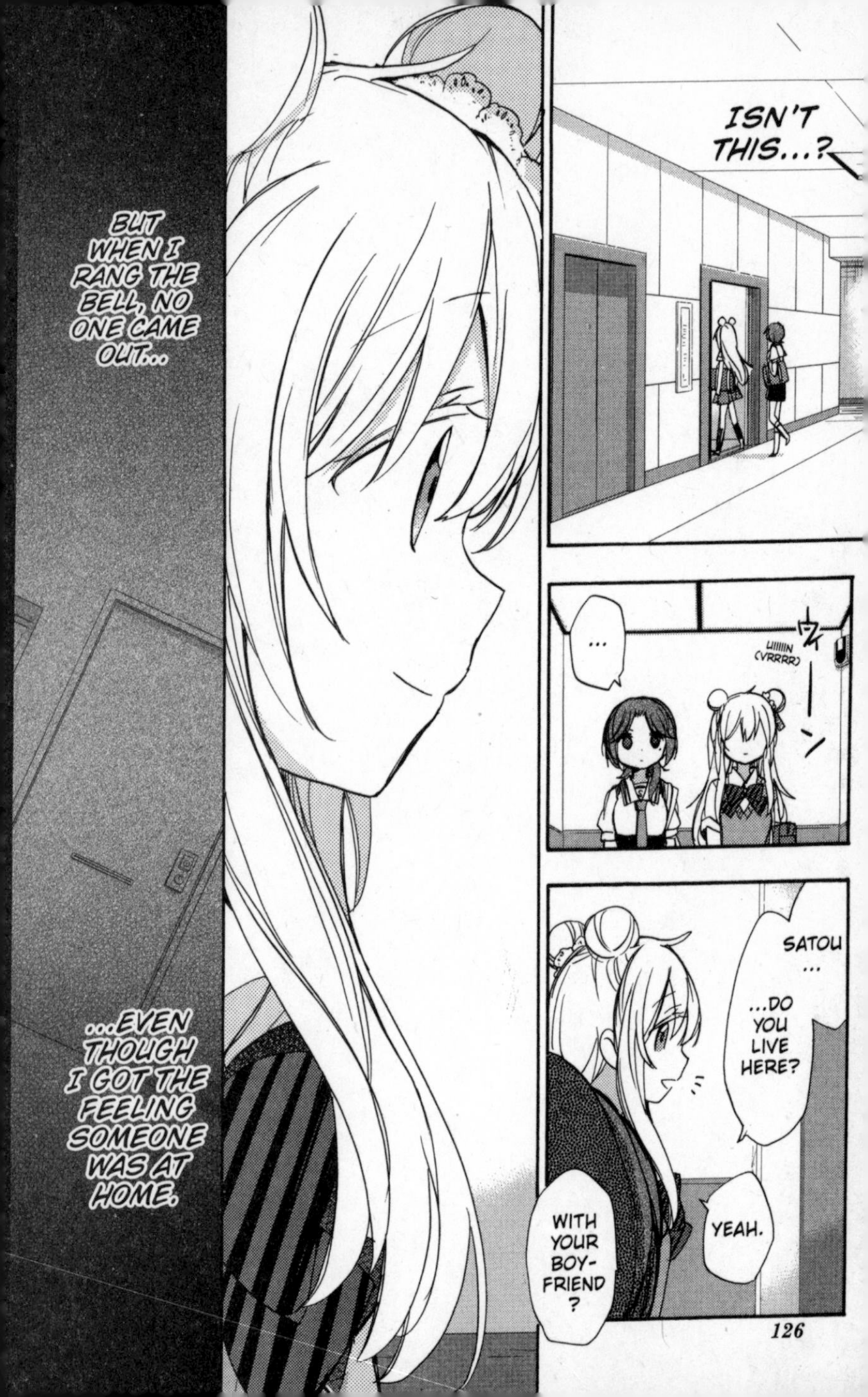
ISN'T THIS...?
UIIIIIN (VRRRR)
...
SATOU ...
...DO YOU LIVE HERE?
YEAH.
WITH YOUR BOY-FRIEND?
BUT WHEN I RANG THE BELL, NO ONE CAME OUT...
...EVEN THOUGH I GOT THE FEELING SOMEONE WAS AT HOME.

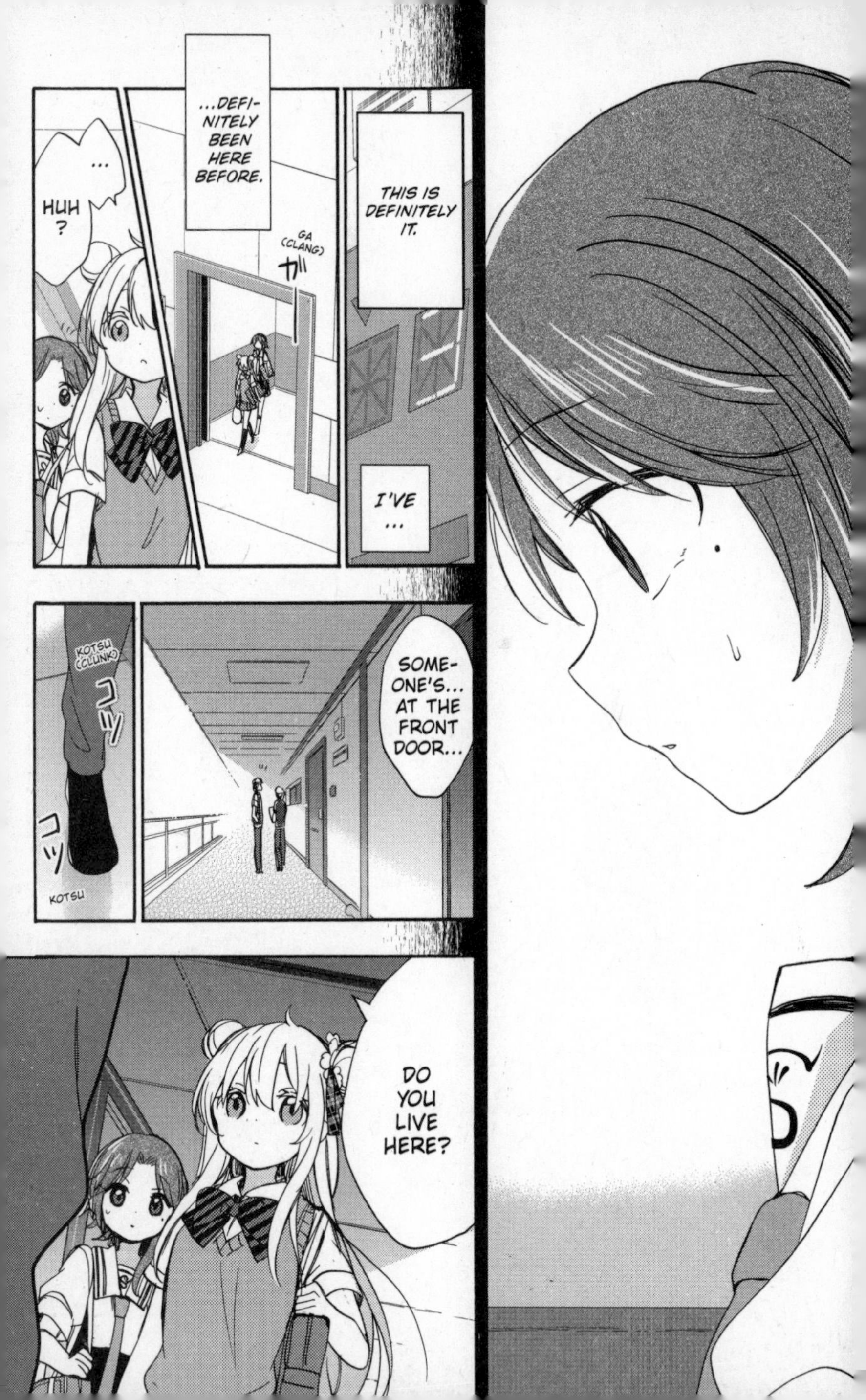
THIS IS DEFINITELY IT.
I'VE ...
...DEFINITELY BEEN HERE BEFORE.
GA (CLANG)
ガ
...
HUH?
SOME-ONE'S... AT THE FRONT DOOR...
KOTSU (CLUNK)
コツ
コツ
KOTSU
DO YOU LIVE HERE?

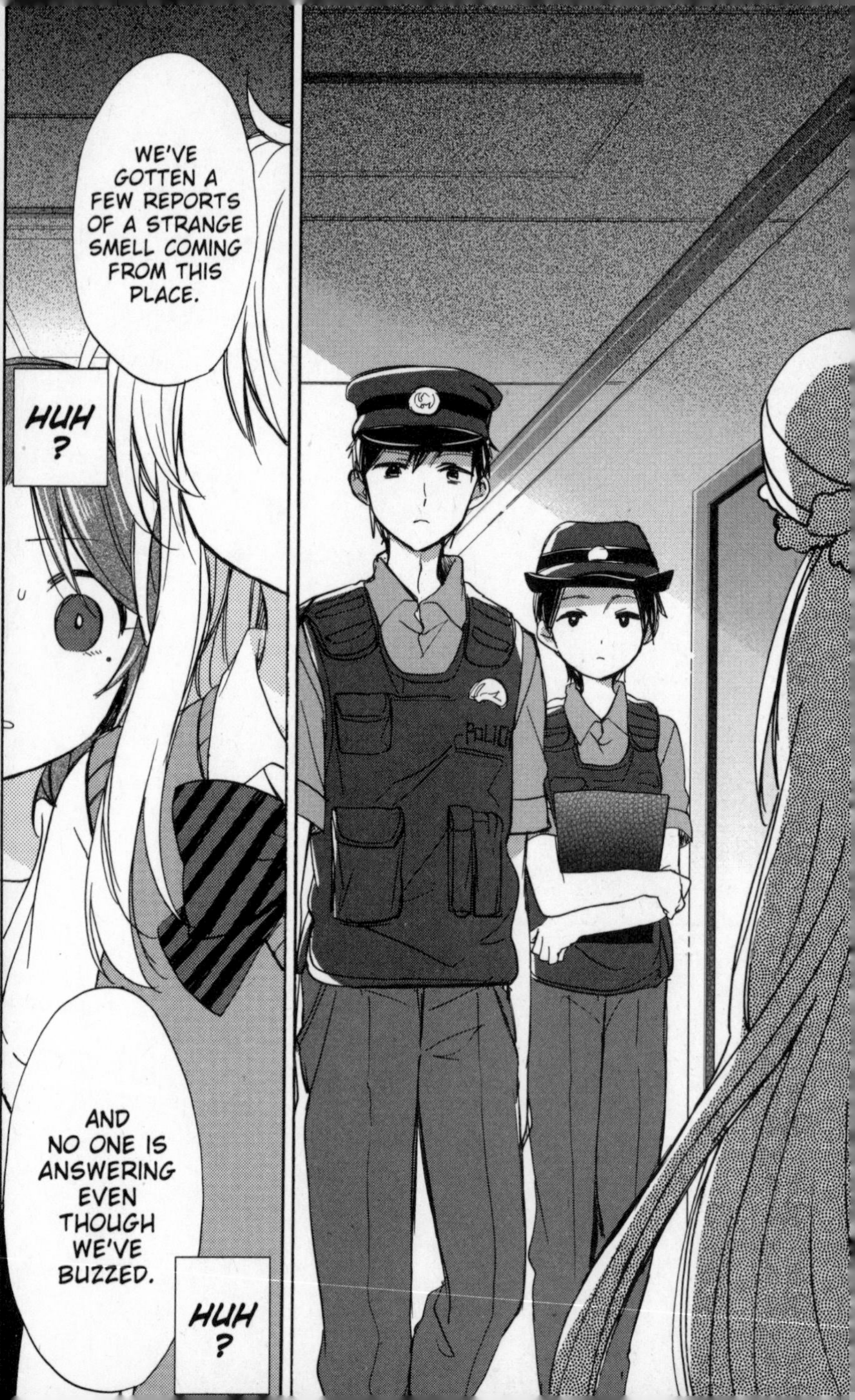
WE'VE GOTTEN A FEW REPORTS OF A STRANGE SMELL COMING FROM THIS PLACE.
HUH ?
AND NO ONE IS ANSWERING EVEN THOUGH WE'VE BUZZED.
HUH ?

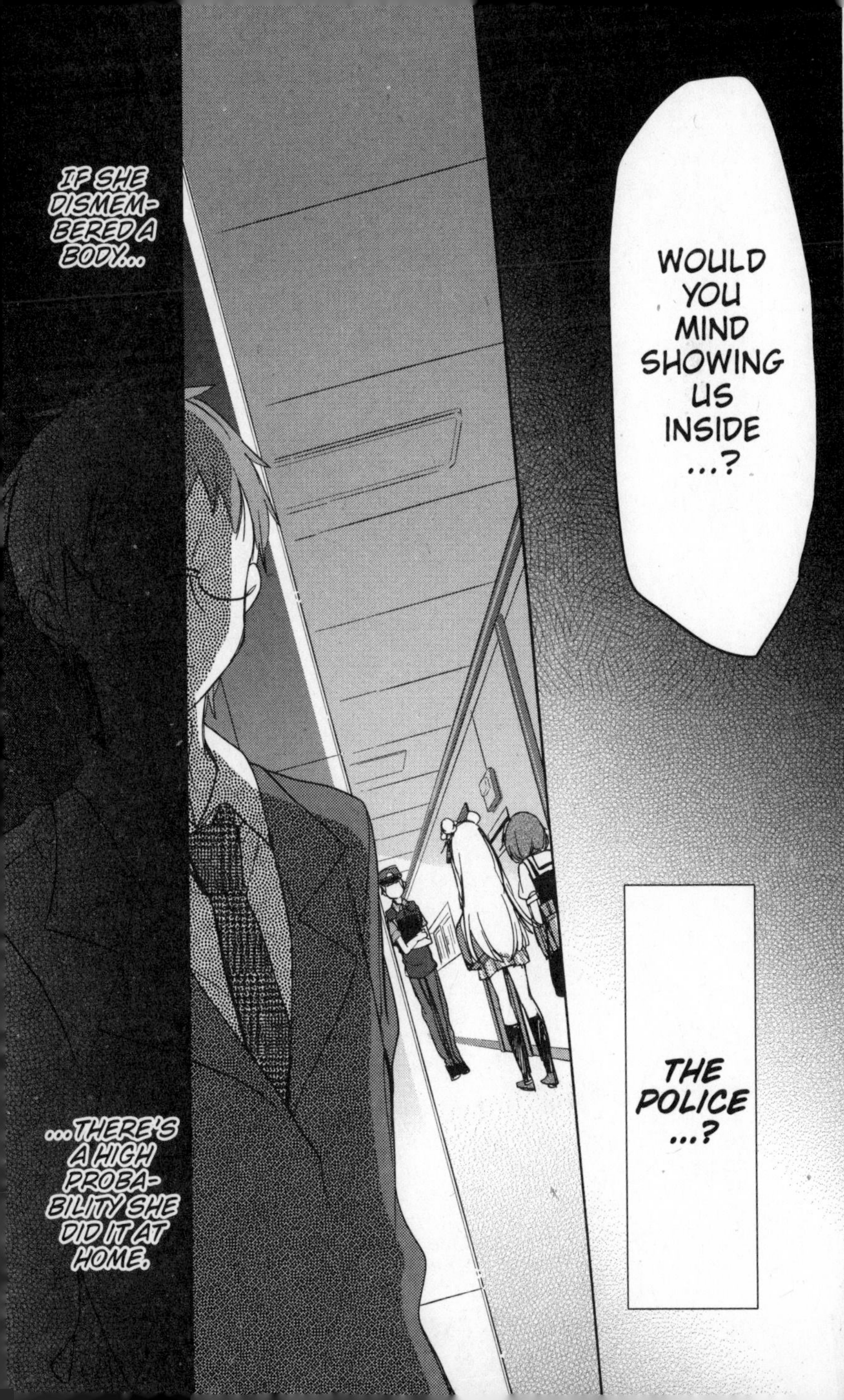
WOULD YOU MIND SHOWING US INSIDE ...?
THE POLICE ...?
IF SHE DISMEMBERED A BODY...
...THERE'S A HIGH PROBABILITY SHE DID IT AT HOME.

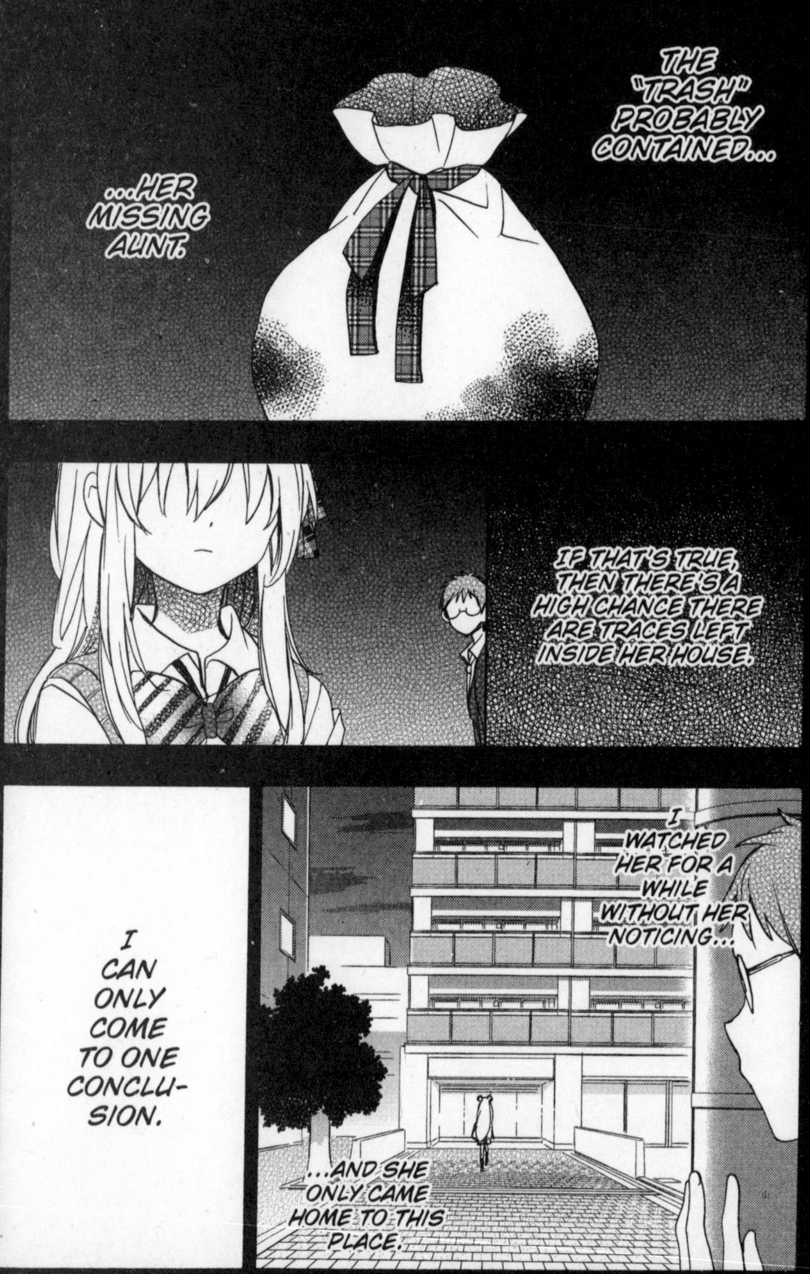
THE "TRASH" PROBABLY CONTAINED...
...HER MISSING AUNT.
IF THAT'S TRUE, THEN THERE'S A HIGH CHANCE THERE ARE TRACES LEFT INSIDE HER HOUSE.
I WATCHED HER FOR A WHILE WITHOUT HER NOTICING...
...AND SHE ONLY CAME HOME TO THIS PLACE.
I CAN ONLY COME TO ONE CONCLUSION.

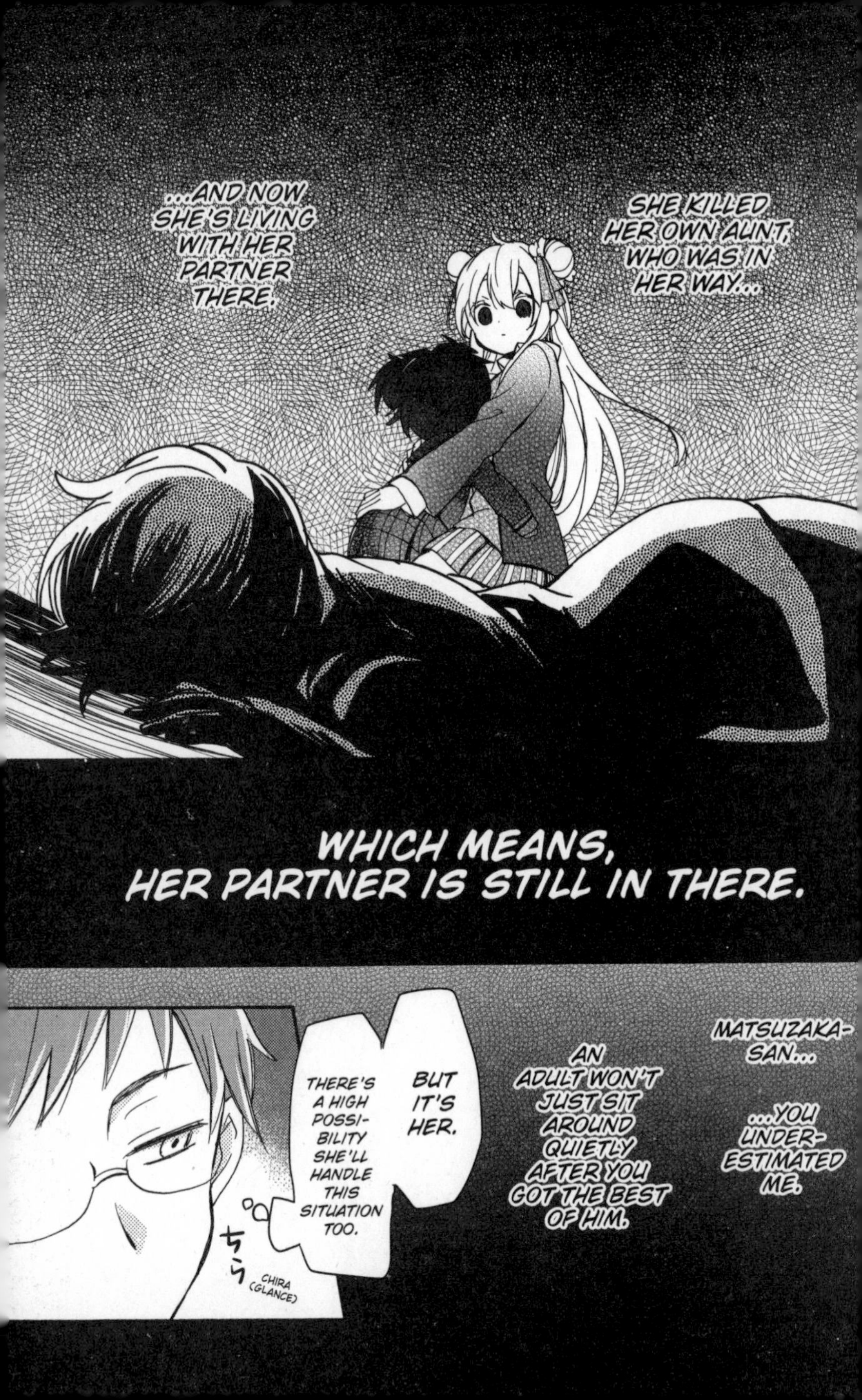
SHE KILLED HER OWN AUNT, WHO WAS IN HER WAY...
...AND NOW SHE'S LIVING WITH HER PARTNER THERE.
WHICH MEANS, HER PARTNER IS STILL IN THERE.
MATSUZAKA-SAN...
...YOU UNDER-ESTIMATED ME.
AN ADULT WON'T JUST SIT AROUND QUIETLY AFTER YOU GOT THE BEST OF HIM.
BUT IT'S HER.
THERE'S A HIGH POSSI-BILITY SHE'LL HANDLE THIS SITUATION TOO.
ちら
CHIRA (GLANCE)

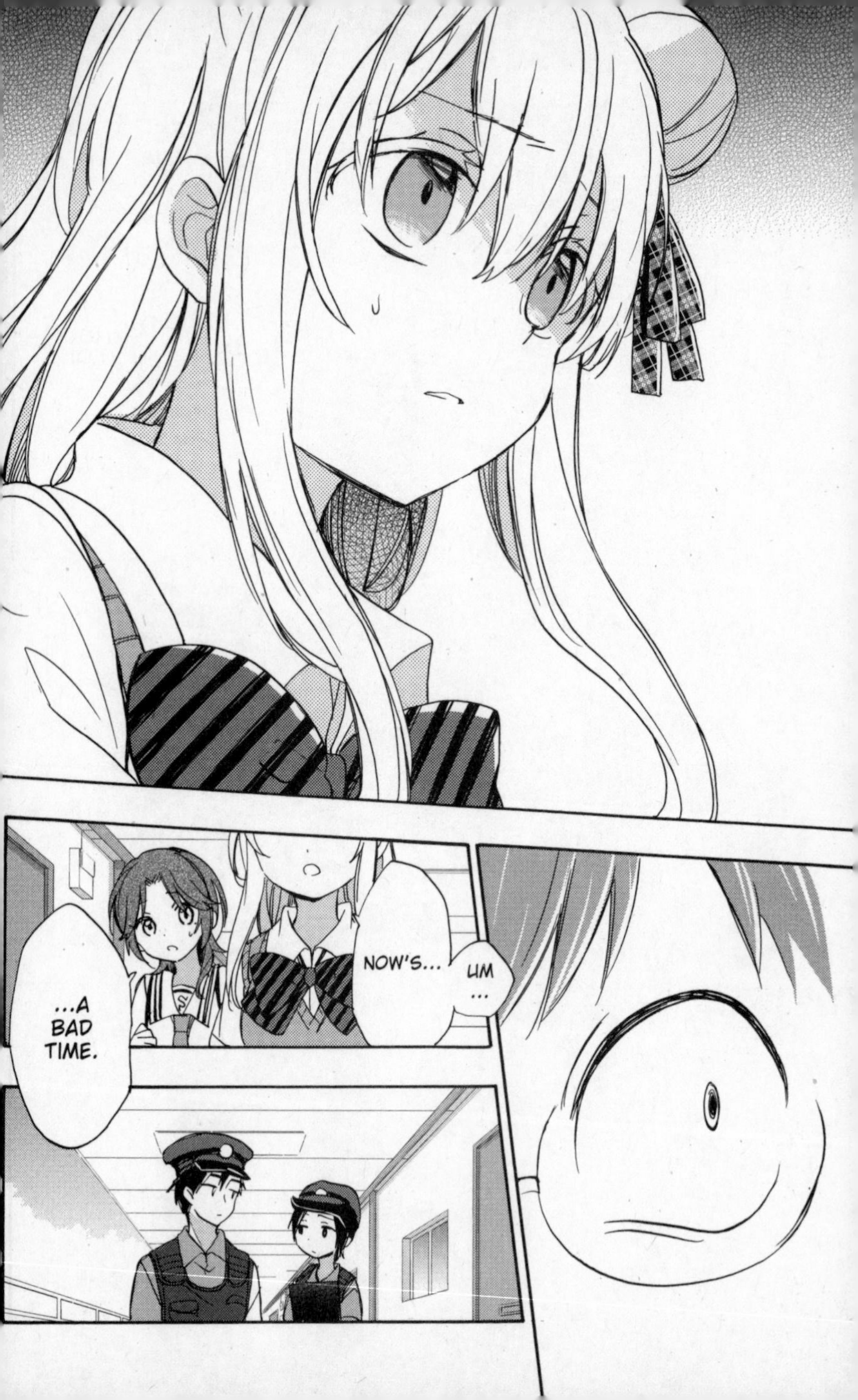
UM...
NOW'S...
...A BAD TIME.

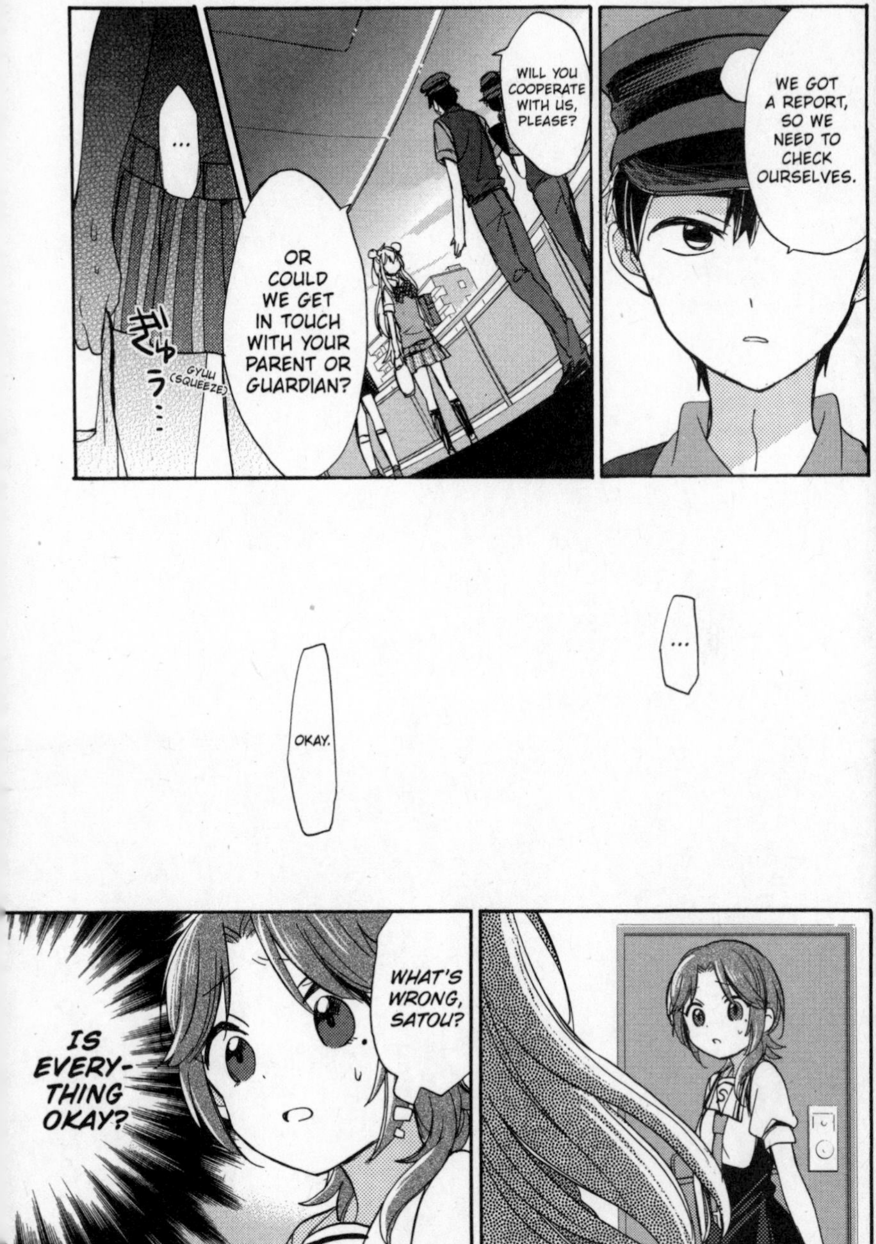
WE GOT A REPORT, SO WE NEED TO CHECK OURSELVES.
WILL YOU COOPERATE WITH US, PLEASE?
OR COULD WE GET IN TOUCH WITH YOUR PARENT OR GUARDIAN?
...
ぎゅぅ…
GYUU (SQUEEZE)
...
OKAY.
WHAT'S WRONG, SATOU?
IS EVERY-THING OKAY?

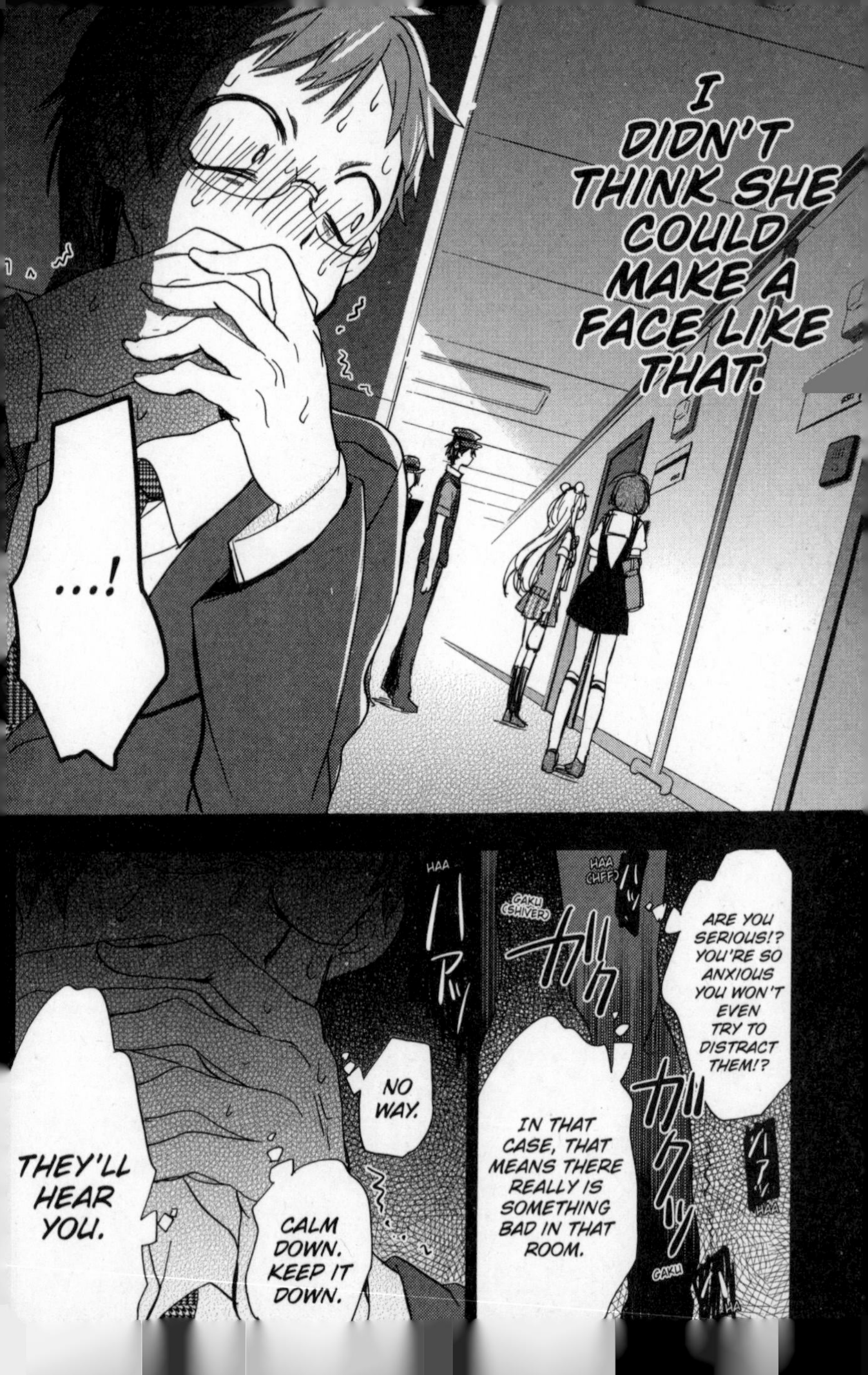
I DIDN'T THINK SHE COULD MAKE A FACE LIKE THAT.
...!
HAA (HFF)
GAKU (SHIVER)
ARE YOU SERIOUS!? YOU'RE SO ANXIOUS YOU WON'T EVEN TRY TO DISTRACT THEM!?
IN THAT CASE, THAT MEANS THERE REALLY IS SOMETHING BAD IN THAT ROOM.
HAA
GAKU
HA
HAA
NO WAY.
CALM DOWN. KEEP IT DOWN.
THEY'LL HEAR YOU.

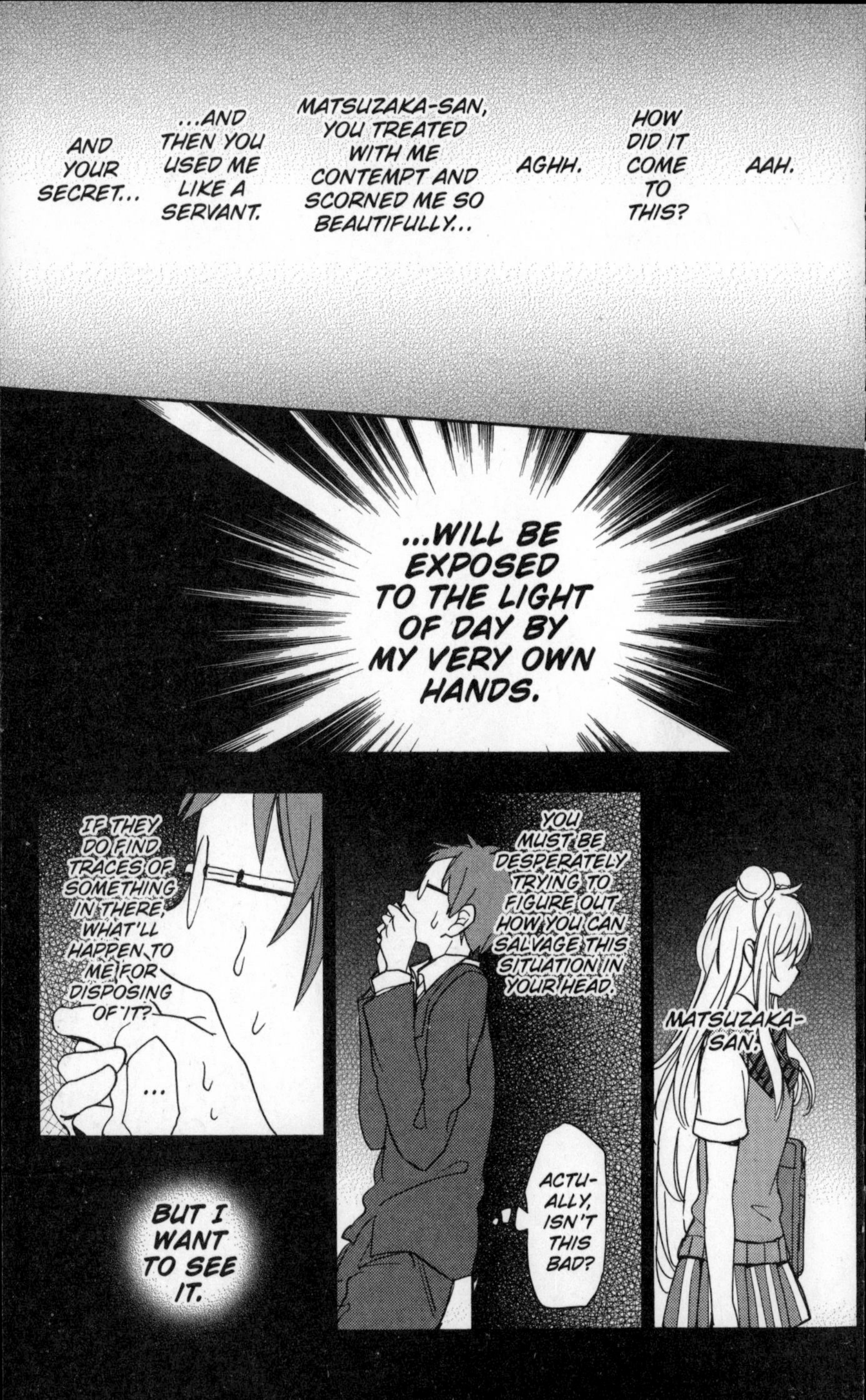
AAH.
HOW DID IT COME TO THIS?
AGHH.
MATSUZAKA-SAN, YOU TREATED WITH ME CONTEMPT AND SCORNED ME SO BEAUTIFULLY...
...AND THEN YOU USED ME LIKE A SERVANT.
AND YOUR SECRET...
...WILL BE EXPOSED TO THE LIGHT OF DAY BY MY VERY OWN HANDS.
MATSUZAKA-SAN.
YOU MUST BE DESPERATELY TRYING TO FIGURE OUT HOW YOU CAN SALVAGE THIS SITUATION IN YOUR HEAD.
ACTU-ALLY, ISN'T THIS BAD?
IF THEY DO FIND TRACES OF SOMETHING IN THERE, WHAT'LL HAPPEN TO ME FOR DISPOSING OF IT?
...
BUT I WANT TO SEE IT.

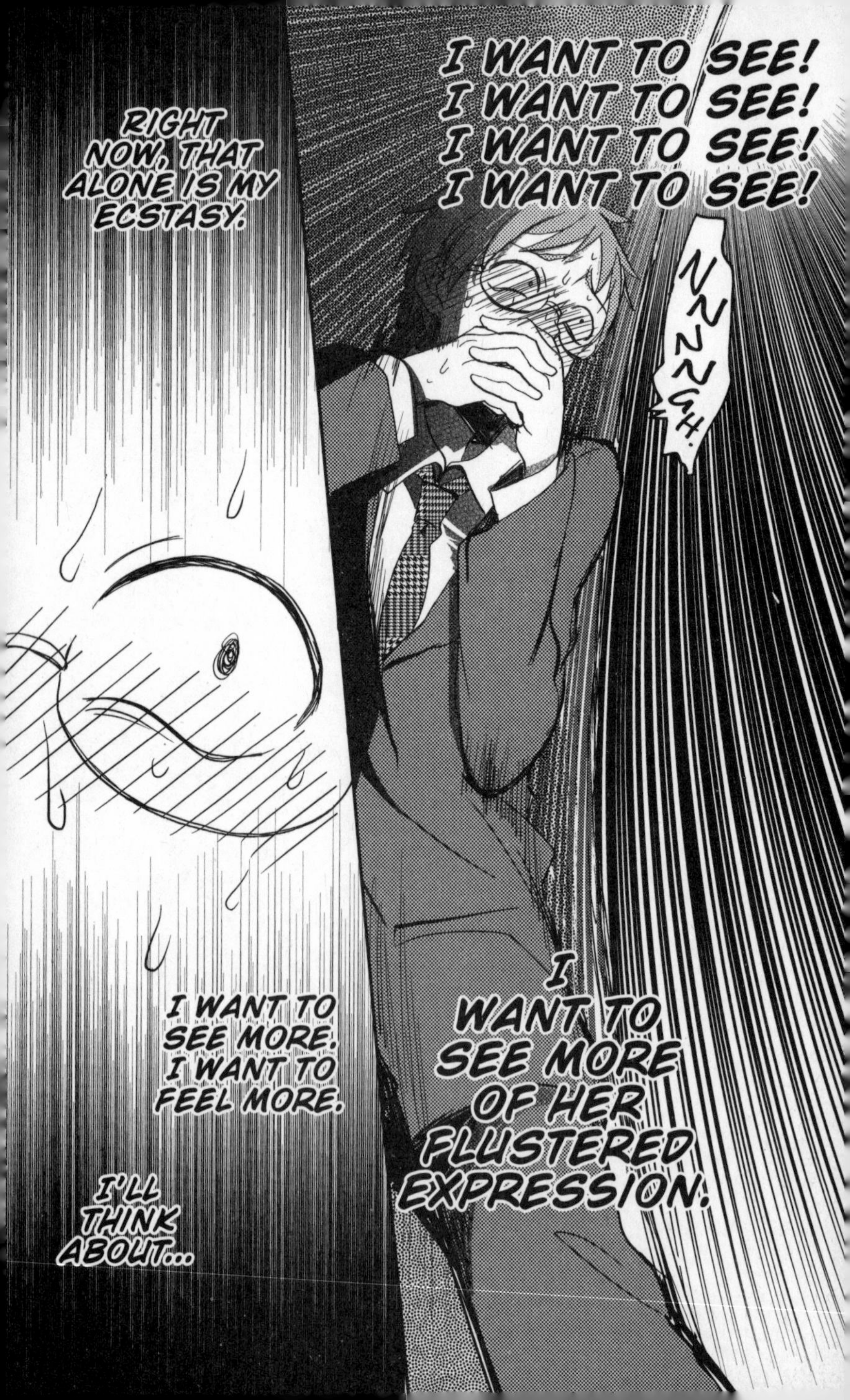
I WANT TO SEE! I WANT TO SEE! I WANT TO SEE! I WANT TO SEE!
NNNNGH.
I WANT TO SEE MORE OF HER FLUSTERED EXPRESSION.
RIGHT NOW, THAT ALONE IS MY ECSTASY.
I WANT TO SEE MORE. I WANT TO FEEL MORE.
I'LL THINK ABOUT...

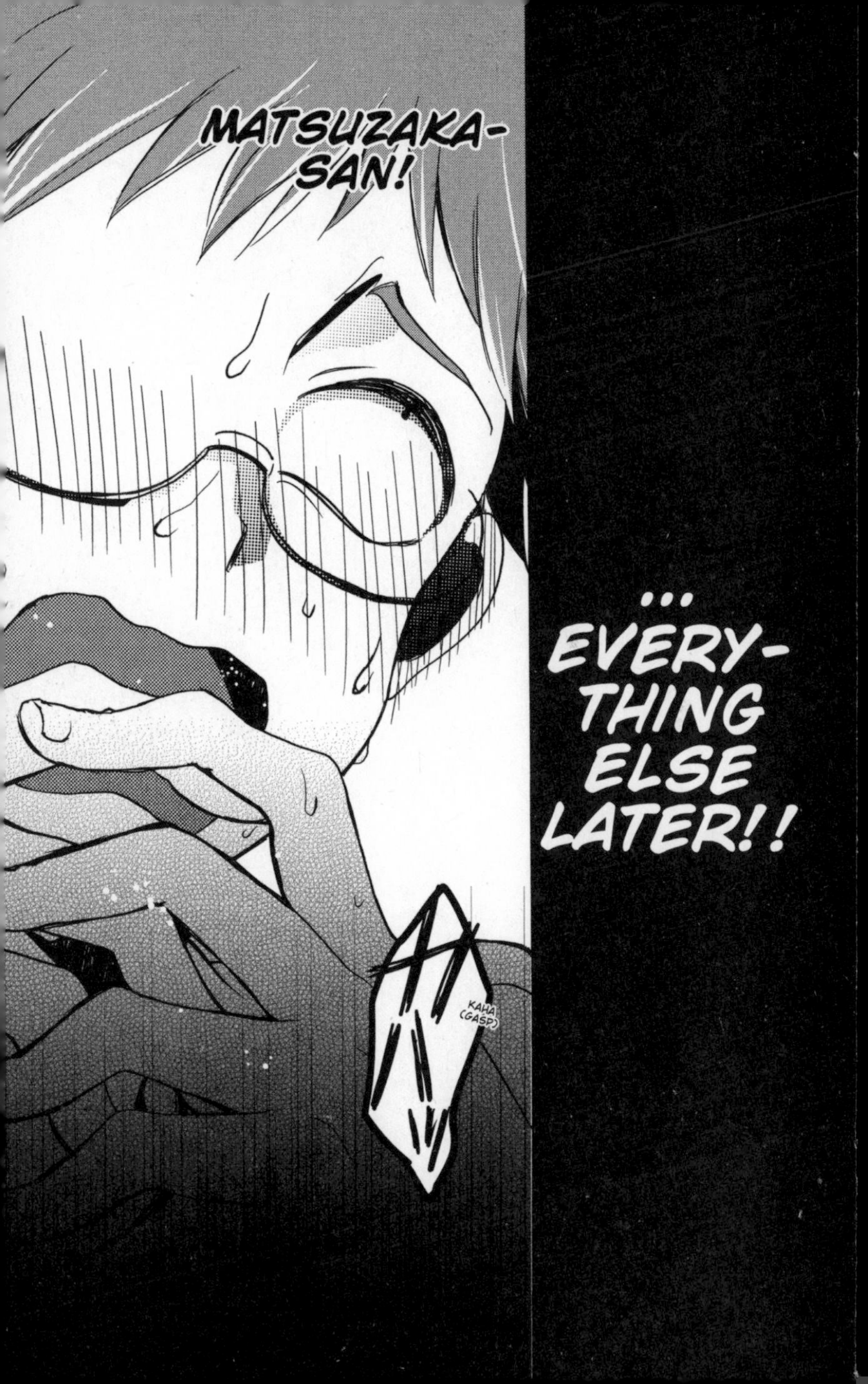
...EVERY-THING ELSE LATER!!
MATSUZAKA-SAN!
KAHA (GASP)

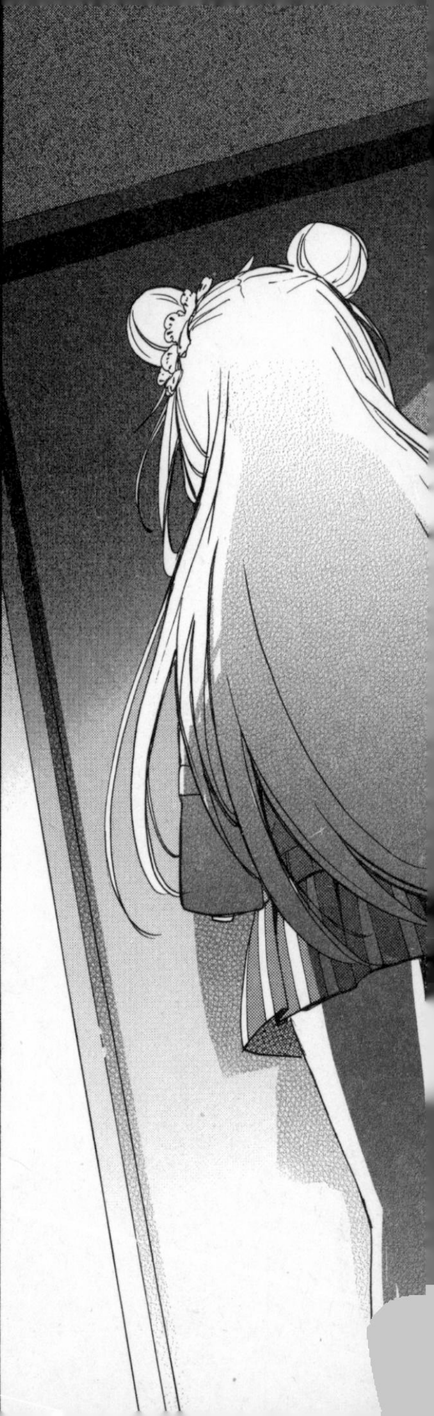
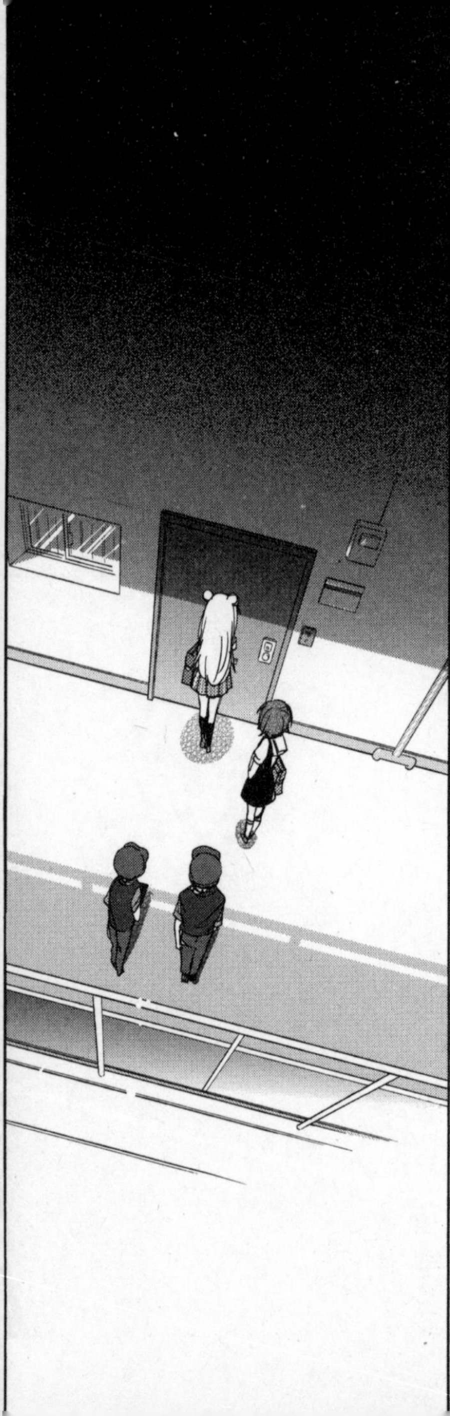

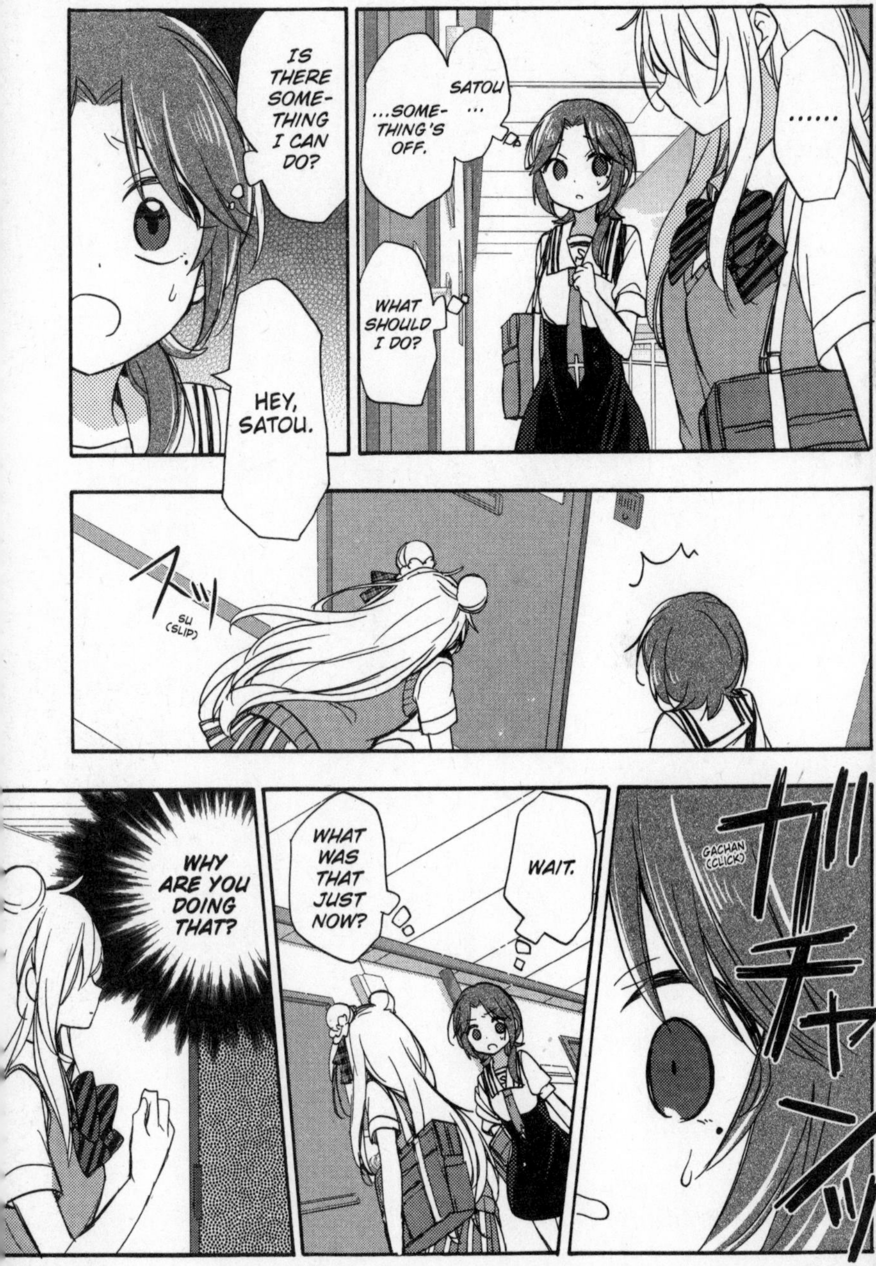
......
SATOU ...
...SOME-THING'S OFF.
WHAT SHOULD I DO?
IS THERE SOME-THING I CAN DO?
HEY, SATOU.
SU (SLIP)
GACHAN (CLICK)
WAIT.
WHAT WAS THAT JUST NOW?
WHY ARE YOU DOING THAT?

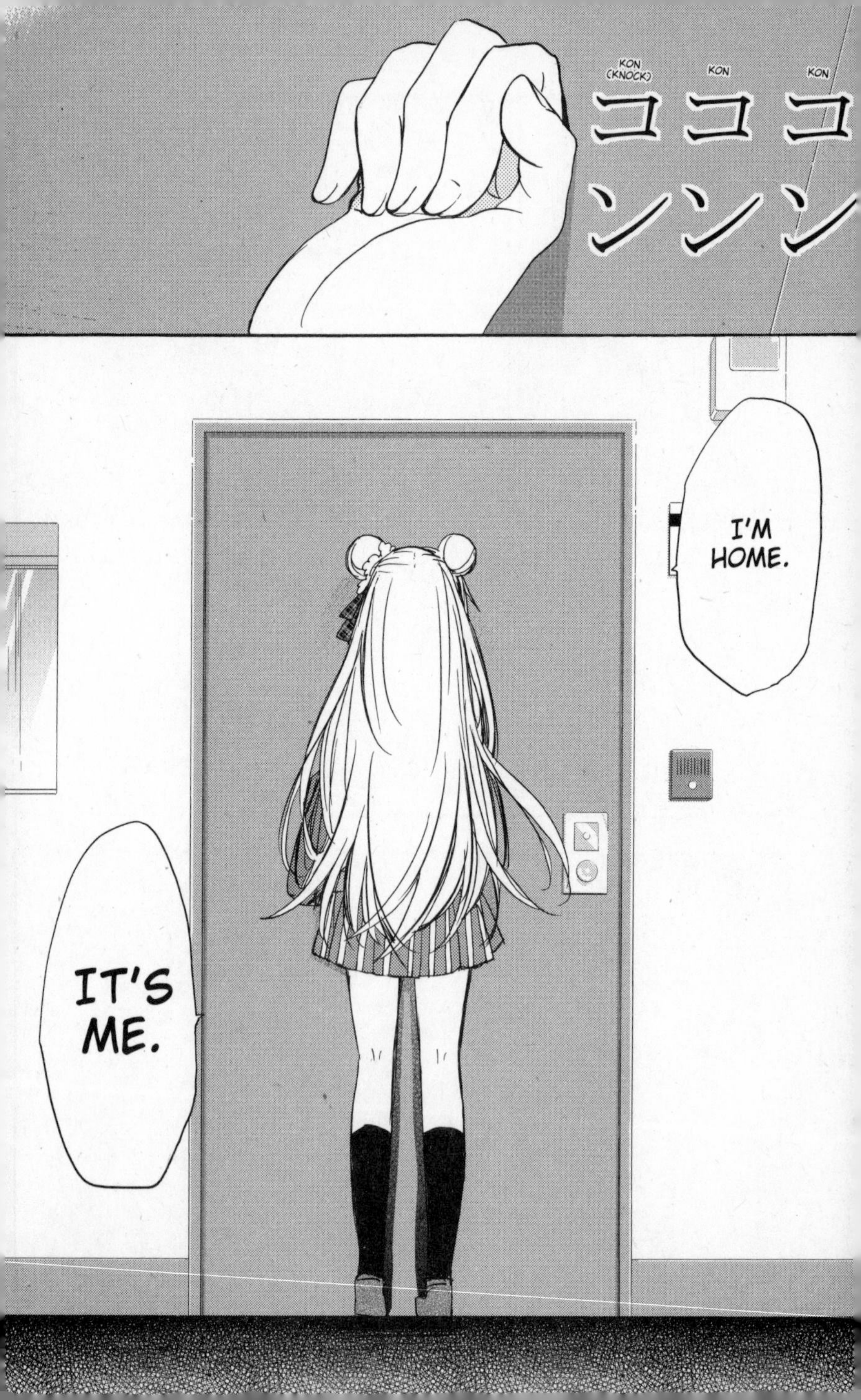
コンコンコン
KON (KNOCK) KON KON
I'M HOME.
IT'S ME.

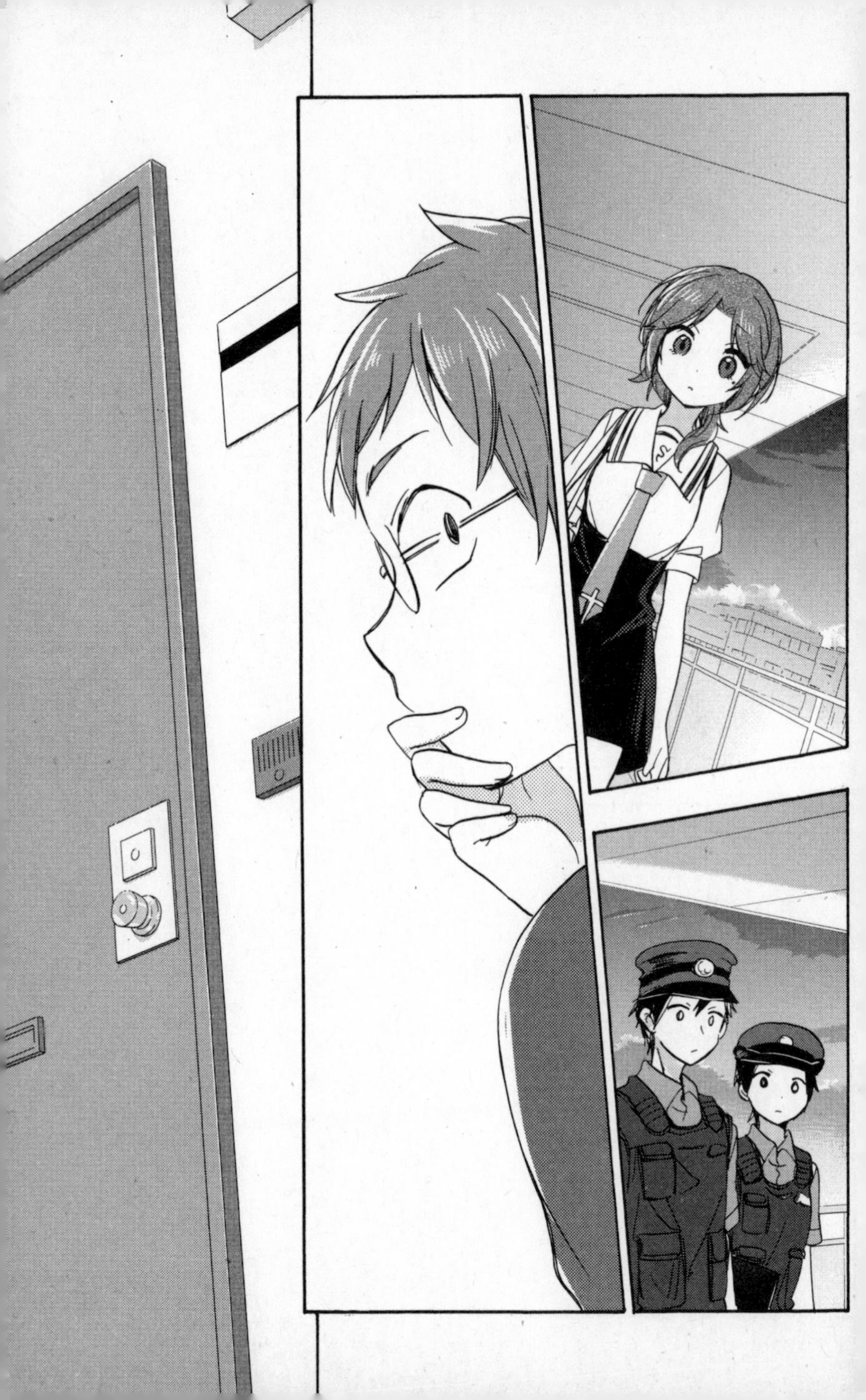

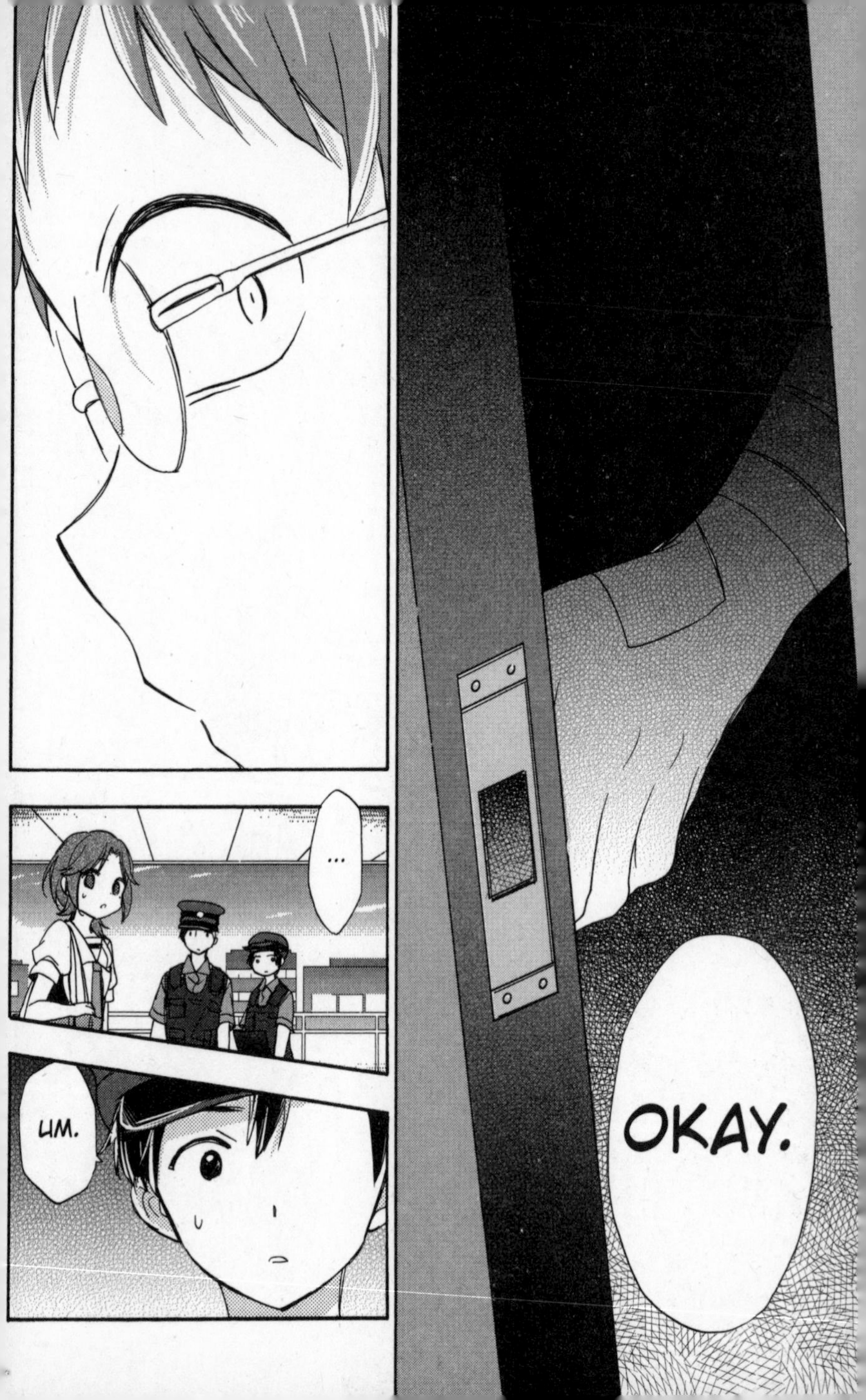
OKAY.
...
UM.

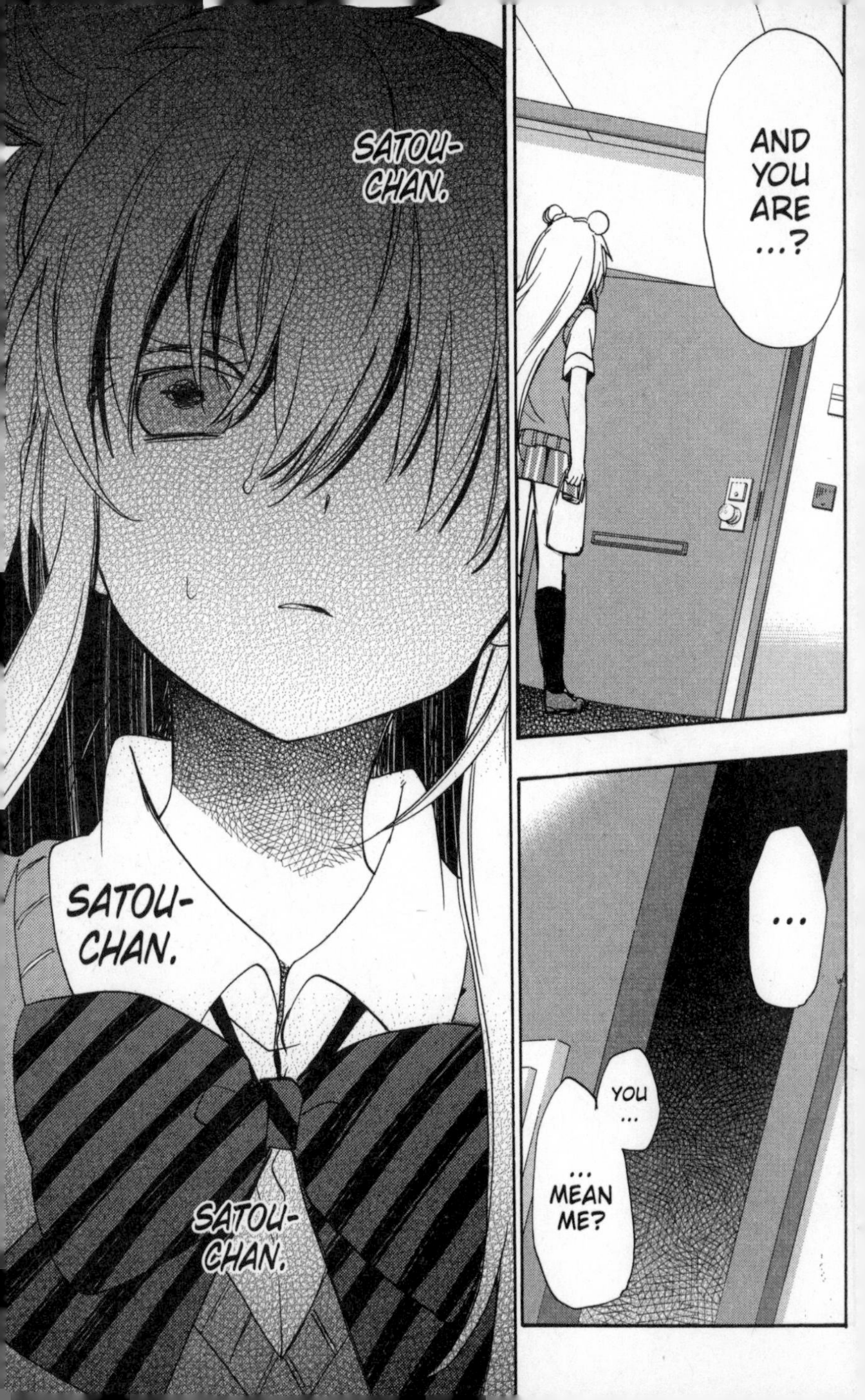
AND YOU ARE ...?
...
YOU ...
... MEAN ME?
SATOU-CHAN.
SATOU-CHAN.
SATOU-CHAN.

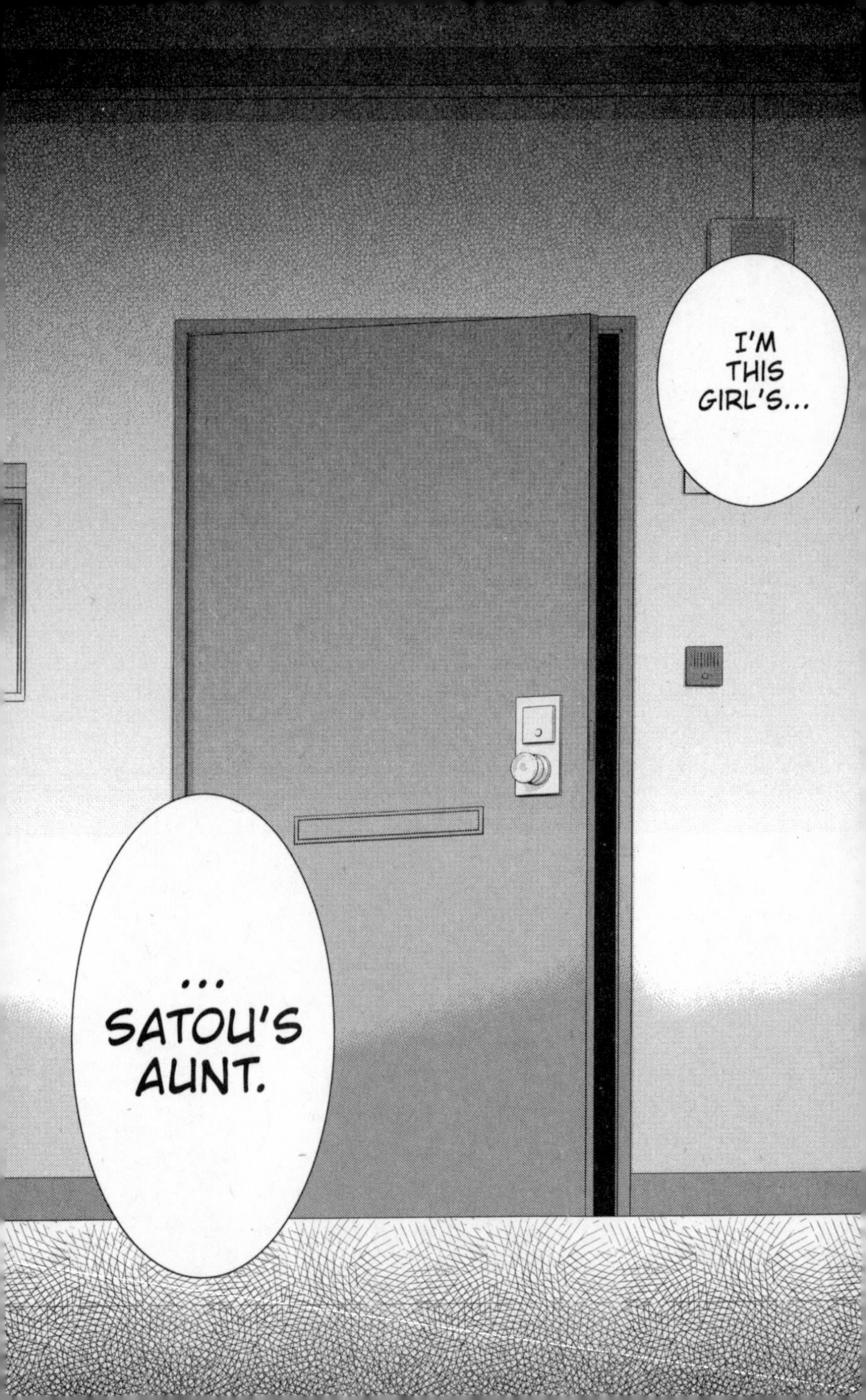
I'M THIS GIRL'S...
...SATOU'S AUNT.

Happy
Sugar
Life

Happy
Sugar
Life

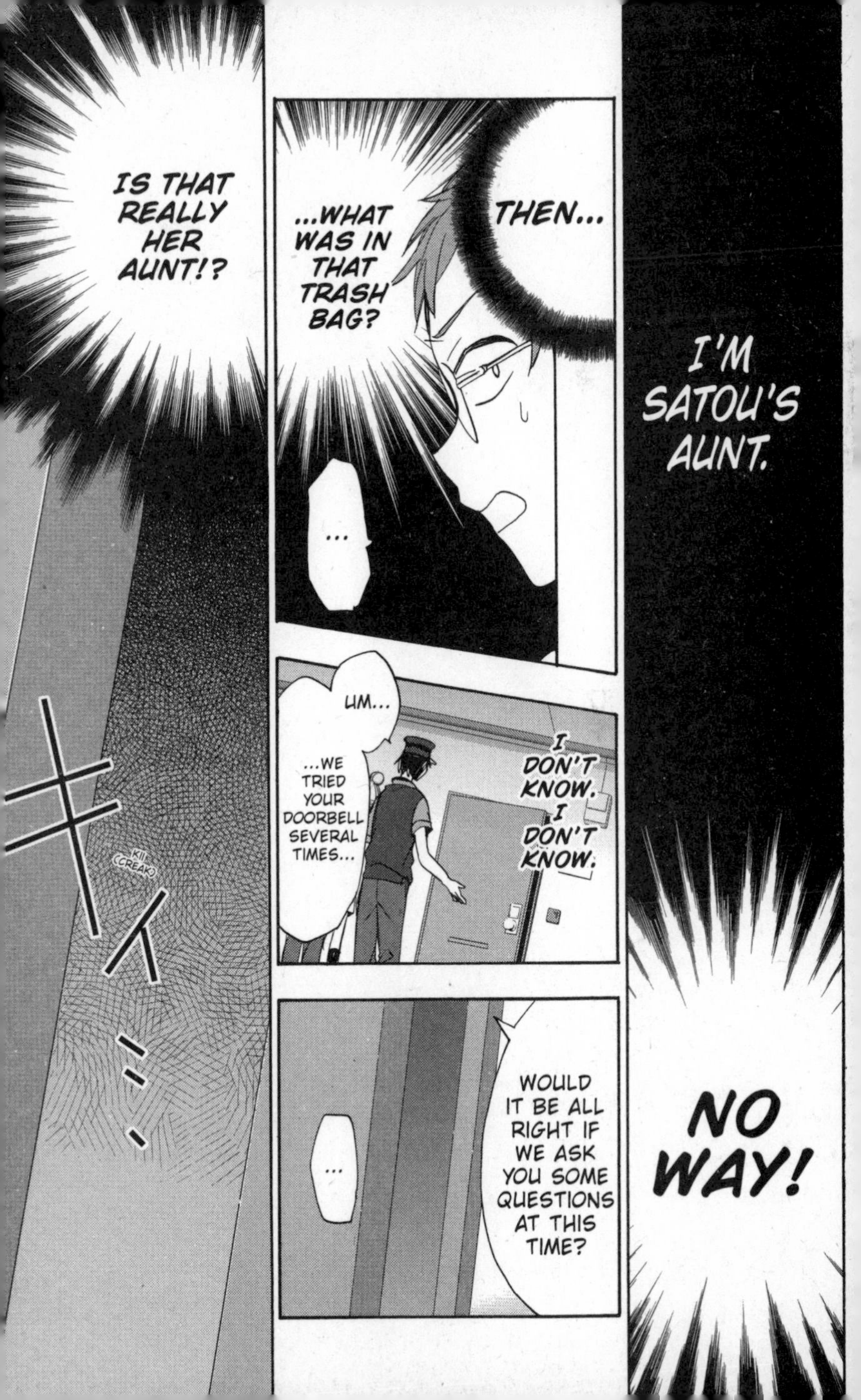
I'M SATOU'S AUNT.
NO WAY!
THEN...
...WHAT WAS IN THAT TRASH BAG?
...
UM...
I DON'T KNOW. I DON'T KNOW.
...WE TRIED YOUR DOORBELL SEVERAL TIMES...
WOULD IT BE ALL RIGHT IF WE ASK YOU SOME QUESTIONS AT THIS TIME?
...
IS THAT REALLY HER AUNT!?
KII (CREAK)

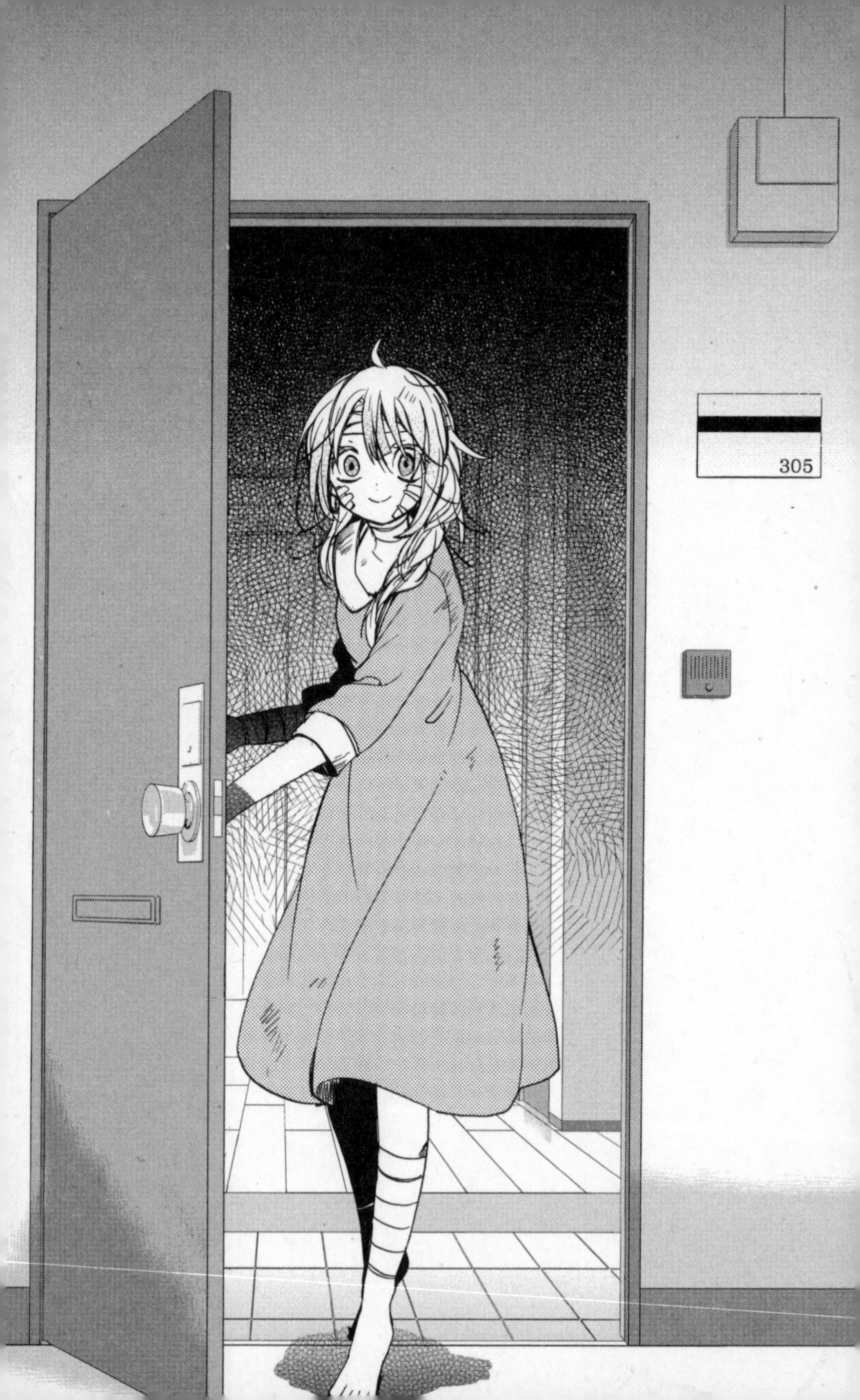
305

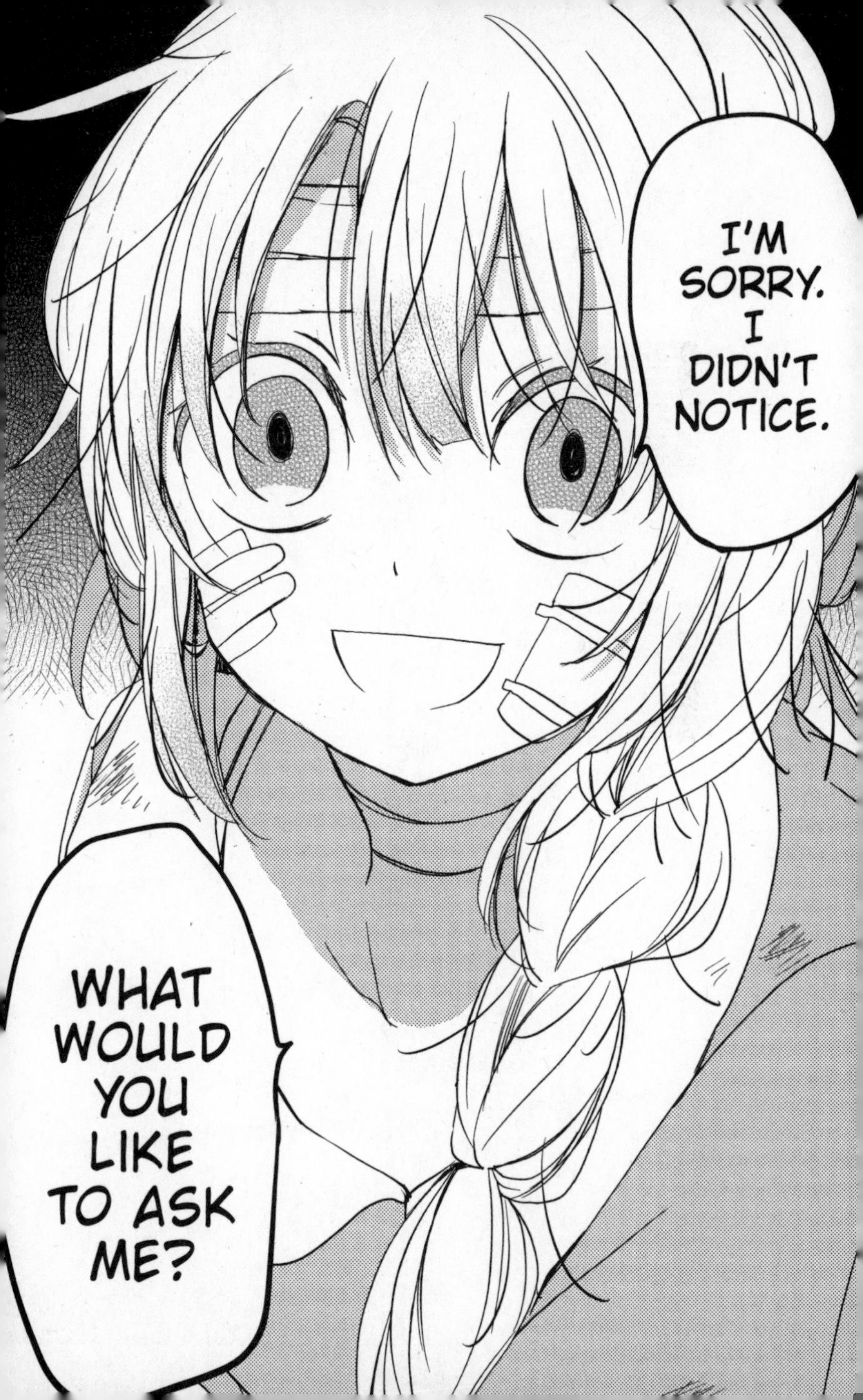
I'M SORRY. I DIDN'T NOTICE.
WHAT WOULD YOU LIKE TO ASK ME?

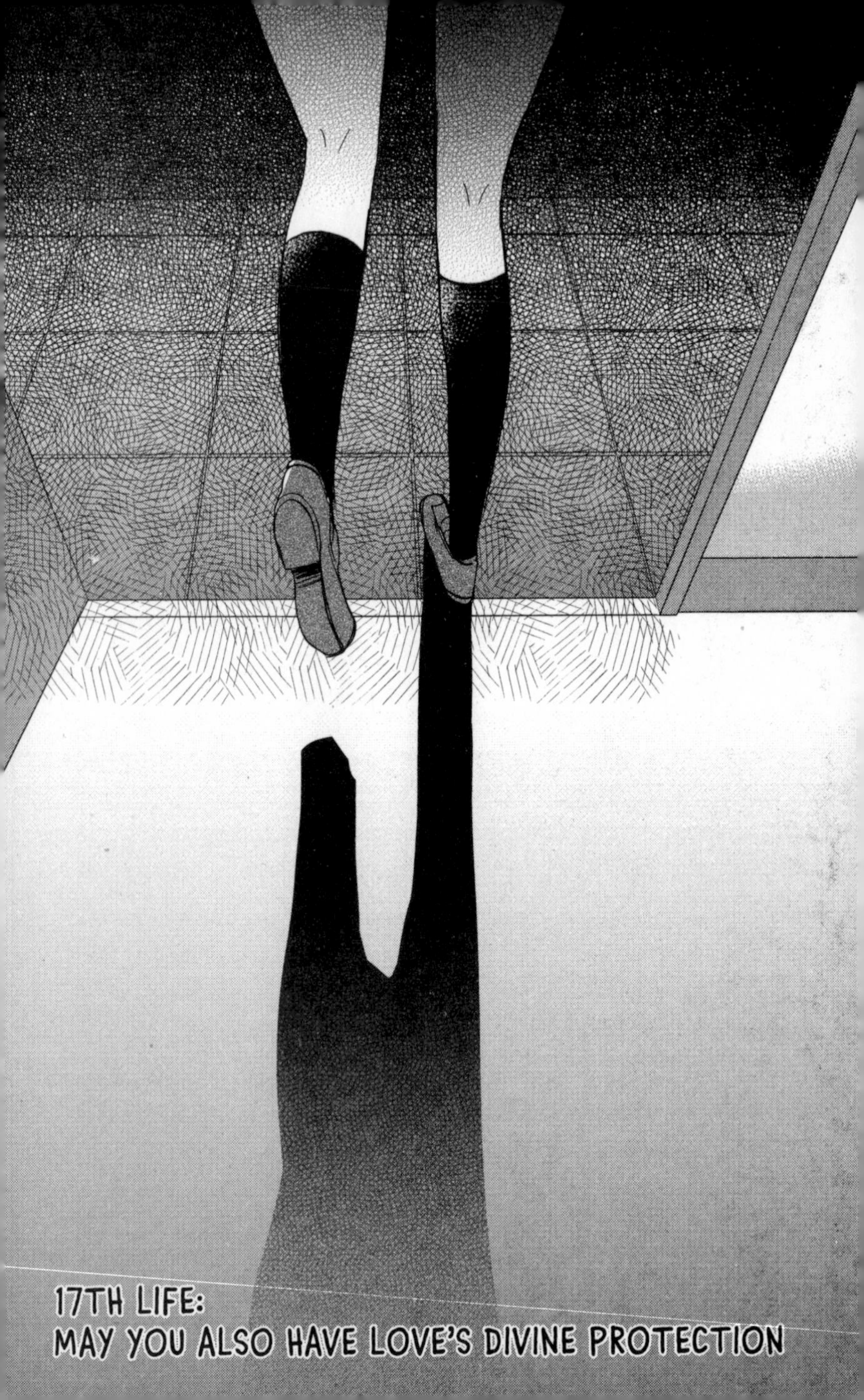

17TH LIFE:
MAY YOU ALSO HAVE LOVE'S DIVINE PROTECTION

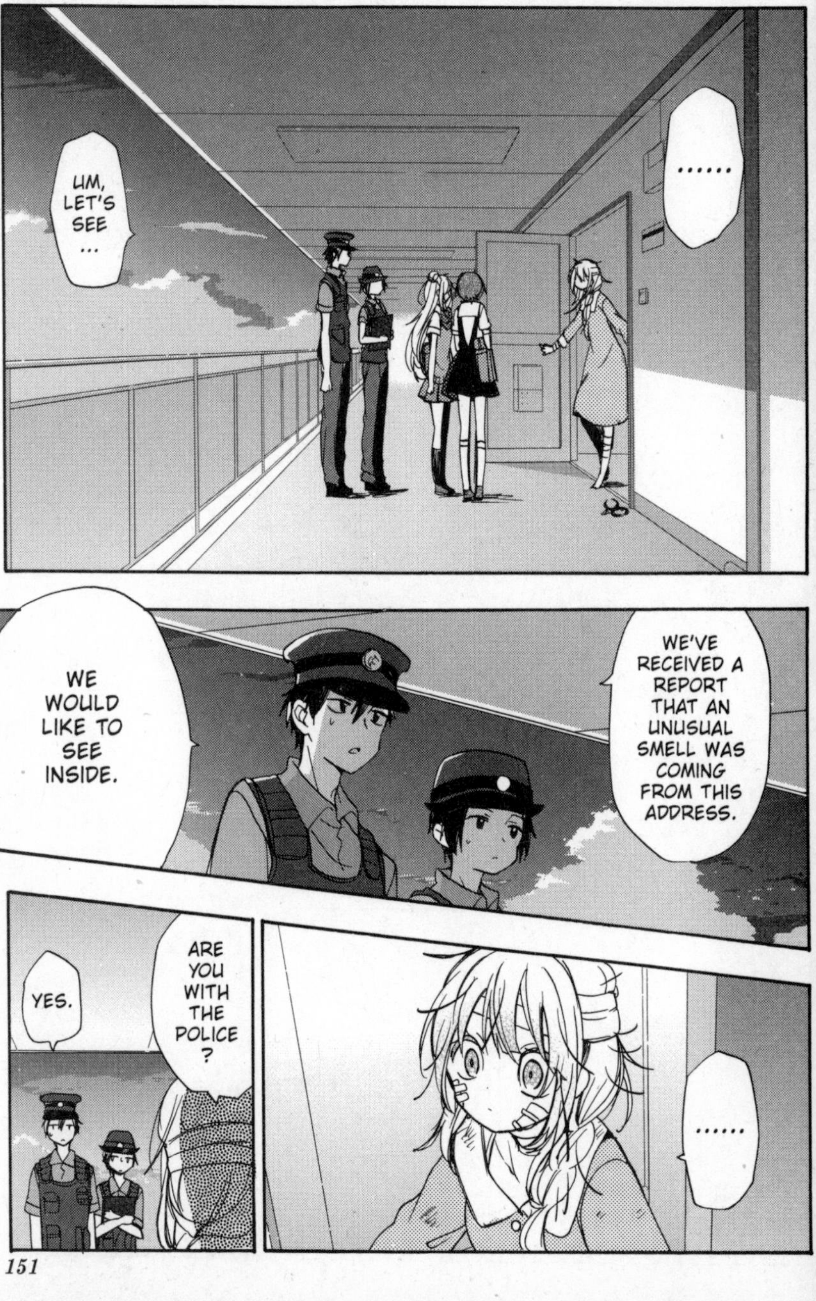
......
UM, LET'S SEE ...
WE'VE RECEIVED A REPORT THAT AN UNUSUAL SMELL WAS COMING FROM THIS ADDRESS.
WE WOULD LIKE TO SEE INSIDE.
......
ARE YOU WITH THE POLICE?
YES.

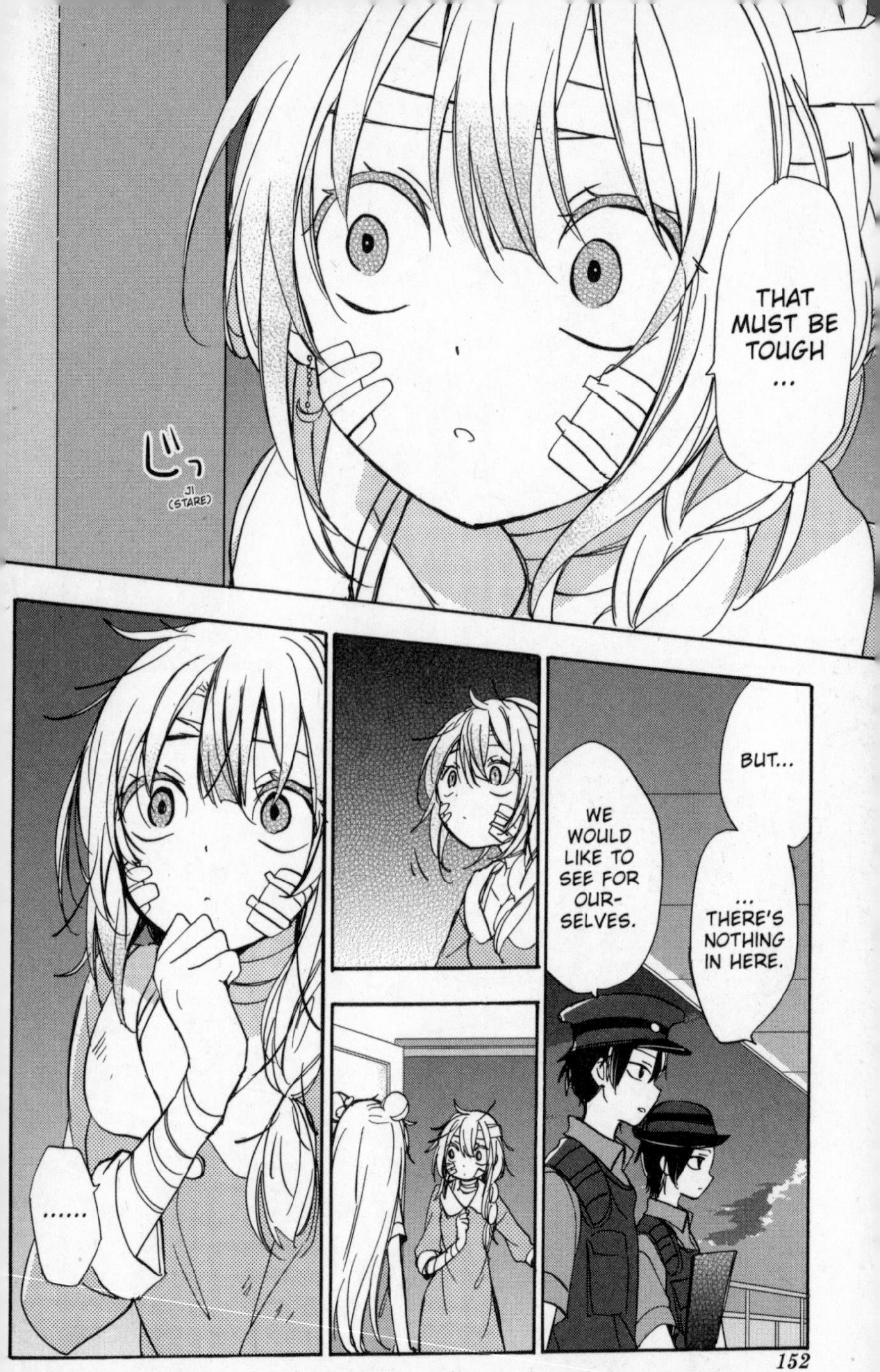
THAT MUST BE TOUGH ...
じっ
JI (STARE)
BUT...
... THERE'S NOTHING IN HERE.
WE WOULD LIKE TO SEE FOR OUR-SELVES.
......

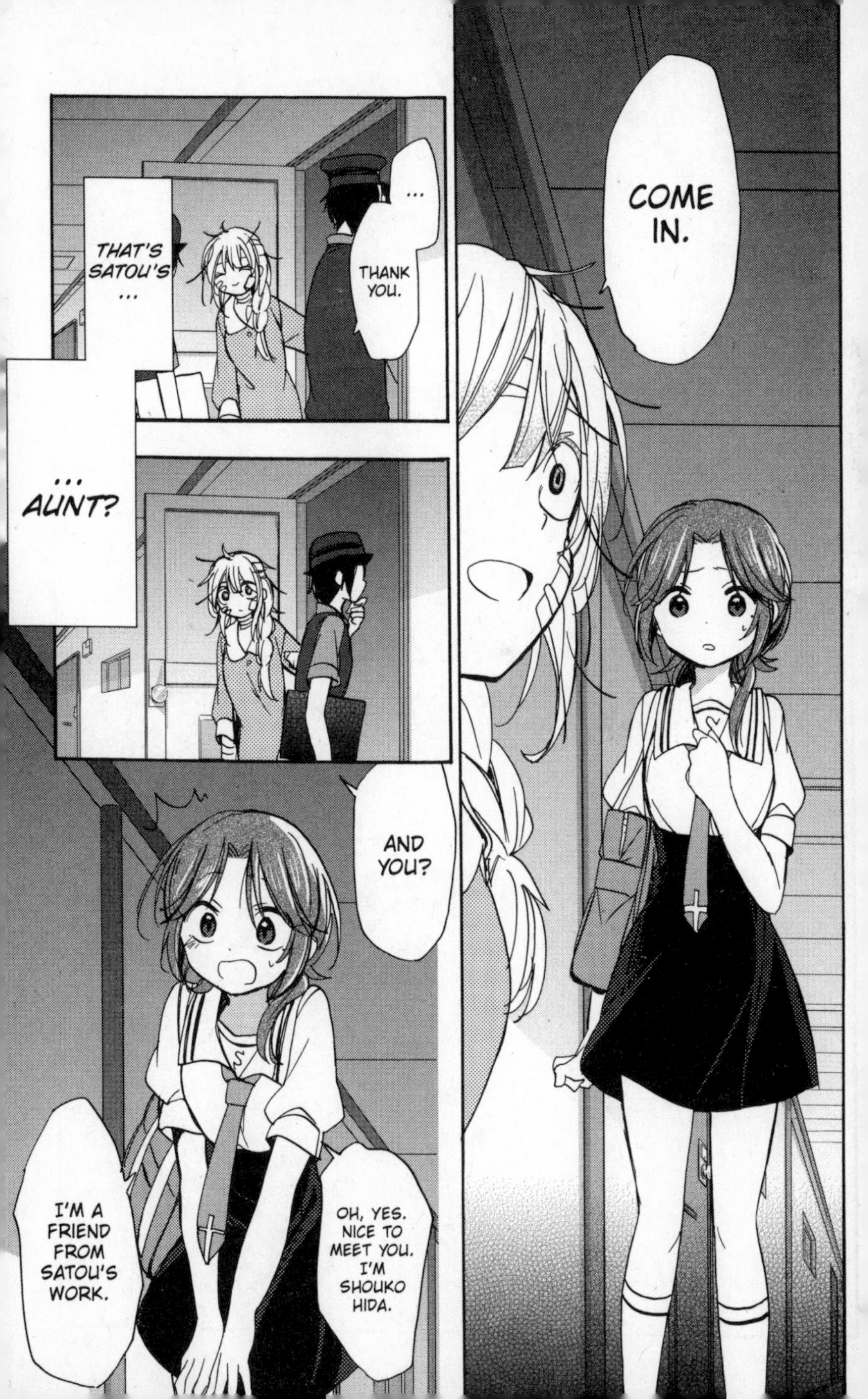
COME IN.
...
THANK YOU.
THAT'S SATOU'S ...
... AUNT?
AND YOU?
OH, YES. NICE TO MEET YOU. I'M SHOUKO HIDA.
I'M A FRIEND FROM SATOU'S WORK.

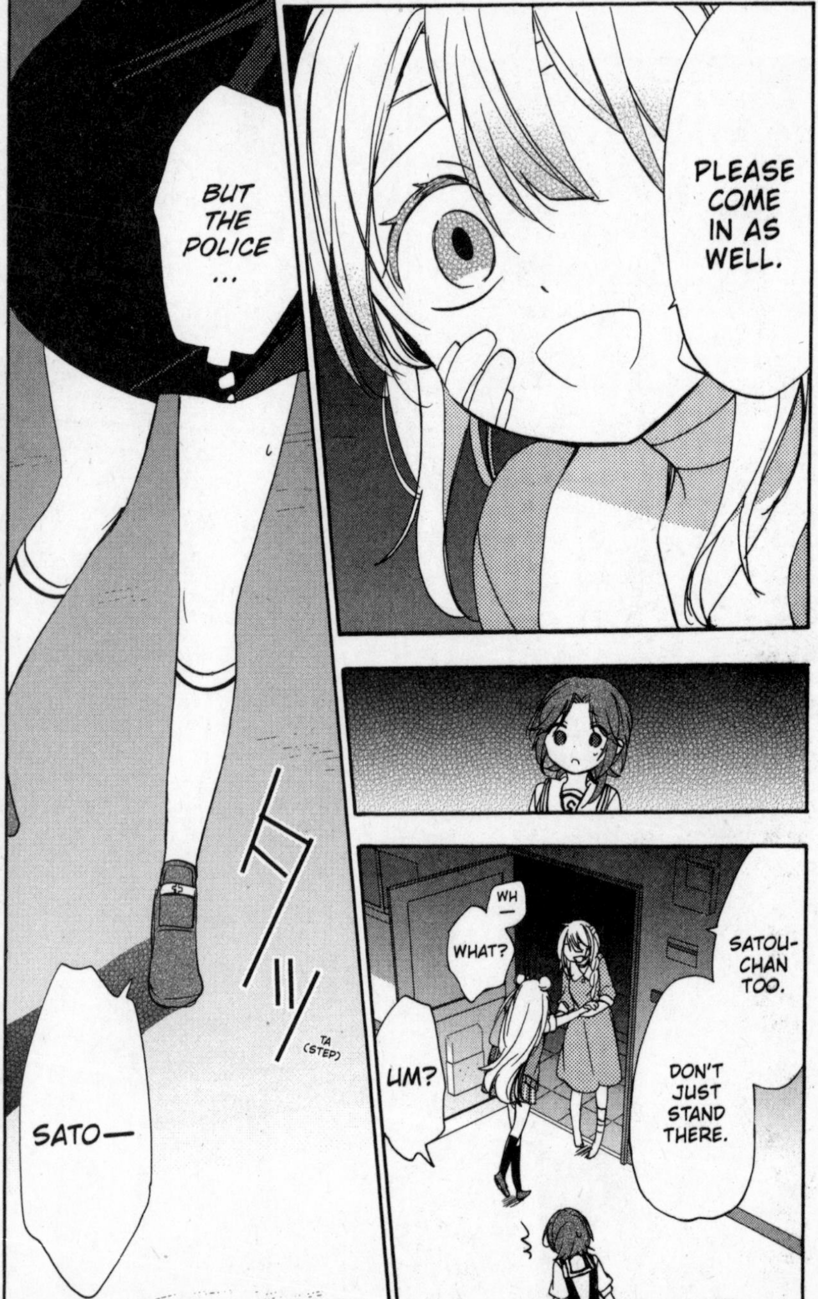
PLEASE COME IN AS WELL.
SATOU-CHAN TOO.
DON'T JUST STAND THERE.
WH— WHAT?
UM?
BUT THE POLICE ...
TA (STEP)
SATO—

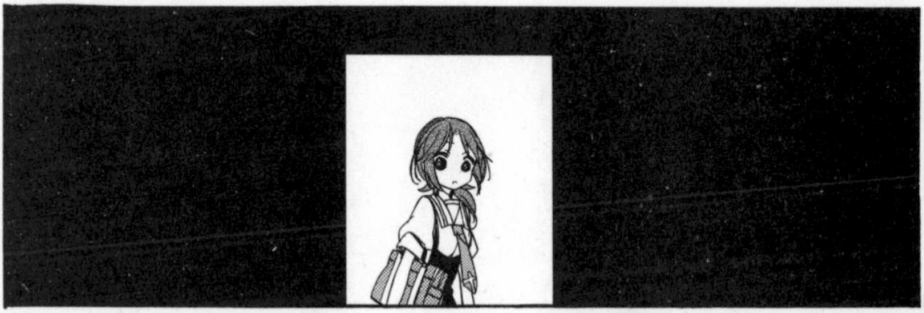
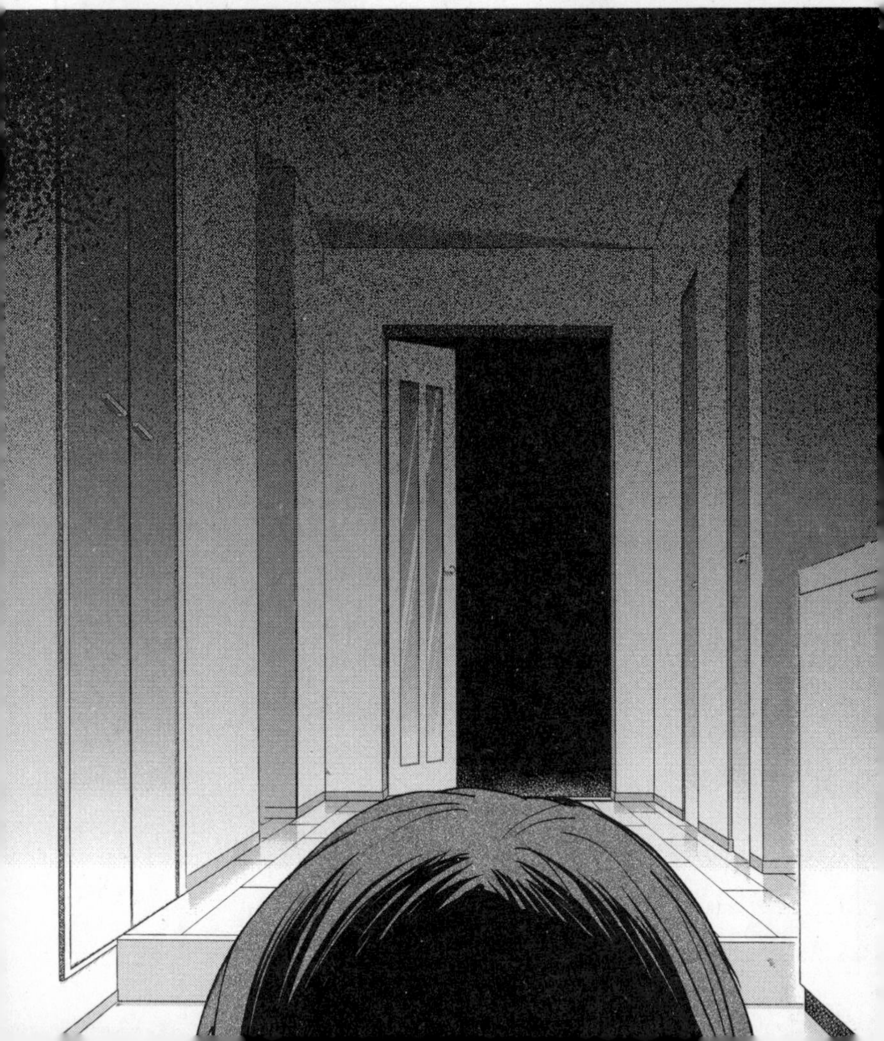

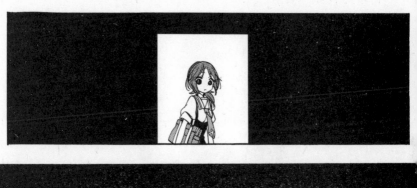

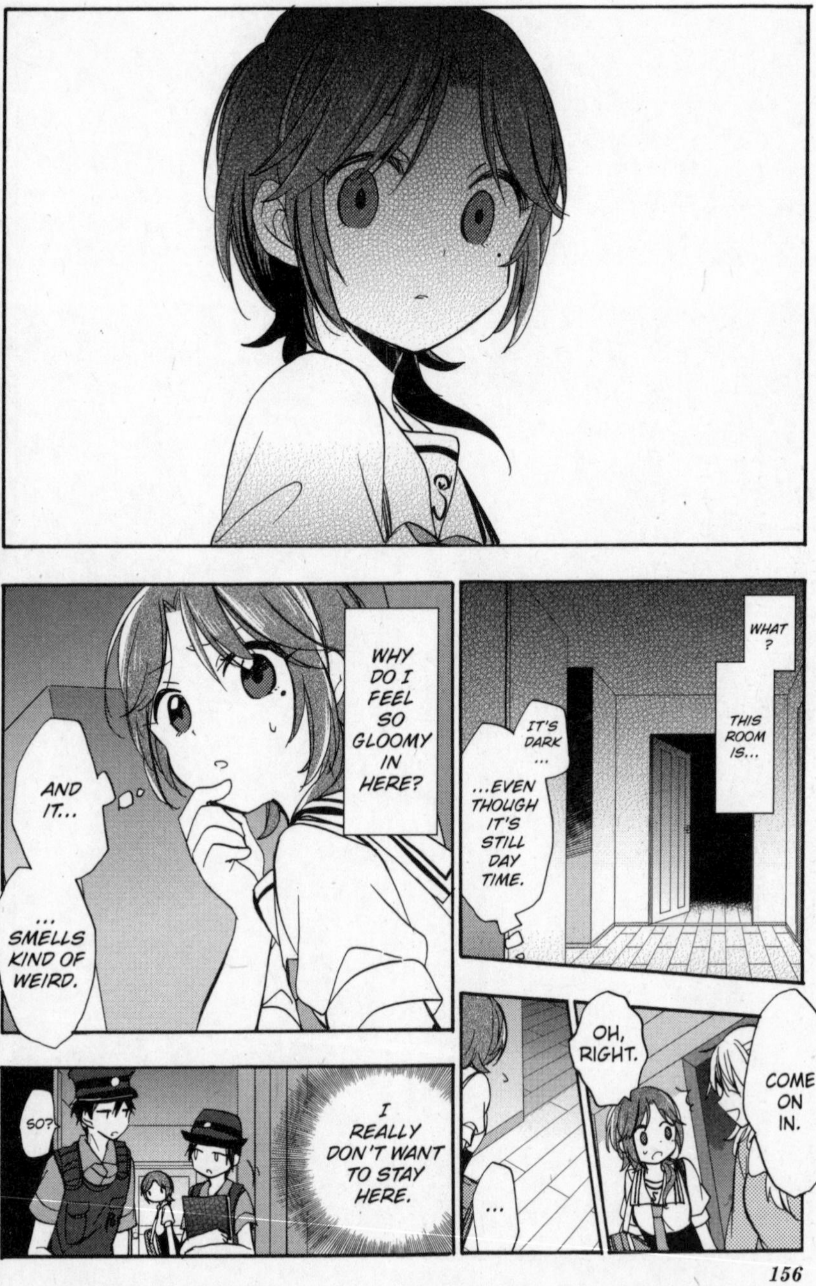
WHAT?
THIS ROOM IS...
IT'S DARK...
...EVEN THOUGH IT'S STILL DAY TIME.
WHY DO I FEEL SO GLOOMY IN HERE?
AND IT...
...SMELLS KIND OF WEIRD.
COME ON IN.
OH, RIGHT.
...
SO?
I REALLY DON'T WANT TO STAY HERE.

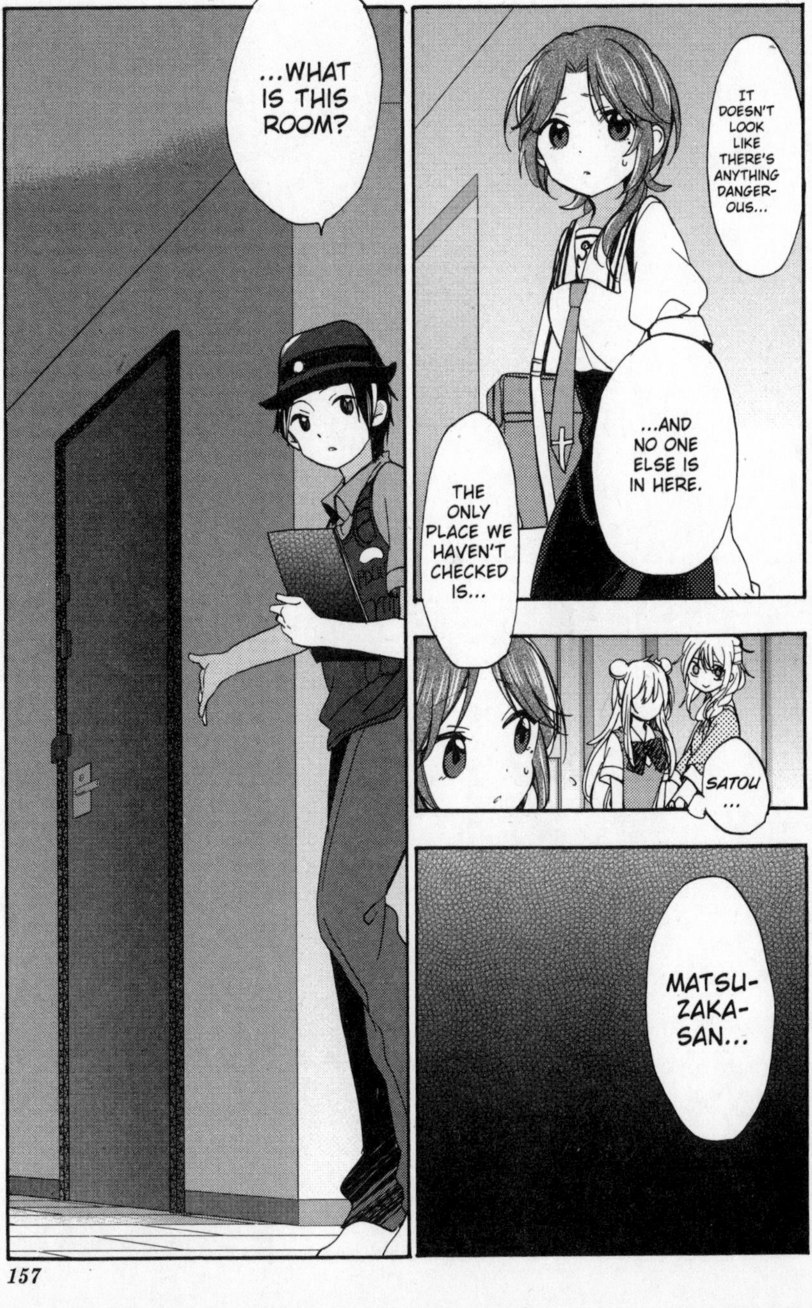
IT DOESN'T LOOK LIKE THERE'S ANYTHING DANGER-OUS...
...AND NO ONE ELSE IS IN HERE.
THE ONLY PLACE WE HAVEN'T CHECKED IS...
SATOU...
MATSU-ZAKA-SAN...
...WHAT IS THIS ROOM?

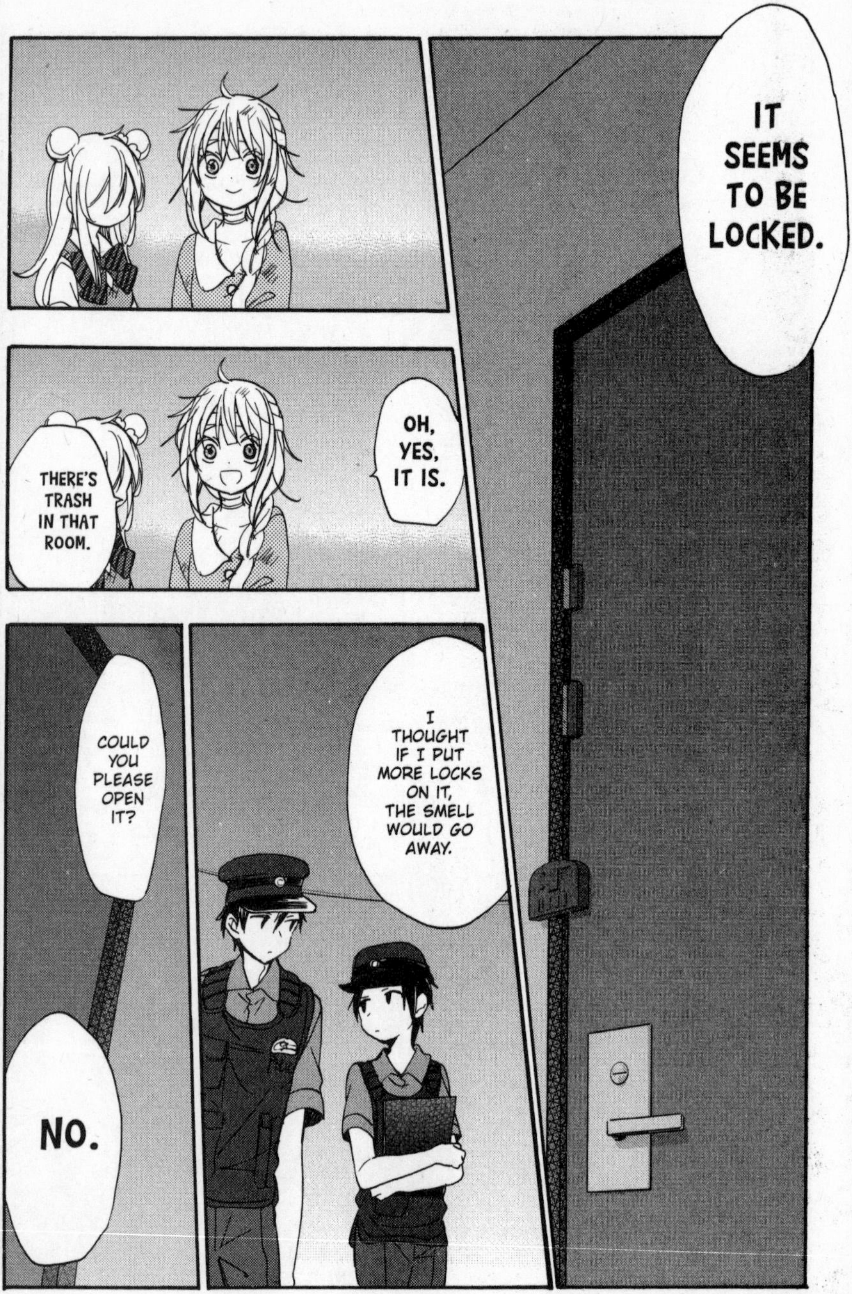
IT SEEMS TO BE LOCKED.
OH, YES, IT IS.
THERE'S TRASH IN THAT ROOM.
I THOUGHT IF I PUT MORE LOCKS ON IT, THE SMELL WOULD GO AWAY.
COULD YOU PLEASE OPEN IT?
NO.

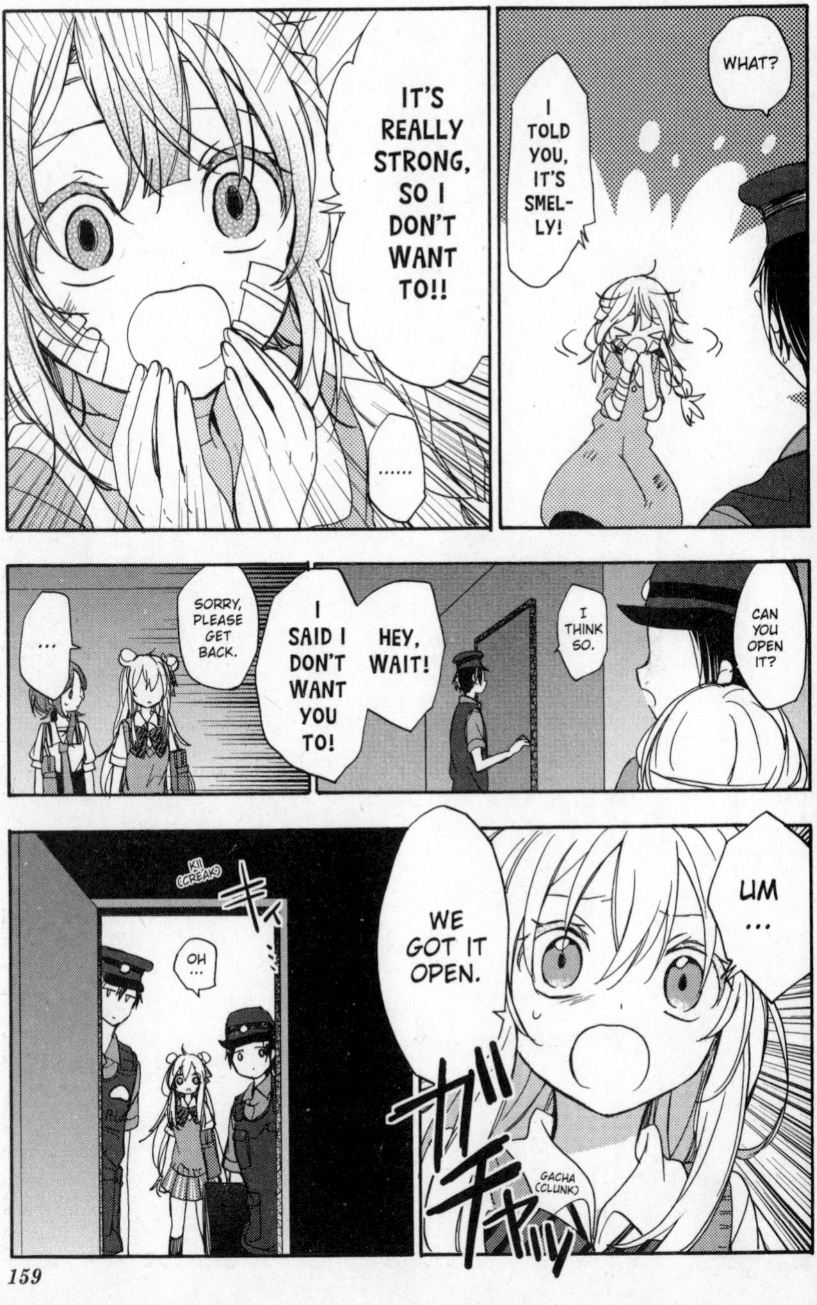
WHAT?
I TOLD YOU, IT'S SMEL-LY!
IT'S REALLY STRONG, SO I DON'T WANT TO!!
......
CAN YOU OPEN IT?
I THINK SO.
HEY, WAIT!
I SAID I DON'T WANT YOU TO!
SORRY, PLEASE GET BACK.
...
UM ...
WE GOT IT OPEN.
GACHA (CLUNK)
KII (CREAK)
OH ...

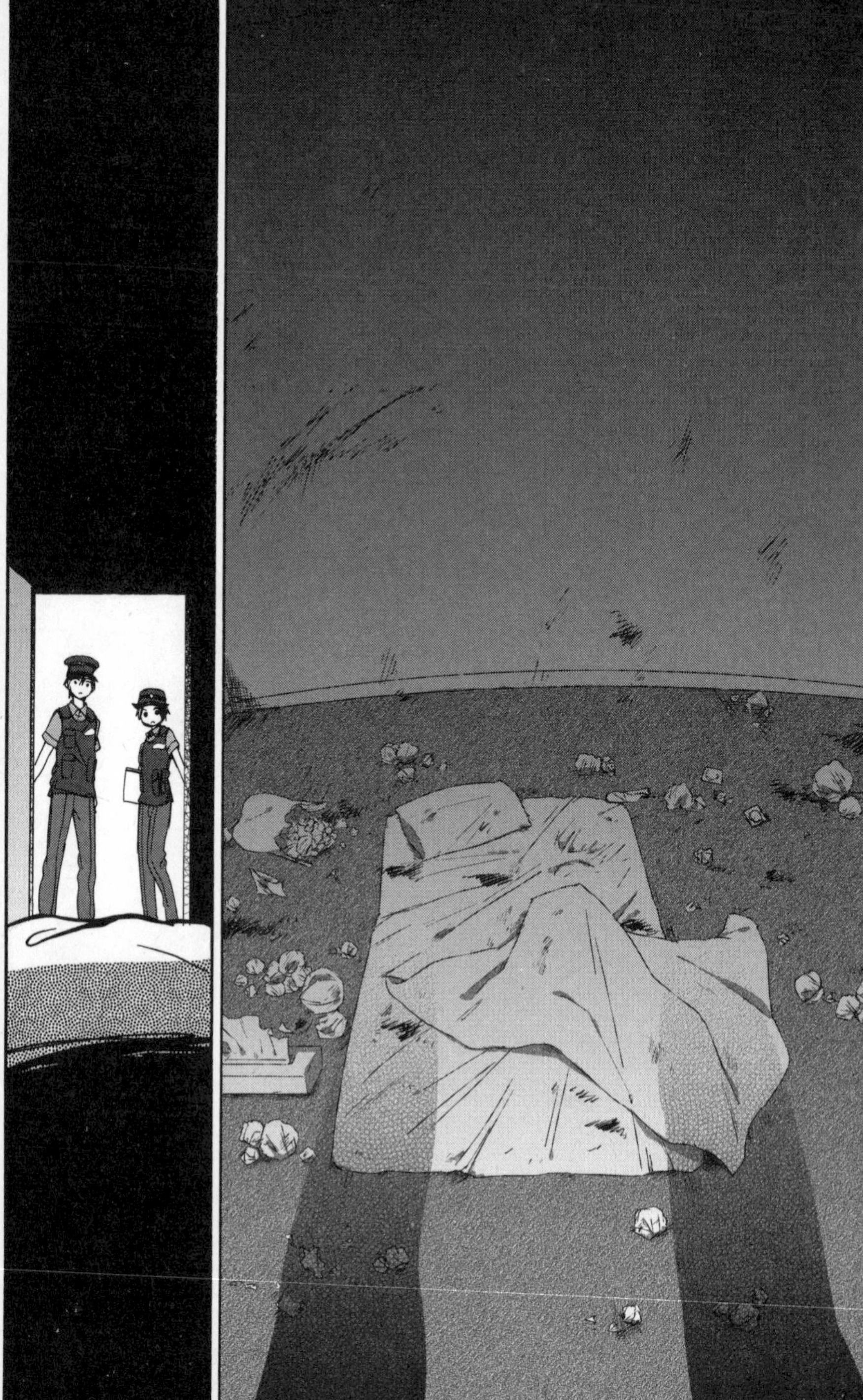

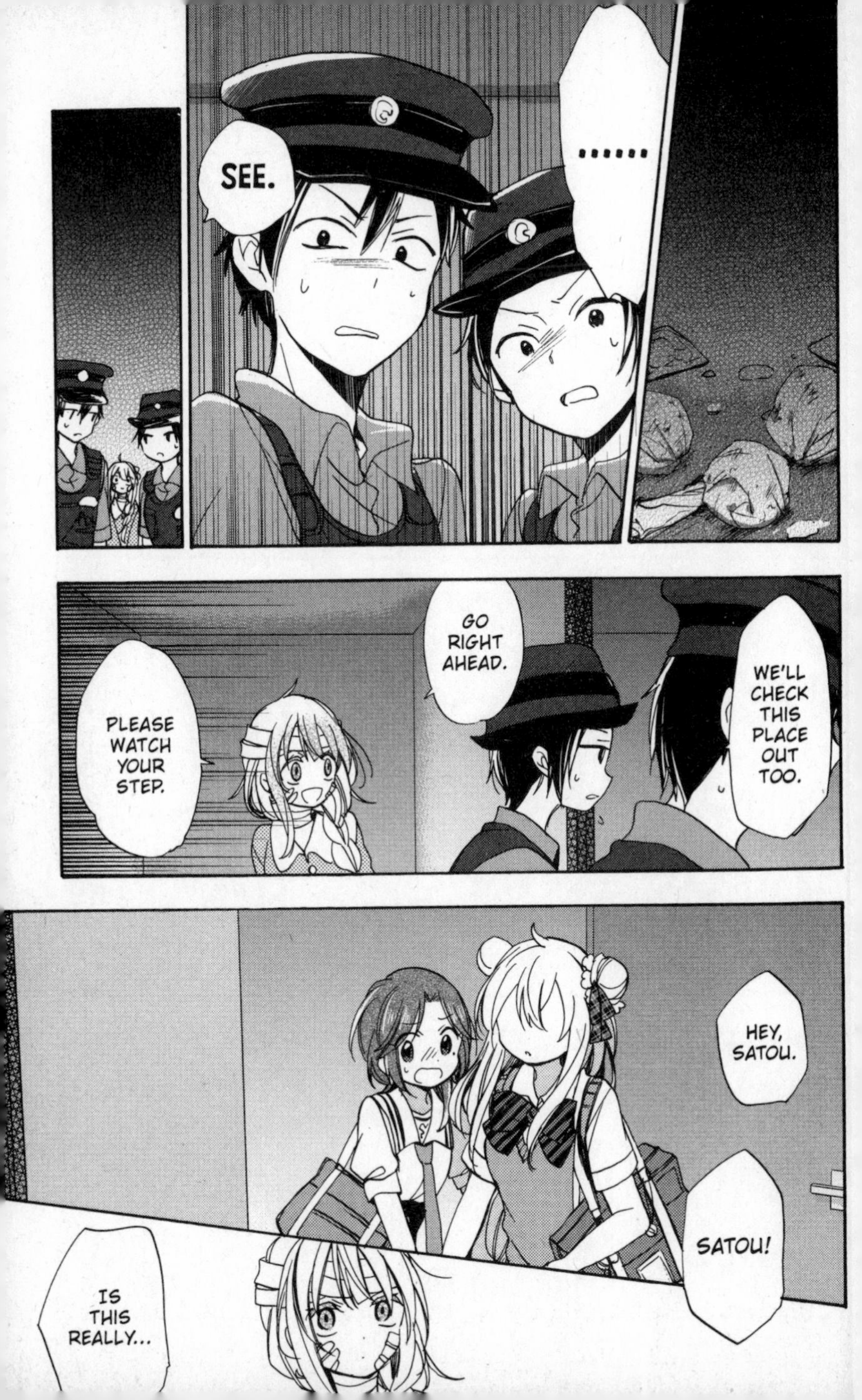
......
SEE.
WE'LL CHECK THIS PLACE OUT TOO.
GO RIGHT AHEAD.
PLEASE WATCH YOUR STEP.
HEY, SATOU.
SATOU!
IS THIS REALLY...

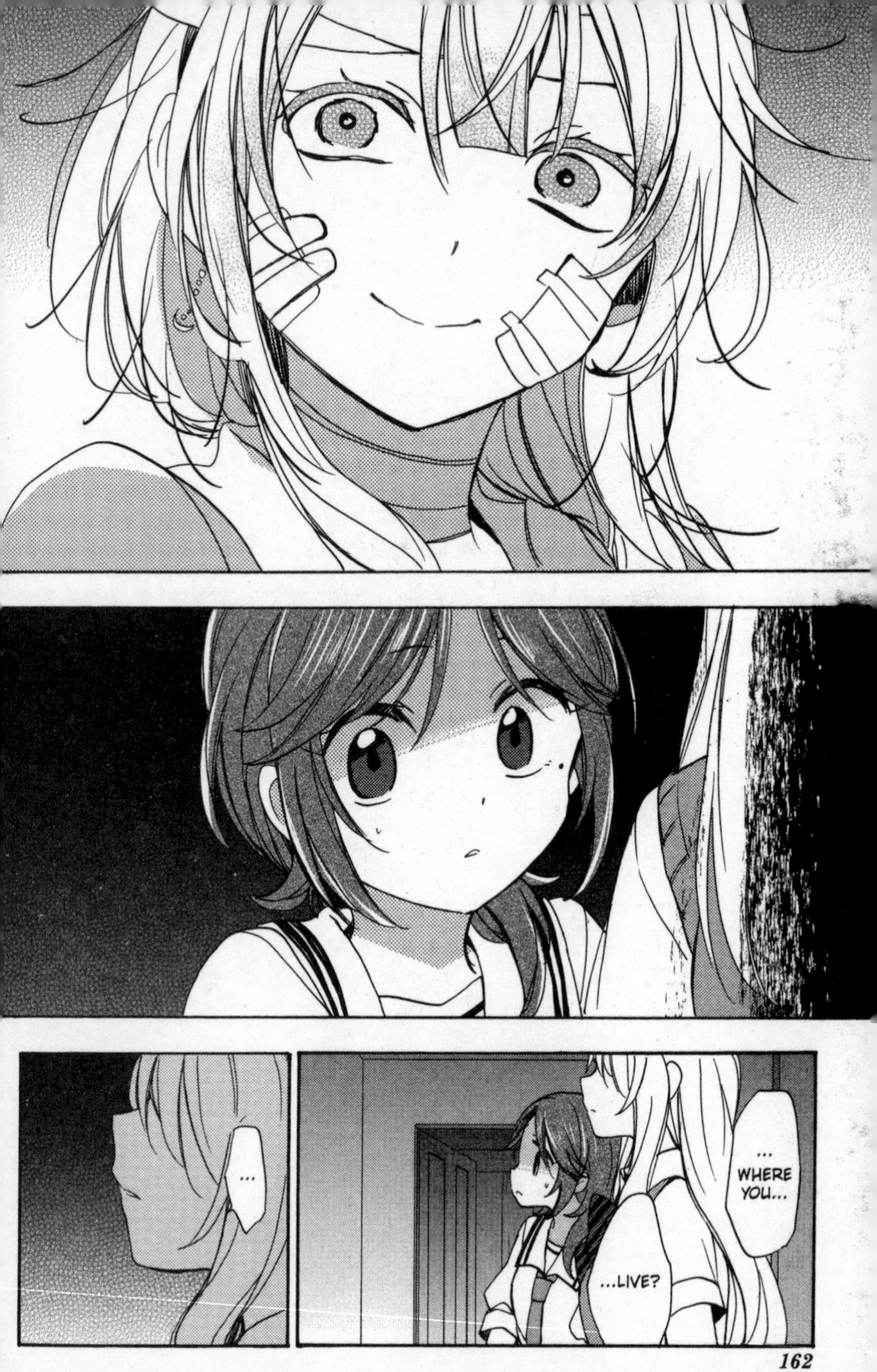
...
WHERE
YOU...
...LIVE?
...

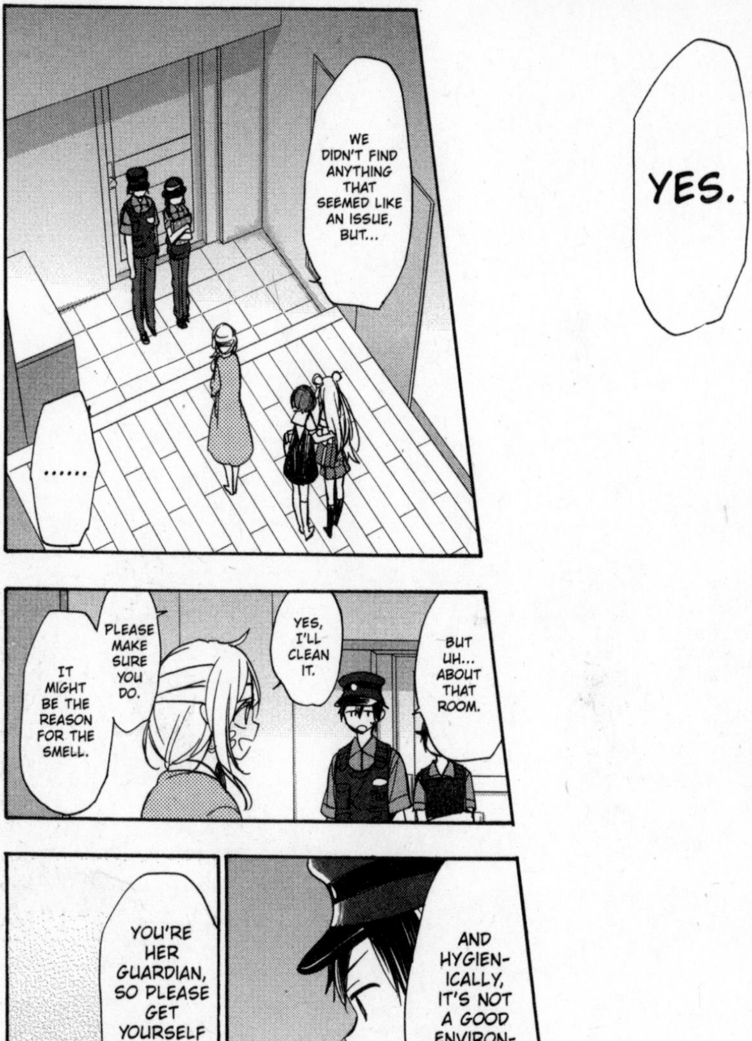
YES.
WE DIDN'T FIND ANYTHING THAT SEEMED LIKE AN ISSUE, BUT...
......
BUT UH... ABOUT THAT ROOM.
YES, I'LL CLEAN IT.
PLEASE MAKE SURE YOU DO.
IT MIGHT BE THE REASON FOR THE SMELL.
AND HYGIEN-ICALLY, IT'S NOT A GOOD ENVIRON-MENT FOR A CHILD.
YOU'RE HER GUARDIAN, SO PLEASE GET YOURSELF TOGETHER.
HA HA.

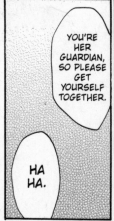

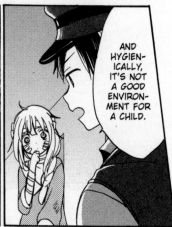

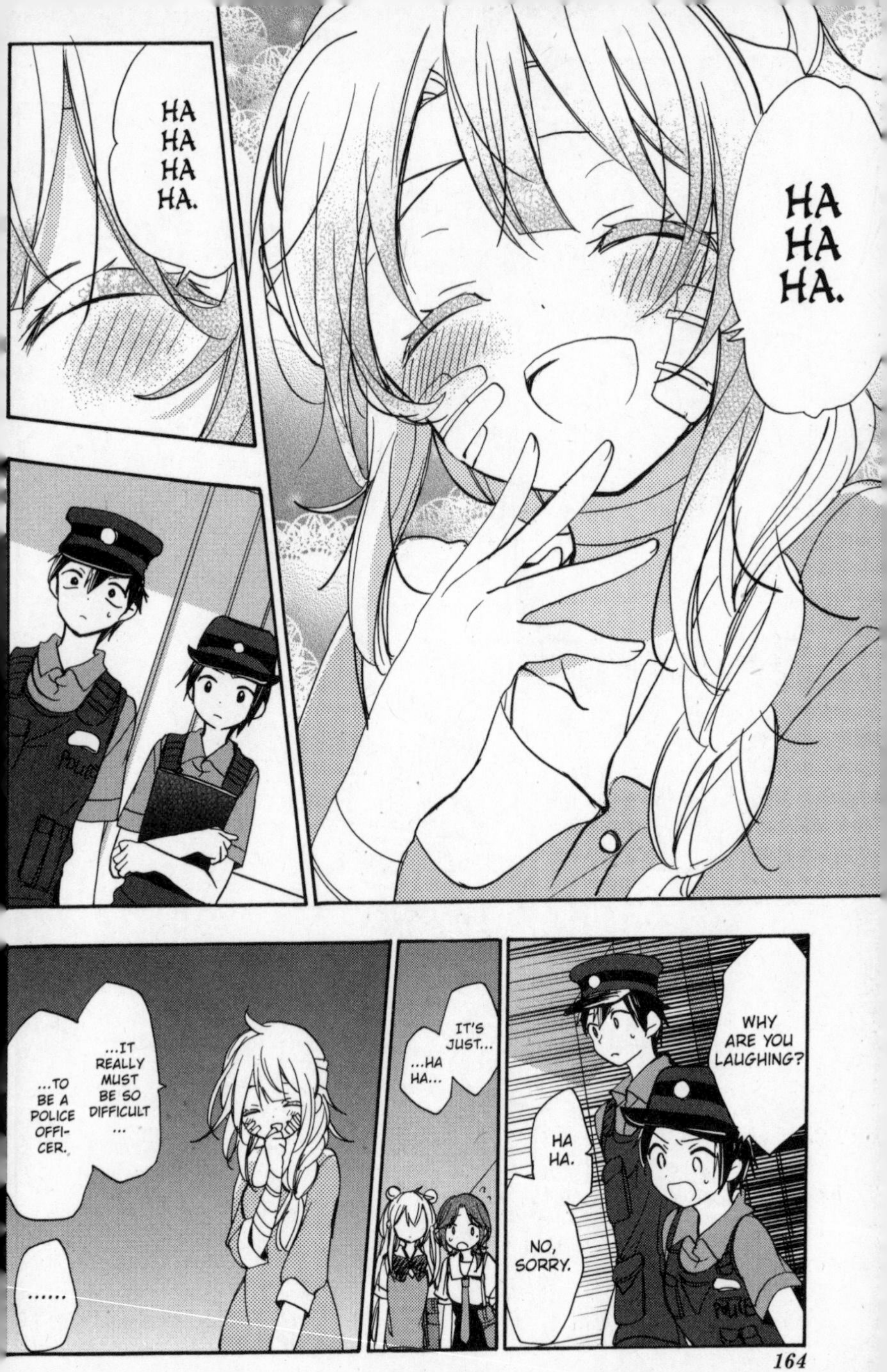
HA HA HA.
HA HA HA HA.
WHY ARE YOU LAUGHING?
HA HA.
NO, SORRY.
IT'S JUST...
...HA HA...
...IT REALLY MUST BE SO DIFFICULT ...
...TO BE A POLICE OFFICER.
......

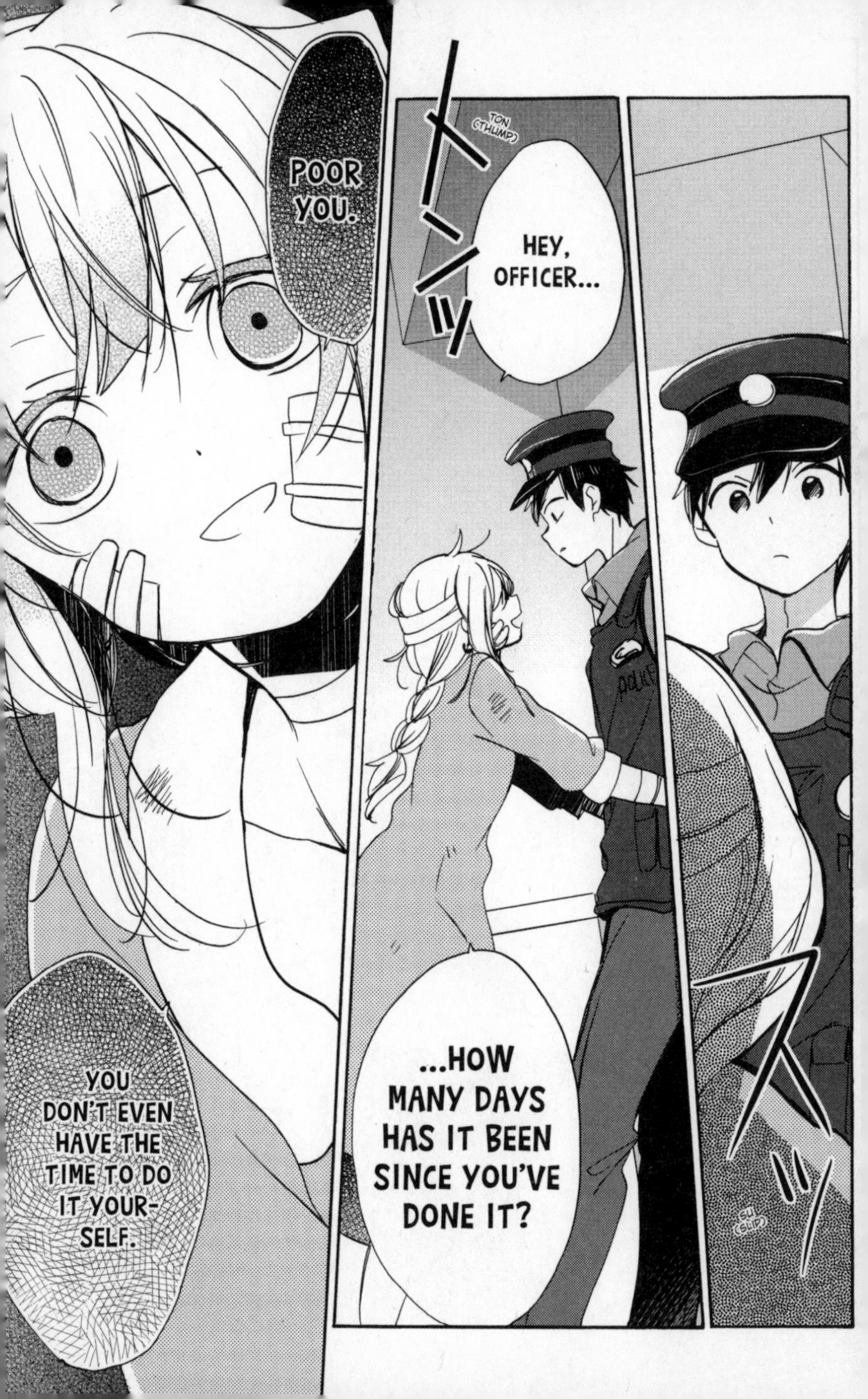
SU (SLIP)
TON (THUMP)
HEY, OFFICER...
...HOW MANY DAYS HAS IT BEEN SINCE YOU'VE DONE IT?
POOR YOU.
YOU DON'T EVEN HAVE THE TIME TO DO IT YOURSELF.

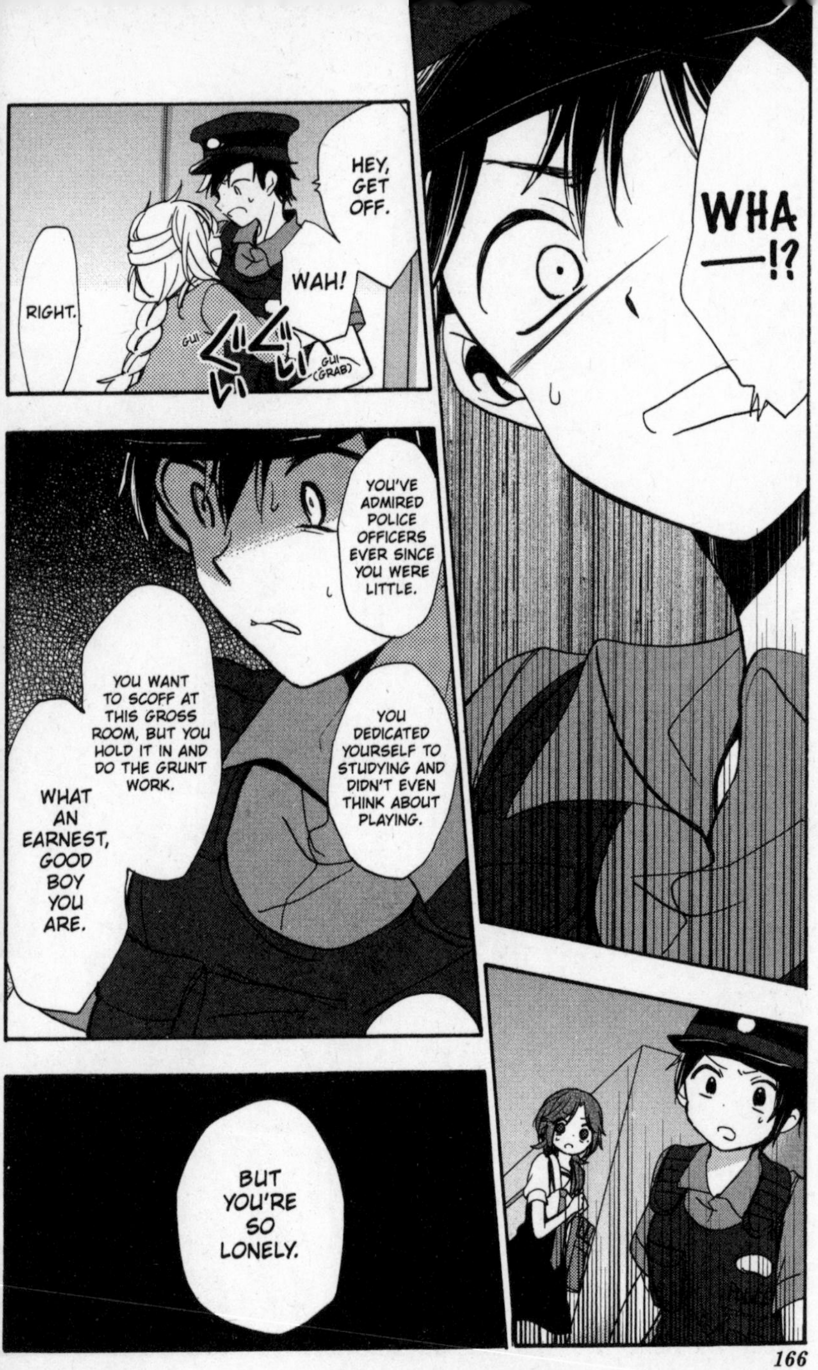
WHA—!?
HEY, GET OFF.
WAH!
GUI
GUI (GRAB)
RIGHT.
YOU'VE ADMIRED POLICE OFFICERS EVER SINCE YOU WERE LITTLE.
YOU DEDICATED YOURSELF TO STUDYING AND DIDN'T EVEN THINK ABOUT PLAYING.
YOU WANT TO SCOFF AT THIS GROSS ROOM, BUT YOU HOLD IT IN AND DO THE GRUNT WORK.
WHAT AN EARNEST, GOOD BOY YOU ARE.
BUT YOU'RE SO LONELY.

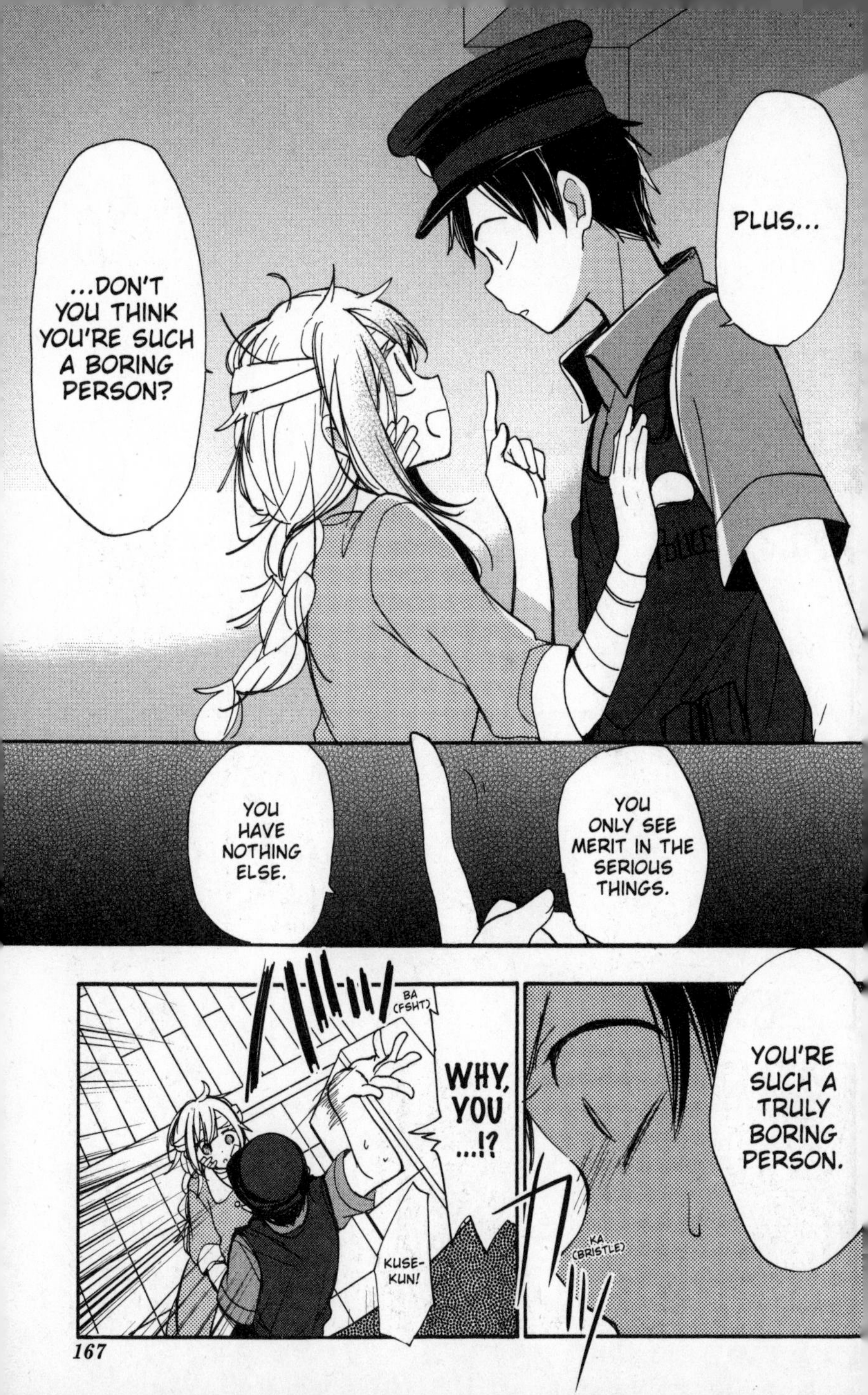
PLUS...
...DON'T YOU THINK YOU'RE SUCH A BORING PERSON?
YOU ONLY SEE MERIT IN THE SERIOUS THINGS.
YOU HAVE NOTHING ELSE.
YOU'RE SUCH A TRULY BORING PERSON.
KA (BRISTLE)
BA (FSHT)
WHY, YOU ...!?
KUSE-KUN!

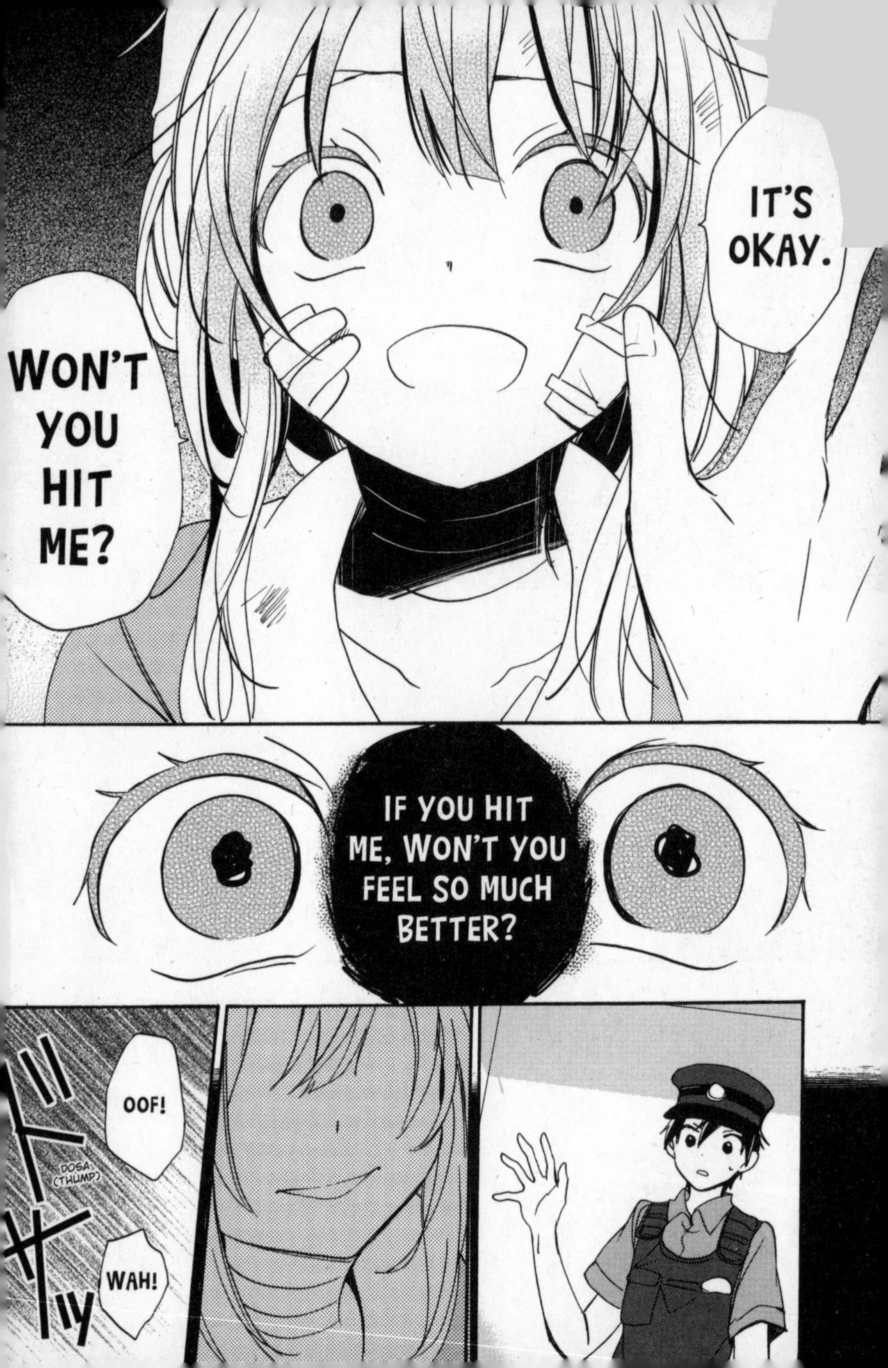
IT'S OKAY.
WON'T YOU HIT ME?
IF YOU HIT ME, WON'T YOU FEEL SO MUCH BETTER?
OOF!
DOSA (THUMP)
WAH!

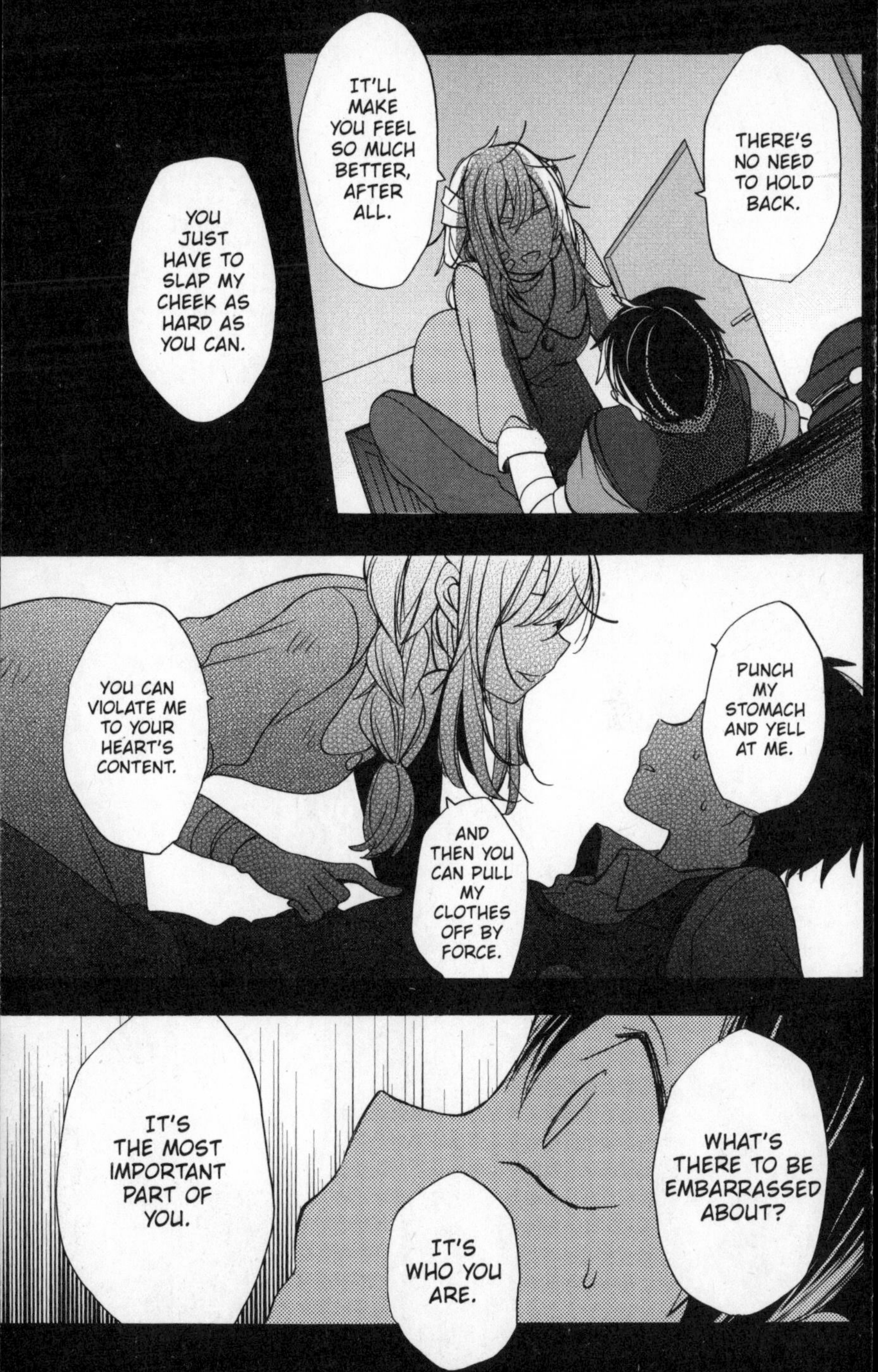
THERE'S NO NEED TO HOLD BACK.
IT'LL MAKE YOU FEEL SO MUCH BETTER, AFTER ALL.
YOU JUST HAVE TO SLAP MY CHEEK AS HARD AS YOU CAN.
PUNCH MY STOMACH AND YELL AT ME.
AND THEN YOU CAN PULL MY CLOTHES OFF BY FORCE.
YOU CAN VIOLATE ME TO YOUR HEART'S CONTENT.
WHAT'S THERE TO BE EMBARRASSED ABOUT?
IT'S WHO YOU ARE.
IT'S THE MOST IMPORTANT PART OF YOU.

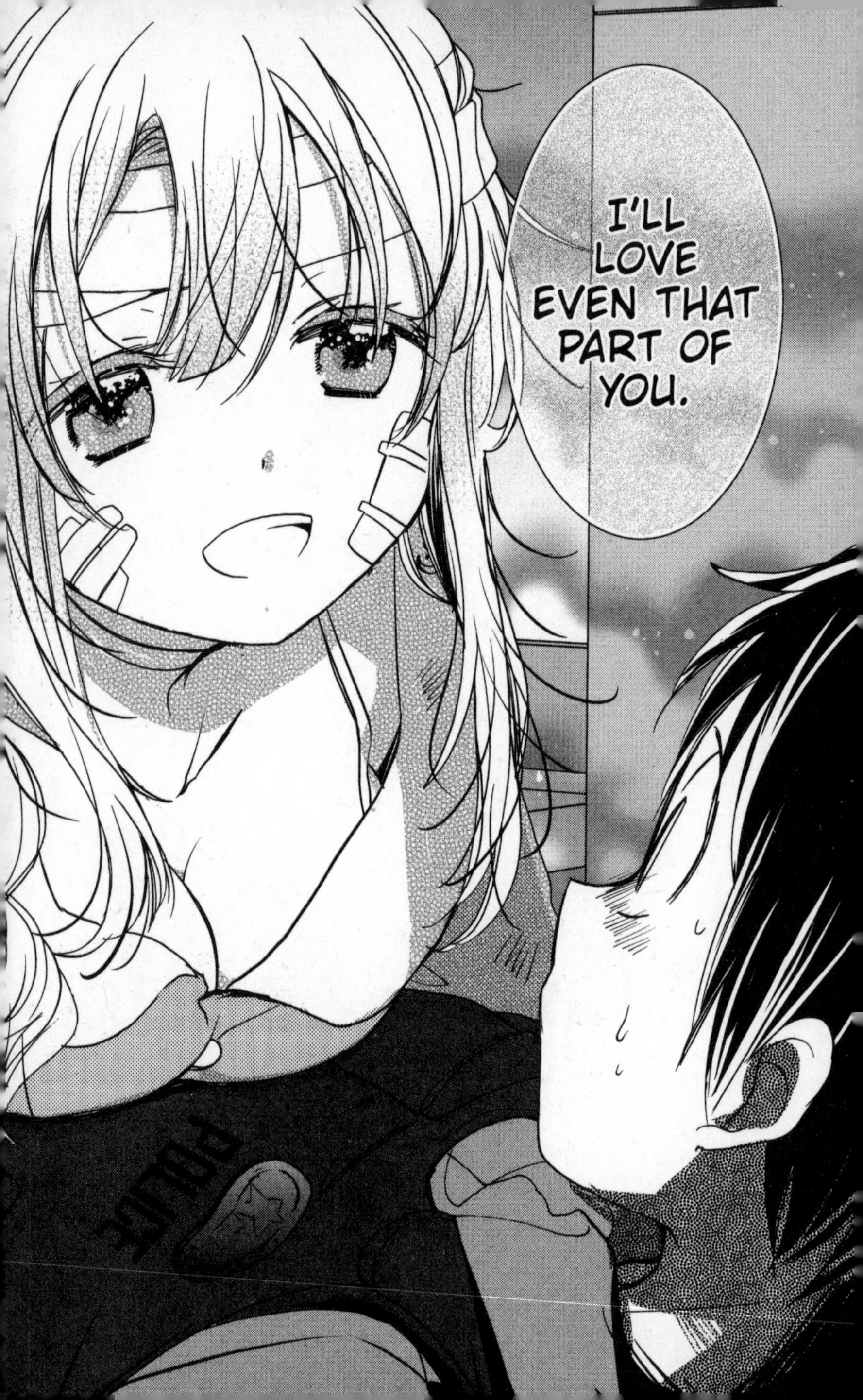
I'LL LOVE EVEN THAT PART OF YOU.

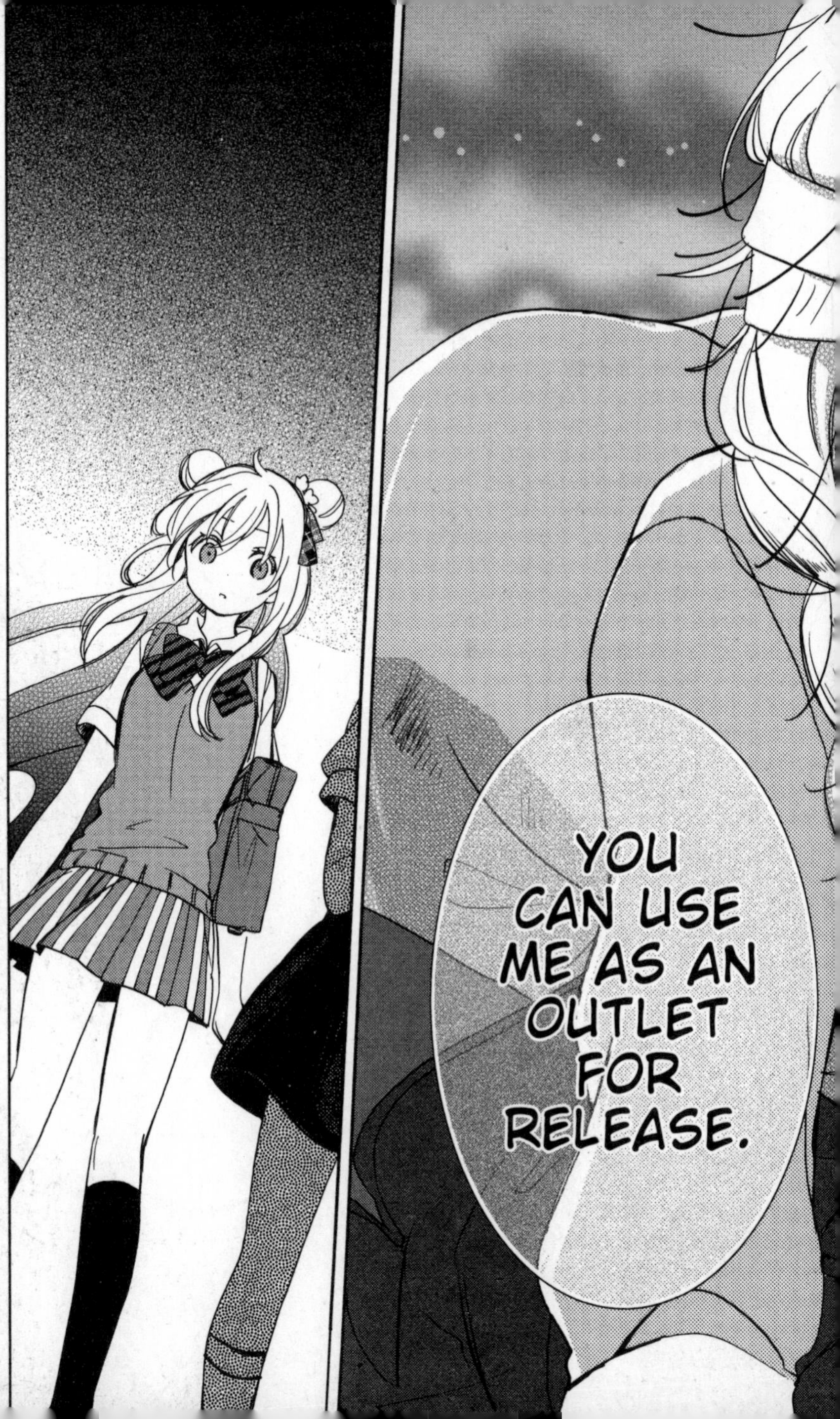
YOU CAN USE ME AS AN OUTLET FOR RELEASE.

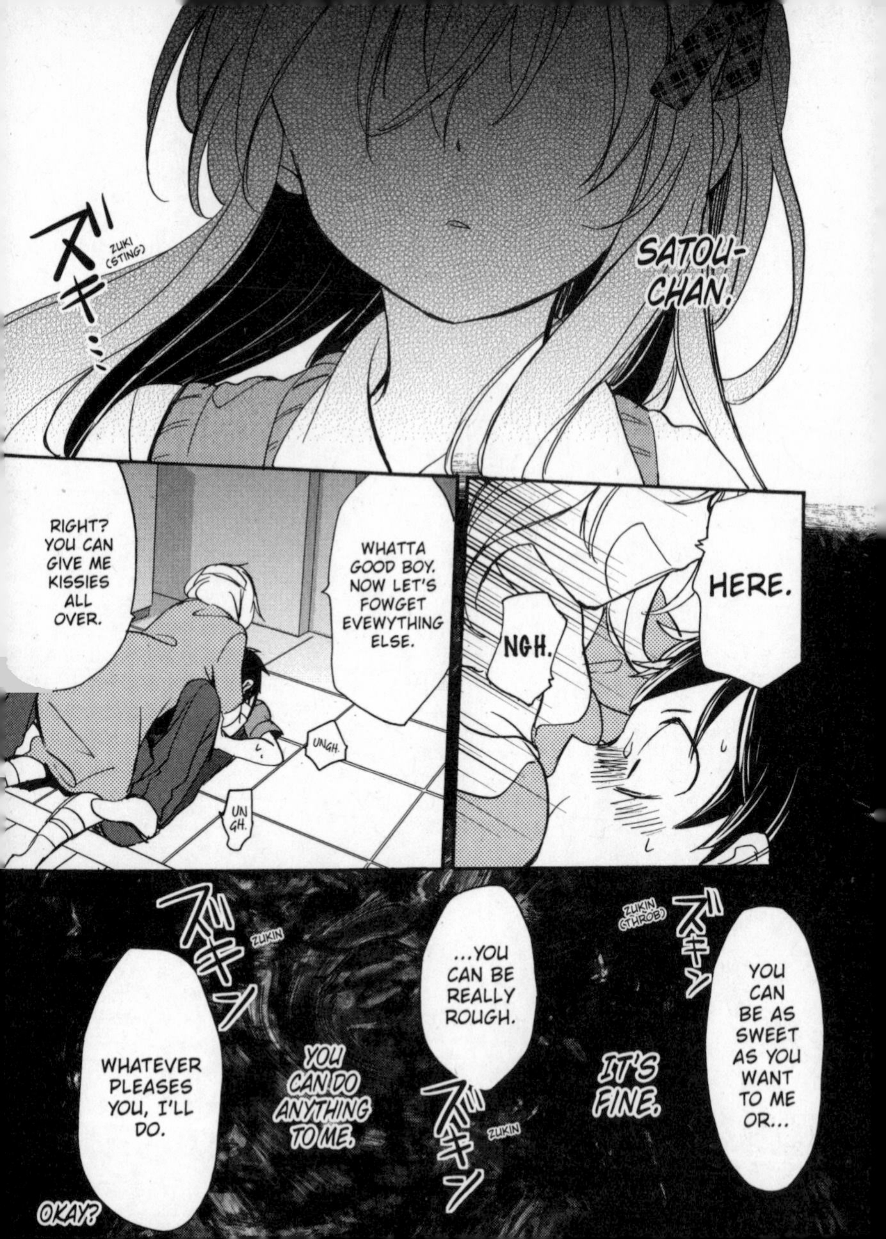
SATOU-CHAN.
ズキ…
ZUKI (STING)
HERE.
NGH.
WHATTA GOOD BOY. NOW LET'S FOWGET EVEWYTHING ELSE.
RIGHT? YOU CAN GIVE ME KISSIES ALL OVER.
UNGH.
UN GH.
ズキン
ZUKIN (THROB)
YOU CAN BE AS SWEET AS YOU WANT TO ME OR...
IT'S FINE.
...YOU CAN BE REALLY ROUGH.
ズキン
ZUKIN
YOU CAN DO ANYTHING TO ME.
ズキン
ZUKIN
WHATEVER PLEASES YOU, I'LL DO.
OKAY?

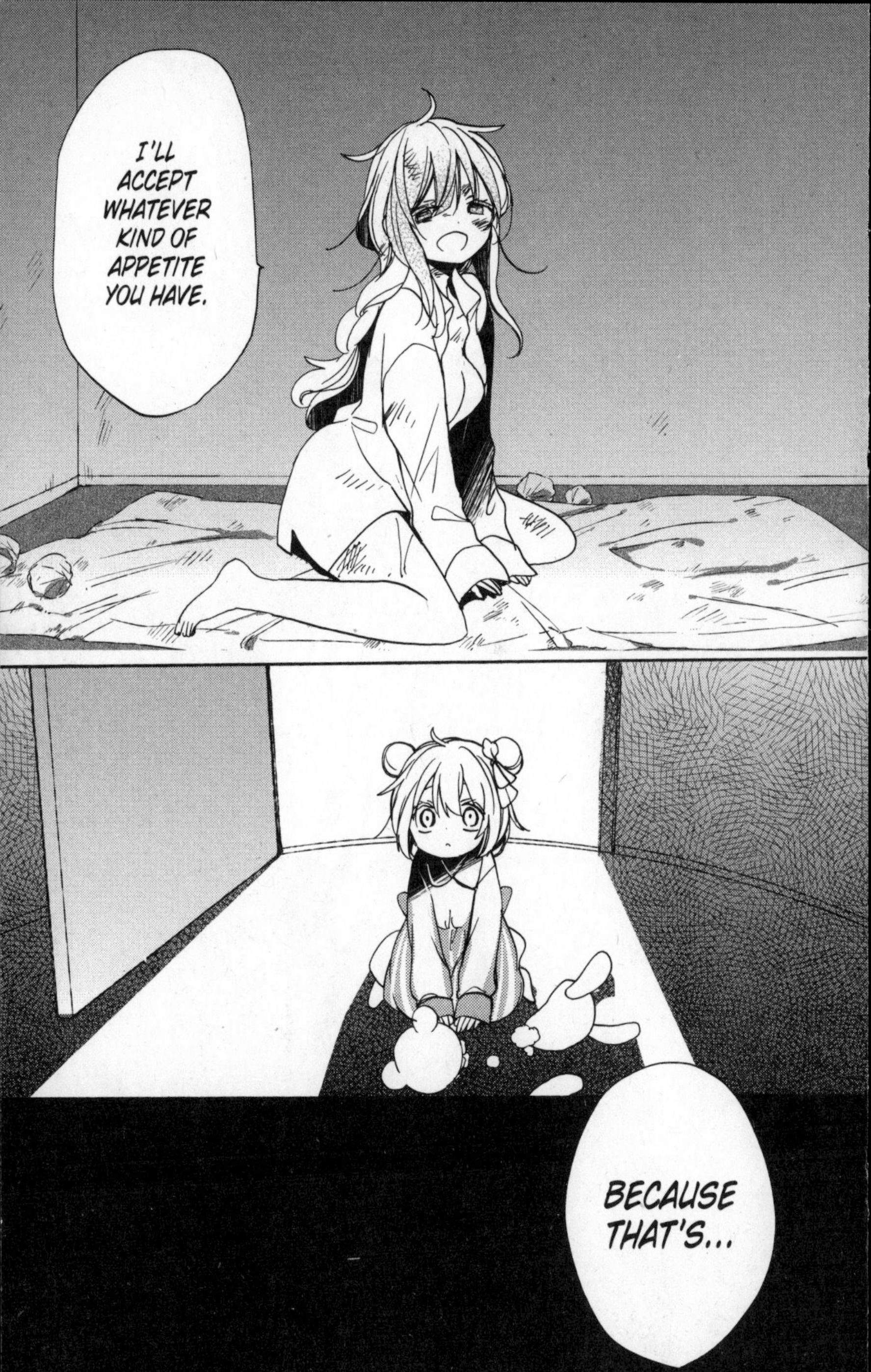
I'LL ACCEPT WHATEVER KIND OF APPETITE YOU HAVE.
BECAUSE THAT'S...

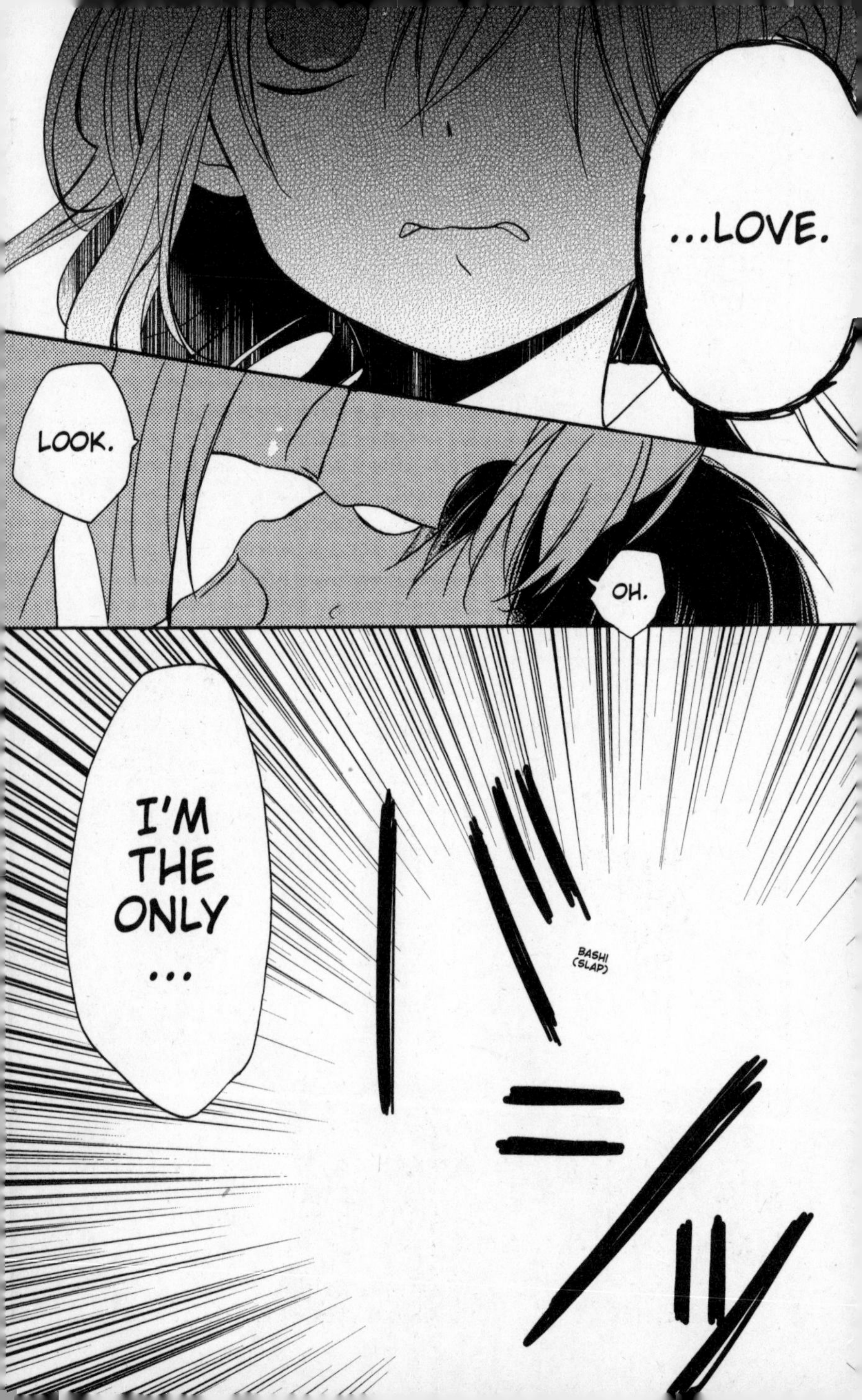
...LOVE.
OH.
LOOK.
BASHI (SLAP)
I'M THE ONLY ...

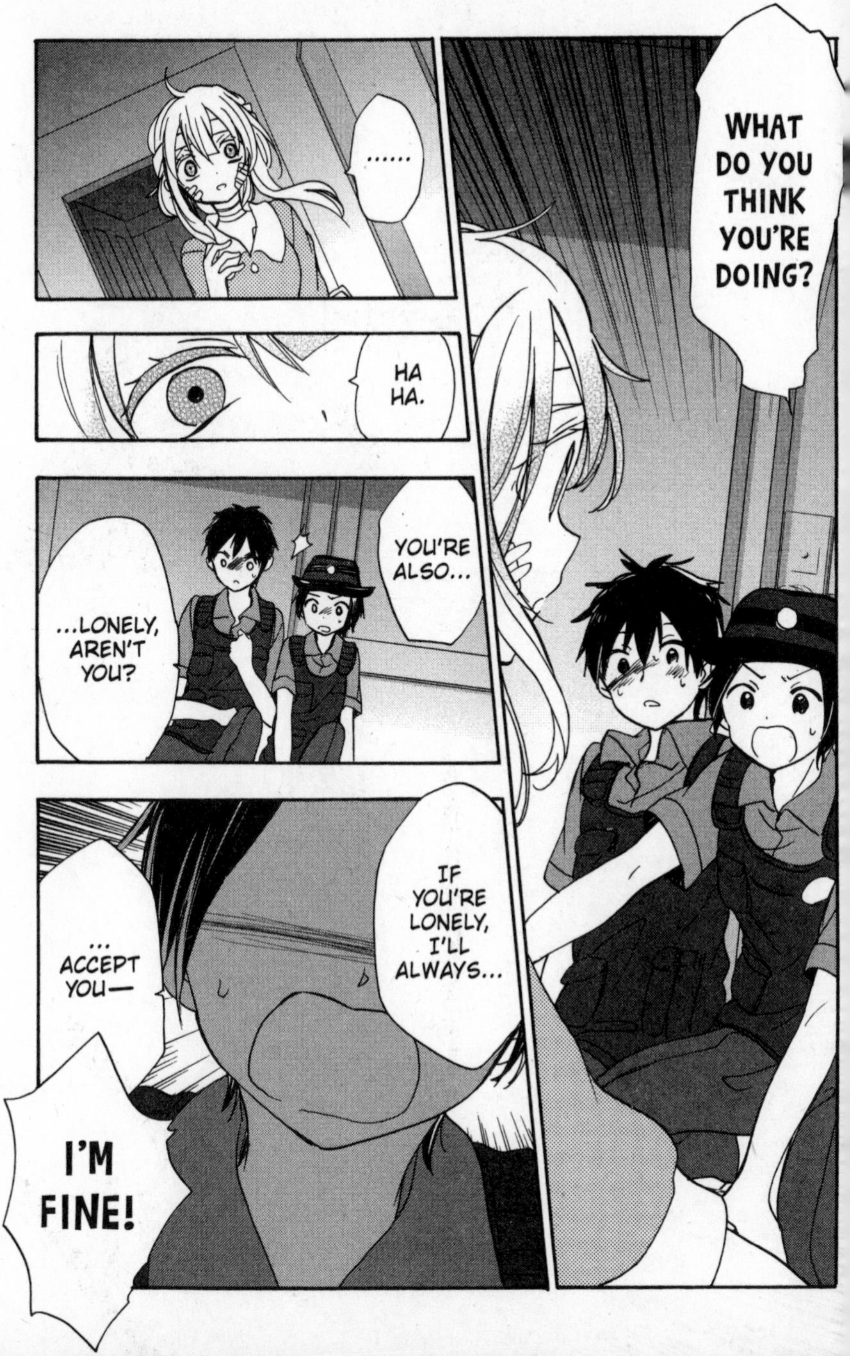
WHAT DO YOU THINK YOU'RE DOING?
......
HA HA.
YOU'RE ALSO...
...LONELY, AREN'T YOU?
IF YOU'RE LONELY, I'LL ALWAYS...
...ACCEPT YOU—
I'M FINE!

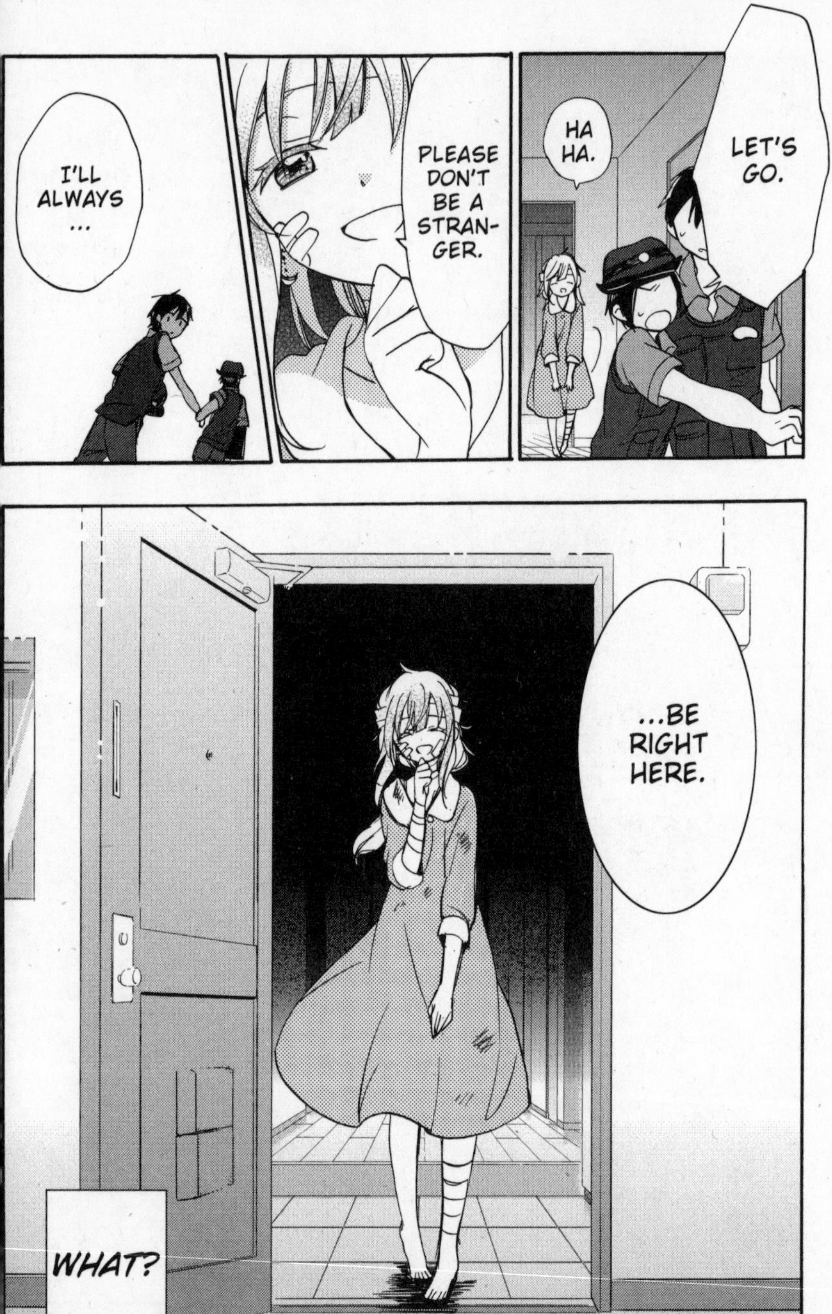
LET'S GO.
HA HA.
PLEASE DON'T BE A STRANGER.
I'LL ALWAYS ...
...BE RIGHT HERE.
WHAT?

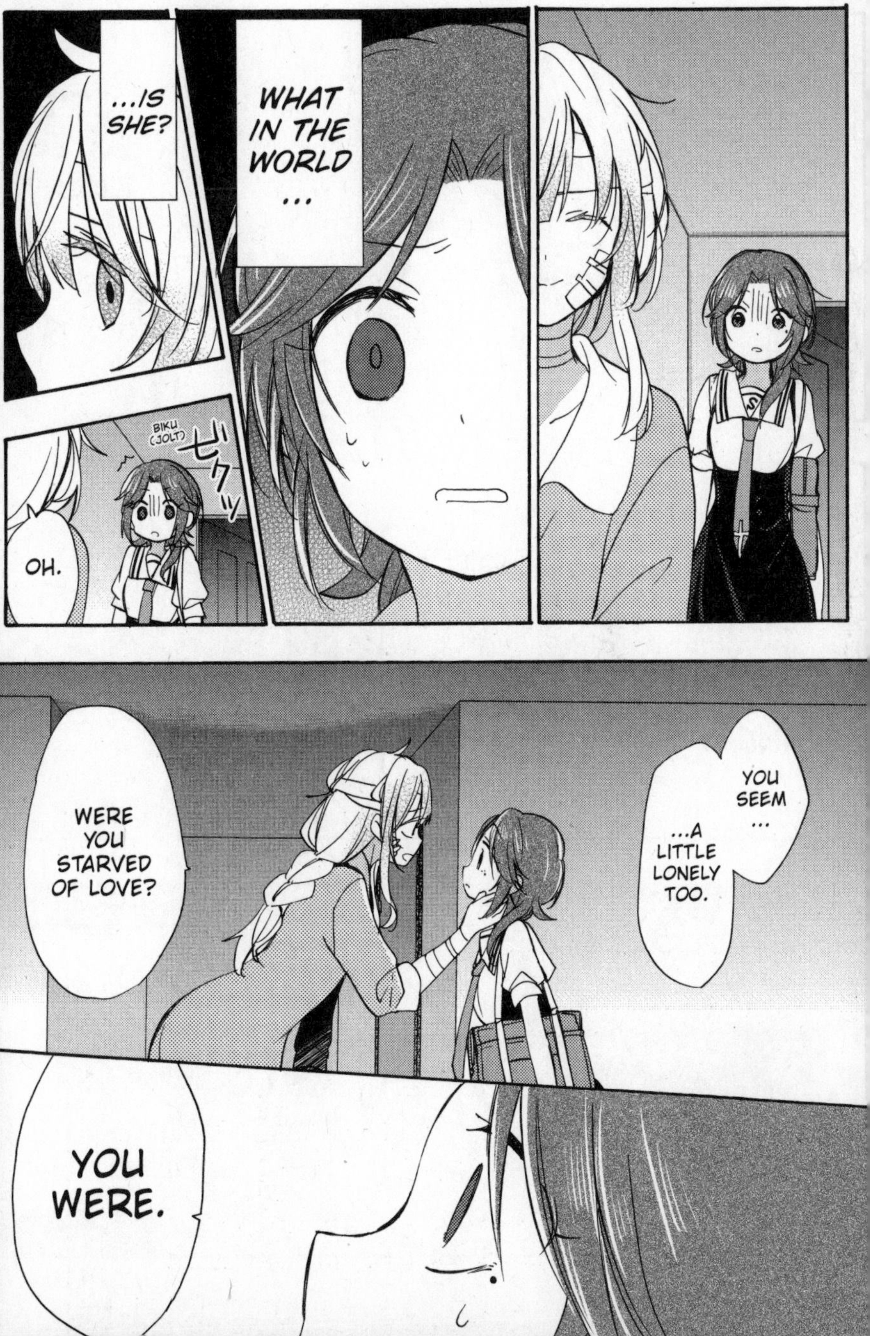
WHAT IN THE WORLD ...
...IS SHE?
BIKU (JOLT)
OH.
YOU SEEM ... ...A LITTLE LONELY TOO.
WERE YOU STARVED OF LOVE?
YOU WERE.

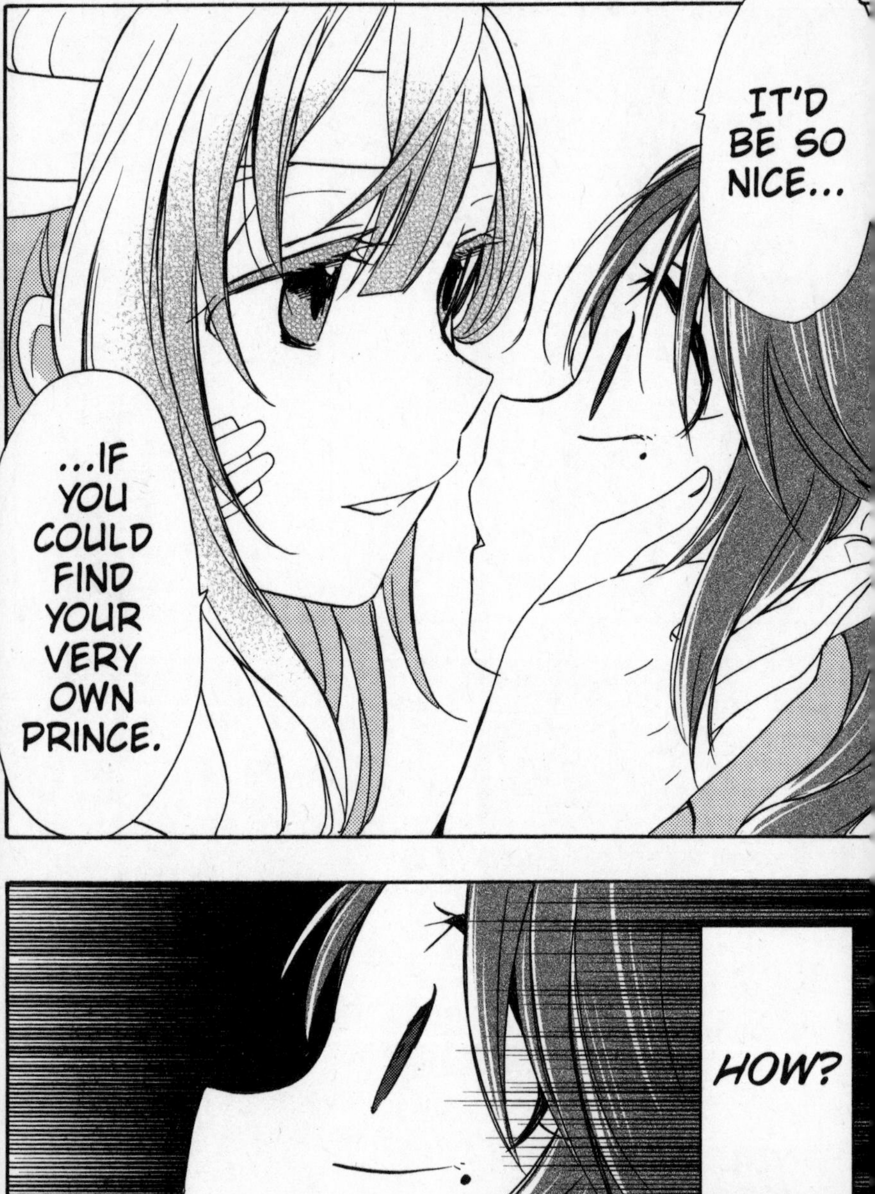
IT'D BE SO NICE...
...IF YOU COULD FIND YOUR VERY OWN PRINCE.
HOW?

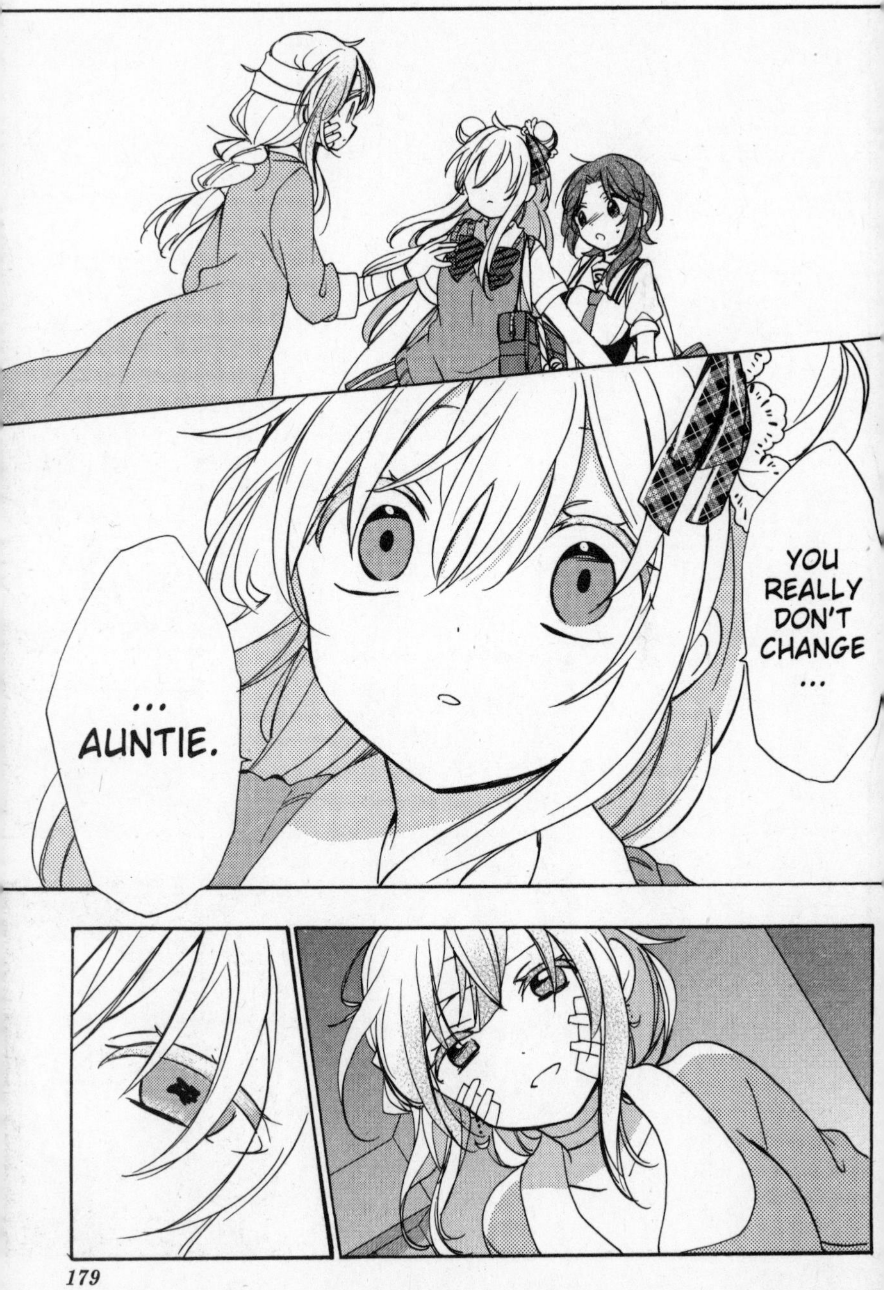
YOU REALLY DON'T CHANGE ...
... AUNTIE.

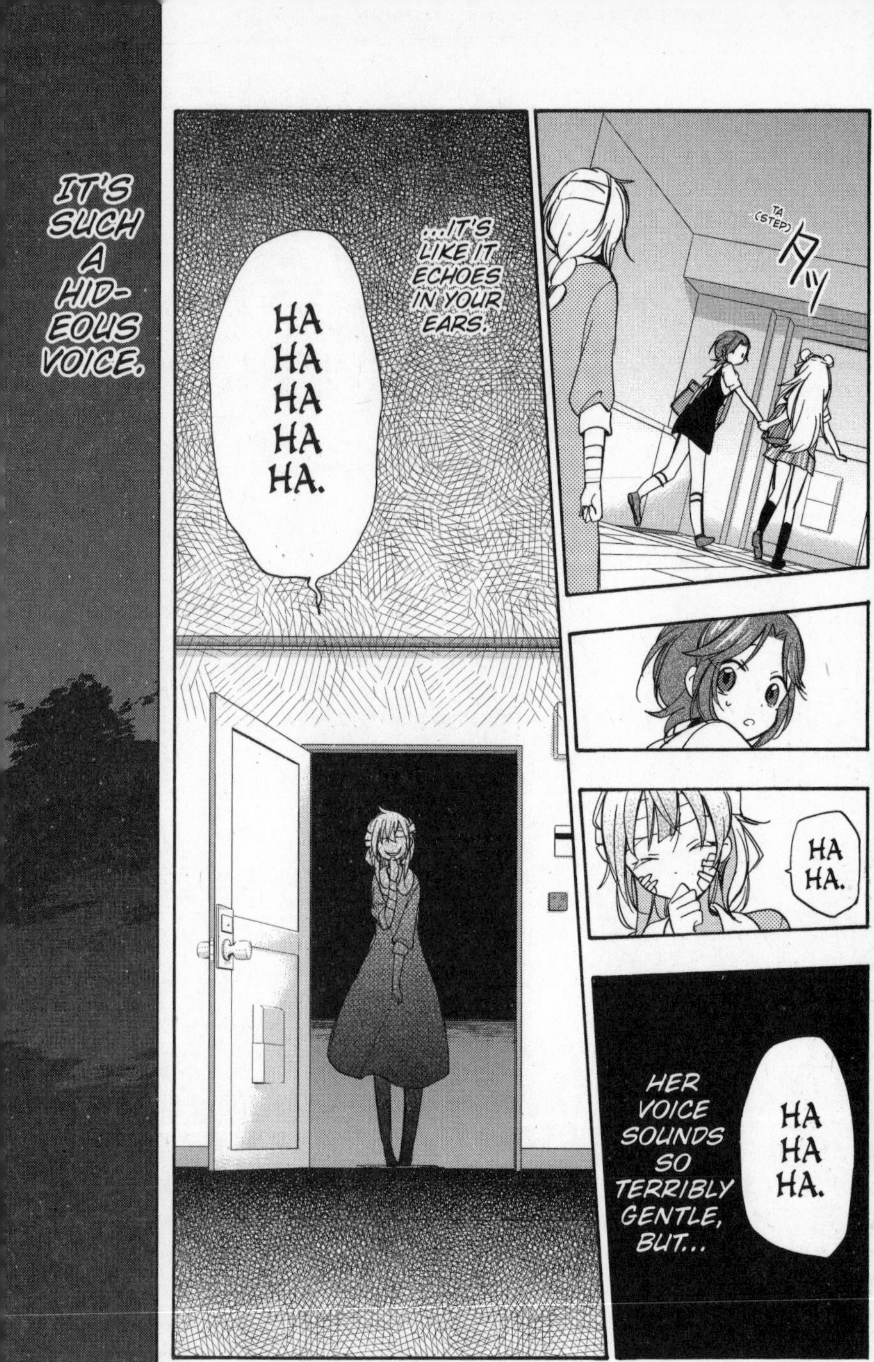
TA (STEP)
タッ
HA HA.
HA HA HA.
HER VOICE SOUNDS SO TERRIBLY GENTLE, BUT...
...IT'S LIKE IT ECHOES IN YOUR EARS.
HA HA HA HA HA.
IT'S SUCH A HID-EOUS VOICE.

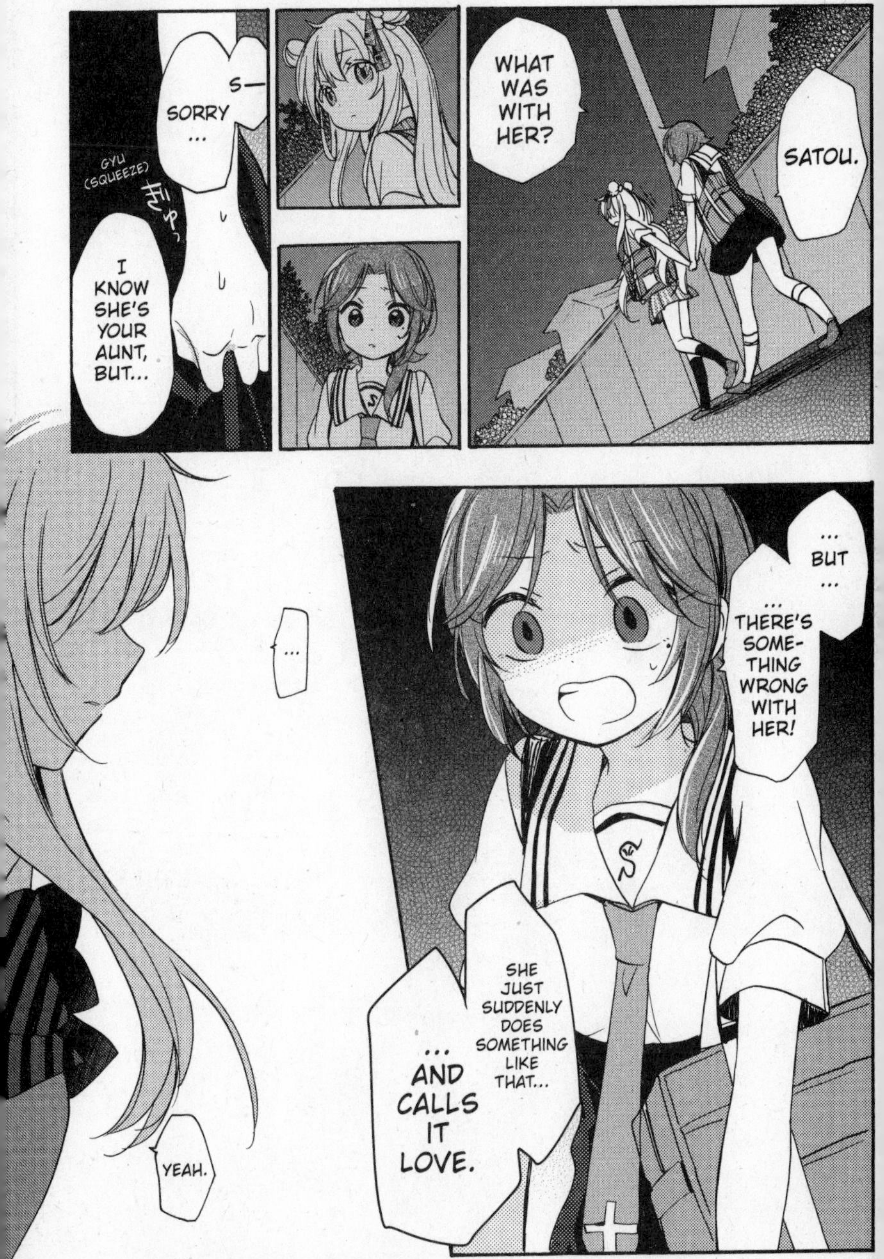
SATOU.
WHAT WAS WITH HER?
S— SORRY ...
GYU (SQUEEZE)
ぎゅっ
I KNOW SHE'S YOUR AUNT, BUT...
... BUT ...
... THERE'S SOME-THING WRONG WITH HER!
SHE JUST SUDDENLY DOES SOMETHING LIKE THAT...
... AND CALLS IT LOVE.
...
YEAH.

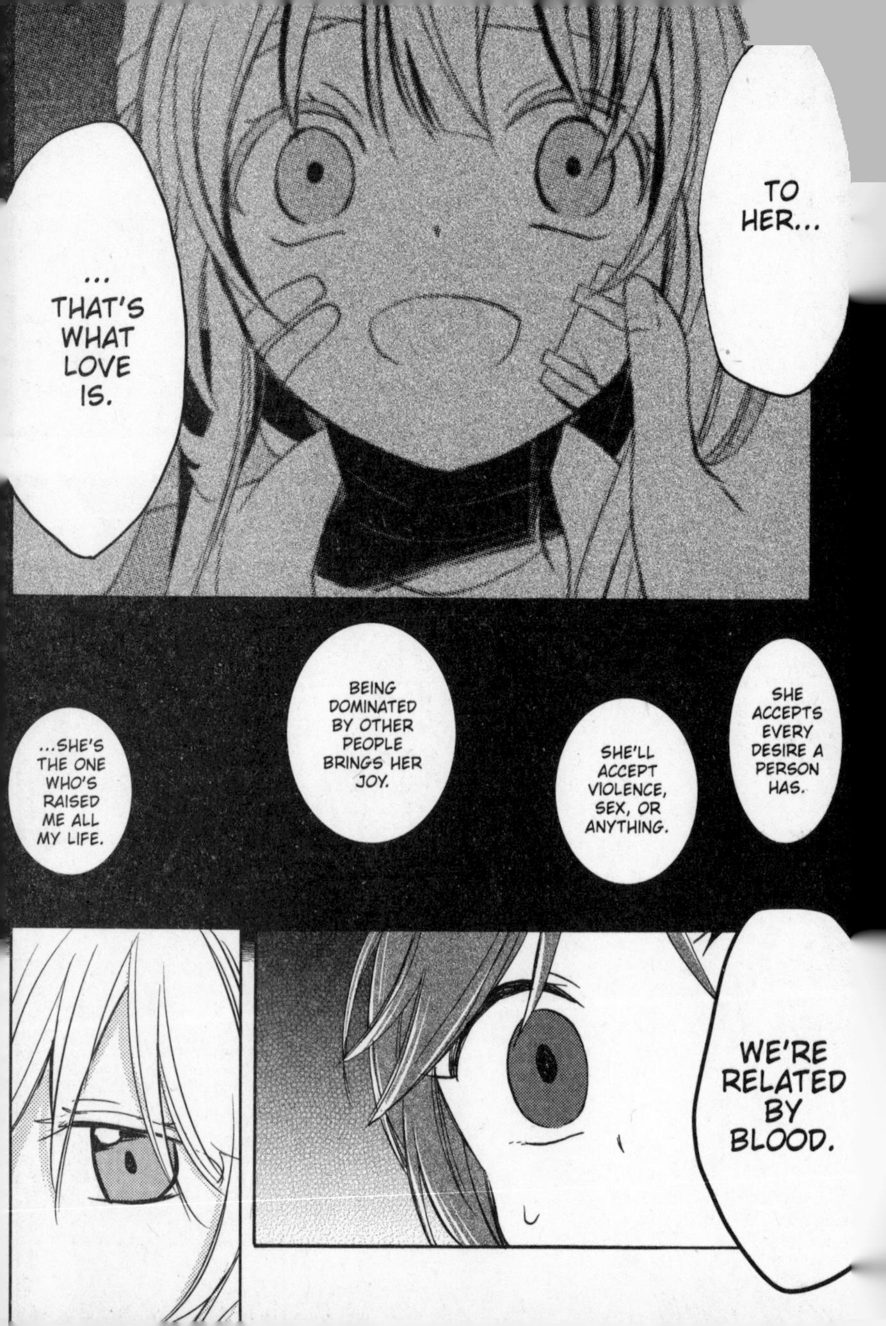
TO HER...
...THAT'S WHAT LOVE IS.
SHE ACCEPTS EVERY DESIRE A PERSON HAS.
SHE'LL ACCEPT VIOLENCE, SEX, OR ANYTHING.
BEING DOMINATED BY OTHER PEOPLE BRINGS HER JOY.
...SHE'S THE ONE WHO'S RAISED ME ALL MY LIFE.
WE'RE RELATED BY BLOOD.

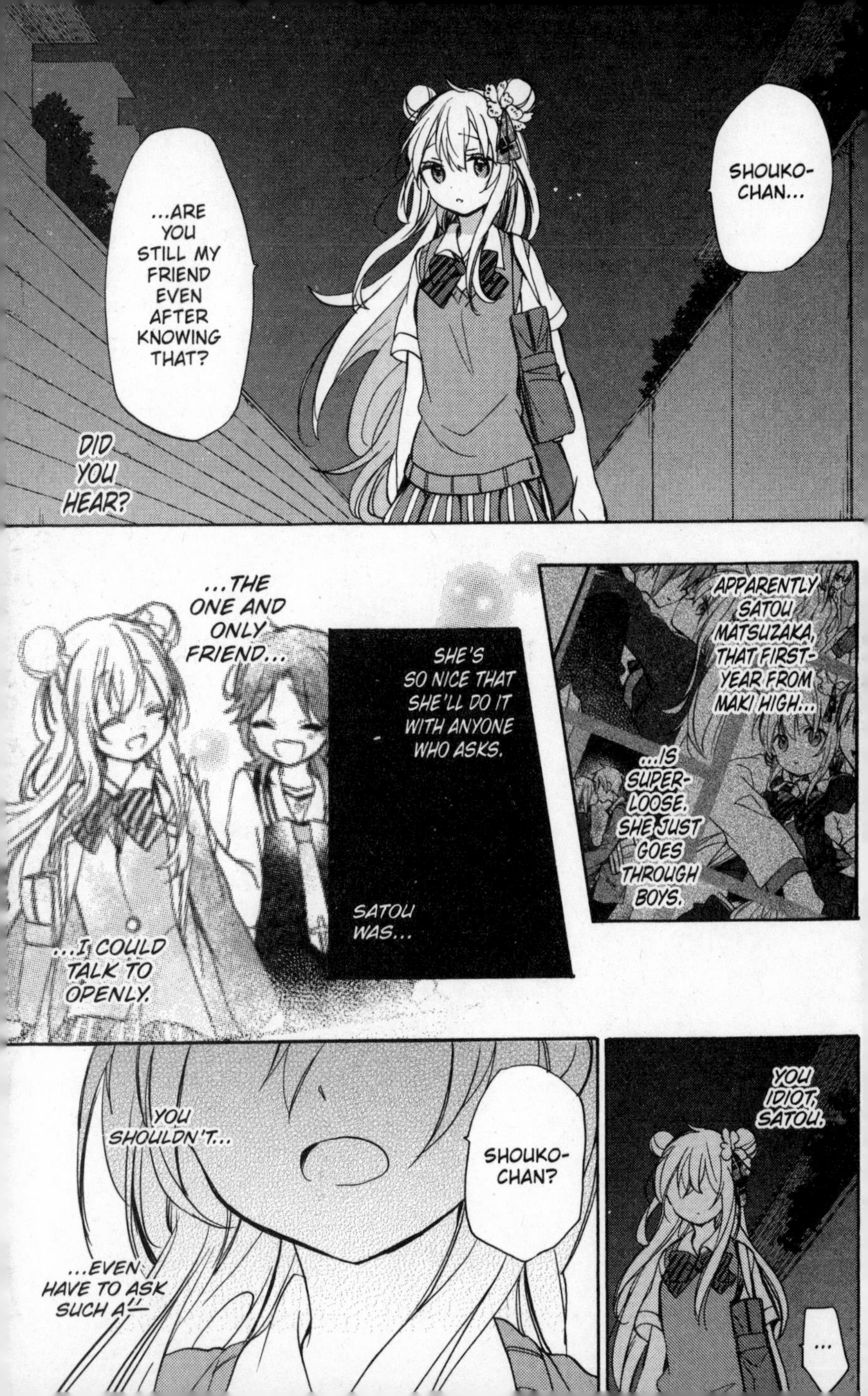
SHOUKO-CHAN...
...ARE YOU STILL MY FRIEND EVEN AFTER KNOWING THAT?
DID YOU HEAR?
APPARENTLY SATOU MATSUZAKA, THAT FIRST-YEAR FROM MAKI HIGH...
...IS SUPER-LOOSE. SHE JUST GOES THROUGH BOYS.
SHE'S SO NICE THAT SHE'LL DO IT WITH ANYONE WHO ASKS.
SATOU WAS...
...THE ONE AND ONLY FRIEND...
...I COULD TALK TO OPENLY.
YOU IDIOT, SATOU.
...
SHOUKO-CHAN?
YOU SHOULDN'T...
...EVEN HAVE TO ASK SUCH A--

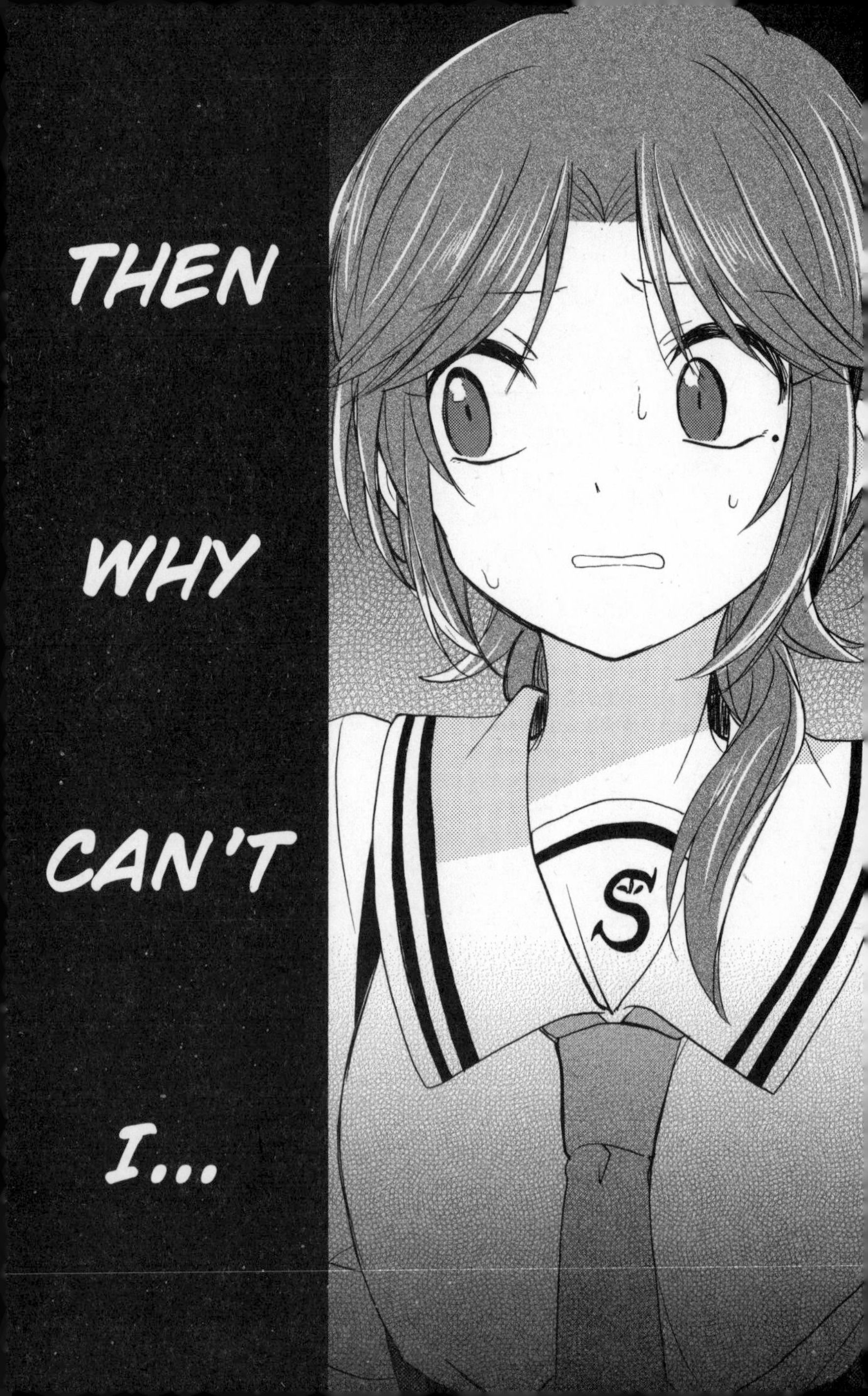
THEN WHY CAN'T I...

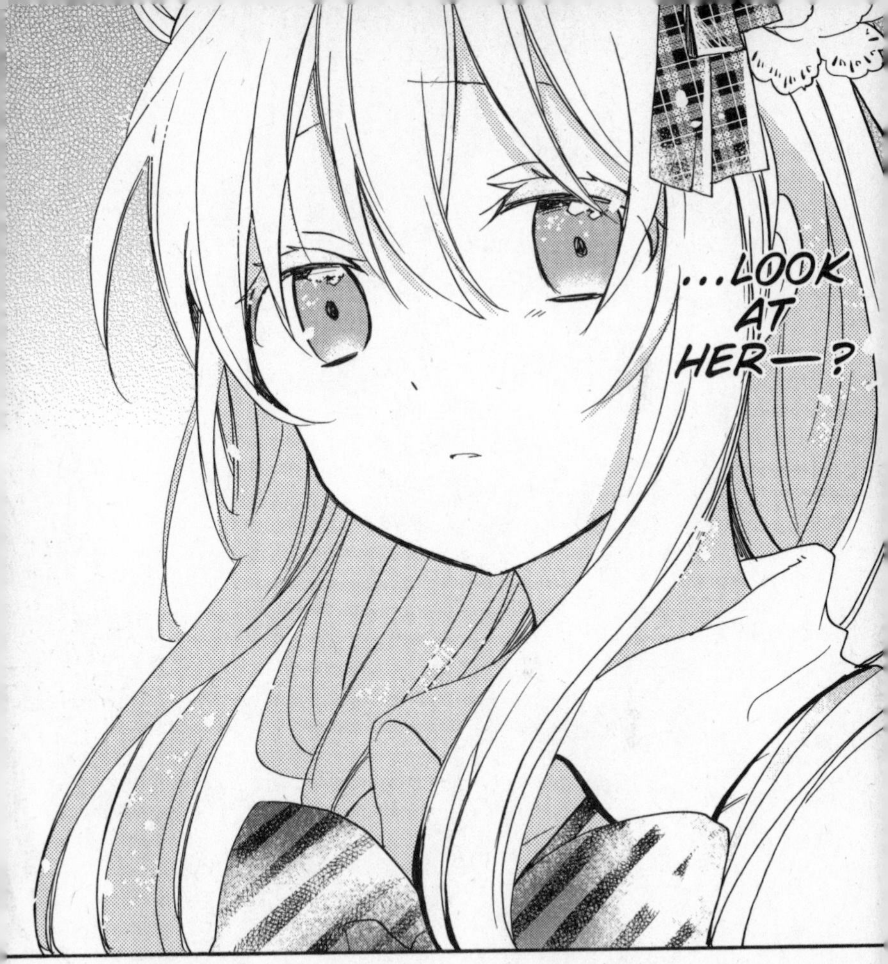
...LOOK AT HER—?
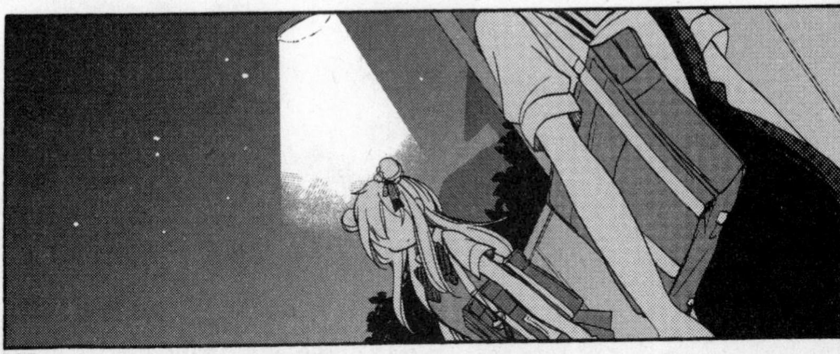

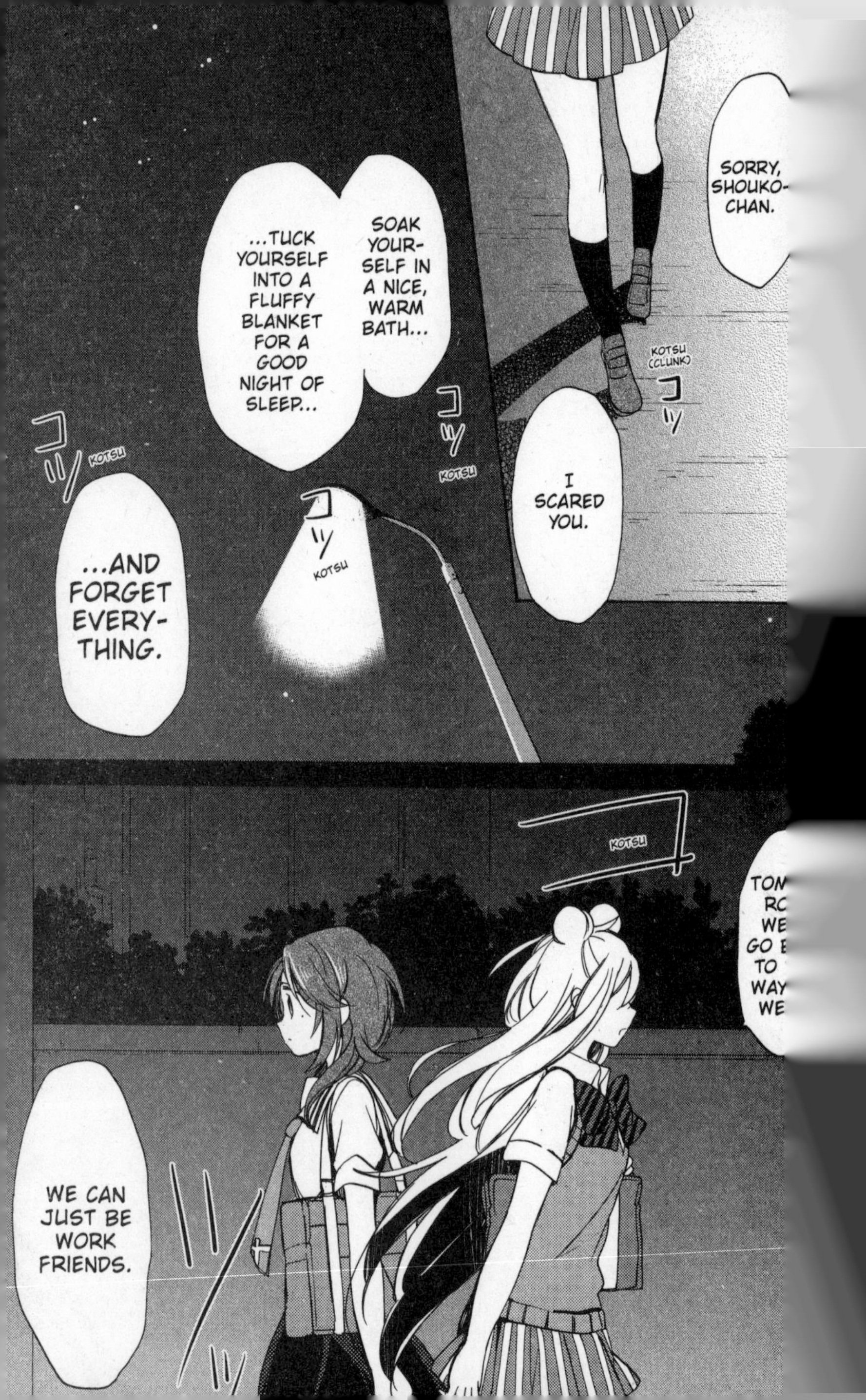
SORRY, SHOUKO-CHAN.
KOTSU (CLUNK)
I SCARED YOU.
SOAK YOURSELF IN A NICE, WARM BATH...
...TUCK YOURSELF INTO A FLUFFY BLANKET FOR A GOOD NIGHT OF SLEEP...
KOTSU
KOTSU
KOTSU
...AND FORGET EVERYTHING.
KOTSU
WE CAN JUST BE WORK FRIENDS.

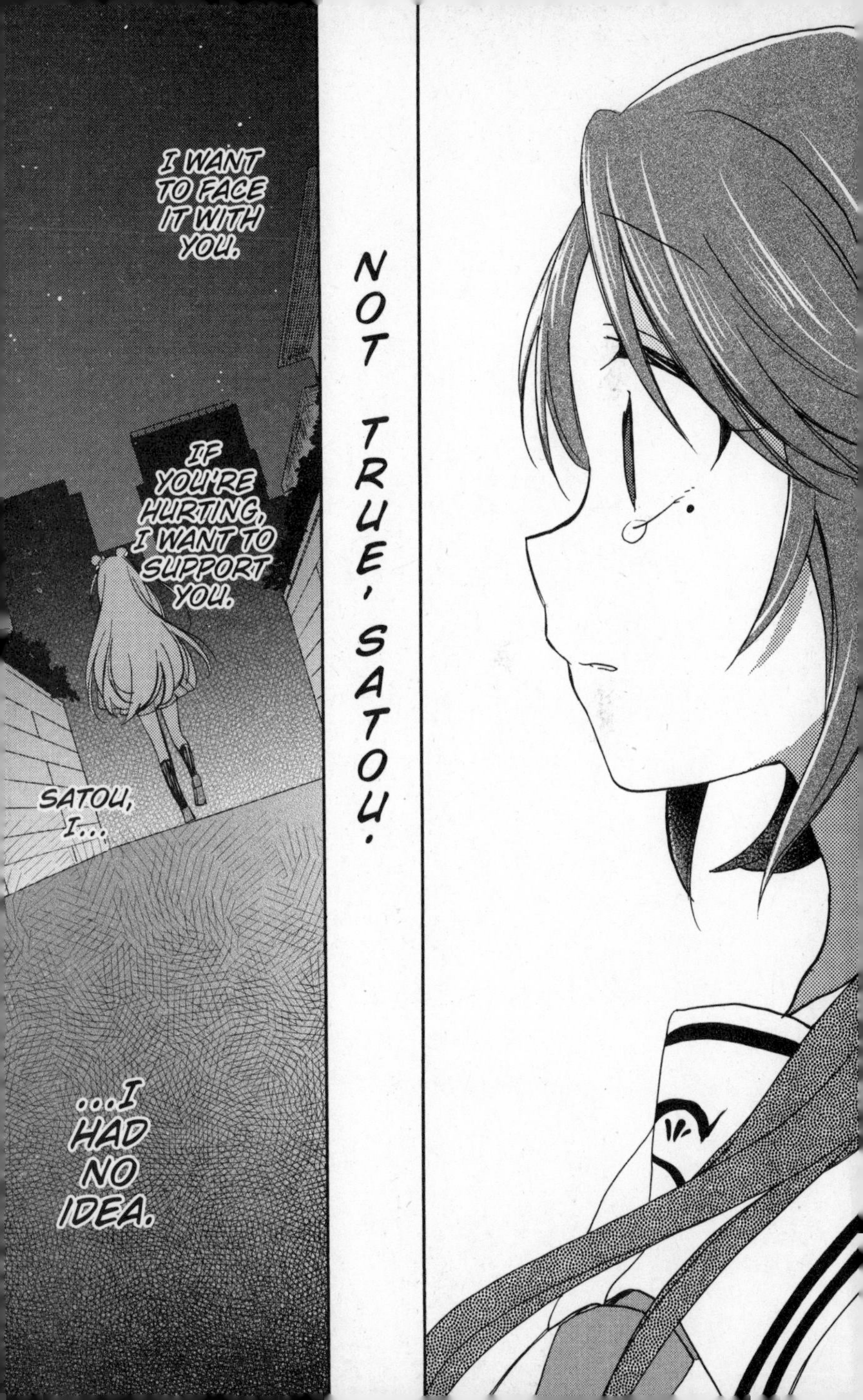
NOT TRUE, SATOU.
I WANT TO FACE IT WITH YOU.
IF YOU'RE HURTING, I WANT TO SUPPORT YOU.
SATOU, I...
...I HAD NO IDEA.

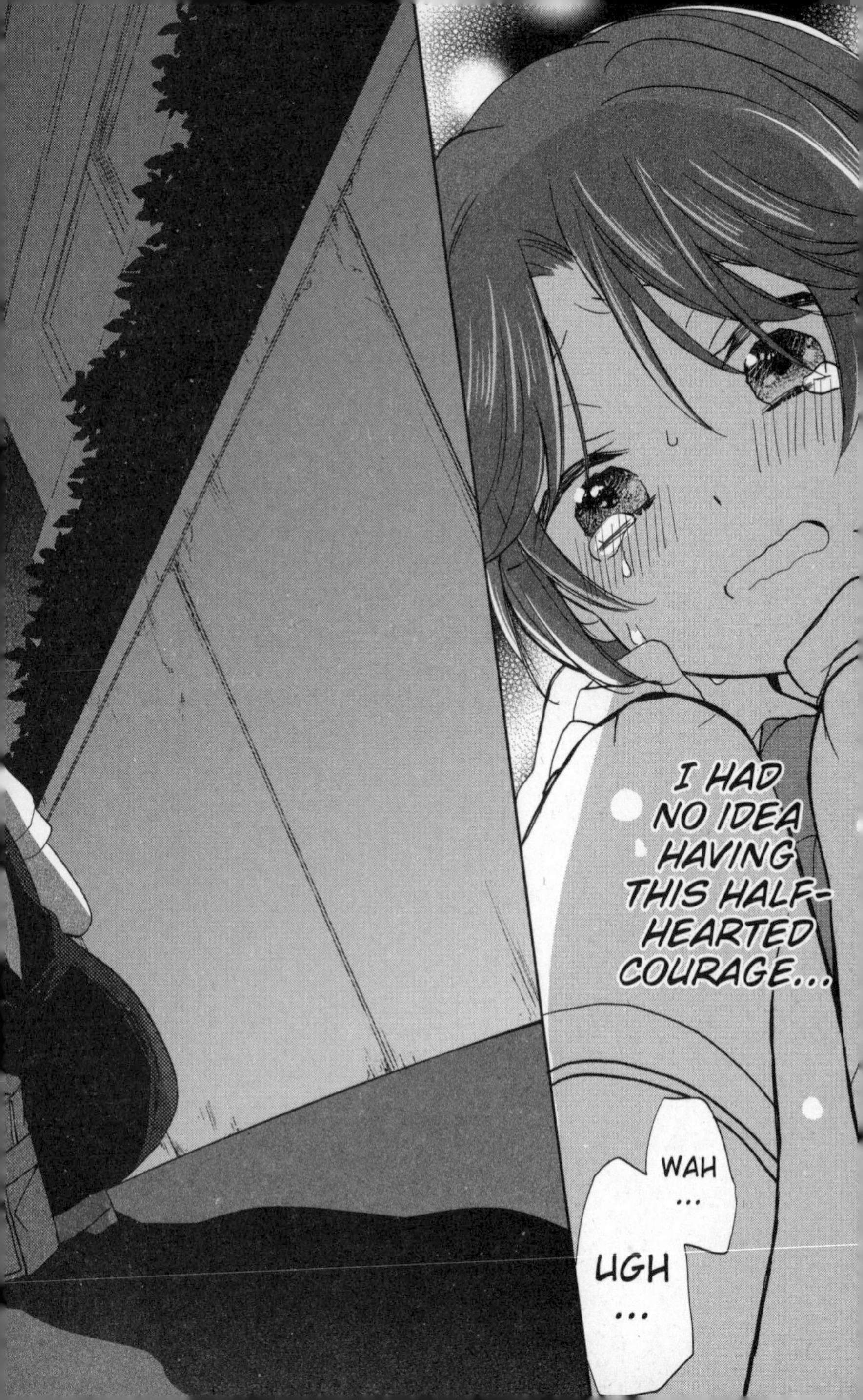
I HAD NO IDEA HAVING THIS HALF-HEARTED COURAGE...
WAH ...
UGH ...

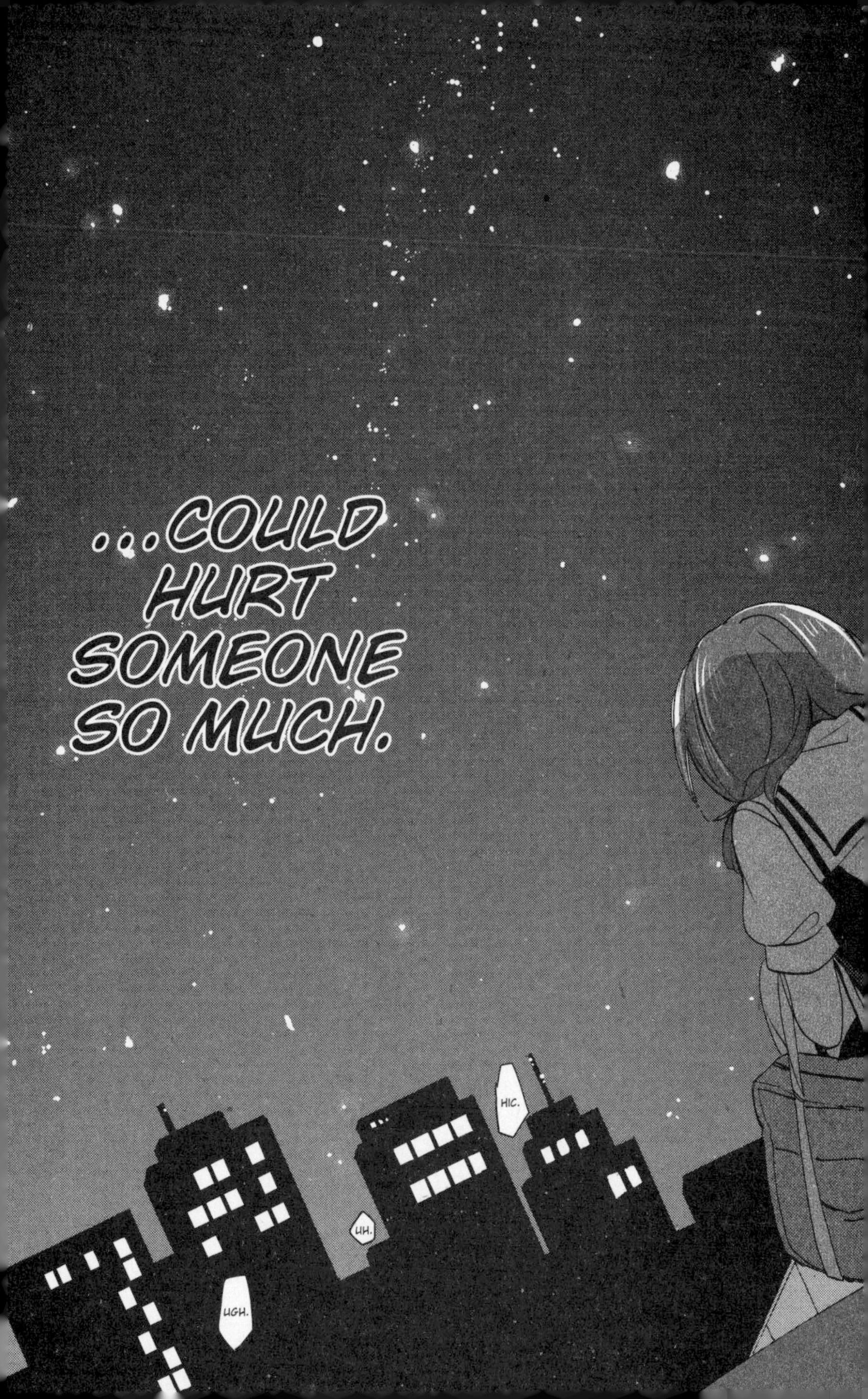
...COULD HURT SOMEONE SO MUCH.
HIC.
UH.
UGH.

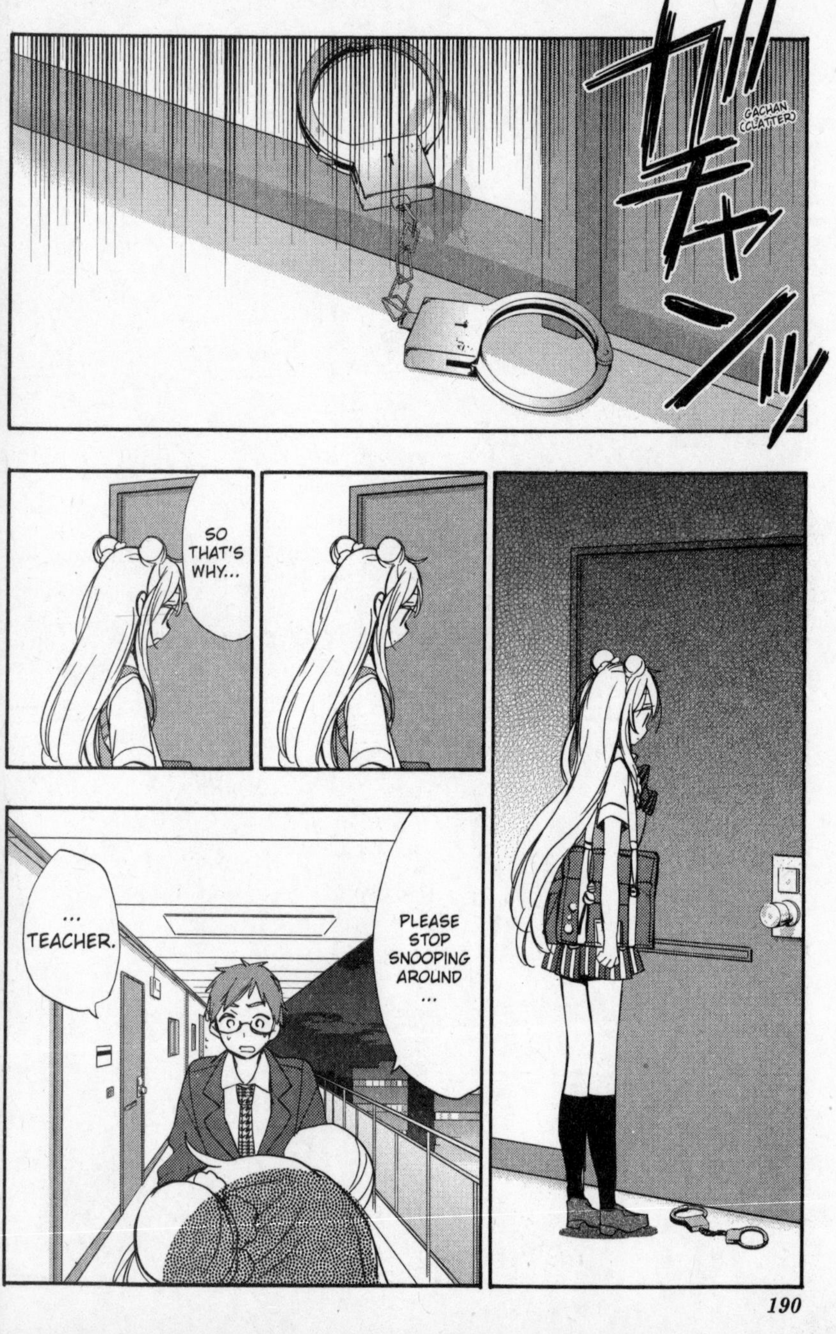
GACHAN (CLATTER)
SO THAT'S WHY...
PLEASE STOP SNOOPING AROUND ...
... TEACHER.

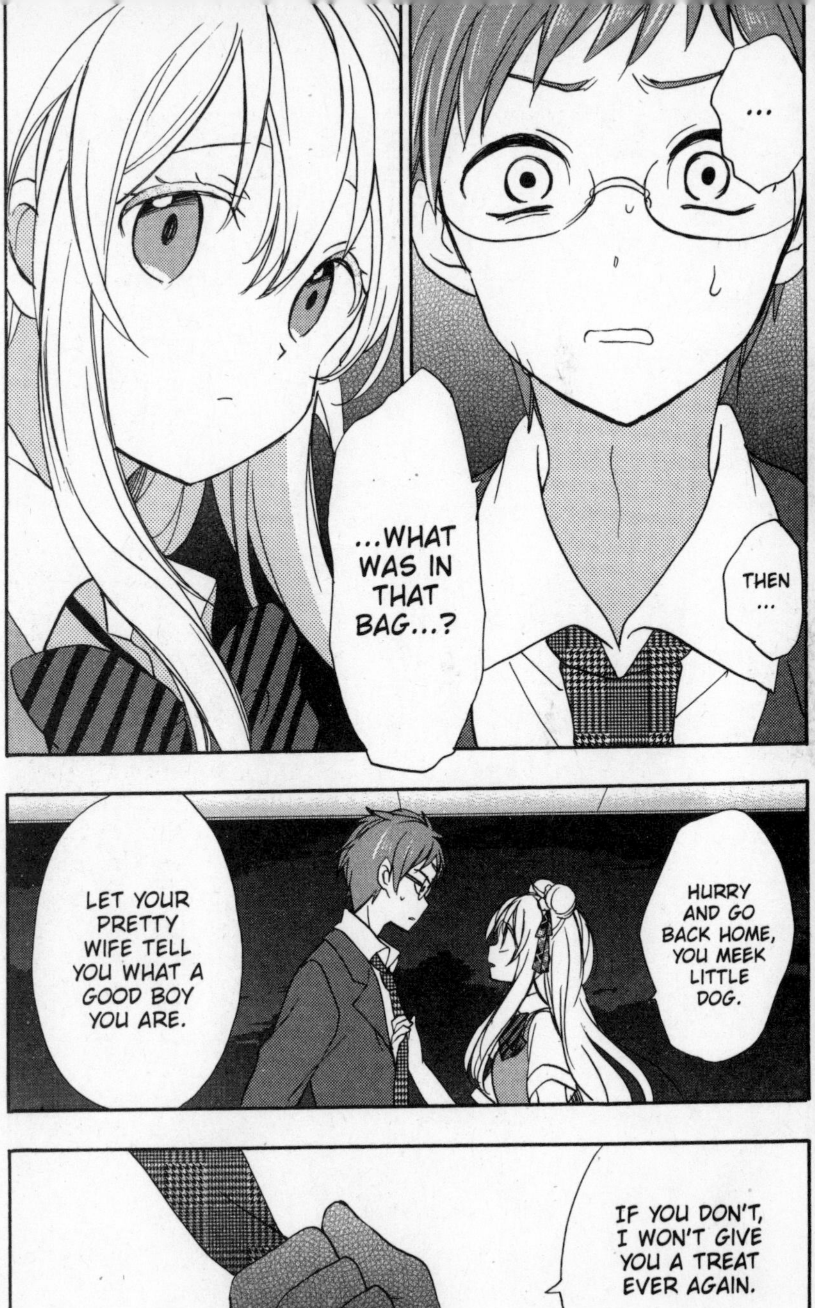
...
THEN ...
...WHAT WAS IN THAT BAG...?
HURRY AND GO BACK HOME, YOU MEEK LITTLE DOG.
LET YOUR PRETTY WIFE TELL YOU WHAT A GOOD BOY YOU ARE.
IF YOU DON'T, I WON'T GIVE YOU A TREAT EVER AGAIN.

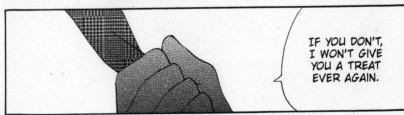

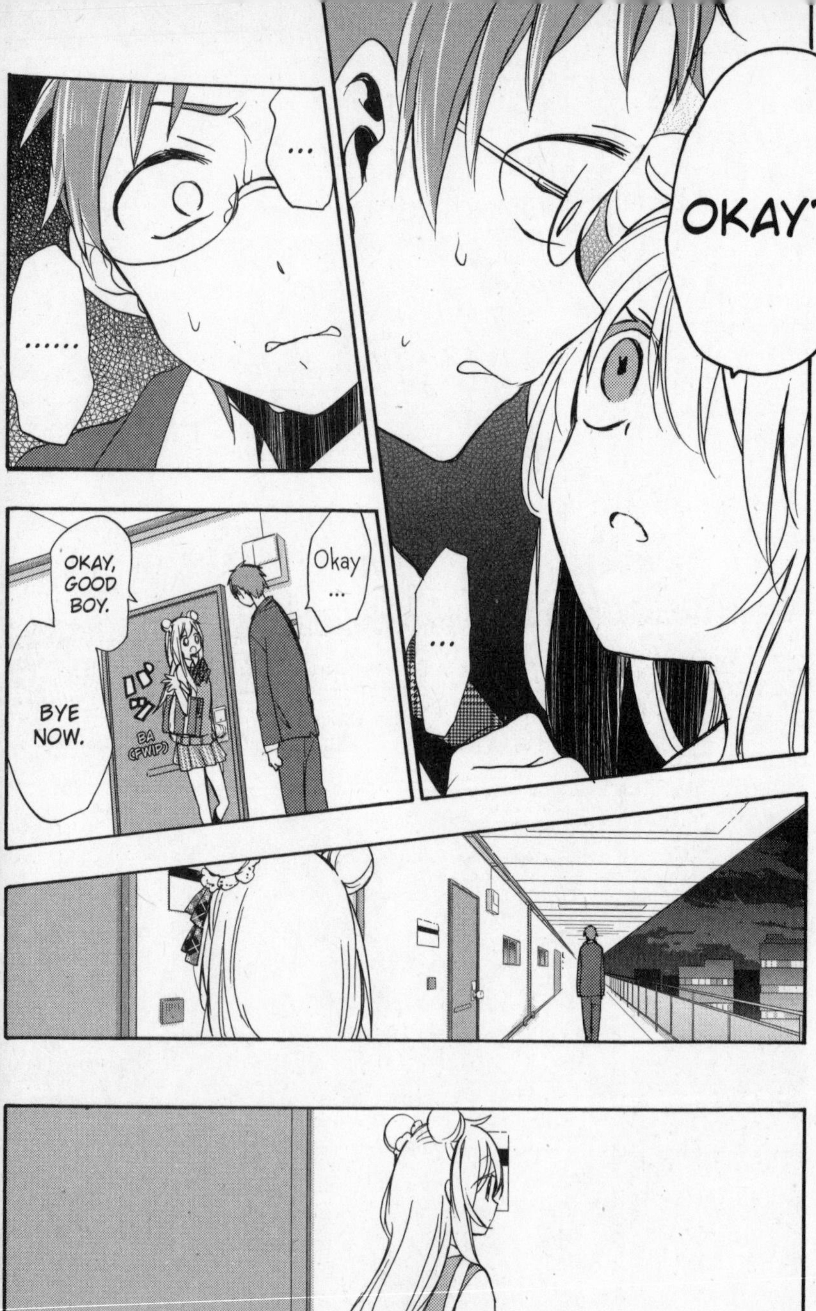
OKAY?
...
...
......
Okay ...
OKAY, GOOD BOY.
BA (FWIP)
BYE NOW.

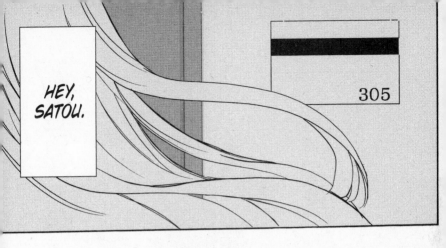

HEY, SATOU.

305

MAYBE
...

KAN

KAN

...
THERE'S
SOME-
THING
WRONG
WITH
YOU
TOO.

KAN

KAN

THERE'S
SOME-
THING
WRONG
WITH
YOUR
AUNT.

HEY.

KAN
(CLUNK)

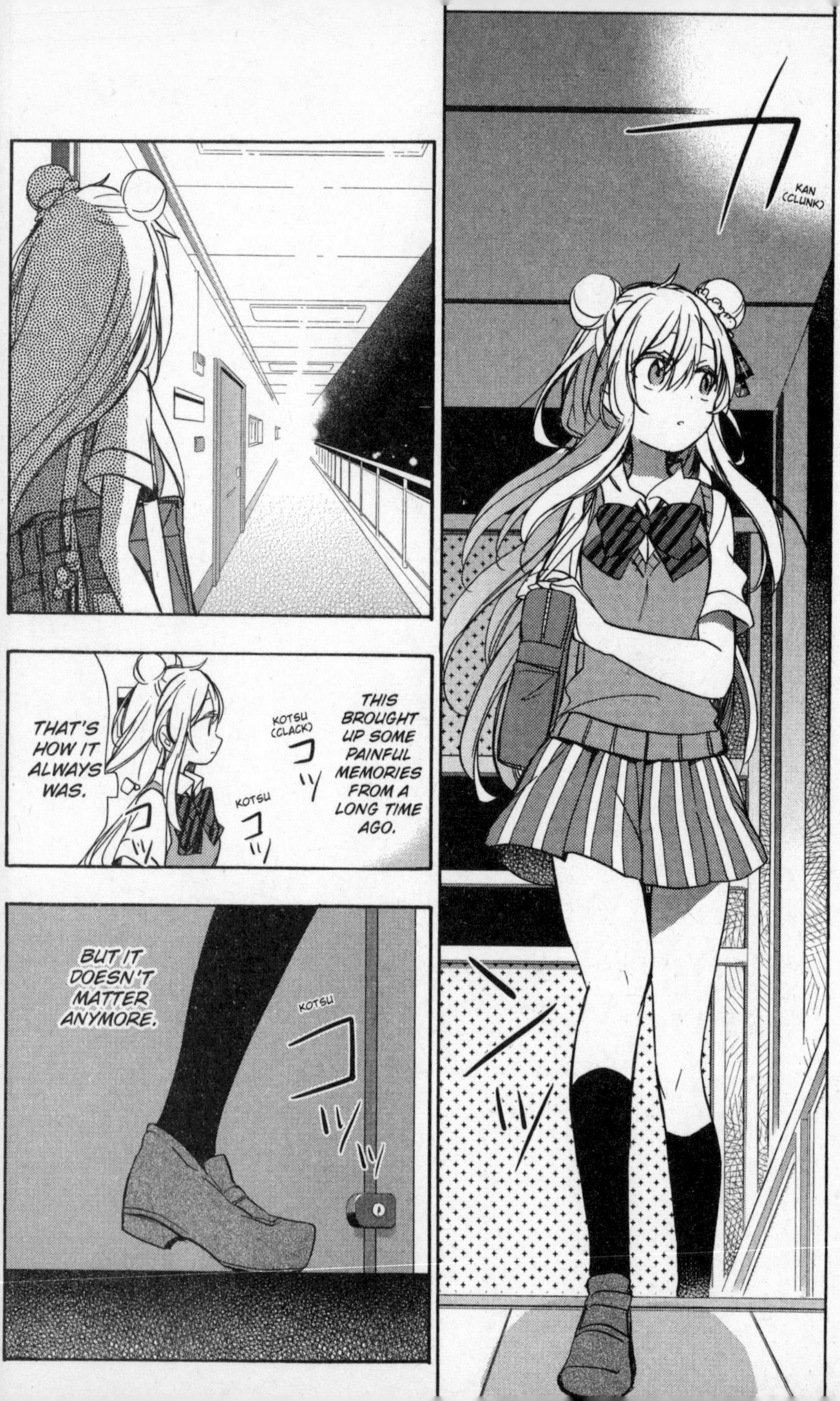
THIS BROUGHT UP SOME PAINFUL MEMORIES FROM A LONG TIME AGO.
KOTSU (CLACK)
KOTSU
THAT'S HOW IT ALWAYS WAS.
KOTSU
BUT IT DOESN'T MATTER ANYMORE.
KAN (CLUNK)

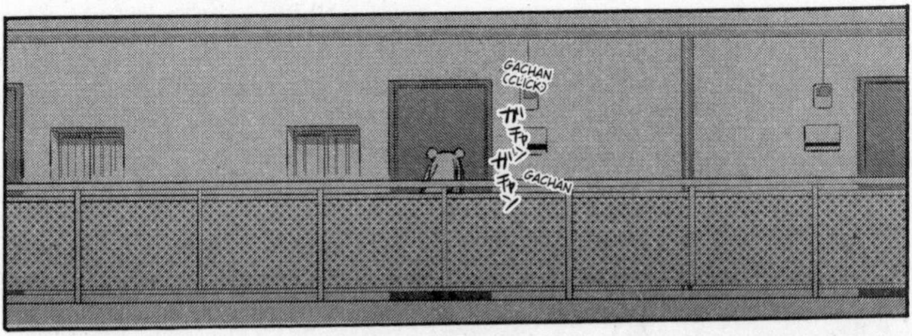
GACHAN (CLICK)
ガチャン
GACHAN
ガチャン
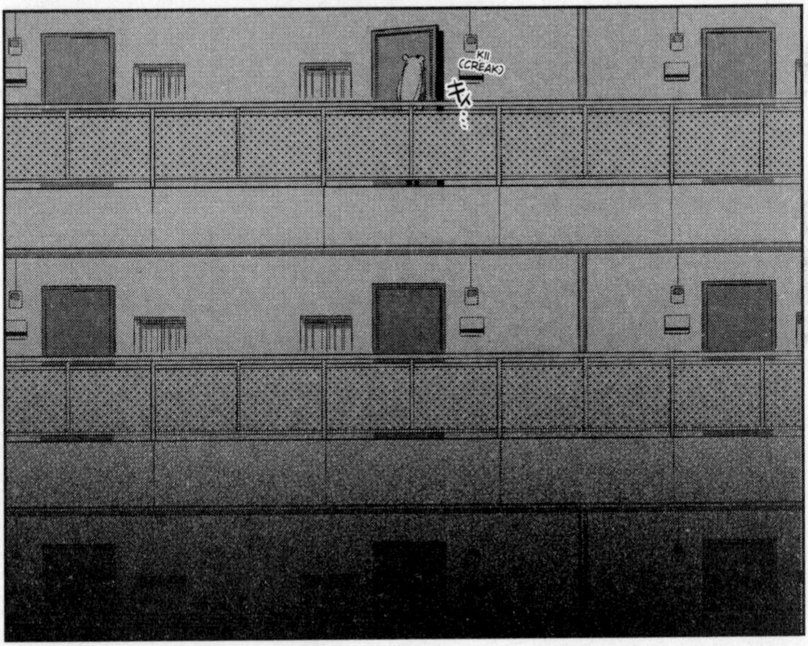
KII (CREAK)
キィ…
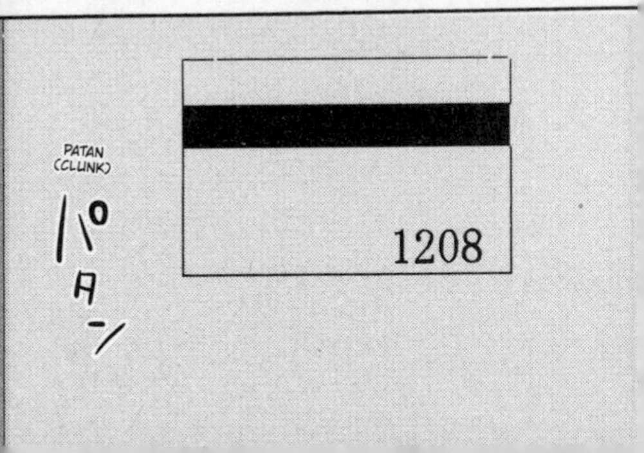
1208
PATAN (CLUNK)
パタン
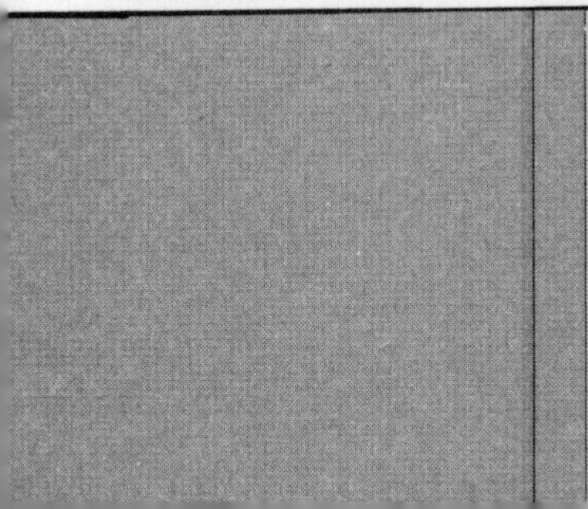

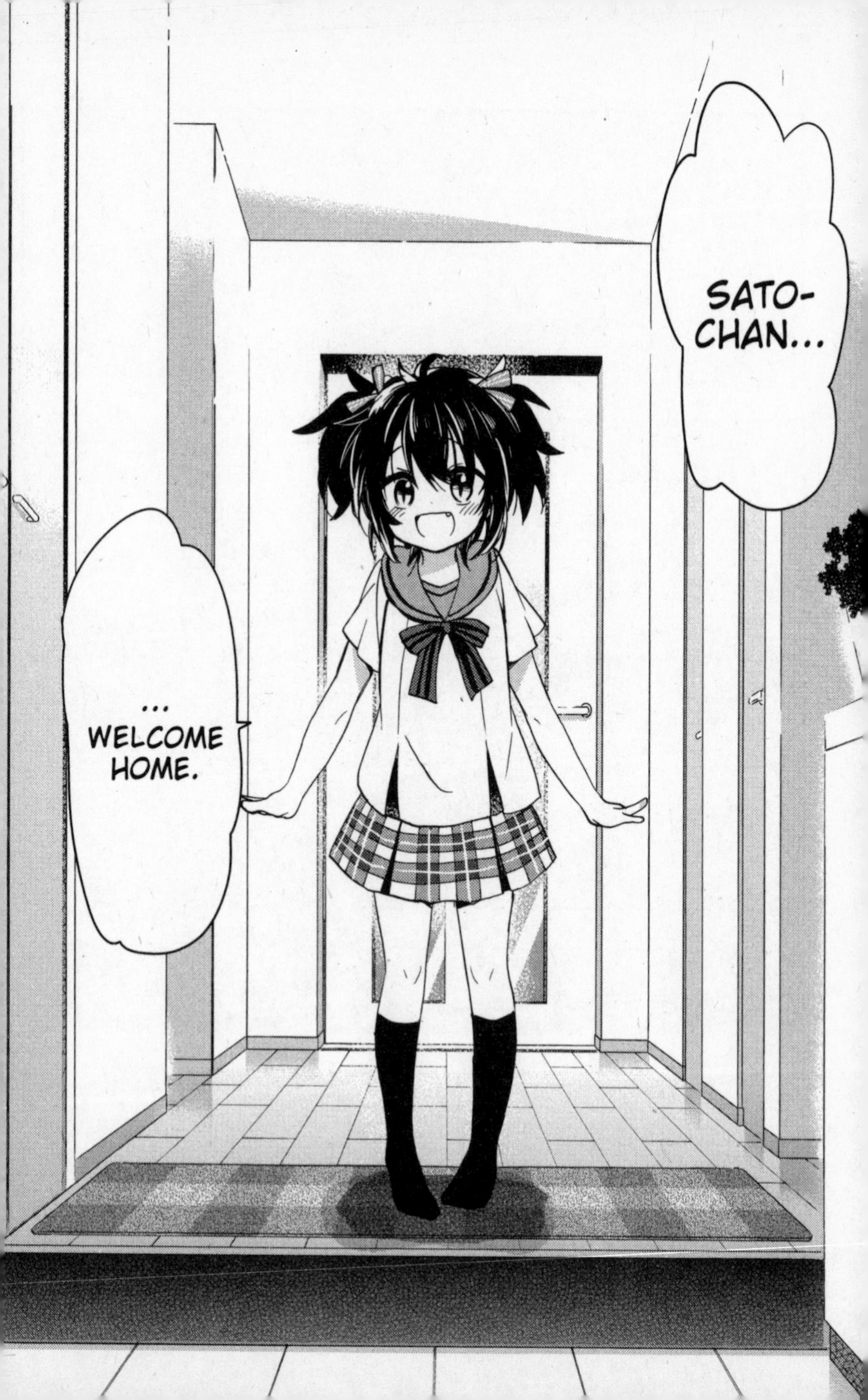
SATO-CHAN...
...WELCOME HOME.

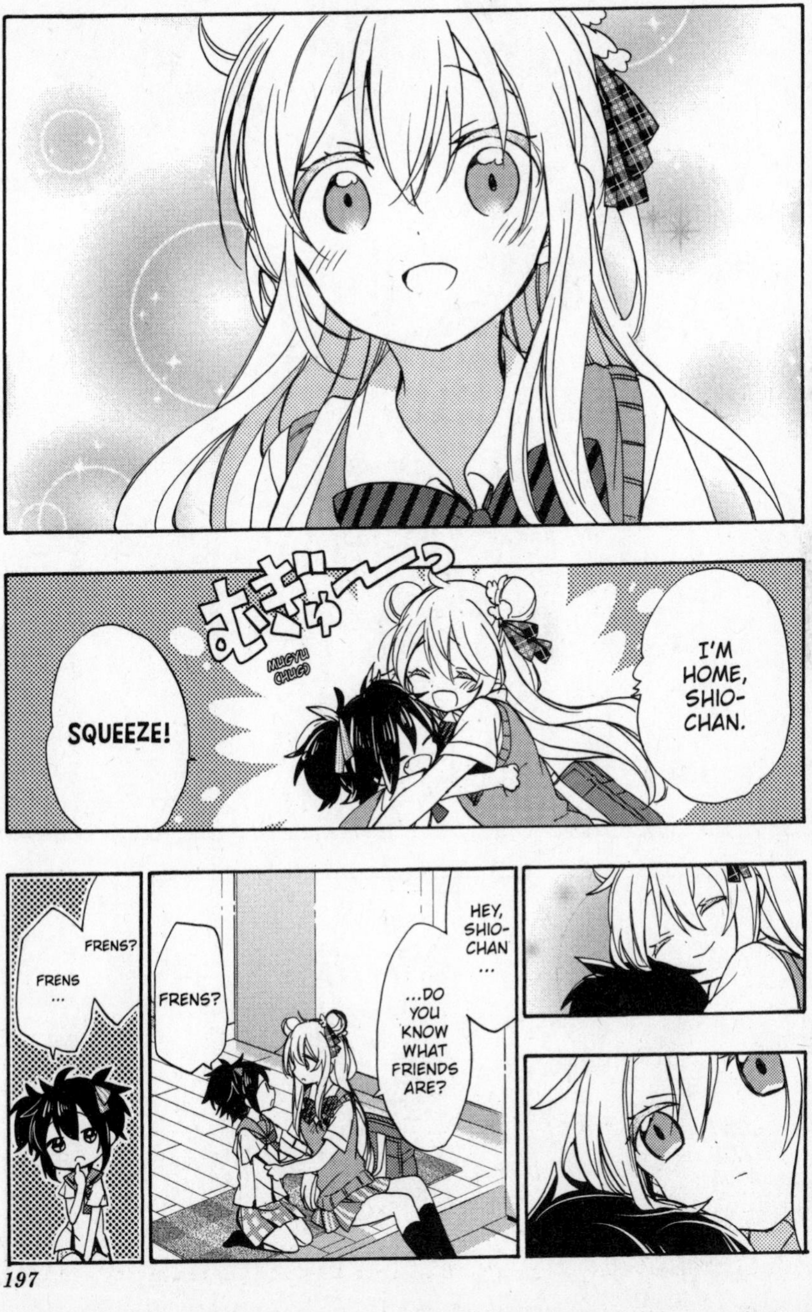
I'M HOME, SHIO-CHAN.
むぎゅ～っ
MUGYU (HUG)
SQUEEZE!
HEY, SHIO-CHAN ...
...DO YOU KNOW WHAT FRIENDS ARE?
FRENS?
FRENS?
FRENS ...

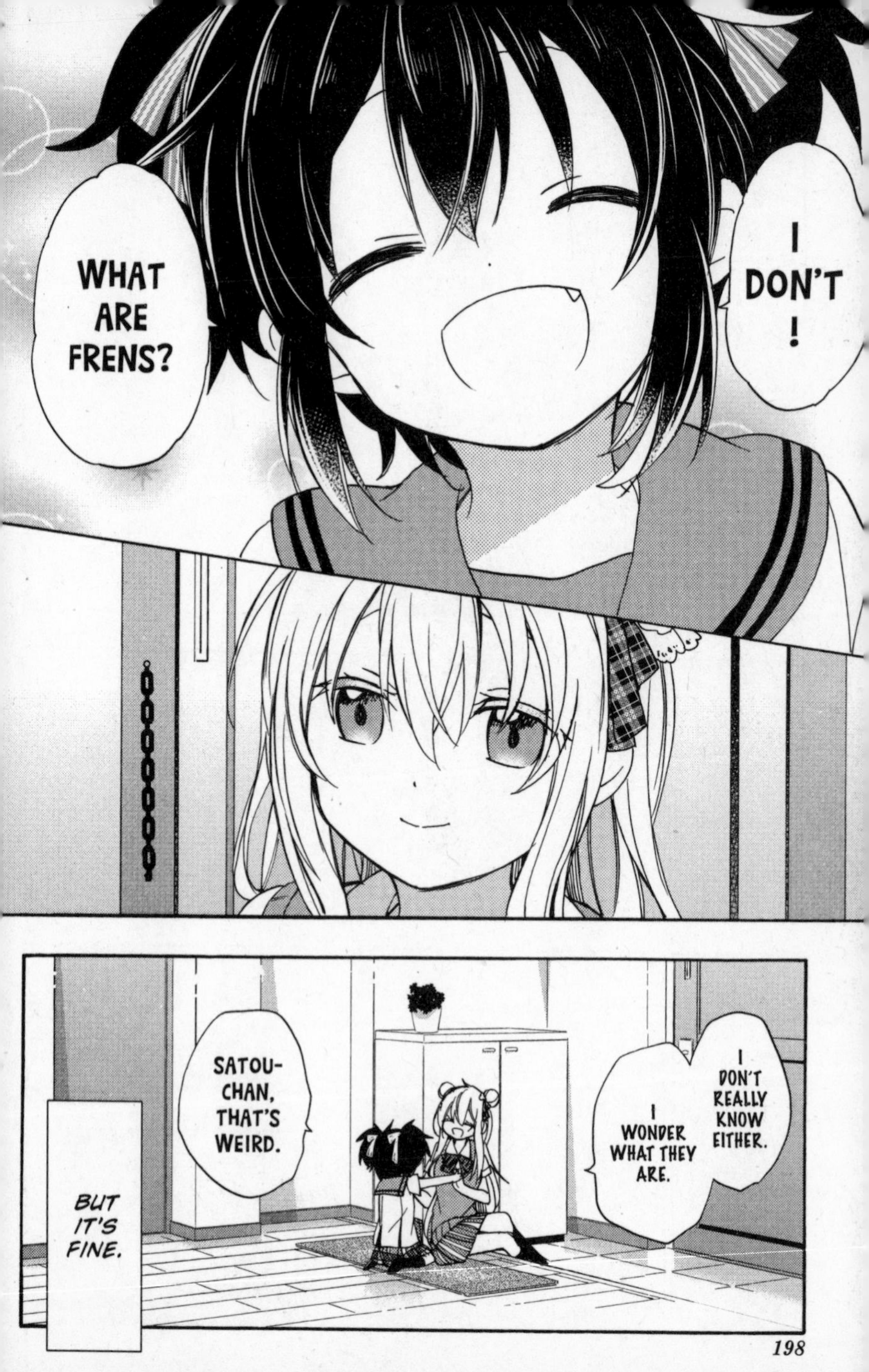
I DON'T !
WHAT ARE FRENS?
I DON'T REALLY KNOW EITHER.
I WONDER WHAT THEY ARE.
SATOU-CHAN, THAT'S WEIRD.
BUT IT'S FINE.

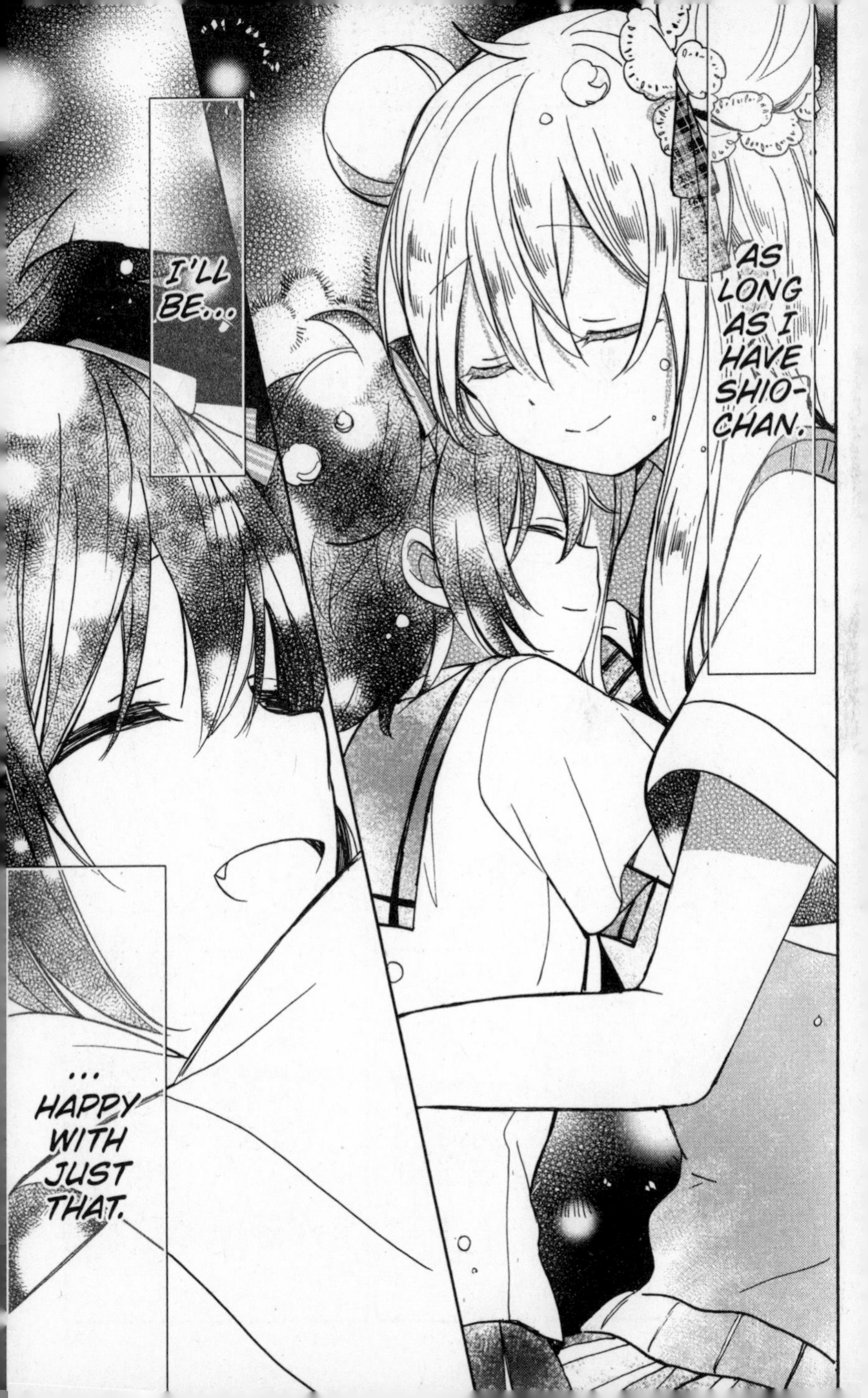
AS LONG AS I HAVE SHIO-CHAN.
I'LL BE...
...HAPPY WITH JUST THAT.

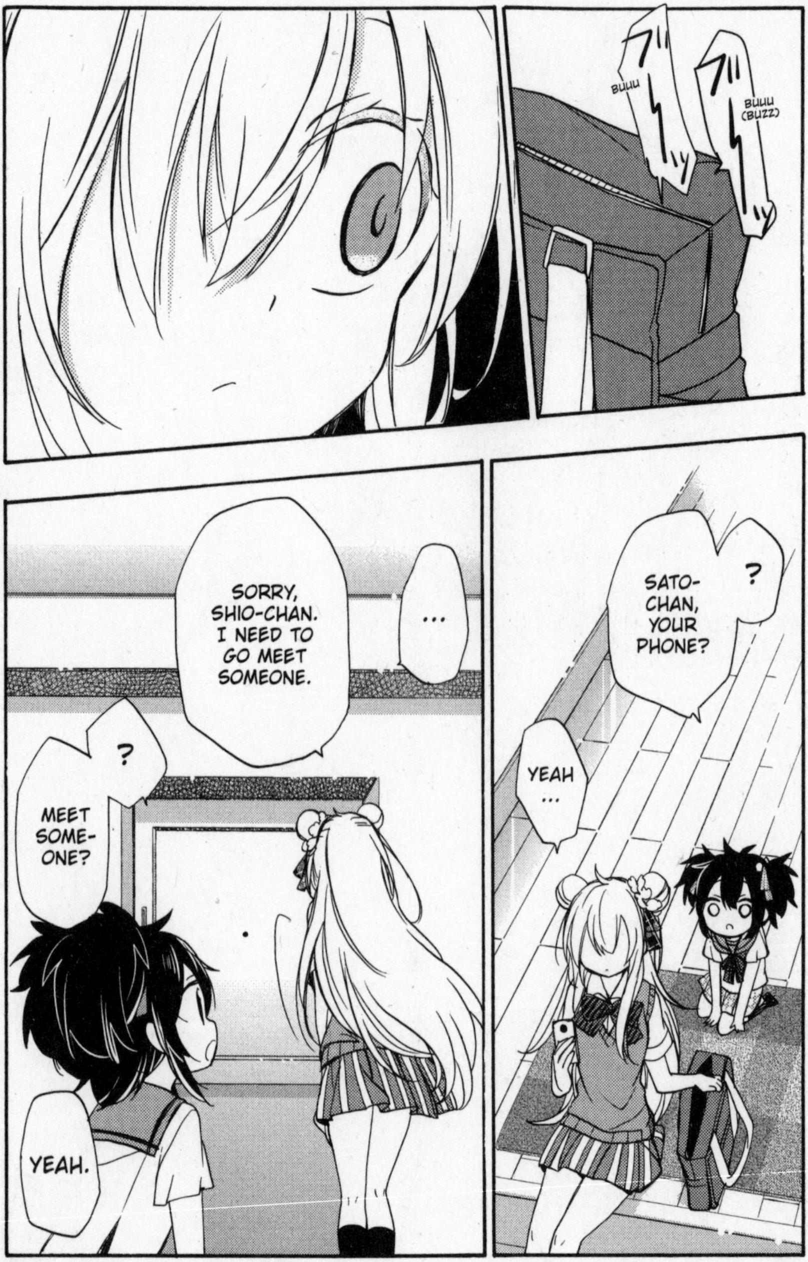
BUUU (BUZZ)
BUUU
SATO-CHAN, YOUR PHONE?
?
YEAH ...
...
SORRY, SHIO-CHAN. I NEED TO GO MEET SOMEONE.
?
MEET SOME-ONE?
YEAH.

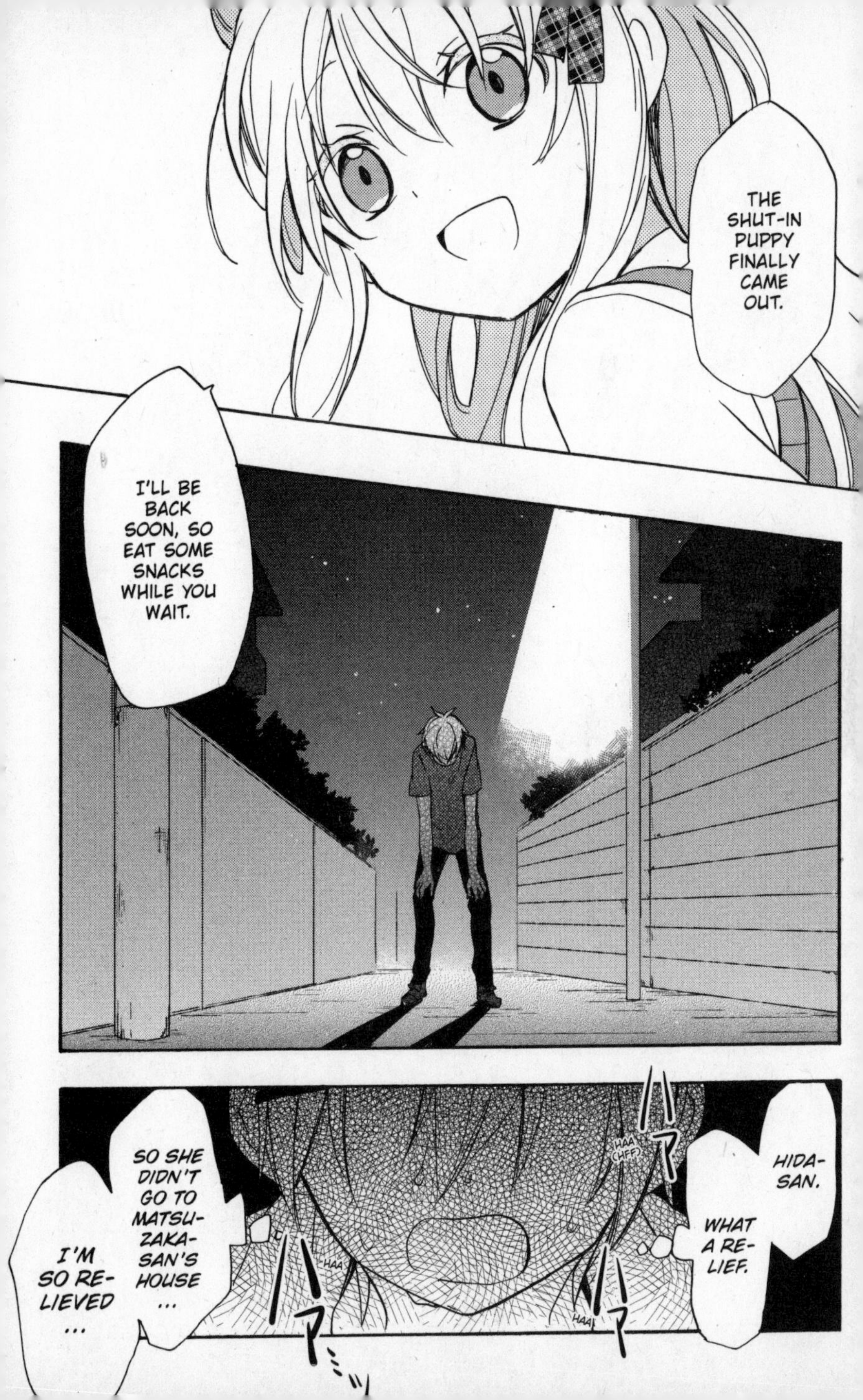
THE SHUT-IN PUPPY FINALLY CAME OUT.
I'LL BE BACK SOON, SO EAT SOME SNACKS WHILE YOU WAIT.
HIDA-SAN.
WHAT A RE-LIEF.
HAA CHFF
SO SHE DIDN'T GO TO MATSU-ZAKA-SAN'S HOUSE ...
I'M SO RE-LIEVED ...
HAA
HAA

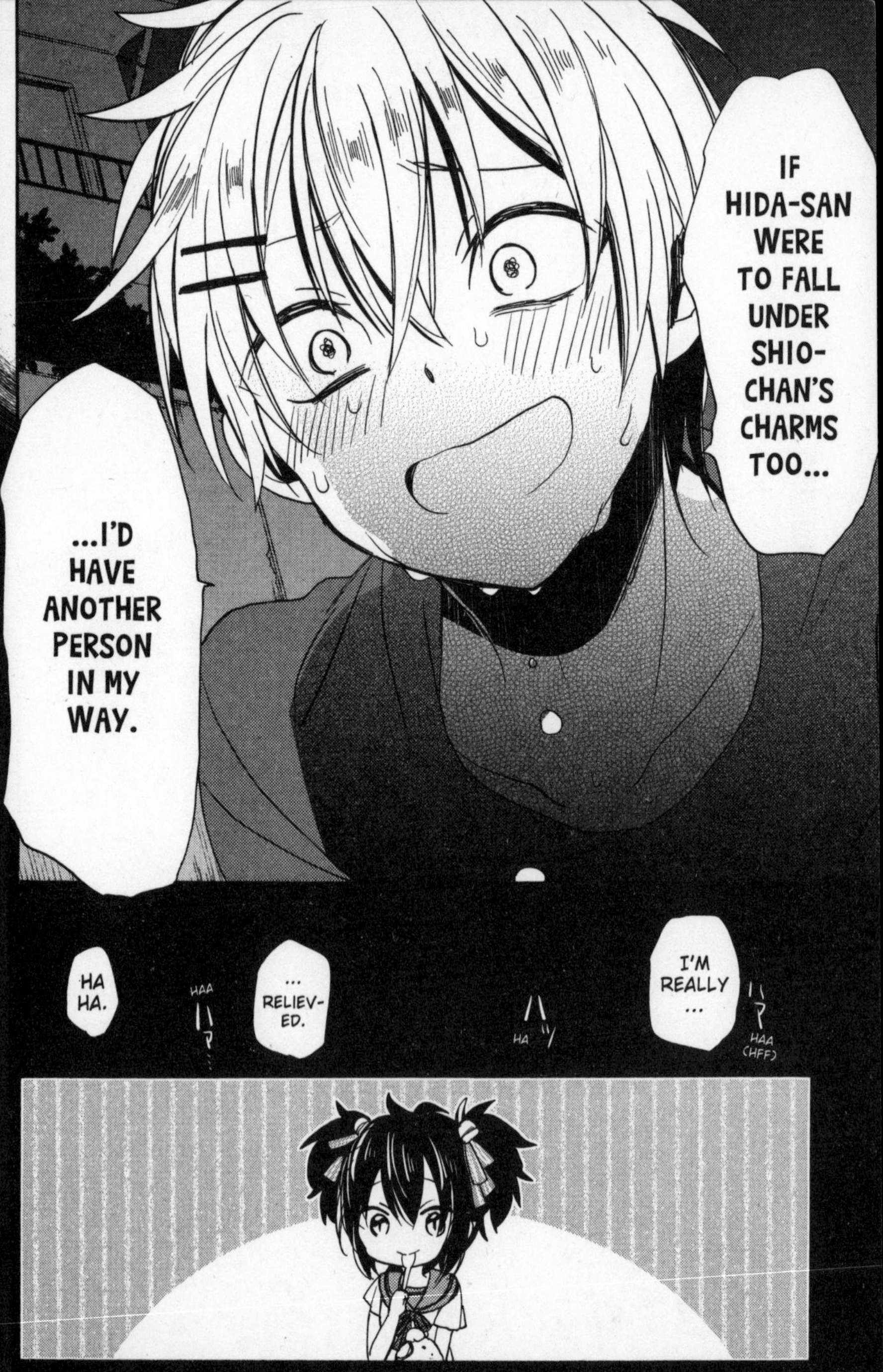
IF HIDA-SAN WERE TO FALL UNDER SHIO-CHAN'S CHARMS TOO...
...I'D HAVE ANOTHER PERSON IN MY WAY.
HAA (HFF)
I'M REALLY ...
HA
... RELIEV-ED.
HAA
HA HA.

HAPPY SUGAR LIFE VOLUME 4 END

Happy
Sugar
Life

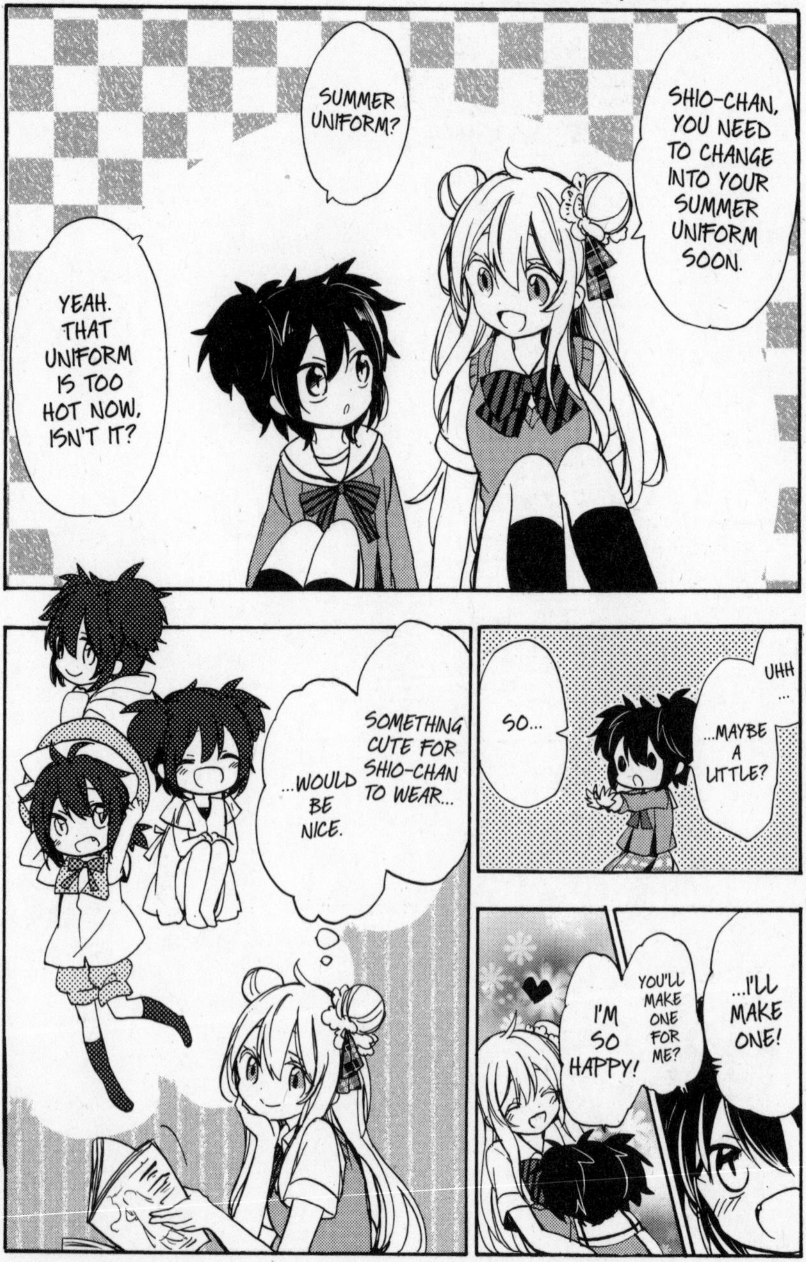
SHIO-CHAN, YOU NEED TO CHANGE INTO YOUR SUMMER UNIFORM SOON.
SUMMER UNIFORM?
YEAH. THAT UNIFORM IS TOO HOT NOW, ISN'T IT?
UHH ... ...MAYBE A LITTLE?
SO...
SOMETHING CUTE FOR SHIO-CHAN TO WEAR...
...WOULD BE NICE.
...I'LL MAKE ONE!
YOU'LL MAKE ONE FOR ME?
I'M SO HAPPY!

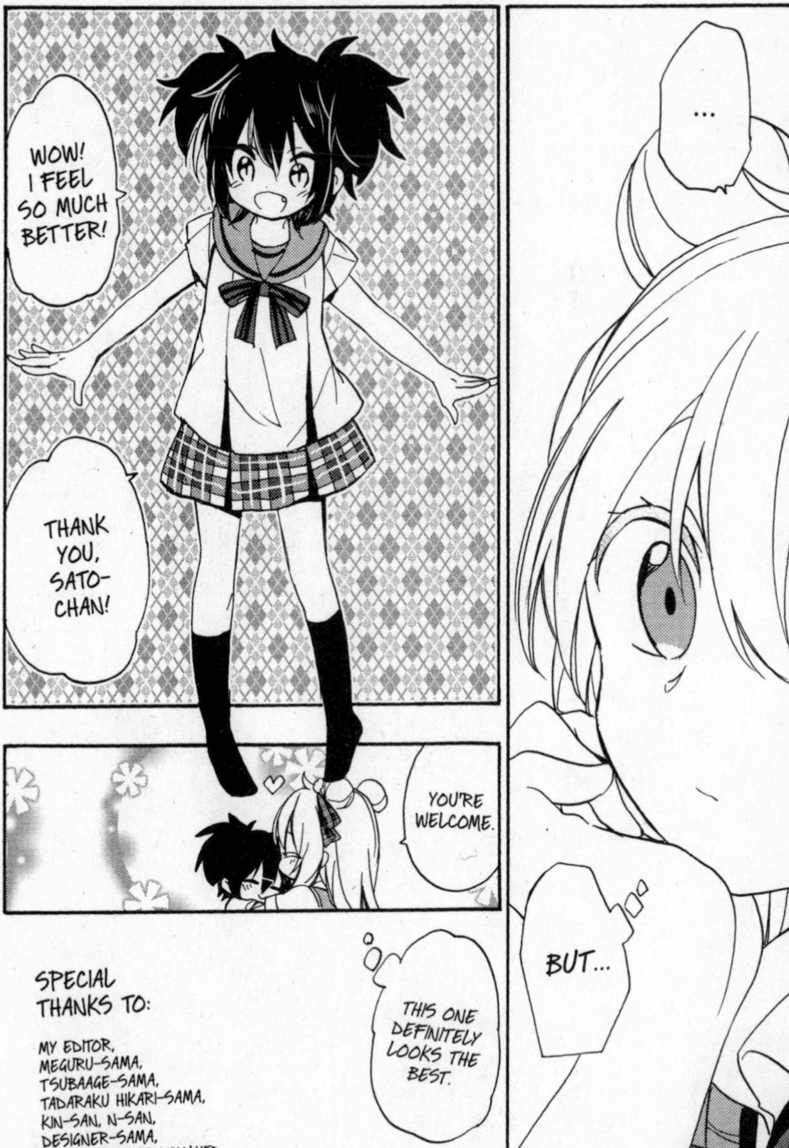
WOW! I FEEL SO MUCH BETTER!
THANK YOU, SATO-CHAN!
YOU'RE WELCOME.
...
BUT...
THIS ONE DEFINITELY LOOKS THE BEST.

SPECIAL THANKS TO:

MY EDITOR,
MEGURU-SAMA,
TSUBAAGE-SAMA,
TADARAKU HIKARI-SAMA,
KIN-SAN, N-SAN,
DESIGNER-SAMA,
EVERYONE ELSE INVOLVED,
THE READERS.

I HOPE TO SEE YOU IN THE NEXT VOLUME.

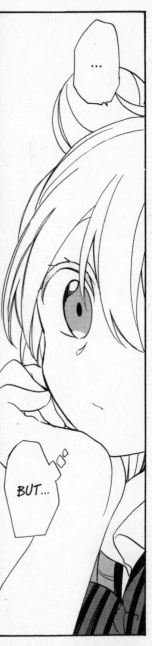

es on.

Volume 5 coming May 2020!

Life go

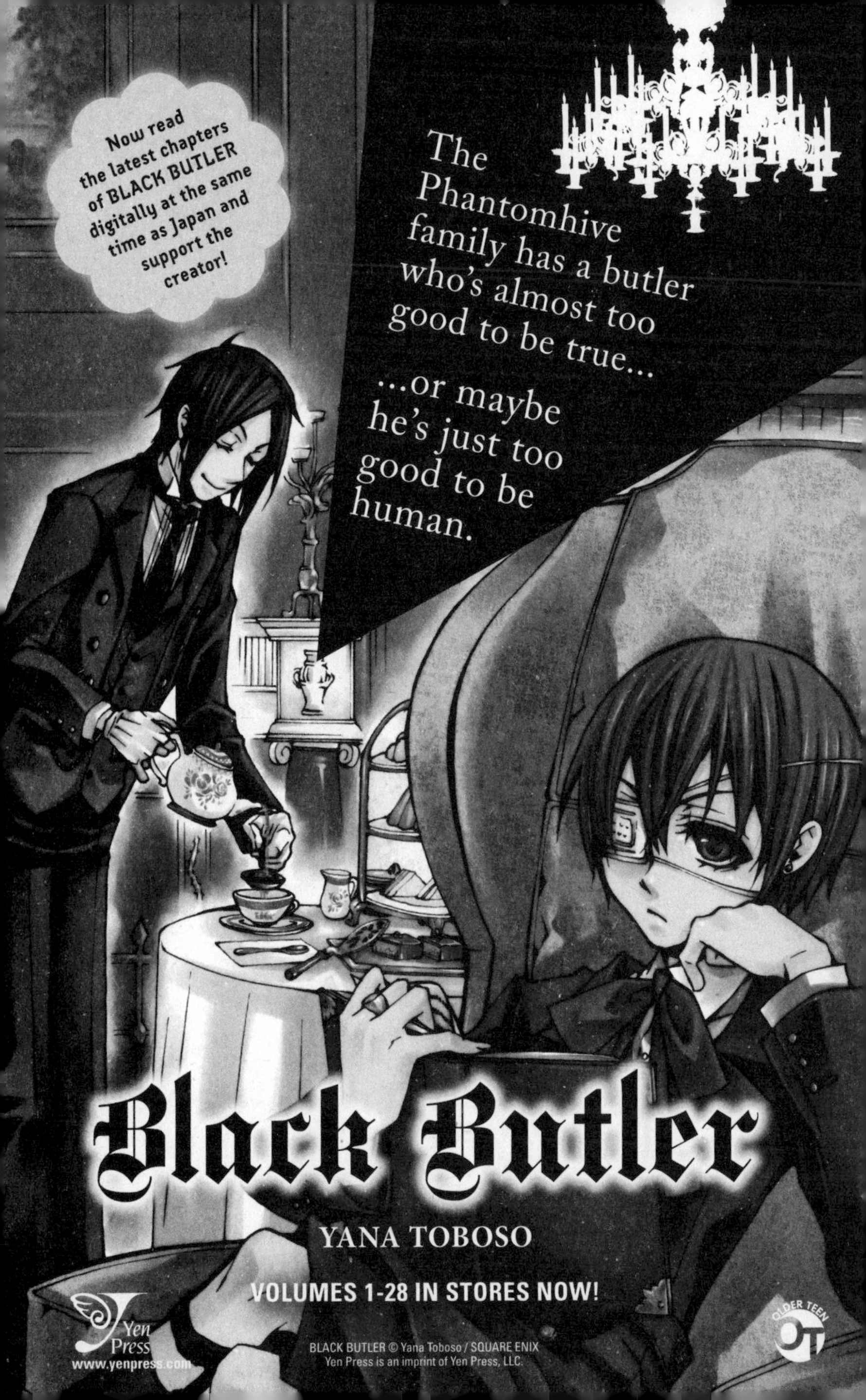
Now read the latest chapters of BLACK BUTLER digitally at the same time as Japan and support the creator!
The Phantomhive family has a butler who's almost too good to be true...
...or maybe he's just too good to be human.
Black Butler
YANA TOBOSO
VOLUMES 1-28 IN STORES NOW!
Yen Press
www.yenpress.com
BLACK BUTLER © Yana Toboso / SQUARE ENIX
Yen Press is an imprint of Yen Press, LLC.
OLDER TEEN
OT

Happy Sugar Life 4

Tomiyaki Kagisora

Translation: **JAN MITSUKO CASH**

Lettering: **NICOLE DOCHYCH**

HAPPY SUGAR LIFE vol. 4 ©2016 Tomiyaki Kagisora / SQUARE ENIX CO., LTD. First published in Japan in 2016 by SQUARE ENIX CO., LTD. English translation rights arranged with SQUARE ENIX CO., LTD. and Yen Press, LLC through Tuttle-Mori Agency, Inc.

English translation ©2020 by SQUARE ENIX CO., LTD.

Yen Press
150 West 30th Street, 19th Floor
New York, NY 10001

Visit us at yenpress.com
facebook.com/yenpress
twitter.com/yenpress
yenpress.tumblr.com
instagram.com/yenpress

First Yen Press Edition: February 2020

Yen Press is an imprint of Yen Press, LLC.
The Yen Press name and logo are trademarks of Yen Press, LLC.

The publisher is not responsible for websites (or their content) that are not owned by the publisher.

Library of Congress Control Number: 2019932474

ISBNs: 978-1-9753-0333-4 (paperback)
978-1-9753-8713-6 (ebook)

10 9 8 7 6 5 4 3 2 1

WOR

Printed in the United States of America